P9-DBN-285

Broadcast News Writing and Reporting

Second Edition

Broadcast News Writing and Reporting

Second Edition

Peter E. Mayeux
University of Nebraska—Lincoln

WAVELAND
PRESS, INC.
Prospect Heights, Illinois

For information about this book, write or call:

Waveland Press, Inc.
P.O. Box 400
Prospect Heights, Illinois 60070
(847) 634-0081
www.waveland.com

Copyright © 1996 by Peter E. Mayeux
2000 reissued by Waveland Press, Inc.

ISBN 1-57766-146-X

All rights reserved. No part of this book may be reproduced, stored in a retrieval system, or transmitted in any form or by any means without permission in writing from the publisher.

Printed in the United States of America

7   6   5   4   3   2

Contents

Chapter 7 — Sentences 128

Chapter 8 — Rewriting Copy 142

Part Two — Sources 161

Chapter 9 — Identifying and Organizing News Sources 161

Part Five Laws and Ethics 378

Chapter 19 Laws and Regulations 378

Chapter 20 Ethics and Judgment 391

Preface

This revised edition remains true to the objectives and goals stated in the first edition: to offer a concise but thorough introduction to the basic approaches and techniques used in broadcast newswriting and reporting. The essentials are presented, but specialized, contemporary reporting and writing techniques are also described and illustrated. The role and responsibility of the broadcast journalist, especially in small- and medium-market news operations, continue to be emphasized.

This second edition was developed based on the advice offered by the students, teachers, and broadcast journalists who have used the first edition over the last several years. Their contributions are acknowledged later.

To update and enhance the quality of this edition, hundreds of electronic media news operations were contacted—in small and large markets, at radio and television stations as well as cable news operations, and at specialized syndicated news services. New photographs, news copy, and personal narratives about story coverage have been integrated into this revised edition.

Several adjustments have been made in this revised edition:

- *Career information* has been moved to an appendix and expanded; broadcast journalism professionals offer advice about where to look for internships and full-time jobs, how to prepare résumé and audition material, and how to handle the rigors of a challenging, ever-changing broadcast news industry. Insights from more than 15 professional broadcast journalists help assess current and future developments in the broadcast news industry.

- *Writing chapters* have been fine-tuned; additional writing samples have been collected from award-winning local stations and cable and regional news outlets; ''weak/ better'' writing examples have been added to better illustrate specific writing style points. When available, transcripts of soundbites were included in the news copy shown.

- *Radio and television reporting chapters* received special attention. Digital audio editing and the use of natural or location sound are further illustrated in Chapter 12, ''Radio Reporting.'' Chapter 13, ''Television Reporting,'' illustrates how sound and picture can combine into an effective television news story; also added are suggestions about using graphics, preparing effective stand-ups and reporter packages, improving lead-ins to soundbites, and adjusting to one-person television news coverage situations.

- *Narratives* have been collected from additional radio and television reporters in various markets. They provide firsthand insights about how to handle various types of news reporting and writing situations. Throughout the book, you learn what to do from seasoned, experienced, in-the-field reporters.

- *Technology and delivery systems information* associated with broadcast news has been added to several chapters. Included now is material about video news releases, databases, computer networks, electronic bulletin boards, and nonlinear video editing systems, as well as equipment updates since the first edition.

• New sections discuss *news coverage and presentation in the 1990s,* and assess the marketing and management tactics developing in the broadcast news industry.

An instructor's manual/workbook, keyed to this revised edition, is now available to help teachers use this edition more effectively. Included is a collection of strategies and approaches that have worked in a variety of teaching situations. Also included are sets of syllabi to help organize a full-semester course, brief comments and suggestions about using each chapter in the revised edition, ready-to-use exercises, and sample student work for several exercises, some of which are in the textbook and some that are not.

To conserve space, several exercises planned for the second edition were moved to the instructor's manual/workbook. To receive the full benefits of this revised edition, teachers are encouraged to order this supplementary publication available at no cost from Brown & Benchmark. Whether new or simply revised from the first edition, *all* exercises, assignments, and projects have been used and refined in actual classroom assignment situations.

Although the content of the book has been updated and strengthened, the structure of the book has not changed. The book is divided into five major parts. Part One (Writing) reviews the form and style of broadcast copy as well as specific requirements for broadcast news leads and stories. Individual chapters are devoted to key elements in effective broadcast newswriting: words, sentences, and rewriting. Part Two (Sources) identifies sources for news and suggests how to organize and develop key news sources. Part Three (Reporting) examines how a broadcast newsroom is organized, reviews the personnel assigned to monitor and execute story coverage, and then focuses closely on specific techniques and practices used in radio, television, and live reporting that relate to both radio and television news broadcasts. Part Four (Coverage) offers insights about routine as well as special kinds of broadcast news coverage and also traces the development of features and the preparation of newscasts. Part Five (Laws and Ethics) provides, in *one* place, the key legal constraints and responsibilities as well as ethical concerns and situations often encountered by a broadcast journalist. Do not infer from the placement of this part that the author believes laws and ethics to be the last concern of a journalist; they should be the *first* concern. Laws and ethics are considered *throughout* the book.

Three appendices supplement the chapter discussions and add dimension to the topics presented. A new appendix, ''Careers,'' offers advice from several professional broadcast journalists about how to prepare for careers in broadcast journalism; internships and résumé and audition tape preparation are emphasized. A second appendix presents the codes of ethics from three professional journalism organizations, including the Radio-Television News Directors Association. A third appendix contains an updated bibliography of books and related material for supplemental reading.

Each chapter provides the following: an introduction to the topics discussed; description and illustration of main points; a summary of the topics discussed; and suggested exercises, assignments, and projects.

The self-test and group-directed activities suggested at the end of each chapter are designed to sharpen and refine writing and reporting skills. Various kinds of items are used: fact sheets, reporter's notes, official reports, news releases, shot sheets and notes (for television coverage), and practical news-related scenarios or interactive case studies designed to encourage the discussion of various kinds of reporting and coverage situations and to provide interesting role-playing opportunities.

These exercises and projects provide a review of basic skills as well as opportunities for more advanced work for those who are interested in specific techniques or for those who have prior news experience and want to sharpen specific kinds of advanced skills. The exercises and assignments offer variety, flexibility, and challenge, so that the reader can begin to *think* and *respond* to situations as a professional broadcast journalist.

Minor adjustments have been made in some of the news copy presented in this book. These adjustments have been made to provide a more uniform presentation of essential broadcast newswriting principles, to accommodate book design considerations, and to avoid potentially sensitive legal situations. Copy adjustments or changes were *not* made when the author felt that the original news copy needed to be displayed as it was originally used.

This book provides an opportunity for the reader to develop the judgment and skills needed to write and report broadcast news in an accurate, clear, understandable, reasonably complete, and interesting manner. The working news professional (in either print or broadcast media) will discover that this book pro-vides the basics as well as some of the complexities and refinements associated with this specialized form of writing and reporting. For the veteran as well as the prospective broadcast newswriter and reporter, this book offers an opportunity to review, practice, and refine essential broadcast newswriting and reporting skills.

Acknowledgments

This revised edition would not have been possible without the help of many dedicated broadcast journalists. Some of the people who helped provide material have since changed jobs. The affiliations listed in this edition applied at the time the individuals supplied material. Also, the facilities shown in this book may have changed since photographs were supplied to the author.

Thanks to the following for their assistance with this second edition: Nan Siemer and Patrick C. Anastasi, WTOP Newsradio, Washington, DC; Cary Pfeffer, KCAL-TV, Hollywood, CA; Charles Osgood and Audrey Forman, *The Osgood File;* Mike Beecher, KFVS-TV, Cape Girardeau, MO; Mike DeMarco and Brian Gann, KVOO, Tulsa; Lorraine Marchand, NIDDK; Malin Jennings, ICI; F. Gifford ("Frank Gentry"), Mutual Broadcasting System; Ray Lockhart, PROPHET Systems, Inc. and KOGA Radio, Ogallala, NE; Judith and Ralph King, Compromter, Inc. and Franz*Hatlem Design Group, LaCrosse, WI; Jim Gold and Nick Peters, Medialink NY and Europe; Kim Engebretsen, CNN; Wayne Lynch, News Channel 8, Maryland, Virginia, Washington, DC; Ann Ferrell and Peter Murray, Capital Cities/ABC, Inc.; Tom Petner and Mariann A. Stefanik, WTAE-TV, Pittsburgh; Robin Briley Cowan, KXLY-TV, Spokane, WA; Charles H. Cooper, National Press Photographers Association, Inc.; Loren Tobia and John Sullivan, KMTV; John Clark, Steve Murphy, and Mike Plews, WOWT, Omaha.

A very special thanks is extended to former students who contributed many items for this second edition. Some also contributed material to the first edition. The newsroom affiliations noted here were the ones in place when their contributions were made for this revised edition: Sue Breding, Los Angeles; Sheila Hyland, WTAE-TV, Pittsburgh; Todd G. Smith, Bonneville International, Inc., Washington, DC; David Ahrendts, ABC News, Chicago; Mike McKnight, WOWT, Omaha; Laurie Krueger, KVOO, Tulsa; Jill Kelley Petersen, WKRC-TV, Cincinnati; Dennis Lyon, KXAS-TV, Fort Worth; Essex J. Porter, KIRO, Seattle; Phil Witt, WDAF-TV, Kansas City; Gary Shapiro and Barb Simon, KUSA-TV; Ben Hall, KFVS-TV, Carbondale, IL; Ann Pedersen Gleeson, WCCO-TV, Minneapolis; Don Browers, Steve Spriester, John Glenn, John Atkinson, Peggy Rupprecht, Barry Kriha, Amy Kennedy, and Traci Jones, KMTV, Omaha; Dan Dillon, KFDI, Wichita, KS; Scot Witt, WDCB Radio, Glen Ellyn, IL; John Holden, Miami; Brian Barks and Paul Sterba, KKAR, Omaha; Jim Ballard, University of Nebraska–Lincoln; Dennis Wilden and Mike O'Keefe, WOWT, Omaha; Leslie Strong; and Kevin McMahon.

The suggestions offered by the following reviewers were very helpful as the second edition was planned: Dale Cressman, Lyndon State College; Don Edwards, Syracuse University; Jim Foust, Bowling Green State University; Luett Hanson, Kent State University; Michael Murray, University of Missouri–St. Louis; and John Rhodes, William Paterson College.

I continue to appreciate the encouragement and assistance provided by colleagues in the College of Journalism and Mass Communications at the University of Nebraska–Lincoln: Larry Walklin, Tom Spann, Rick Alloway, Jerry Renaud, Hubert Brown, Laurie Thomas Lee, Pat Lehecka, Marylu Dughman, George Tuck, Nancy Mitchell, and Will Norton, Jr.

I remain grateful for the first edition contributions of the following: James L. Hoyt, Robert M. Steele, Louise Benjamin, Benjamin Silver, R. Neale Copple, Doris Moses, Mary Jane Bruce, Bryce Anderson, Laurie Benson, Linda Shinn, Keith Groteluschen, Bob Cullinan, Deborah Holmes, Steve Roth,

Dan Staehr, Barry Bernson, Gary Wordlaw, Kay Salz, Martin Silverstein, Ed Norden, David King, Joe Connolly, Merrilee Cox, Gary W. Nunn, Chuck Roberts, Bob Furnad, Paul Varian, Robert R. Siegenthaler, Michael Castengera, Cary Pfeffer, Adrienne Abbott, Butch Montoya, Dan Day, Dan Perkes, John Lippmann, Joe Steele, Chris Eskridge, Don Bryant, Bob Priddy, Tyler Cox, Betsy Braziel, Reid Johnson, Doug Stone, Cheryl Peterson, John Altenbern, Arles Hendershott, Mary Baker, Mark Martin, Richard Warner, Jane M. Rulon, Julie Dean, John Moncrief, Bob Cockrum, Dale Woolery, Nancy Cope, Jon Mangum, Ken Beck, J. Spencer Kinard, Bob Campbell, Anne Clausen, Pat Turner, David C. Maurer, Len Kehl, Anita Shaw, Paul Vann Ehlis, Gene T. Brodeur, Jeff Grimes, Brian Peterson, Bill Polish, Harvey Kercheval, Mike Morgan, Bob Agnew, Donald Bonin, Steve Johnson, Gay Cantrell, Melanie Miller, Rich Hawkins, Bob Brogan, Bill Flanagan, Dr. Brian Patrick McDonough, John Denney, Diane Gonzolas, Tina Nisi, David Fitzgibbon, Jan Dorn, Cliff Gauldin and Geri Austin.

All of these individuals and organizations will not necessarily agree with everything contained in this book. And, obviously, none of them is responsible for errors, omissions, or opinions expressed by the author.

This book continues to be dedicated to my wife, Sue, and my son, Ben. I sincerely appreciate their never-ending patience, understanding, and encouragement.

Chapter 1

Introduction

Broadcast journalism is a career as vital as the world around us. Radio and television transmit actuality, the sights and sounds of events as they happen, of history being made. We witness armed conflict in a distant nation at suppertime. We follow the progress of a tornado or power blackout via battery radio. The realities of oppression and terrorism fill our eyes and our ears, but these same media also bring us the triumph of an Olympic moment or a scientific breakthrough that benefits all humanity. Never before have there been such immediate and complete instruments for reporting our lives.[1]

News and information surround us every day. We are exposed to literally thousands of messages and impressions that inform, entertain, tempt, confuse, persuade, and often irritate us. We gather thoughts, ideas, impressions, and information in an effort to apply what we learn and understand to the ever-changing and challenging situations in our hectic lives.

We are experiencing an information explosion that is unparalleled in history. This may frighten some, but it should invigorate those who want to participate fully in what will surely be a challenging, but rewarding, opportunity for personal and professional success. You would not be reading this if you did not share at least some part of this vision and commitment for the future.

This first chapter provides an overview of broadcast news. It examines the importance of news and the expectations of broadcast news audiences. Since newsworthiness is an important audience expectation, you will examine how information is selected for radio and television news stories. You will also review some of the changes and influences of the 1990s to see how technology and audience demands have influenced broadcast news. Reviews of new presentation strategies and initiatives give you a glimpse into the future of broadcast news. Essential characteristics of broadcast news are also outlined. This introductory chapter provides a broad perspective that allows you to better understand and appreciate broadcast news.

Importance of News

News is important to practically everyone. A tax increase affects your pocketbook; the eruption of an armed conflict in a distant part of the world may threaten a loved one or affect your financial investments; a weather forecast of rain today will determine whether local farmers plant or harvest their crops. Each news item affects, in some way, the person seeing or hearing that news report.

Researchers have tried to identify why people rely on broadcast news reports. Some simply want to stay informed, to catch up with what has happened. Others want to know what to expect during the day. Some claim that broadcast news reports provide a variety of information in a short time. Still others indicate that such reports get them thinking.[2]

One study reaffirmed the belief that for most people, broadcast news, especially television, is a primary source of news and information. People tend to believe what they see reported on the air. Americans tend to look forward to television news reports each day. Watching television is second only to talking with friends, neighbors, and co-workers among activities that most Americans anticipate doing during the day.[3]

Today's audience can select from a variety of media to obtain information as well as entertainment. People continue to rely on traditional and established media outlets such as newspapers, magazines, radio, and television stations, but now they can also choose to view a videocassette at home or at work to expand skills and knowledge. Perhaps a personal satellite receiving dish is anchored outside the home to receive signals from any number of off-air broadcast stations as well as various private sources. Home computer users rely on sophisticated software and telephone modem connections to tap intricate databases and manage personal finances. Stereo systems have expanded to include compact discs as well as multiple-speaker Dolby® sound recordings.

The competition to capture today's audiences is severe. More choices are available now than ever before, and the variety of choices and the level of sophistication are expected to increase as the years progress.

No matter how the audience receives news and information, different people need different kinds of material at different times for different reasons. In the morning, you want to know what happened overnight while you slept, and you want to know the current weather forecast to better plan your day's activities. Noontime is a time to update your information, and by evening you will want a recap of the day's events. At times you will want to focus in-depth on specific stories to obtain better insight into events and how they will shape your life. Most people need general news and information, but some require specialized information such as financial, medical, and agricultural news.

The audience has begun to develop very personalized and flexible media-use patterns. Studies show that those who read a daily newspaper listen regularly to radio news while in the car, watch daily television newscasts, and also read a weekly news magazine. The demands of today's audience are fulfilled by any number of media usage combinations.

The setting or environment in which the audience receives news and information often is not ideal. There are distractions; other activities are often under way at the same time as news reports are heard or seen. Those who prepare news reports struggle continually to determine what the audience needs and wants and how to deliver that information in the best manner and at the best time for the audience.

Expectations of News Reports

To better prepare responsible and competitive broadcast news reports, you need to know what the audience wants and expects. Otherwise, you will not be able to determine the stories to report and how to present these reports.

Accuracy

Listeners and viewers expect accurate reporting, and you should expect it of yourself. The desire for accuracy needs to become part of your journalistic integrity and responsibility. Once you present inaccurate information, you lose credibility. There are too many other places where the public can obtain accurate news reports.

Your job is to report the news as accurately and as fairly as you can, no matter how unpopular the facts might be. Reporting a charge of child molestation against a local minister or an accusation of graft against a popular public official is not pleasant. But such stories are reported regularly. Too much is at stake for these reports not to be accurate.

Be diligent in your commitment to honest, accurate, fair reporting. Take the time to check and recheck facts so that you can be certain about the information you gather and report. In a traffic fatality story, for example, it is important to have the correct address and name of the victim. An inaccuracy in this kind of story causes too much unnecessary consternation.

Inaccuracy leads to mistrust by the audience. Carelessness, laziness, missed facts, distortions, and the use of speculation and rumor are all paths leading to inaccuracies.

Objectivity and Fairness

Reporters are human beings; therefore, it may be difficult for them to be completely objective, but they can be fair. A group of reporters could observe the same testimony in a court case, for example, and review the same legal brief outlining the specifics about the case and still file differing stories about what was observed and experienced. One reporter might emphasize evidence offered by a few key witnesses; another might focus on the responses by the defendant's attorney; still another might provide reactions by attorneys and witnesses outside the courtroom. All of these reports would provide some information about the court case, but a single report may not be the best example of objective reporting about the various aspects of the trial.

Good reporters try to put aside personal biases and beliefs when covering news. In news stories, listeners and viewers expect fair, objective reporting of the facts, not the reporter's opinion about the story. Again, credibility is important. Fair, objective reporting is one way to ensure credibility.

Completeness

The broadcast journalist cannot always present all sides in a controversy. Deadlines necessitate shortcuts. Limited time may prevent an interview with that extra source who might provide needed insight into a situation. The reporter is forced to make quick decisions about the path of story coverage. Balance and perspective are needed in every story, but often they give way to deadlines, pressures, speed, and brevity.

You may obtain a complete report about a particular incident or situation only after reading or checking various media reports and after the audience forms judgments. As a broadcast journalist, try to provide the most complete report possible, knowing that there is always more that could be said.

Clarity

Broadcast news must be reported clearly and concisely. Too many other activities compete for the audience's time and attention. Unlike newspaper readers, viewers and listeners cannot reread stories. Your story must be clear the first (and probably the only) time it is seen or heard.

Choose your words carefully. Shape and design your reports to meet and exceed audience expectations. Later chapters will describe and illustrate specific techniques for improving clarity in broadcast stories.

Identification and Attribution

Sometimes you must attribute or identify sources of information in a story; at other times, attribution is not needed. A listener or viewer will be more likely to accept a statement from your local mayor about downtown redevelopment than an off-handed comment by the manager of a local fast-food franchise. Your source must be knowledgeable and must be cited and identified clearly in your news story; your credibility as a reporter depends on it. Chapter 2 presents specific techniques for providing attribution.

News Judgment

Simply stated, news is what people need and want to know. Events and situations that are considered newsworthy have certain characteristics in common. All news stories will not have all of the common characteristics, but they will all have some of them. Newsworthiness increases proportionately to the number of such characteristics an individual story contains.

The broadcast journalist has to determine newsworthiness during each phase of the process of gathering, writing, reporting, and editing the news. An assignment editor in a newsroom must select stories for reporters to cover. Once on the scene, the reporter needs to know the questions to ask at a news conference or at the scene of a fire or traffic accident to obtain the most newsworthy information. Then facts must be sifted, selected, and shaped into a final report. Audio- and videotape excerpts must be chosen to enhance the story on the air. Even the length and placement of individual stories within newscasts are determined by an assessment of newsworthiness.

Several factors shape news judgment. These include the background and experience of the reporter, the requirements of the news organization, the size of the broadcast market in which the station operates, and the needs and expectations of the audience. News judgment is adjusted to reflect these and other factors active at the time. Judge each story on its own merits, but also consider factors such as the day of the week, time of day, and the availability of other news stories.

To decide what is newsworthy, apply common sense and basic broadcast journalism principles to available current events. Once you understand the essential criteria used to determine newsworthiness, you must apply those criteria to specific situations and circumstances. Eventually, through experience, you will learn to recognize the newsworthy elements of each story. Learn from your mistakes, and compare your instincts with those of more-experienced journalists.

Proximity, prominence, timeliness, impact, conflict, controversy, uniqueness, human interest, suspense, the need to update earlier stories, and available sound or pictures are the primary characteristics that determine newsworthiness.

Proximity

It is important to consider where a story occurred. Listeners and viewers are more interested in what affects them personally, directly, and locally than in events happening in some distant location. Thus, they tend to consider local news to be more newsworthy than stories from faraway countries. However, some events capture the interest and imagination of an audience no matter where they happen. Examples include disaster stories, national elections, and space shots.

Examples of stories that affect your local audience include a local tax increase or property tax assessment, a local garbage strike that affects how you handle refuse, street closings within your community that determine how you route your travel around town, and the local weather forecast that influences your decision to walk to work or take the bus. All of these items emphasize *local* news that affects your audience directly.

You can convert distant stories into important local stories, and thus increase this measure of proximity, by developing local angles on major world and national stories. For example, a major company has a manufacturing plant in your community, and the national office has just decided to close all of its plants, including the local one that employs one-third of your community's residents. Providing a local angle on this story is important. In this way, you maintain the proximity element and newsworthiness becomes more evident. Chapter 8 shows how to localize news stories.

Prominence

People want to know about other people, especially well-known or prominent people. The more prominent or visible the person involved in a story, the more newsworthy that story becomes. Prominent locations such as the U.S. Capitol or the site of arms negotiations or events such as national telethons or a presidential speech to the United Nations also increase newsworthiness.

The president of the United States, a governor, a U.S. senator, or even a movie star or famous athlete commands more attention because of the importance of the individual's occupation, position, or notoriety. They have become celebrities. When the governor of your state leaves for a governor's conference, that becomes a news item; when you leave for a trip to the same location, hardly anyone notices, and it certainly does not merit attention on the evening newscast.

Timeliness

When an event occurs is sometimes just as important as how it happened, who was involved, or where it took place. People expect broadcast news to provide immediacy, instant or live reports on important events, today's news today. If you report preliminary information about a major fire in your downtown area earlier in the day, later newscasts had best present the latest information about that fire. Broadcast news must provide timely information.

Impact

Consider also the impact, significance, or consequence of a news event on the lives, welfare, or future of those in your listening or viewing area. Generally, the more people affected by a news story, the more newsworthy that story becomes. When a train carrying toxic chemicals derails and sends dangerous clouds billowing into a five-mile area, people abandon their homes. This directly affects the lives of these residents, and the lives of their relatives and friends. The story has impact.

Conflict

Physical as well as ethical and emotional conflicts can cause clashes between people. Such confrontations heighten news interest. The conflicts may be within an individual (e.g., overcoming a physical handicap or kicking a deadly drug habit), between individuals (e.g., an argument that erupts into a fatal shooting), between groups of individuals (e.g., arguments between pro-life and pro-choice factions on the steps of a state capitol), even between nations (e.g., armed confrontations between countries in the Middle East). Values and priorities are at stake when conflicts develop. The broadcast journalist must know how to recognize conflicts, assess their value, determine their newsworthiness, and prepare a compelling story.

Controversy

Some stories are controversial; many stories are not. Controversy may be evident in stories such as the site selection for a new city landfill or a residence for mentally retarded citizens, or the awarding of road construction contracts to relatives of public officials. Controversy tends to fuel interest in a particular story, but it needs to be handled carefully.

Uniqueness

Often an event or situation is considered news because it is unusual, out-of-the-ordinary, unique. An old journalism axiom states that it is not news if a dog bites a man, but it is news if a man bites a dog. That does not happen every day. In a similar way, airplane crashes are reported on newscasts, but the thousands of safe flights every day are not. The unusual event, the airplane crash, makes the newscast.

Viewers and listeners are curious about other people, even those who are not necessarily well known. They like to empathize with the problems of others and share in their achievements. Such stories feature the human side of the news and help balance a news broadcast.

Human Interest

Suspense heightens newsworthiness. Some events become newsworthy because people are uncertain about the outcome and want to know how an event was resolved. Many people report for work in the morning bleary-eyed after spending the night watching election returns roll in for an important political race or catching the extra innings in a tight baseball game. People are curious to know if a small child survived a complicated heart transplant operation or if the hostages in a touchy terrorist situation are safe again.

Suspense

Stories are sometimes broadcast because they update earlier news items. By providing brief updates on developing stories, news broadcasts assure listeners and viewers that they know the latest developments. Examples include current damage and fatality statistics from a natural disaster, such as an earthquake, flood, tornado, or hurricane; the current status of a civil disturbance; the latest rescue efforts in a major subway accident; the latest charges made in a local fraud or bribe-taking situation that has become complex and extended.

Updating

Some stories are considered newsworthy for radio and television because sound or pictures are available to better illustrate the story. The story might have had news value anyway, but when you have a telephone recording of a bank official being robbed or a videotape of a routine rescue exercise that turns into a fatal crash with multiple fatalities, then the story becomes especially newsworthy. Sound and picture tend to heighten the impact and news value of a story. Ethical concerns arise, however, about the use of such material; these are discussed in Chapter 20.

Available Sound or Pictures

This decade has presented interesting challenges for broadcast news operations around the country. Audiences now demand news and information tailored to specific needs and timetables, offered at convenient times, and presented in an easy-to-use, cost-effective, and efficient manner. Viewers with interactive television systems can use teletext systems, which are described later in this chapter, to "produce" or assemble their own newscast by selecting only the stories that interest them.

News in the '90s

Although economic downturns early in the 1990s caused radio and television station newsrooms to decrease their staff size and operating budgets, this situation also compelled news operations to explore new initiatives and strategies to better use available resources and respond to audience demands. Radio and television stations have begun working with former rivals in the newspaper and cable industries. This has created news operations in which personnel from various media work together, combine and share writing and reporting responsibilities, and provide reports that are versatile, well written, interesting, attractive, memorable, and often compelling.

The 1990s has also altered the way newsrooms prepare and deliver broadcast news. They continue to try to do more with less, looking for additional revenue opportunities without significant increases in operating expenses. This has led to reliance on cooperative newsgathering alliances, syndicated news services, and combined print and broadcast news operations. This, in turn, has spurred such developments as local television station newsrooms producing five-minute news summaries for use between cable network programs, and regional cable news channels now operating in approximately a half-dozen large urban areas. Cable news operations, in turn, have helped simplify and streamline electronic news operations. Fiber-optics technology allows cable systems to prepare a special newscast tailored to the specific needs of thousands of homes in a specific area of the local cable system. Cable subscribers are beginning to enjoy the chance to customize the news and information they receive as they select and arrange story items to suit individual tastes and needs.

Special Characteristics of Broadcast News

Despite moves designed to integrate or merge print and electronic news operations, each medium of communication offers special opportunities, challenges, and responsibilities. Similarities exist between media, but so do significant differences.

The broadcast media can reach millions of people simultaneously. They can touch a life directly. Radio and television news broadcasts also require teamwork to produce programs that are credible and easily understood. These fleeting sounds and pictures are quickly replaced by those of the next story, then the next story, and so on.

No one works alone in broadcast news. The skills and talents of one person meld with those of others to provide a well-written and skillfully produced news report. Teamwork is necessary in any news operation, but the nature and requirements of broadcast news production make close teamwork essential.

Listeners and viewers must trust and believe what they hear and see in broadcast news stories. A special kind of responsibility is involved in coming into the homes and lives of people. As a professional journalist, you should also remember the trust that has been established and do all that you can to enhance belief in the facts that you present.

A conversational writing style is used in broadcast news to make stories easy to understand and remember; the ear is less patient than the eye. You will have to skip details and present only the essential facts of each story. A thorough discussion of this writing style is provided in Chapter 2 and Chapters 4 through 8.

ABC Newsroom, New York. © 1993 Copyright Capital Cities/ABC, Inc. Photo by Maria Melin.

The transitory nature of broadcast news often causes consternation. Broadcast audiences consume news and information quicker and with less regard than do the audiences of perhaps any other media. Broadcast news involves continuous deadlines. Live, on-the-scene reporting is commonplace. Nothing stands still. No matter how much time, energy, effort, sweat, and worry you put into gathering facts and preparing an effective news report, the next deadline and the next newscast loom ahead. Eventually another story or new facts will bump your story from the newscast. It is the nature of the business. The sounds, images, and impressions in a story are replaced quickly with others that help capture the interest and imagination of the audience. News developments never stop.

Although limited time is available to provide full coverage in broadcast news stories, journalists can blend news and information into a variety of audience life-styles. For many, broadcast news reports, especially those on television, are the only source of information. The challenge for broadcast journalists is to provide as much pertinent information as possible, given time constraints.

New Technologies   Technology has always been an integral part of broadcast news. Microphones, cameras, recorders, audio boards, and other equipment have been a part of broadcast newsgathering and reporting since the broadcast industry began. New technology is changing the way broadcast news is compiled, written, edited, and presented. The possibilities seem limitless. Technology is making available sophisticated, flexible systems that allow broadcast journalists to do their jobs better. The following paragraphs describe a few of the major technologies.

Computers are becoming more common in broadcast newsrooms. Word-processing programs help writers compose, edit, move, store, send, and receive information. Journalists can now receive large volumes of information at high speed from wire services or data banks (enormous information reservoirs) and compile the information into usable news stories. Some newsrooms file stories on floppy disks. Others use computers to perform practically all routine newsroom operations, including scheduling, writing, filing, and budgeting. The need for paper in broadcast newsrooms is fast declining because broadcast news scripts can be written on and read from the computer screen. The use of computers in broadcast news is described more fully in Chapter 2.

Networks and even local stations have begun to depend on satellite systems. Networks can provide several signals concurrently that stations can monitor and record for later use. Some networks are experimenting with high-speed transmissions that permit the reception of more material in a shorter time. Local stations receive all major network signals and wire service transmissions via satellite. Stations can swap stories by sharing satellite time and creating state and regional newsgathering alliances. Local television stations have invested heavily in mobile satellite trucks to allow reporters to cover stories live from just about anywhere.

Touch-screen technology increases the capabilities of broadcast news. When this technology is combined with other forms of automation, it is possible to coordinate a news broadcast from a central location such as a producer's or a newscaster's desk, or add sophisticated graphics to a television weathercast.

Cellular phones are indispensable in broadcast news coverage. They provide high-quality, high-capacity service to reporters in the field, who can file stories and check assignments with their newsrooms without interrupting their transmissions. When attached to a laptop computer, a cellular phone allows a field reporter to transmit news copy directly to the newsroom.

Video camera and editing technology maximize the efficiency and improve the quality of television news coverage. Small-format video systems include equipment that is simple, light, compact, durable, affordable, and easy to handle. Electronic videotape editing is fast, efficient, and sophisticated. Picture quality is improving, while camera size, complexity, and the need for maintenance are diminishing.

Teletext capabilities make good use of the television signal. Teletext is a system that uses part of the existing television signal to transmit information that can be received on a conventional television set. The viewer selects the information category desired through a special keypad device. These transmissions replace part of the television picture and can offer sports scores, news headlines, weather information, stock prices, or any number of informational items. Because of the limited space available in a television signal, most teletext systems can include only about 100 pages of information.

A more interactive system, videotext, uses a mainframe computer and telephone connections to provide almost unlimited information capacity. Teletext has generated more interest outside the United States. Although only a modest number of U.S. stations offer teletext services, interest seems to be increasing.

Within the decade, high-definition television (HDTV) is expected to influence newsroom equipment purchases as did color film, which replaced black and white, and electronic newsgathering (ENG) equipment, which replaced film in the 1970s. Although a HDTV system will produce high-quality television pictures, the cameras, recorders, and editing equipment that broadcast newsrooms use will have to change to accommodate HDTV requirements. Broadcast journalists will have to learn the HDTV system and adjust their reporting and writing techniques accordingly.

Fiber optics now make television newsgathering from remote locations as simple as making a telephone call. Cable news operations can plug into a fiber-optic line underground or on a nearby telephone pole and provide high-quality pictures in an efficient, cost-effective manner. These transmissions avoid some of the interference from atmospheric conditions that is often encountered with traditional broadcast signals or microwave links.

Video dialtone and digital compression technologies increase the delivery system possibilities for television news. Cooperative ventures by telephone companies, cable systems, and television stations have become commonplace. All-news cable channels, video-on-demand, and customized television news reports are becoming routine for viewers around the country.

Remember, however, that new technology will not replace good journalists. Knowledgeable, experienced news reporters, editors, producers, videographers, and news managers will continue to be at the heart of a professional news operation. Technology simply gives them more-sophisticated tools with which to do their jobs. Technology also creates new challenges and requires further refinement of reporting skills such as live reports from a news scene.

The Future

What is the future of broadcast news? What will electronic news reporting be like in the next century? How can you possibly prepare yourself for an industry that seems to change so quickly and so radically?

Certainly technological changes will help shape broadcast news in the future. They always have. New electronic tools and techniques will help make the broadcast journalist's job even more flexible and easier than now.

Broadcast news specialists predict that integrated information systems that combine the strengths of television, cable, and print will be developed to produce a wide variety of programs and stories aimed at the needs of very narrow audiences. Round-the-clock news services, especially on special cable channels, in almost all the major urban areas, will accommodate news-on-demand requirements.

How can radio and television news be expected to survive and even succeed in this competitive, ever-changing environment? The best advice so far is that broadcast newsrooms diversify what they do, respond to audience demands in terms of story ideas and availabilities, and maintain a distinctive, high-quality product that continues to emphasize strong community involvement and high competitive standards.

As a prospective journalist, how should you prepare yourself for this challenging industry? Appendix A, "Careers," helps you to identify your qualifications. A variety of professional broadcast journalists offer advice about career planning steps that you should follow and about how to prepare job application material such as résumés, cover letters, and audition tapes.

Summary

This chapter introduced the work of the broadcast journalist. Broadcast news competes with other media for the time and attention of millions of people each day. Viewers and listeners expect news reports to be accurate, fair, clear, and as complete as possible.

Throughout the newsgathering and writing process, newsworthiness is determined by several criteria, including proximity, prominence, timeliness, impact, conflict, controversy, uniqueness, human interest, suspense, the need for updates, and the availability of picture or sound to accompany a story.

The 1990s have altered the way broadcast news is prepared and delivered. Print and electronic news operations have begun to work together to respond to increasing audience demands for high-quality, flexible information systems.

Radio and television news coverage maintain distinctive identities. Teamwork and coordination are still required to prepare stories that listeners and viewers easily understand and readily believe.

New technologies have streamlined the broadcast journalist's work. These technologies include computers, satellites, cellular telephone systems, teletext and videotext, and high-quality video equipment using such systems as video dialtones and digital compression.

The future for broadcast news is challenging. Technology and audience demands will influence changes within the industry.

Exercises

1. For one day, keep a log of your use of the mass media. Include what you saw and heard on radio and television, in newspapers and magazines, and on billboards, buses, and so forth. Indicate the following: what you saw or heard, when you saw or heard it, what you were doing at the time, and any observations you had. Report your findings.

2. Read today's edition of a local daily newspaper and note the important world and national stories reported. Indicate the length of each story (in column inches) and whether graphic material was used (i.e., photographs, charts, graphs, maps, etc.). Indicate why you believe each story is especially newsworthy (see the section titled "News Judgment" in this chapter).

3. Complete Exercise 2 and then monitor a network radio or television newscast for a comparable time period. For example, monitor early morning newscasts if using a morning newspaper or early evening newscasts if using an afternoon newspaper. Indicate the following: the length of each story, the use of sound or picture, and why you believe each story was especially newsworthy (see the section titled "News Judgment" in this chapter). Compare and contrast the newspaper and the broadcast coverage. Report your findings.

Notes

1. Vernon A. Stone, *Careers in Broadcast News: What Electronic Journalists Do,* 5th ed. (Washington, D.C.: Radio-Television News Directors Association, 1987), 1.

2. Summary of a survey conducted by Reymour & Gersin Associates commissioned by the Associated Press. "AP Study Deflates News Perceptions," *Radio & Records,* September 4, 1987, 42.

3. Steven Miller, "TV: America's Most Trusted Source of News," *BPME Image,* May/June 1987, 50–52. *America's Watching: The 1987 TIO/Roper Report* was conducted as part of the regular Roper Reports opinion polls.

Part One

Writing

Chapter 2

Broadcast Newswriting Style

Those involved in the evolution, development, and refinement of broadcast newswriting styles and techniques recognize that broadcast news involves a team effort. Because several sets of hands handle the same piece of copy, the copy must be consistent, clear, and easy to read in both form and style. To ensure this, a uniform set of rules is needed. The listener or viewer cannot reread broadcast news copy. Clarity is crucial. The effectiveness of broadcast news copy hinges on the newscaster's ability to read the words written in a believable and convincing manner. Thus, you must write copy to avoid hesitations and mistakes by the newscaster.

This chapter reviews the essential elements of broadcast newswriting style: the importance of spelling; the use of regular capitalization; making the copy more readable and expressive through the use of punctuation, emphasis, and pronunciation help for difficult words; effective use of numbers; making abbreviations clear; noting clearly the sources of information; and editing broadcast copy so it can be read easily on the air. The chapter describes the use of computers in handling broadcast news copy and provides exercises to help test your skills.

Chapter 3 covers scripting formats and the mechanics of copy preparation. Chapters 2 and 3 are companion chapters that will help you prepare broadcast news copy in acceptable style and form.

The guidelines provided in Chapters 2 and 3 reflect standard usage in most broadcast newsrooms. However, each newsroom has its own preferences, and writing styles may vary from newsroom to newsroom. Chapters 2 and 3 offer a workable set of rules that you can easily modify as needed. Remember that you are trying to reach your audience with specific information presented in a clear, concise, and interesting manner. In accomplishing this objective, *how* you write your copy is as important as what you have to say and how you tell the story.

Spelling

Spelling is an essential part of basic language usage. You might argue that correct spelling is not important because the audience does not see the words in broadcast copy. But television news reports often display words on the screen, and even for radio, correct spelling shows that you care enough about your work to spell words correctly. Some experienced broadcast newswriters often develop codes and abbreviations for common spellings such as *nite* for *night, tho* for *though, nuff* for *enough.* However, these shortcuts will not be acceptable when you write copy to be read by someone who is not familiar with your shorthand.

Incorrect spelling distracts the newscaster and may cause unnecessary and distracting pauses, hesitations, and even stumbling on the air. Misspellings cast doubt on the quality and accuracy of the information presented. They also embarrass the news operation and the newswriter.

Take steps to solve your spelling problems. Concentrate on what you write. Learn or review the principles of phonics and how they help determine the spelling of common words. Use a dictionary on a regular basis. Keep a list of words you routinely misspell. Check this list often and delete those words you have mastered. Be persistent; do not become discouraged. Correct spelling is important!

Capitalization

Use regular upper- and lowercase letters when typing broadcast news stories. Follow the generally accepted rules for capitalization. By doing this, you can easily recognize the beginnings of sentences, proper nouns, street names, and so forth. It will be easy to start using FULL CAPS later if required; simply lock the shift key on the keyboard. Wire services may provide copy in FULL CAPS, but this is done for mechanical reasons, not necessarily to improve readability. Some newsrooms prefer FULL CAPS throughout.

It should be easier for a newscaster to read this sentence:

```
City Council President Marv Bailey says the Evans Street
project should be completed in December.
```

than this sentence:

```
CITY COUNCIL PRESIDENT MARV BAILEY SAYS THE EVANS STREET
PROJECT SHOULD BE COMPLETED IN DECEMBER.
```

Typing

Broadcast news copy must be clean, readable and *typed*. Whether you use conventional typewriters or computer systems, you must be able to demonstrate reasonable typing speed and skills. Handwritten news stories are not acceptable. News stories must be written so fast and handled by so many different people that efficient typing skills are essential.

Typed characters are displayed in various fonts and styles: Elite is too small to be easily read; pica is satisfactory and used often; great primer, executive size, or orator is the best, especially in television for on-camera use. Notice how easy it is to read words typed in larger and bolder typeface:

Times Roman style—The City Council passed the resolution.

`Courier style—The City Council passed the resolution.`

Helvetica Light style—The City Council passed the resolution.

Double-space your copy. This allows enough room for the newscaster to see the words clearly and for copyediting. Single-spacing is too confining; triple-spacing is unnecessary for most broadcast copy applications.

Chapter 3 will illustrate how to arrange your copy pages, set margins, provide copy headings, and time your copy.

Split Words and Sentences

Read these two sentences out loud:

`The President says he will veto the bill. He not-`
`ed the budget is too large already.`

This should be easier to read:

`The President says he will veto the bill.`
`He noted the budget is too large already.`

In the first example, notice how your eye must jump from the first to the second line to complete the thought and the sentence. Such jumps make copy difficult for the newscaster to read aloud without unnatural hesitations and pauses.

Do not hyphenate words between lines in broadcast copy. Type the entire word either at the end of one line or at the beginning of the next. Also, finish one sentence on a page before beginning the next sentence on the following page. Your copy will be easier to read aloud if you follow these guidelines.

Punctuation

Use good judgment, common sense, and practicality as guidelines when using punctuation in broadcast news copy. Punctuation gives the newscaster clues about the meaning, emphasis, and interpretation of the copy.

When speaking aloud, you punctuate constantly with body language. Your listeners hear commas, dashes, question marks, exclamation points, and quotation marks as you whisper, shout, wave your arms, roll your eyes, and wrinkle your brow. In broadcast newswriting, punctuation plays the role of body language.

Correct use of punctuation avoids ambiguity and adds clarity. WMAR-TV in Baltimore identifies the purpose of broadcast news copy punctuation as follows: "The only excuse for punctuation in your script is the help it gives the anchor in reading, and ultimately, so the viewers can better understand what they hear."[1] The sparse use of punctuation keeps sentences short.

There are approximately 30 main punctuation marks, but you'll need to use only about eight for most broadcast writing situations. Do *not* use the following: semicolons (;); exclamation points (!); and brackets ([ ]). Use question marks (?) only to indicate crucial copy interpretations or to indicate that the newscaster should use a rising inflection pattern. Parentheses (( )) are used in phonetic spelling; to bracket things such as length of time of stories, actualities, or soundbites; and often to indicate that a story continues on to another page (MORE/MORE). Information bracketed by parentheses is not to be read aloud.

Learn to use the following punctuation marks effectively: periods (.); commas (,); colons (:); apostrophes ('); hyphens (-); double dashes (--); ellipses (. . .); and quotation marks (" ").

A *period* signals the end of a single thought and the need for a moderate pause. Always place a period at the end of a sentence.

`Eighteen New Yorkers lost their lives in traffic accidents`
`over the weekend.`

A *comma* separates words, phrases, or clauses in a sentence. You can use it to indicate emphasis and to improve clarity when parenthetical phrases (thoughts that supplement the main idea in a sentence) are used. A comma indicates the need for a slight pause by the newscaster.

`The State Board of Education, meeting in special session,`
`considered several items. These included plans for`
`construction of new classrooms, proposals for budget items,`
`and negotiations for teachers' contracts.`

Avoid using *colons* when listing several items in a sentence. The audience may forget the idea you are trying to communicate if the list is too long.

`Agenda items for the next meeting include the following: next`
`year's budget, labor disputes, and environmental protection`
`plans.`

This sentence could be rewritten into several shorter sentences:

```
Several items will be on the agenda at the next meeting. The
board is expected to vote on next year's budget. Labor disputes
will be examined. And board members will discuss environmental
protection plans for the area.
```

Apostrophes form contractions in broadcast copy. An apostrophe replaces a missing letter or number when words or numbers are pushed together. This makes the copy sound more natural, more conversational. Use contractions to join pronouns and verbs:

```
It's a special rock 'n' roll salute to the '80s.
```

Do not use contractions to join nouns and verbs:

```
The governor'll say Iowans'll be better for the experience.
```

Do not use contractions when clarity or emphasis is needed:

```
The governor says he will veto the bill.
```

Hyphens help connect closely related letters, words, or numerals or make a combination of words easier to read aloud. Hyphens appear frequently in broadcast news copy. Clarity of expression often overrides other language rules. Here are acceptable examples of hyphenated letters, words, and numerals:

```
A-B-A                two-to-one vote      out-of-state
one-of-a-kind        142-million          family-owned
semi-professional    two-thirds           re-elect
```

Periods and commas indicate pauses, separate different thoughts, and help the newscaster to interpret broadcast news copy better. But the newscaster often overlooks these very common punctuation marks. Sometimes, using double dashes and ellipses is better. Many broadcast writers use these two punctuation marks interchangeably; however, each has a distinctive function.

Double dashes consist of a single space on either side of two consecutive hyphens (--). Double dashes can help emphasize, clarify, or qualify the previous thought or denote an abrupt change in the thought in a sentence:

```
City officials are concerned about the accident -- one of the
worst ever recorded in the city.
```

Double dashes can also set off lists of items that normally might be separated by commas:

```
The coach listed several qualifications -- determination,
talent, team play -- that determine success in high school
sports.
```

Ellipses consist of three consecutive dots (. . .). They are used in print to indicate that portions of the original material have been deleted for condensation. You should use ellipses in broadcast news copy to add a brief phrase or clarifying thought to an already complete sentence or idea and to signal the newscaster to pause a moment and let vocal inflection drop as the additional phrase is read.

```
State patrol officials stress they will use force at the
nuclear power plant . . . unless the situation improves
overnight.
```

Do not use ellipses as a substitute for commas or other standard punctuation marks:

```
The Oregon Legislature took action on a number of bills today
. . . a new state personnel action program . . . a five-year
road construction program . . . and a comprehensive health
care package for state employees.
```

To write the following would be better:

```
The Oregon Legislature took action on several bills today. A
new state personnel action program was approved. The five-year
road construction program was amended. And legislators
decided to offer state employees a comprehensive health care
package.
```

Emphasis

You can indicate words that need special emphasis or stress. However, do this sparingly and only to clarify the meaning of a word or phrase or to convey an essential idea more accurately.

Read the following sentence several times, emphasizing a *different* word *each* time you read the sentence out loud:

```
How will people know what to do?
```

Notice how the meaning and interpretation of the sentence shift as you emphasize a different word. If this were a direct quote, and if it were important to clarify the thought by noting the word to emphasize, you could indicate this emphasis in the copy.

Indicate the word to be emphasized by <u>underlining</u> the word or typing it in FULL CAPS.

```
The Fire Chief expressed his frustration -- by asking, how
will people know what to do?
```

or

```
The Fire Chief expressed his frustration -- by asking, HOW
will people know what to do?
```

Most word-processing computer systems provide **highlighting** (bold) or reverse printing (e.g., white on black) capabilities to indicate emphasis.

Pronouncers

Provide pronunciation assistance in your copy for unusual or difficult-to-pronounce names, places, terms, and objects. Help the newscaster avoid embarrassment and read these words correctly and smoothly. Do not provide such help for words the average journalist should already know or for words that are not crucial to communicating the idea of the story. You can avoid many foreign references by rewriting the story to eliminate the foreign word. Correct pronunciation of local names is especially important. Provide such help only when you are certain you know how the word should be pronounced; never guess at the correct pronunciation!

Determine how to pronounce the word in question. Ask the news source you interview how to pronounce her name. Ask experienced newsroom journalists how to handle a troublesome local street name. Consult a local specialist who can help with a foreign word or scientific term. Monitor network newscasts and notice how prominent names are pronounced. Be aware that wire services frequently provide pronunciation guides for names in the news.

Use commonsense easy-to-read notations to indicate correct pronunciations. Here are the basic sounds represented by the phonetic symbols identified by the wire services for use in pronouncers:

Vowel Sounds

		Consonant Sounds
a—bat, apple	oh—go, oval	g—got, beg
ah—father, arm	oo—food, two	j—job, gem
aw—raw, saw	ow—scout, crowd	k—keep, cap
ay—fate, ace	oy—boy, join	ch—chair, butcher
e, eh—bed	u—curl, foot	sh—shut, fashion
ee—feel, tea	uh—puff	zh—vision, mirage
i, ih—pin, middle	yoo—fume, few	th—thin, path
y, eye—ice, time, guide		kh—guttural k^2

Indicate the correct pronunciation of a word by typing the phonetic spelling in parentheses directly after or directly above the actual spelling. Do this *each* time the word is used in the same story. Place hyphens between syllables and indicate the accented syllable with FULL CAPS. Here are examples:

```
Iberville (IH-bur-ville) Parish deputies have the bank
surrounded.
```

```
Three men were arrested in the drug raid. They are Cyrus Wesely
(WES-lee), Arnold Goeking (GOH-king), and Vernon Freauf
(FREE-uhf).
```

If all of the words in a name will need pronunciation help, type the entire name on one line, and then indicate the correct pronunciation using the system already suggested.

Finally, read your copy out loud. Trust your ears more than your eyes. Determine whether the copy is easier to read now that you have provided a pronouncer. If it isn't, try again or rewrite the sentence to avoid using the word needing pronunciation help.

Numbers

Use numbers sparingly in broadcast news stories. The audience often has difficulty remembering or appreciating the numbers used. If you use too many numbers, listeners or viewers may be distracted from the next idea or thought and soon may lose the meaning of the story.

Guidelines

Here are guidelines for using numbers in broadcast news stories:

a. Eliminate as many numbers as possible from stories without distorting or omitting essential facts.
b. Exercise good judgment; use only essential numbers.
c. Round off large numbers whenever possible; they are easier to remember when they are heard.
d. Write numbers clearly so that they can be read and understood easily the *first* time.
e. Write numbers in a consistent and functional style; remember numbers are meant to be heard and not read by the audience; write them as they are to be read aloud.
f. Indicate the significance of the numbers used by relating them to the audience's interests, concerns, and life-styles and by putting the numbers into a context that is easily understood.

Writing Style

The following paragraphs present specific suggestions for writing numbers in broadcast news copy.

Use words for numbers one through eleven, and use numerals for numbers 12 through 999.

Use a combination of words and numerals for numbers one-thousand and above. Use hyphens to connect words and numerals to make it easier for the newscaster to "see" and read a number easily. For example, write *75-thousand, seven-million, 134-million,* and *four-trillion.* Notice that numbers one through eleven continue to be written as words even in some of these large word-number combinations.

Use words for all symbols associated with numbers. This would include dollars, cents, degrees, pounds, percent, feet, miles, minutes, hours, Roman numerals, mathematical symbols, and all metric measurements such as liters and kilometers. Thus you would write *17-dollars, 50 cents, 70-degrees, 145 pounds, 45 percent, 85 miles, 18 minutes, Louis the 16th, 16 plus 14 equals 30, four liters.* Hyphens can be added to help indicate the connection between related words and numbers (as in *17-dollars* and *70-degrees*).

Use precise numbers only when they are important:

```
The Bearcats edged the Wolverines 48-to-44 last night in the
championship game.
```

Use approximations like *slightly more than, almost, about,* and *close to* to make large numbers more easily understood:

```
The City Council budget is just over 20 million dollars [rather
than writing $20,030,234.54].
```

When possible, use generic time references. In the examples that follow, you could make the first sentence easier to remember by rewriting it in the form of the second:

```
Tuesday state senators will consider the 1998 budget for the
state.
```

```
Tomorrow state senators will consider next year's budget for
the state [if you wrote this on a Monday in 1997].
```

Make numbers have impact and meaning for the audience. In the following examples, the distance has more meaning in the second sentence:

```
The plane skidded 300 feet before grinding to a halt.
```

```
The plane skidded the length of a football field before
grinding to a halt.
```

In the next examples, the statistic would be more understandable and have more impact if it were presented as shown in the second sentence:

`Auto prices increased two percent last month.`

`It will cost you about 400-dollars more to buy a new car today than it did last month.`

You can use this same technique for stories concerning cost-of-living increases, gasoline prices, and tax increases or declines. Phrases like *doubled, cut in half, dropped 50 percent,* and *dipped sharply* help make the statistic more meaningful and more easily remembered.

Always write fractions as words instead of numbers. Thus ⅔ becomes *two-thirds,* and *3.1* becomes *three-point-one. 5/10%* could be written *five-tenths of a percent,* or better as *five-tenths of one percent* to avoid having *a* sound like *8.*

Convert decimals to regular fractions if equivalents can be written. For example, *.75* can be written as *three-fourths.* Use the word *point* to indicate the position of the decimal point in a number. For example, *The market closed at 3610.35 today* becomes *The market closed as 36-10-point-35 today.*

Use suffixes for ordinal numbers. Thus, write *12th vote, March 23rd,* and *142nd Street,* but use words for the ordinal numbers one through eleven. Thus, write *tenth, third,* and *second.*

Use hyphens to separate numbers used in dates, street addresses, and telephone numbers. Thus, *1996* becomes *19-96, 2141 Elm Street* becomes *21-41 Elm Street,* and *472-3046* becomes *4-7-2 30-46.* Write the numbers as they should be read for clarity and ease of understanding.

Use hyphens when writing ages as well. Here is an example of the standard style for writing ages:

`The accused murderer is identified as 23-year-old Ellen Griffin.`

Notice how hyphens join the words that refer to her age. Since the words are related, hyphens are used.

If a number *begins* a sentence, use *words* to write the number. For example,

`Twenty-three-year-old Ellen Griffin is the accused murderer.`

Make references to time as clear as possible. For example, write *six tonight* instead of *six P.M. tonight,* and write *shortly before midnight* instead of *eleven 57 P.M. tonight.*

Use *zero* instead of *oh* when writing *0* (except when referring to time). For example, write *The Cougars beat the Tigers 52-to-zero,* but write *The rocket launched at exactly 12-oh-four.*

Round off numbers and use approximations whenever possible, but use exact numbers for items like sport scores, market statistics, and election returns when precision is required. For example, write *Ted Mathison defeated Mary Henry by a wide margin, 345-to-16.*

Abbreviations

Eliminate most abbreviations from broadcast news copy. Use abbreviations only if they are likely to be clearly understood when heard the first time and when the newscaster is not likely to stumble or hesitate on the abbreviation. When in doubt, don't abbreviate.

Common abbreviations, like Mr., Mrs., and Dr., are helpful. Do not attempt spelled-out phonetic forms such as *mister* and *missus.* They will confuse the newscaster.

If you have reason to believe the audience will not understand an abbreviation, use the full name or designation the first time it appears in the copy; then use the abbreviation in subsequent references, as in the following example:

```
The Environmental Protection Agency today . . . The E-P-A
. . .
```

An abbreviation is sometimes easier to understand than the full name or designation. For example, *A-F-L C-I-O* is generally recognizable as a labor organization; *American Federation of Labor and Congress of Industrial Organizations* would not have the same instant name recognition. *Y-M-C-A* is more readily understood than *Young Men's Christian Association.*

Do not abbreviate such items as Christmas, governmental titles, religious titles, books of the Bible, names of states and countries, months of the year, days of the week, and addresses.

Do not use symbols in lieu of words. For example, do not write & for *and,* # for *number,* or % for *percent.*

Use hyphens, not periods, to separate the letters in abbreviations. Write F-B-I instead of F.B.I.

Acronyms

An acronym is a word formed from the first letters of each significant word in an organization's name or designation. Acronyms like *SEATO, NATO, NASA, UNICEF,* and *OPEC* are written in FULL CAPS without hyphens separating individual letters. Use only acronyms that are readily understood when read aloud as single words.

Attribution

It is important to attribute, or name the source of, the significant information in broadcast news stories. Using attribution adds credibility and clarity to a story and helps avoid legal liability problems for the reporter/writer as well as the newsmaker and those affected most directly by the story. Never leave a doubt as to whose words are used.

Use attribution when:

    a. There is uncertainty about the source of information.
    b. An opinion is expressed.
    c. Potentially inflammatory statements are made.
    d. Facts may be suspect and questioned in the future.
    e. Story information may be potentially controversial.

Attribution is not necessary when facts are obvious or easily verified:

`Memorial Day services were held at the state capitol this`
`morning.`

Attributing obvious facts in a story makes the copy pedantic and confusing and disrupts the flow of the story.

When using attribution in a story, present it in an honest, responsible, and complete manner. All three characteristics should be evident each time attribution is used.

Be honest and accurate in naming the source and indicating the manner in which the comment was made. Variations of the verb *to say* can provide simple, direct, and unambiguous references. However, when substituting verbs like *emphasizes, claims, charges, accuses,* and so forth, be careful to reflect accurately and objectively the tone and meaning of the comment made. For example, in the following sentence, using *points out* instead of *charges* would change the tone and implication of the governor's comment.

`The Governor charges that the Revenue Department has concealed`
`tax receipt projections for the last three years.`

A responsible journalist cites the most knowledgeable, authoritative source available. Avoid references to "informed or anonymous sources" or a variation of "a high source in the mayor's office." There are occasions, however, when such attribution is used. (The following is © CBS Inc. 1981. All Rights Reserved.) CBS News acknowledges that the use of anonymous sources is an indispensable tool in newsgathering but cautions that the practice must be balanced against the potential for abuse and the public's right to essential story information. CBS indicates that anonymous sources should be used only when there is no other way to gather or report the information, when the information is factual and sufficiently newsworthy, and the source is highly reliable for the specific story in question.[3]

When the source is identified, be certain that the identification is as clear and complete as possible. In broadcast news, provide the title or position of the source, the full name of the source, and *then* the comment. Attribution precedes the comment made:

```
Superintendent of Public Schools Phil Grant emphasizes that
schools will open despite the teachers' strike.
```

If the source's title or position is lengthy, a separate sentence may be necessary:

```
Carl Frost is the Coordinator of the Environmental and Natural
Resources Policy Division. Frost claims that only low-level
nuclear waste will be deposited at the site.
```

In most cases, use the full title of the source when that source is first cited in the story. Then use an abbreviated title or just the source's last name in subsequent references:

```
Mayor Frank Harris will meet with the City Council this
afternoon. Harris is expected to present next year's budget
proposal.
```

Exceptions include religious titles such as Rabbi Goldstein or Reverend Jerry Trams, which you should always use with the name of the source. Eliminate most middle initials and the use of *Junior* and *Senior* unless the source regularly uses them or if they are necessary for accurate identification. If a source is best known by a nickname, put the nickname in parentheses in the copy:

```
Charged with murder was Willard (Spooky) Landry.
```

Occasionally, especially in foreign news stories, the title or position of the source is more important than the name of the source, or the name may be obscure and irrelevant to the essential facts of a story. For example, knowing that Saddam Ali Hussein is the ambassador to the United States from a small Persian Gulf country that is threatening to bomb American ships is not crucial. Simply refer to the ambassador by title and eliminate his name; using his name would probably confuse most listeners or viewers.

The need for clarity may cause you to eliminate or at least modify long, complex titles in broadcast news stories.

```
The Principal Associate Deputy Attorney General for the U.S.
Justice Department, Ami Brewster, says . . .
```

can be simplified by writing:

`A high ranking Justice Department official says . . .`

followed by a sentence that indicates the specific name of the official along with an abbreviated job title.

`He is a member of the Citizens Advisory Committee for the`
`statewide Department of Environmental Control . . .`

could be improved by writing:

`He's a member of a citizens' environmental advisory group . . .`

Never start a story with attribution from an unfamiliar source. Such attribution is wasted and tends to confuse the audience. Instead, use the title and name as attribution in the second or third sentence of the story. For example:

`Local wildlife advocates have a new ally. County Extension Agent`
`Norm Galaxie wants local wildlife to have better homes . . .`

In all cases, attribution precedes the comment. This technique "sets up" the comment and prepares the audience for the statement or comment that follows.

Use taped comments and statements whenever possible. If these are not available, use direct quotes or partial quotes sparingly and only if they add impact or color to the story. Be certain that the quotation is indicated clearly, as in the following example, by using phrases like *as she put it, in these words, quoting now, calling it,* and so forth, because the audience doesn't see the quotation marks.

`The Mayor says the proposal is -- in his words -- worthless.`

Do not use phrases like *quote* and *end quote* or *unquote.* This technique is awkward, distracting, and seldom used today.

If a quotation is divided into several sections (partial quotes), be certain to note when you resume the quotation:

`The Mayor says -- quoting now -- the proposal is worthless.`
`Mayor Harris continued by saying that the differences he has`
`had with the City Council over the last few weeks can be worked`
`out. No reaction yet from City Council members.`

Paraphrase or summarize comments that the newscaster or reporter can say in less time and with greater clarity and directness. Using the word *said* does not necessarily indicate that the words are quoted. They may be paraphrased.

```
The president says the modified program will be in place next
year.
```

Attribution is an essential part of broadcast newswriting and reporting practices and you need to provide it honestly, responsibly, and fully and in a form that is brief and clearly understood when read aloud.

Corrections and Broadcast Editing Marks

Providing news copy that is clean and easy to read is important. The limited number of editing marks available to broadcast newswriters and reporters should be used sparingly, with regard for time constraints and common sense. Ideally, you should retype copy if too many corrections are noted, but time pressures often prevent following this advice. The intricate array of copyediting symbols used in the print media are not acceptable for broadcast copy. Remember that the newscaster must be able to read the copy aloud smoothly and accurately.

Note any broadcast copyediting marks simply, clearly, boldly, and neatly in the main body of the copy, using block printing rather than script or cursive style. The basic editing marks available for broadcast news copy are shown in Figure 2.1.

Although you may not need to use broadcast copyediting symbols on a regular basis now, you should still learn them because not every newsroom in which you will work will have computers to handle routine copyediting tasks.

Computers in the Newsroom

The editing marks just described may not be necessary once broadcast newsrooms become completely "electronic." Although movements toward electronic news processing and electronic newsrooms are noticeable, small- and medium-market newsrooms (where most broadcast news careers begin) will be the last to convert to these systems. Also, in many cases, job applicants still take writing tests on typewriters rather than computer terminals. Figure 2.2 shows some of the functions handled by newsroom computers.

Knowing basic broadcast newswriting style, even when using computers, is still important. Computers and other technology free the journalist to concentrate on gathering and writing the news and on the content of the story.

The computer systems being used in broadcast newsrooms can perform marvelous functions like those listed here:

a. Wire copy can be transferred or "dumped" into newsroom computers for later rewriting and updates.
b. Computers can load numbers such as sports scores and election return results directly into character generators that can interface with sophisticated graphics systems to provide striking visual material for television newscasts.

1. To separate words run together, use a single slanted line:

    Senators passed the bill this/morning.

2. To close up space between letters in the <u>same</u> word, use curved lines <u>both</u> above <u>and</u> below the gap:

    Senators passed the bill this morn◡ing.

3. To delete a word or phrase, black out the unwanted material <u>completely</u> and bridge the gap with a <u>single</u> line above the connecting words:

    Senators passed the ~~crucial~~ bill this morning.

4. To insert a word or phrase, print the entire word boldly above the line and funnel it into the proper place in the sentence:

    Senators passed *THE*↓bill this morning.

5. To correct a misspelled word, black it out <u>completely</u>, print boldly the correct version of the <u>entire word</u> above the line and funnel the correction into the proper place in the sentence.

    Senators passed the *BILL*~~____~~ this morning.

6. To close up space when a word, a phrase, or an entire sentence is deleted, black out completely the portion to be deleted, and then use a curved line to connect the two parts of the finished sentence:

    Senators ~~were in conference most of the morning but eventually~~ passed the bill this morning.

7. To insert a missing punctuation mark, simply provide the missing notation neatly but boldly at the proper place in the copy: Senators passed the bill this morning.

Figure 2.1 Basic broadcast news copyediting marks.

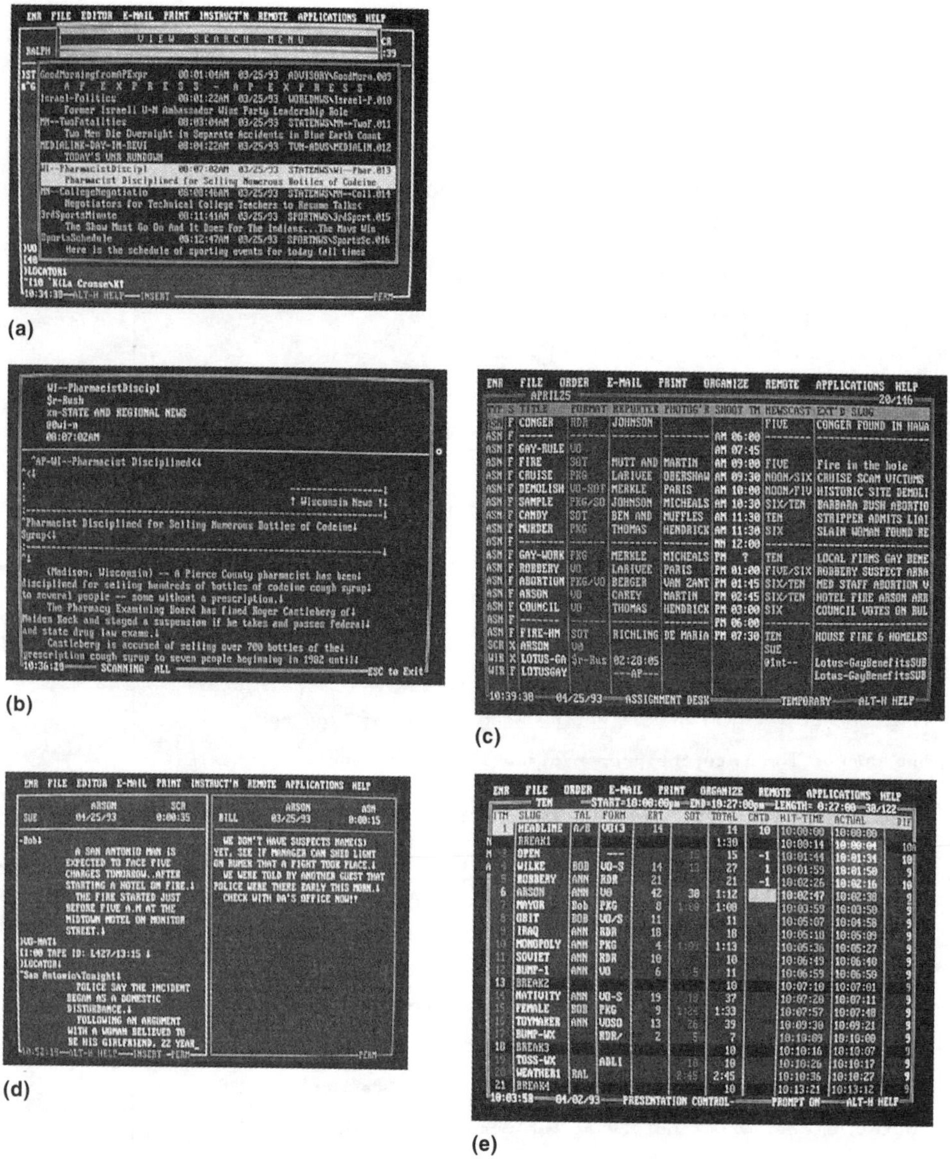

(a)

(b)

(c)

(d)

(e)

Figure 2.2 Computers can help streamline the flow of information in a newsroom. Once a particular wire story is identified (a), the full story can be reviewed, edited, stored, and retrieved (b). Customized assignment boards simplify story coverage tracking (c). Word-processing functions make entering script instructions easy for the writer who simply fills in the requested information (d). Computers help producers maintain control over a newscast from the preliminary rundown through the on-air presentation (e). Illustrations courtesy of Comprompter Incorporated.

c. Original stories can be written directly onto the screen, and news copy can then be added, deleted, moved, and saved as needed.

d. Computers can be interconnected so that reporters both in the field and in the newsroom can communicate directly with newsroom supervisors to provide story coverage information. Electronic notepads help users capture, organize, and communicate ideas and information. These small, portable devices allow free-form note taking, drawing, calculating, scheduling, and communicating.

e. Previous stories can be retrieved directly from computer files.

f. Newsroom personnel activities can be coordinated by using story assignment lists and updates, future story file notations, personnel addresses and phone numbers, news sources and contacts, updates of newsroom policies and procedures, and so forth.

g. Once the reading speed on an individual newscaster has been determined, a computer can calculate the reading time of each story, add the length of any tape used, and provide an estimated total length for a particular story.

h. Once stories have been checked and edited, they can be written onto teleprompter copy for on-camera use or read directly off the computer screen in radio newsrooms.

i. Cues for editing audio or video material can be entered on computer.

j. Producers can use computers to generate the lineups for newscasts, noting the length of each story to be used as well as the available tape material that will accompany each story in a newscast.

k. With a modem or telephone connection, newsroom computers can tap vast data base files that provide resource and background information that is otherwise not readily available.

Computers help broadcast newsrooms generate, store, and retrieve news material. The capabilities just listed vary with the computer system and software packages used. More newsrooms will become completely computerized as costs decline and as the efficiency of the electronic newsroom becomes more apparent.

Computer literacy is important. Prospective employers will expect you to know more about computers than simply how to type a research paper on a word processor. If a computer system is not available in your school's newsroom, visit a nearby radio or television station that has a newsroom computer system and see how computers are used to process information quickly and efficiently. Many self-taught and instructional opportunities are also available using computer discs, instructional videotapes, and commercial computer learning centers. You must learn to use computers.

NewsChannel 8, Maryland • Virginia • Washington, DC Photo courtesy of Wayne Lynch.

Summary

This chapter reviewed basic broadcast newswriting style. Always use correct spelling in broadcast copy. Use regular upper- and lowercase letters when typing broadcast news stories, and use the largest, boldest type size available. Never split words between lines or sentences between pages in broadcast copy.

Good judgment, common sense, and practical usage are the guidelines when using punctuation marks; each punctuation mark should make the copy easier to read and understand when read aloud. If it is important to indicate that a word or phrase needs special emphasis, underline the words or type them in FULL CAPS. Use commonsense, easy-to-read notations in parentheses directly above or immediately after words that are difficult to pronounce.

Use numbers sparingly; when you do use them, write them in a consistent way and always try to indicate the significance of the numbers included. Use words for numbers one through eleven, numerals for 12 through 999, and a combination of numerals and words (separated by hyphens) for numbers one-

thousand and above. Use approximations as often and as accurately as possible.

Use abbreviations sparingly but clearly. If the abbreviation is not well known, provide the full name the first time; then use the abbreviation in subsequent references. Acronyms are abbreviations meant to be read as single words.

Attribution adds credibility and clarity to stories and avoids potential legal problems. Obvious facts do not need attribution, but comments in which opinions are expressed or which include facts that may be questioned later always require that sources be named. Make the attribution clear, complete, and honest. Provide the title or position of the source, the name of the source, and *then* the statement made. Attribution can be shortened after the first reference.

The limited number of broadcast editing marks available should be used only when necessary and only when the edited copy is still easy to read and understand. Newsroom computers help generate, store, and retrieve news material. They also streamline the copyediting process.

Exercises

1. Using the guidelines provided in this chapter, correct the following story segments to conform with standard *broadcast* newswriting style and practice:

a. RESCUE WORKERS ARE DIGGING THROUGH THE WRECKAGE OF THE UNITED AIRLINES PLANE LOOKING FOR SURVIVORS, ACCORDING TO F.A.A. OFFICIALS.

b. St. senators meeting in special session have passed almost fifty bills in one day

c. Several issues will be discussed by the mayfield city council tonight; water rights, rezoning ordinances, liability insurance.

d. Congress'll consider the legislation after christmas.

e. The low level waste site is opposed by environmental groups.

f. School board members indicate they will oppose the change; even if it means doing without textbooks next school year

g. Observers claim that the governors statement was dramatic; the most dramatic he has ever made.

h. Phillip Yates claims he didn't rob the clerk at the bank. 27 yr. old Phillip, also known as ''Bolero'' is charged with 6 counts of robbery.

i. Judge Hastings says he won't review the controversial suit.

j. thirteen thousand and fourteen dollars and twenty-two cents. [written in the middle of a sentence]

k. The cost of living rose .5% last month.

l. Gasoline prices increased ¼% last month.

m. Local taxes will increase ½ of 1% next year.

n. 3.75

o. October 16

p. November 23

q. State Police are searching for Melvin C. Douglas, 19, who's address is listed as 1256 22 street.

r. If you would like to send messages to the 4 yr. old heart transplant patient, call 567–2389 or write to griffin memorial hospital 907 west 2nd avenue in Olwine.

s. The parade is scheduled for 6 o'clock p.m. tonite.

t. The Nigerian pres. and his cabinet will visit several midwestern states this week, Kansas, okla., iowa, & Nebr.

u. The bills signed on mon. will take effect next febr.

v. $512.23 [written in the middle of a sentence]

w. Missus Evelyn Tremain was the m.c. for the banquet.

x. u.s.d.a.

y. a.m.a.

z. The occasion has special religious significance, according to Rabbi Albert Wurlitzer. Wurlitzer adds that special events are planned to mark the day.

aa. Helen Roberts, united way coordinator, says ''local residents can expect the new shelter to be open by tues.''

bb. gov. Thomas stresses that ''the legislation is unnecessary.''

cc. In Washington, d.c., u.s.senator Elliot Avery (D., NM) told reporters, ''the situation in the mideast looks grim. We will have to continue our high profile in the area. Our government is doing everything possible to protect Americans in the area.''

dd. ''We will continue to negotiate with the kidnappers. The situation is not hopeless,'' according to Moammar Asahi, the Associate Director for Overseas Affairs and the Tibetan Ambassador to the United States.

ee. ''The issue is not dead,'' according to Harry Burnett, Chief Prosecutor.

Notes

1. WMAR-TV *Channel 2 News Stylebook* (Baltimore, MD: WMAR-TV, n.d.), 9.

2. James R. Hood and Brad Kalbfeld, eds., *The Associated Press Broadcast News Handbook* (New York: The Associated Press, 1982), 230.

3. CBS News, *CBS News Standards* (New York: CBS News, n.d.), 37B.

Broadcast News Copy Mechanics and Scripting Formats

This is a companion chapter to Chapter 2, ''Broadcast Newswriting Style.'' Together, they indicate the principal guidelines for broadcast newswriting style and mechanics—how to put words on paper in standard form in broadcast newsrooms. This essential information is presented in one place early in this book. If a question arises about recommended writing style or scripting format, these two chapters will help you to review important guidelines. They serve as a foundation for later chapters that concern other aspects of broadcast newswriting and reporting. Use what you need as you need it. Come back to Chapter 3 to check your newswriting style and copy format practices as you explore other scripting techniques.

Remember that Chapters 2 and 3 concern only basic writing style and scripting formats for both radio and television news. Other chapters in this book, especially Chapters 12 (''Radio Reporting'') and 13 (''Television Reporting''), will describe and illustrate effective techniques for applying these fundamental elements to broadcast news coverage, writing, and reporting.

Also understand that only basic news copy formats will be presented and that each broadcast operation will have its own copy format requirements as well as unique terms to describe the sound and picture components of broadcast news copy. The scripting formats and requirements of several broadcast news operations have been examined. The chapter presents a composite of these formats with some variations that you may encounter. If you learn the basic formats recommended, you should be able to adapt to the requirements of other newsrooms with only a minimum amount of instruction. In this and later chapters, when news copy from a variety of newsrooms is reproduced without changes, you will notice variations in copy style and format.

No matter how complete and well illustrated an individual stylebook might be, not every situation can be covered. A stylebook is a guideline and is not meant to place a chokehold on your scripting efforts. Some situations will not be covered with a policy; some policies will not work under certain situations. Some situations will require common sense and good judgment rather than a strict rule in a guidebook.

You might find that you begin to feel overwhelmed by the large number of terms and abbreviations used in broadcast news copy. Unfortunately, this "shorthand" is used in newsrooms throughout the country. Alternative terms are provided when they are in common use. To help yourself understand, remember, and use these terms and abbreviations, you might find it useful to underline or highlight terms and abbreviations presented *in italics* in the text.

Thus, this chapter presents the principal types of radio and television news copy and scripting formats. Essential copy mechanics are presented first—page layout, headings and copy slugs, margins, and timing. Then each type of format is defined, described, and illustrated. The principal radio formats presented are the following: readers, copy with actualities, voicers, wraps, live reports, and stories using natural sound. The principal television formats illustrated are the following: readers, copy with graphics, voice-overs, copy with soundbites, reporter packages, and on-set and live reports. Alternative copy formats will also be presented. The exercises at the end of this chapter will help you to review and identify the characteristics of each scripting format.

Copy Mechanics

Standardizing the selection and placement of story information on a page of broadcast news copy is important. Each news story is easier to handle and process through the various steps necessary if each piece of copy is presented in a uniform manner.

General Guidelines

Here are guidelines for preparing *both* radio and television news copy pages:

a. Select a soft grade of paper to avoid distracting noise near microphones. Pastel-colored pages are used in television to avoid problems with glare caused by lights.
b. Type on only one side of standard size sheets of 8½″ × 11″ unruled paper. Some newsroom supervisors find they get more tightly written stories if they chop 8½″ × 11″ sheets in half. 8½″ × 5½″ makes for shorter stories (12 lines max.) and a lot less waste. This practice is more common in radio than in television news operations.
c. Type only one story per page. This provides flexibility when decisions are made about the order of stories in a newscast. Television newsrooms often use "copy books" (preassembled sets of paper producing duplicate copies of each story for distribution to key news production personnel).
d. If a story continues to a second page, write (*MORE*) at the bottom of the first page and a notation at the top of the next page indicating the continuation of the same story (e.g., *ADD 1, 2–2–2–2, Page 2*, or *Page 2 of 3*). Some newsrooms use a heavy dark arrow at the bottom of the first page pointing to the right. ———→
e. Do not split sentences between news copy pages.

 f. Leave at least a one-inch margin on the left and right and a one-to two-inch margin at the top of the page.

 g. Use standard margin settings: a 65-space line for radio and two columns for television—a 20-space column on the left side of the page for video production notations and a 25-space column on the right side of the page for audio notations, including the words that will be read aloud. These are approximate margin settings based on the use of the medium-size Courier style shown in Chapter 2 (see ''Typing''). Different fonts and letter sizes are available and will influence margin settings and timing notations (discussed later in this chapter).

 h. Double-space all copy to be read aloud.

 i. Single-space all other copy notations.

 j. Follow standard capitalization rules for copy read aloud, but use FULL CAPS for all production notations. As noted in Chapter 2, some newsrooms prefer FULL CAPS throughout.

 k. Indent all paragraphs two to five spaces. Some newsrooms prefer that an extra space divide paragraphs with no indentation.

 l. Identify each story with a *copy slug,* a term described later.

 m. A few spaces below the last line of each story, use an *end mark* to indicate the end of each story. Common end marks are: -0-, -30-, ###, or the writer's initials.

Copy Slugs

In only a few words, a copy slug must identify the specific nature of a news story. In effect, the copy slug is the ''file folder'' label or identification for each story. Story slugs often must be very short—for instance, only eight characters on an IBM newsroom computer system—because of computer file limits.

Copy slugs are typed in FULL CAPS and single-spaced in either a stacked arrangement at the top left or spread across the top line of each copy page. If stories are typed on individual sheets of paper, radio tends to use the first system, whereas television and most computerized newsrooms favor the second arrangement. Both methods accomplish the same objective—to identify and to monitor the flow of individual stories in a newsroom. Here is an example of each type of copy slug arrangement:

Stacked Slug   **Line Slug**
REYNOLDS MURDER REYNOLDS MURDER 10/21 5p RB
10/21 5p
R. BROWN

Specific information must be provided in each copy slug: a brief but clear identification of the story item; the date of the story; the time the story was prepared; and the identification of the writer of each story. Each piece of the copy slug is important.

KRLN LOCAL NEWS   Date 6/24   Subj: INCLINE RAILWAY   0600

(CANON CITY)- - -MECHANICAL PROBLEMS WITH THE INCLINE RAILWAY AT THE ROYAL GORGE BRIDGE 0700

WEST OF CANON CITY CAUSED SOME INCONVENIENCE TO A GROUP OF TOURISTS YESTERDAY BUT   0800

RESULTED IN NO SERIOUS INJURIES. ROYAL GORGE SPOKESMAN BEN HART SAID A PROBLEM WITH

THE TRANSPORT SYSTEM AT THE TOP OF THE INCLINE BROUGHT THE RAIL CARS TO A SUDDEN HALT

ABOUT 3 O'CLOCK YESTERDAY AFTERNOON. KRLN ASKED HART WHERE THE CARS STOPPED? . . . .

. . . . (INCLINE RAILWAY . . . . CUT 1 . . . . 6 SEC . . . . . . OUT: MIDDLE OF THE TRACK)

Figure 3.1   Example of a story slug. Courtesy of KRLN, Canon City, Colorado.

In less than three or four words, the writer must identify the essential nature of the story. If you have several traffic accidents to report in one newscast, do not use *ACCIDENT* as the story slug; use the location of the accident or the name of the fatality or some other specific reference to distinguish that particular accident from other accident stories (e.g., *ELM STREET CRASH* or *PHILLIPS FATALITY*). If the copy provides another angle or aspect to an important local story or will be used as a follow-up to a previous report, consider using the same original story slug but adding notations like *—UPDATE, —NEXT DAY, —FOLLOW-UP*, or *—NEIGHBORS, —FAMILY ANGLE, —SUSPECT B.G.*

Indicate a date and time for each story. Some newsrooms want the date and time the story was *written*. Others prefer that you indicate the specific newscast date and time in which the story will be *used*. Some newsrooms add these date and time notations at the top or along the margins of the copy. Notice these kinds of notations on the KRLN copy in Figure 3.1.

This technique is especially useful in small news operations where one person coordinates all newsroom activities. Other station personnel, especially on-air personalities, often read news copy when the one-person news staff is out covering stories or collecting the mail. By having these newscast times noted on the copy, others can verify that a story has been used and can monitor the emphasis placed on certain kinds of stories in daily newscasts.

The writer's name or initials are included in the copy slug not only to note who wrote the story but also to indicate who probably knows the story best and could provide additional details if needed.

Timing Copy

Indicating the length of each story on the copy page is helpful. This can be done by noting (either at the top right or at the bottom of the story) the total number of lines written as well as the length of the tape material included. If the story is longer than 60 seconds, separate minutes and seconds by a colon (e.g., 1:21 or 01:53). The abbreviation *TRT* (total running time) may be used to indicate the total length of a single story. Here are sample timing notations:

8 lines	12 lines	TRT = 2:05
:30	:45	
	(+ :08 actuality)	
	TRT = :53	

Entire newscasts can be pretimed just by counting the number of lines in each story, adding the time for the tape material to be used, and calculating the reading speed of the newscaster.

If the reading speed of the newscaster who will be reading the copy is not known, time each story by reading it aloud and using a stopwatch to determine the length of each item. As an alternative, you could use approximations. Using the margin settings indicated earlier, one line of radio copy takes about four seconds to read aloud, and one line of television copy takes about one second to read aloud. Thus, 16 lines of radio copy yield a 60-second story, and a 15-second radio story requires about four lines of copy. Remember, these are only approximations. It is better to know precisely the reading speed of the newscaster who will be reading the copy.

The font used to type or print news copy will also influence timing. If the typeface is large, you can place only a few words on each line of copy. If the typeface is small, you can place more words on each line of copy, but timing calculations will have to be adjusted. Larger typefaces are useful for on-camera television anchors who have to read copy from a teleprompter from a distance of sometimes 10 to 18 feet. Here is how a few typical typefaces would look on paper:

14 point courier

18 point courier

24 point courier

Newsroom computers can now perform timing calculations automatically once typeface information as well as the reading speed of each newscaster have been determined and loaded into the computer. Using this system, the writer simply writes the copy, indicates the newscaster assigned to read the copy, and the computer does the rest, automatically! Chapter 2 illustrated how computers can be used to generate and process stories in broadcast newsrooms.

Radio Scripting Formats	A news story in a radio broadcast can be presented in several ways. This section describes and illustrates each basic scripting format to show the placement and form for key copy notations. A single news item is presented in different forms, progressing from the most simple to the most complex. The same story facts are presented in different ways or formats. The *use* of these basic copy formats is explained further in Chapter 12, "Radio Reporting."

Readers

A *reader* is a story delivered or told by the newscaster without the use of any additional audio. The entire story is told by the newscaster. Figure 3.2 shows an example of a reader.

Actualities

An *actuality* (also called a *soundbite*) is a short taped comment from someone associated directly with the development of a news story. It could be an excerpt from a speech or news conference, a police officer's description of an accident, the comments of a local homeowner displaced by a building project. To better identify the actuality, provide the first few words of the comment (the *in-cue*), the last words heard (the *out-cue* or *end-cue*), the exact length of the actuality, and a brief summary of what was said (the *summary*). Most newsrooms assign a number to the tape on which the actuality is recorded. Figure 3.3 is the same story shown in Figure 3.2, but scripted to include an actuality.

Some newsrooms use fewer copy notations. A common practice is to indicate the number of the tape that contains the actuality or voicer report, the first few words of the open or in-cue, the length of the recorded material, and the last few words of the close or out-cue. Figure 3.4 shows this abbreviated set of notations used on ABC Radio news copy.

Some newsrooms require the reporter or writer to type out the entire actuality or soundbite and to place this transcript *on* the main copy page. This practice has also gained favor with television newsrooms; the transcripts are used to encode information for special receivers used by hearing-impaired viewers. When available, transcripts of soundbites are provided for radio and television news copy used throughout this book.

Radio network newsrooms often provide additional precision and copy flexibility by *attaching* to the main copy page a verbatim transcript of an actuality. These *verbatim sheets* are used instead of the summary suggested earlier. Figure 3.5 shows the verbatim sheet for the story in Figure 3.4.

Voicers

When a *voicer* is used, the newscaster or anchor reads a short lead-in to the item and then the reporter who wrote the story provides all of the essential details. No actualities or other audio elements are included in the main body of the report, only the voice of the reporter. Generally, voicers are recorded. However, voicers or single-voice reports can be done as part of live broadcasts.

```
DERAILMENT                                    9 LINES
10/21   9A                                    :30
S. BROWN


        Traffic was blocked for more then two hours this morning on

North 70th Street after a Union Pacific train derailed.

        U-P spokesman Jeff Harris says the company has no idea what

happened. Harris adds that it was fortunate no cars or trucks

were near the crossing when the train left the tracks about five

this morning. No injuries are reported.

        Union Pacific has cancelled all rail traffic between Omaha

and Denver until the wreckage is cleared. Harris says that should

take about 24 hours. Investigation into the accident continues.


                              ###
```

Figure 3.2 Sample radio copy format for a reader.

```
DERAILMENT                              6 LINES
10/21   9A                              + :12 ACTUALITY
S. BROWN                                TRT= :30


     Traffic was blocked for more then two hours this morning on

North 70th Street after a Union Pacific train derailed.

     U-P spokesman Jeff Harris says the company has no idea what

happened.

--------------------------------------------------------------------------------

          Cart # 102-A

          In Cue: "We really don't know...."

          Out Cue: "...a real disaster."

          Length: 12-seconds

          Summary:  Harris says that it was fortunate
          no cars or trucks were near the crossing when
          the train left the tracks about five this
          morning. No injuries are reported.

--------------------------------------------------------------------------------


     Union Pacific has cancelled all rail traffic between Omaha

and Denver until the wreckage is cleared. Harris says that should

take about 24 hours. Investigation into the accident continues.


                              ###
```

Figure 3.3   Sample radio copy format for use of an actuality.

hardt Tue Oct 20 17:48 page 2

-0-

SEEMS THE PENTAGON WAS MAKING HOME-MOVIES OF YESTERDAY'S U-S NAVY ATTACK ON 2-OF IRAN'S OIL PLATFORMS IN THE GULF! ABC'S BOB ZELNICK GOT A LOOK AT THE MOVIES TODAY:

CAT# 127

O; THE FOOTAGE

(5) T; 23

C; ABOARD THE SHIPS

IRAN IS STILL THREATENING TO GET-BACK AT THE U-S FOR THE ATTACK ON ITS OIL PLATFORMS.

Figure 3.4 Example of abbreviated copy notations for a voicer. Courtesy of ABC Contemporary Network.

```
CAT#  WHO              NC  CODE       SLUG            ? RUNS PROCESSED

127  BOB ZELNICK       ABCrruuu   WHAT FOOTAGE SHOWS  Q  :23 Oct 20 16:45
  WHAT:

WHERE:PENTAGON            EVENT TIME:   445P   FACILITIES/QUAL:DOD AUTO

TAKEN BY:silverst  CREDIT/RESTRICTION:ASK/ZELNICK

OPENS:THE FOOTAGE..           RUNS:23  CLOSE:....THE SHIPS.

NEWSCALL DESCRIPTION:
========================================================================

THE DEFENSE DEPARTMENT HAS RELEASED FOOTAGE OF YESTERDAY'S DESTRUCTION OF AN

IRANIAN OIL INSTALLATION - AND MILITARY OUTPOST - IN THE PERSIAN GULF. FROM THE

PENTAGON, ABC'S BOB ZELNICK TELLS US WHAT THE FOOTAGE SHOWS....




VERBATIM: THE FOOTAGE SHOWS THE OVERWHELMING MIGHT OF FOUR DESTROYERS UNLEASHED

AGAINST A VIRTUALLY UNDEFENDED STATIONARY TARGET, BANGING AWAY AT THE ROSTOM

PLATFORM AT WHAT AT TIMES APPEARS LITTLE MORE THAN TARGET PRACTICE. AFTER MORE

THAN A THOUSAND FIVE-INCH SHELLS AND SOME 45 MINUTES OF FIRING, A NAVY

DEMOLITION TEAM MOVES ON TO THE WRECKAGE. THE EXPLOSION FROM ITS CHARGE BRINGS

CHEERS FROM THE MAN ABOARD THE SHIPS.
```

Figure 3.5 The verbatim sheet for the radio copy in Figure 3.4. Courtesy of ABC
Contemporary Network.

Newsrooms tend to standardize the closing to voicers. Here are a few examples: . . . *Ed Jones, Radio 90 News* or . . . *at the Statehouse, Mary Reilly, News 8*. A short summary of the contents of the voicer should be provided in case the recorded report is not heard or for use later when the story needs to be rewritten.

Figure 3.6 is the same story shown in Figures 3.2 and 3.3, but now scripted for a voicer report. Figure 3.7 shows a transcript of the words the reporter recorded on tape when producing the main part of the voicer report.

Wraps

A *wrap* (also called a *voicer wrap* or a *voicer wraparound*) is, in effect, a complete, self-contained story preceded by a brief lead-in by the newscaster. The reporter's recorded comments ''wrap around'' an actuality associated with that particular story. A wrap is similar to a voicer, except an actuality is inserted within the taped report.

Figure 3.8 shows the copy the anchor or newscaster would use to introduce a voicer wrap. Figure 3.9 shows the copy the reporter would use to record the wrap. Some newsrooms attach the two pages for reference, rewriting, and eventual filing. Figures 3.8 and 3.9 illustrate the most complex version of the same story facts reported in different copy formats in Figure 3.2, 3.3, 3.6, and 3.7.

Live Reports

A late-breaking story often involves a reporter's delivery of a *live report* directly from the scene. Use the scripting format suggested for voicers or voicer wraps. When using a modified version of this copy format, the anchor lead-in copy could be written in the same manner, but only note a standard out-cue and approximate length for the live report. No in-cue or summary would be scripted, since this information would not be known in advance.

Figure 3.10 is an example of how the ABC Contemporary Network (ABC/C) scripted a live report. Since ABC/C provides several newscasts to affiliate stations each hour, two lengths are noted for the ''live join'' in the figure.

Natural Sound

Natural sound (often abbreviated as *Nat Sound* and also called *Location Sound*) provides an audio backdrop or setting for a story. This could be the shouts of demonstrators at the gates of a factory facing a labor strike, the wail of emergency vehicle sirens as survivors are being transported to hospitals after a major airplane crash, the tolling of church bells on Easter morning. Natural sound can be used as a short actuality or included in voicers and wraps. Use the scripting format illustrated earlier that best matches the use of natural sound in a particular story. Chapter 12 offers suggestions and examples for using natural or location sound in radio news stories.

Television Scripting Formats

Since television news production involves a unified team effort, providing complete and consistent details about each story to every member of the team is important. Once the copy for each story has been approved (usually by the newscast producer or managing editor), copies are distributed to various units

```
DERAILMENT                           5 LINES
10/21    9A                          +:20 VOICER WRAP
S. BROWN                             TRT= :32


        Traffic was blocked for more then two hours this morning on

North 70th Street after a Union Pacific train derailed.

        News 11's Sue Brown has details.
-----------------------------------------------------------------

             Cart # 105-V

             In Cue: "U-P spokesman Jeff Harris....

             Out Cue: "...Sue Brown, News 11."

             Length: 20-seconds

             Summary:  U-P spokesman Jeff Harris says the
             company has no idea what happened when the
             train derailed about five this morning. No
             injuries were reported. Sue Brown has learned
             that it will take about 24 hours to clear the
             wreckage.
-----------------------------------------------------------------


        Union Pacific has cancelled all rail traffic between Omaha

and Denver until the wreckage is cleared. Investigation into the

accident continues.


                            ###
```

Figure 3.6   Sample radio copy format for a voicer report.

```
DERAILMENT                                          5 LINES
10/21   9/A                                         :20 VOICER
S. Brown                                            COPY




        U-P spokesman Jeff Harris says the company has no idea what happened.
   Harris adds that it was fortunate no cars or trucks were near the crossing
   when the train left the tracks about five this morning. No injuries are
   reported. It should take about 24 hours to clear the tracks. Sue Brown, News
   11.




                                  ###
```

Figure 3.7 Sample radio copy format used by a reporter to record or produce a voicer report.

or individuals who will help put the story on the air. These include the tele-prompter operator, who will display the copy to be read on-camera by the anchors or newscasters; each of the on-camera newscasters; the director of the newscast; the graphics or CG (character generator) operator, who will prepare the written and graphic material to be inserted on the screen when the story is broadcast; and the ENG (electronic newsgathering) editor, who will edit the videotape to match the script that has been written. Chapter 11, ''Broadcast Newsroom Organization and Operation,'' presents a more complete description of how television news copy is processed and handled.

Become familiar with the terminology and abbreviations that are often used in television news copy. In this chapter, an effort has been made to simplify this production terminology and to present these production elements in progressive steps. Chapter 13 provides a more comprehensive discussion of essential television news production terms.

Television scripting formats are more intricate than radio scripting formats. You must indicate both sound and picture components for each television news story. Except for dramatic and comedy scripts, virtually all television scripts are written in two columns. The left column is primarily for

```
DERAILMENT                        5 LINES
10/21   9A                        +:20 VOICER WRAP
S. BROWN                          TRT= :32


        Traffic was blocked for more then two hours this morning on

North 70th Street after a Union Pacific train derailed.

        News 11's Sue Brown has details.

--------------------------------------------------------------------

                Cart # 105-V

                In Cue: "U-P spokesman Jeff Harris....

                Out Cue: "...Sue Brown, News 11."

                Length: 20-seconds

                Summary:  U-P spokesman Jeff Harris says the
                company has no idea what happened when the
                train derailed about five this morning. No
                injuries were reported. Sue Brown has learned
                that it will take about 24 hours to clear the
                wreckage.

--------------------------------------------------------------------


        Union Pacific has cancelled all rail traffic between Omaha

and Denver until the wreckage is cleared. Investigation into the

accident continues.



                              ###
```

Figure 3.8   Sample radio copy format used by a newscaster to introduce a voicer
wraparound report.

```
DERAILMENT                                    5 LINES + :08 ACT.
10/21  9A                                     TRT = :20
S. Brown                                      VOICER WRAP COPY




        U-P spokesman Jeff Harris says the company has no idea what happened.


   -----------------------------------------------------------------------


   In Cue: "It was fortunate no cars or trucks were near. . . .

   Out Cue: " . . . no injuries reported."

   Length: 08-seconds

   Summary: Harris says it was fortunate no vehicles were near the crossing
   when the train derailed. No injuries reported.
   -----------------------------------------------------------------------



   Harris says it will be about 24 hours before trains run again.

   Sue Brown, News 11.



                                  ###
```

Figure 3.9   Sample radio copy format used by a reporter to record or produce a voicer wraparound report.

```
WALL STREET'S RIDING A POGO STICK ON THE DAY AFTER.

A LIVE-SWITCH TO OUR BOB SCHMIDT AT THE NEW YORK STOCK EXCHANGE GETS THE

NUMBERS...AND THE MOOD:


                SCHMIDT LIVE              Live  Join

                APPROX. :12 AT 12:52P BRIEF

                  LONGER ON 12:56P SHOW



WORLD MARKETS TOOK A NOSE-DIVE, THEN NOSED-UP. CHEMICAL AND MARINE

MIDLAND BANKS ROLLED-BACK THEIR PRIME RATES.
```

Figure 3.10 Example of a radio live report copy format. Courtesy of ABC
Contemporary Network.

the director and identifies what is *seen* on the screen. The right column is for
the on-air talent and those concerned with what is *heard* in a television news
story.

Computer systems offer many features that would be especially useful
when writing and producing television news material. Although one system
may not offer all of them, here are a few of these features: capturing major
wire service material; E-mail communication; script editing; timing calculations; rundown sheets for newscasts; story coverage assignments; news copy
archiving; generating teleprompter copy for anchors; graphics creation,
storage, and retrieval; and control of robotic cameras in the studio.

Presenting a news story in a television broadcast can be done in many
ways. The following sections describe and illustrate each basic television
scripting format to show the placement and form for key copy notations. Although each television scripting format has been isolated for the sake of
clarity, you will soon become aware that these formats are often combined to
prepare a news story for a specific kind of presentation. The *application* of
these basic copy formats will be explained further in Chapter 13, ''Television
Reporting.''

So that you will have a uniform and consistent set of scripting format
guidelines to follow, the requirements used at KCAL-TV in Los Angeles will
be presented. The KCAL-TV guidelines cover each principal type of television
news scripting format. KCAL-TV, along with many other television newsrooms, stores, updates, and retrieves its style guide on computer. This technique makes the newsroom writing guide flexible and current.

You will see only a portion of the KCAL-TV style guide—the sections that deal with television scripting formats and policies. Other portions of the 9News style guide concern the presentation and use of graphics material; general writing style and scripting format preferences; and ethics, standards, and practices. A few examples from other newsrooms will help illustrate some of the scripting format variations often encountered. Have a thorough knowledge of the scripting formats required in the newsroom in which you work.

Figure 3.11 provides essential copy format rules for KCAL-TV news stories.

Readers

Readers in television are essentially the same as in radio. An on-camera anchor reads or tells the story with no additional video.

Here are a few observations about Figure 3.12: Any letters typed outside of the audio column margins will not be seen by the newscaster on the teleprompter system that displays the copy to be read on-camera. This could cause the anchor to stumble. Also notice that the name of the newscaster, Jerry, is typed in both the audio and video columns for further clarity. In some newsrooms, the name of the anchor who will read a particular story is added later, generally by the newscast producer.

At KCAL-TV, the same copy format is used for readers and tags. A *tag* is the copy read just after a complete story or after a particular piece of video is seen. The term *tag* is sometimes replaced with *tag line* or *write-out*. A tag signals the viewer that the story is over and that it is time to move to the next story.

Graphics

Graphics can be used in stories that newscasters read or that individual reporters prepare. The standard practice in most newsrooms is to script the graphics needed and then insert them as the story is broadcast.

Several kinds of graphics material can be used in television news stories. A story might need letters or numbers inserted for names, story locations, and dates. A character generator, or *CG,* is used like a typewriter to electronically produce, store, and then display letters and numbers directly on the screen. Some newsroom computer systems allow the writer or reporter to input CG information from the word-processing and scripting operations directly into a particular piece of graphics equipment, such as a Chyron unit. Although a graphics specialist must still finish the work to prepare an item for on-air use, this preliminary work by the reporter or writer helps ensure that the supers, or on-screen name identifications, used are correct, complete, and timed properly. Unfortunately, this is one more task for the already busy reporter or writer.

An electronic still store, or *ESS,* can produce individual pictures along with letters and numbers that can be designed and then stored into an electronic retrieval system. A specific number is assigned to each CG or ESS so that it can be retrieved when needed. Instead of CG or ESS, some newsrooms use

Slug	Writer	California 9	Status	Time	Changed	By
WRITING-General	jkaufman	Sun Mar 4 20:50	READY	03-90	May 11 02:27	jkaufman

==

Writing

General Rules

>Preserve the assigned slug. Scripts, tape and archive material are collated by slug. Planners, assignment editors, producers, reporters, writers and editors must use the same slug to describe a particular story, or information, scripts and tapes will be lost.

>Script copy is written in "no" mode.

>Instructions, times and cues, whether on the left or right side of the page, are written in video mode. That prevents the computer from calculating them as part of the story length.

>Each sentence is its own paragraph, and should be indented. End each sentence by hitting the RETURN key. Also hit the RETURN key after all video instructions.

>Pronouncers should be typed (in parentheses and in video mode) immediately after the word, name or phrase in question.

>Note on the script the beginning of each VO (like this: ---VO---) and the beginning of each SOT (like this: ---SOT---). On the right side of the script, do not mark times or out-cues of soundbites, points at which the anchor comes back on camera for a live tag to a VO or VO/SOT, and the beginning of each VO when you're effecting from one to another.

>Pages marked with a star (*) are lines in the rundown to show you and the director multiple visual elements within a story. Do not write copy in any page marked with a star. Starred pages will not be printed.

>Pages marked with an "A" are, generally, package scripts. Just prior to air and during the newscast, the producer may designate late-add stories with an "A" or some other letter.

>When your story is complete, move the cursor to the BKTIME column and put an "X" in the first character space. That lets the producer know your copy is ready to be approved and printed.

On writer keyboards, the F17 key will place an "X" in the BKTIME column after the story is saved.

When copy is printed for air, the "X" in the BKTIME column will be replaced with a "*".

Figure 3.11 General rules for KCAL-TV scripting formats. Courtesy of KCAL-TV, Los Angeles.

```
   pfeffer                 Tue Nov 9 16:23 page 1

Slug                    Writer      California 9 Status  Time Changed      By
WRITING Today Copy      jkaufman Sun Mar 4 20:50  READY   03-90 May 11 02:27 jkaufman


 ============================================================================
VO'S, VO/SOT'S, READERS AND PACKAGE INTROS & TAGS FOR TODAY'S NEWSCASTS:

1. Go to the rundown of the newscast in which your story will appear.

   If your story has been placed in the rundown, go to that line and use the
   → key to get into the story.

   If your story is not yet in the rundown, use the NEW STORY key to create a
   form. Enter the SLUG and, in the column marked WR, your initials. Enter
   the TALent, ESS, TAPE and any VIDEO instructions, if you know them.

2. Type your story, following the formats below.
```

Figure 3.11 continued.

```
   pfeffer              Tue Nov 9 16:23  page 1

Slug                 Writer    California 9 Status  Time Changed      By
WRITING-Readers      jkaufman Sun Mar 4 20:50  READY   03-90 May 11 02:27 jkaufman


==========================================================================
     READERS AND PACKAGE TAGS

--------------------------------------------------------------------------

     JERRY ON CAMERA                    (((JERRY)))
                                             THIS IS HOW AN ON-CAMERA READER
                                        SHOULD LOOK.
                                             SIMPLY WRITE THE SCRIPT COPY IN
                                        THIS COLUMN, AND WRITE THE DIRECTOR'S
                                        INSTRUCTIONS IN THE LEFT-HAND COLUMN.
                                             AS IN ALL 9NEWS SCRIPTS, EACH
                                        SENTENCE IS ITS OWN PARAGRAPH, AND
                                        SHOULD BE INDENTED.
                                             COPY IS TYPED IN "NO" MODE AND IN
                                        ALL CAPS.
                                             END EVERY STORY WITH THREE "POUND"
                                        SIGNS IN "VIDEO" MODE.
                                             ###
```

Figure 3.12 Example of the copy format for scripting tags to readers and package reports. Courtesy of KCAL-TV, Los Angeles.

an abbreviation for the manufacturer of a particular piece of graphics equipment, for example, ADDA, Vidifont or VF, CHYRON, DVE, and Quantel.

Instead of a static picture with letters inserted in a box over the shoulder of the anchor, using videotape in this box while the newscaster reads the story is also possible. The videotape (abbreviated VTR or ENG in the video column of the copy) could be shown within this box throughout the story, or it could be used in the box for the opening to the story and then shown full-screen.

Voice-Overs

In a *voice-over* (often abbreviated VO), the copy is read over the edited video, which is shown full-screen. The video used could be CG or ESS material, but often it is videotape that includes natural sound. Both reporters and newscasters can do voice-overs.

A story could begin with a voice-over, but a more common practice is to provide anchor lead-in copy with CG/ESS material and then go to the VO later in the story. Figure 3.13 illustrates this common practice and the copy format used for scripting voice-overs at KCAL-TV.

Soundbites

A television *soundbite* is similar to a radio actuality. In television, however, the viewer both sees and hears the short taped statement made by a person associated directly with a particular story.

The copy notation *SOT* means "sound on tape," a picture with accompanying sound. The SOT excerpt to be used can be noted on the copy in the left or right columns or in both columns. Many newsrooms require specific verbatim notations on script pages that accompany the newscaster's copy. KCAL-TV does not require verbatim notes on news copy that includes soundbites. See Figure 3.14.

Reporter Packages

A *reporter package* in television is similar to a wrap in radio news. A television news package includes the reporter's voice-over narration, soundbites from those associated with the story, and usually a brief segment in which the reporter appears on-camera (called the *stand-up*); generally the stand-up is used in the middle or at the end of the packaged report but in some cases at the beginning of the taped report.

Copy for reporter packages is written in two parts: the anchor's lead-in copy using the appropriate copy format illustrated earlier, and the reporter's copy for the package. The reporter's copy generally includes: CG or ESS information, and the words the reporter will read in the voice-over segments. If required, the reporter's copy might also include: a verbatim transcription of the SOT excerpts to be used and the videotape times for editing.

Figure 3.15 shows how to write an anchor's introduction or lead-in to a package report at KCAL-TV.

Figure 3.16 describes how to write the narration tracks or segments for packages.

```
   pfeffer             Tue Nov 9  16:23  page 1

Slug                 Writer    California 9  Status  Time Changed      By
WRITING-VOs          jkaufman Sun Mar 4 20:50  READY  03-90 May 11 02:27 jkaufman


=======================================================================
   VO

-----------------------------------------------------------------------
   PAT ESS: ELECTION                    ((( PAT )))
        (that's the graphic)                 THIS IS A SAMPLE V-O.
                                             WHEN YOU'RE READY TO INDICATE THE
   VO                                   V-O, DO IT THIS WAY:
     (writers: use FIND key to make     --VO--
     the notation for VO; reporters         ALL OF THIS COPY IS ANCHOR VOICE
     and anchors: use SELECT key)       OVER.
   CH: 9 DOWNTOWN L A                        AS IN ALL 9NEWS SCRIPTS, EACH
                                        SENTENCE IS ITS OWN PARAGRAPH AND
                                        SHOULD BE INDENTED.
                                             COPY IS TYPED IN "NO" MODE AND IN
   TRT: :25                             ALL CAPS.
                 (this indicates the         END THE V-O WITH THREE "POUND"
                 running time of the    SIGNS IN "VIDEO" MODE.
                 story. The editor                         ###
                 will add :10 of pad
                 beyond the time you
                 indicate)
```

Figure 3.13 Example of the copy format for scripting voice-overs. Courtesy of KCAL-TV, Los Angeles.

```
  pfeffer                Tue Nov 9 16:23 page 1

Slug                  Writer    California 9 Status  Time Changed      By
WRITING-V/S/Vs        jkaufman Sun Mar 4 20:50  READY  03-90 May 11 02:27 jkaufman


=======================================================================
      V/S/V


      JANE ESS:HEARTBREAK                 (((JANE)))
                                              THIS IS A SAMPLE VOICE OVER, WITH
                                          SOUND ON TAPE, FOLLOWED BY MORE V-O.
      VO                                      WHEN YOU'RE READY TO INDICATE THE
         (writers: use FIND key to make   V-O, DO IT THIS WAY:
         the VO notation; reporters and   --VO--
         anchors: use SELECT key)             THIS IS ANCHOR V-O.
      CH: 9 EL MONTE                           AS IN ALL 9NEWS SCRIPTS, EACH
                                          SENTENCE IS ITS OWN PARAGRAPH, AND
      :07 SOT                             SHOULD BE INDENTED.
      CH: Smith                               HERE'S THE SOUND:
      Q: . . . here's the out-cue."       --SOT--
      :15 VO                                  (writers: CMD/FIND to make SOT
                                              notation; reporters and anchors:
                                              CMD/SELECT)
      JANE ON CAMERA                      --VO--
                                              MORE COPY FOR VOICE OVER GOES
      TRT: :20                            HERE.
         (this indicates the                 IF THERE'S AN ON-CAMERA TAG, JUST
         running time of the             KEEP WRITING ON THE RIGHT SIDE, AND
         story. The editor               INDICATE THE RETURN ON THE LEFT SIDE.
         will add :10 of pad                            ###
         beyond the time you
         indicate)
```

Figure 3.14 Example of the copy format for scripting stories that contain voice-over/ sound on tape/voice-over segments. Courtesy of KCAL-TV, Los Angeles.

```
     pfeffer              Tue Nov 9  16:23  page 1

Slug                 Writer      California 9  Status  Time Changed     By
WRITING-Pkg Intros   jkaufman Sun Mar 4 20:50  READY   03-90 May 11 02:27 jkaufman


=======================================================================
PACKAGE INTRO


-----------------------------------------------------------------------


     DAVID ESS:RIOT                    (((DAVID)))
          (that's the graphic)               THIS IS A SAMPLE INTRO TO A
                                       PACKAGE.
                                              AS IN ALL 9NEWS SCRIPTS, EACH
                                       SENTENCE IS ITS OWN PARAGRAPH AND
                                       SHOULD BE INDENTED.
                                              COPY IS TYPED IN "NO" MODE AND IN
                                       ALL CAPS.
                                              WHEN YOU'RE READY TO GO TO THE
                                       PACKAGE, DO IT LIKE THIS:
     SOT                               (PKG)
```

Figure 3.15 Example of an anchor's introduction to a television package report.
Courtesy of KCAL-TV, Los Angeles.

Slug   Writer   California 9 Status Time Changed   By
WRITING-Pkg Tracks   jkaufman Sun Mar 4 20:50   READY   03-90 May 11 02:27 jkaufman

==
PACKAGE TRACKS FOR TODAY'S NEWSCASTS

1. Go to the rundown of the newscast in which your story will appear.

   Package tracks are written in pages marked with an "A."
   If your story has been placed in the rundown, go to that line and use the
   → key to get into the story.

   If your story is not yet in the rundown, use the NEW STORY key to create a
   form. In the SLUG column, enter the name of the talent who'll track the
   package, like this:

          (MURPHY PKG)
2. Type your story, following the rules below:

   >Package script copy is written in "video" mode—left and right sides.

   That's so the computer won't time your copy. The computer cannot time a
   package, since the computer doesn't calculate natural sound or soundbites.
   A package written in anything other than "video" mode will throw off the
   producer's backtime.

   >Instructions, times and cues, whether on the left or right side of the
   page, are written in video mode. That prevents the computer from
   calculating them as part of the story length.

   >Each sentence is its own paragraph, and should be indented. End each
   sentence by hitting the RETURN key. Also hit the RETURN key after
   all video instructions.

Figure 3.16 Instructions for writing the tracks or narration portions of a package
report. Courtesy of KCAL-TV, Los Angeles.

Figure 3.17 illustrates how the various components of a package report are scripted. Notice how the final script for this package incorporates many of the television scripting formats already described and illustrated in this chapter.

On-Set and Live Reports

Reporters may appear on the set where the newscast is produced and lead into and out of their own packages. Live reports also often include packages that have been produced before the reporter goes live.

An on-set report may be used when the story details are still developing or when the reporter's coverage needs to be emphasized. The traditional structure of such on-set reports is as follows: both reporter and newscaster shown at the beginning or lead-in to the story; a shot of the reporter alone, identified with CG material; the reporter's lead-in to an edited package; the package report; a closing comment by the reporter; and a return to the anchor and reporter exchanging final comments about the story.

Alternative Scripting Formats

Although KCAL-TV's scripting formats have been used to illustrate a consistent and complete set of television scripting guidelines, you might encounter other scripting formats that are commonly used. For example, you might see a different way to script the tracks presented in a package report, or you might need to learn how to change CG material in a story.

Figure 3.18 shows another way to script the second part of a television package report. It is an excerpt from the stylesheet used at KWTV in Oklahoma City. Compare Figure 3.18 to Figures 3.15, 3.16, and 3.17. The KWTV format in Figure 3.18 was *not* done on a computer system.

You may need to change or add CG or ESS material within the same story. In the left column of Figure 3.19, notice how the Cable News Network (CNN) indicates the contents of each graphic as well as the place in the story where the graphic changes.

```
      pfeffer               Tue Nov 30 21:31 page 1

PAGE TAL    SLUG           VIDEO  ESS        ESS # TAPE  VT WR SOT   TOTAL BKTIME
RO1   DJ/PH TOSS PFEFFER   MONITOR            2-2          LL 0:00 0.21 *
DATE: 931112N COMMENTS: 2186                                          READY


      ===========================================================================
(DAVID)                    (((DAVID)))
ANIM MON;                        AND ONE OF THE
UNHOLY ALLIANCE            HIGHEST RANKING
                          MEMBERS OF THE CATHOLIC
                          CHURCH IS ACCUSED OF
                          HAVING AN "UNHOLY ALLIANCE."
                                 ACCUSED OF SEXUALLY
                          ABUSING A HIGH-SCHOOL
                          STUDENT.
(PAT)                            (((PAT)))
ANIM MON:                        THE ALLEGED INCIDENT
                          HAPPENED ALMOST 20 YEARS
UNHOLY ALLIANCE           AGO.
                                 AND THE MAN WHO'S
                          IN THE HOT SEAT SAYS--NO
                          WAY--
                                 HE DIDN'T DO IT.
ANIM MON:                        UPFRONT TONIGHT,
UPFRONT                   REPORTER CARY PFEFFER
                          EXPLAINS WHY THE SCANDAL
                          COULDN'T HAVE COME AT A
                          WORSE TIME.
CARY ON SET               TOSS PFEFFER--
```

Figure 3.17 Example of a finished set of script material for a package report using the guidelines in Figures 3.15 and 3.16. Courtesy of KCAL-TV, Los Angeles.

```
   pfeffer                Tue Nov 30 21:31 page 1

PAGE TAL   SLUG          VIDEO   ESS        ESS #  TAPE  VT WR SOT    TOTAL BKTIME
RO2  CP    CARDINAL/SEX  ON SET  ON SHAKY   3BXSP PKG    A  CP  0:00  0:12  *
DATE: 931112N COMMENTS: 2186                                                READY


=================================================================================
(CARY)                        (((CARY)))
ESS: ON SHAKY GROUND              THIS CASE IS NOT
                              ONLY AIMED AT A LEADER
                              OF THE CATHOLIC CHURCH,
                              BUT THE MAN WHO IS
                              ACCUSED, CARDINAL JOSEPH
                              BERNARDIN, IS THE MAN IN
                              CHARGE OF INVESTIGATING
                              SEXUAL MISCONDUCT BY
                              OTHERS IN THE CHURCH.
PKG                                 --PKG--
```

Figure 3.17 continued.

```
   pfeffer              Tue Nov 30 21:31 page 2

PAGE TAL   SLUG            VIDEO   ESS      ESS # TAPE  VT WR SOT   TOTAL BKTIME
RO2A       (PFEFFER PKG)                                2:38 2:38
DATE: 931112N COMMENTS: 2186                                          READY


=======================================================================
                          11:30 CNN/11:35:40
                          "I TRY TO LOVE . . .
CG) CHICAGO CATHOLIC
CARDINAL
     Joseph Bernardin      . . . AN OPEN BOOK."
                          (:17)


CG) CHICAGO                     CARDINAL JOSEPH
                          BERNAHDEEN LEADS THE
                          CATHOLIC CHURCH IN
                          CHICAGO . . . HE HAS ALSO
                          HEADED-UP EFFORTS TO
                          CLEAR THE CHURCH OF
                          PEDIFILES AND OTHERS WHO
                          ARE ACCUSED OF SEXUAL
                          MISCONDUCT . . . NOW HE
                          FACES CHARGES HIMSELF
                          FROM A FORMER SEMINARY
                          STUDENT.


CG) ACCUSER               cnn/3pm
     Steven Cook          aircheck/15:38:55
                          "I REMEMBER GOING INTO . . .

                          . . . SEX ON ME . . . PAUSE
                          (:05)" (:22)


                               STEVEN COOK SAYS HE
                          IS JUST NOW REMEMBERING
                          SOME OF THE DETAILS OF
                          WHAT HAPPENED . . . COOK IS
                          SUFFERING FROM AIDS
                          AND HAS FILED A 10
                          MILLION DOLLAR LAWSUIT
                          AGAINST THE CHURCH.

                          11:30 CNN 11:39:10
                          "ALL I CAN SAY . . .

                          . . . TOTAL CONFIDENCE."
                          (:07)
```

Figure 3.17 continued.

```
pfeffer                     Tue Nov 30 21:31 page 3

PAGE TAL   SLUG              VIDEO   ESS       ESS # TAPE  VT WR SOT   TOTAL BKTIME
RO2A       (PFEFFER PKG)                                   2:38 2:38
DATE: 931112N COMMENTS: 2186                                         READY


=====================================================================


PRE-PROD . . .                    AMONG THOSE COMING
                          TO THE AID OF CARDINAL
                          BERNADEEN . . . LOS ANGELES
                          CARDINAL ROGER MAHONEY.
                          --STATEMENT--

                                  A PRELIMINARY
                          INVESTIGATION IS NOW
                          BEING CONDUCTED INTO THE
                          CHARGES BY THE CHURCH.
                                  AN INDEPENDENT
                          INVESTIGATION, SEPARATE
                          FROM CARDINAL BERNADEEN.

                          STAND UP/8:45 (:13)

                                  THE CATHOLIC CHURCH
                          HAS MORE THAN 900
                          MILLION MEMBERS
                          WORLDWIDE, BUT THE SEX
                          LIVES OF PRIESTS AND THE
                          COVER-UP THAT HAS
                          OCCURRED OVER THE YEARS
                          HAS ROCKED THE CHURCH TO
                          ITS FOUNDATION.

NO CYRON!!!! NAT!!!                CAMERA TAPE 1:05
                          "ALREADY THE CHURCH
                          HAS . . .


                          . . . CRISIS, ACTUALLY."
                          (:07)

CG). SHERMAN OAKS                 TERRENCE SWEENEY
                          HAS BEEN SUSPENDED AS A
                          PRIEST . . . HE IS MARRIED
                          AND HAS WRITTEN A BOOK
                          ABOUT THE CHURCH AND
                          MARRIAGE OF PRIESTS.
```

Figure 3.17 continued.

```
PAGE TAL   SLUG           VIDEO  ESS      ESS # TAPE   VT WR SOT   TOTAL BKTIME
RO2A       (PFEFFER PKG)                                           2:38 2:38
DATE: 931112N COMMENTS: 2186                                            READY
```

==

                              HE SAYS CATHOLICS
ARE SLOWLY MOVING TOWARD
DEALING WITH THIS
PROBLEM.

CG) SUSPENDED PRIEST   CAMERA TAPE: 2:11
   Terrance Sweeney   "WHAT HAS HAPPENED IN
THE PAST . . .

                            . . . HAVE FOUND NONE OF
IT." (:16)

CARY   (((CARY)))
ON CAM TAG   TONIGHT, STEVEN COOK
SAYS HE'S BEEN SO
WRONGED—
         HE WANTS THE
CARDINAL TO RESIGN.
###

Figure 3.17   continued.

PAGE	SLUG/TAPE #/SOURCE
	package body

REP/PHT.	DATE/PGM.
kab	7/9

This is the format for a package body. I don't care if you
type it in all caps, or upper and lower letters. Just make
sure you can read it. Leave some space at the left side of
your package bodies for supers. For instance if right about
here my audio track talked about Mrs. Alice Simpson who lives
on a lonely country road called Lonely Street in Edmond, and
I knew that the video was going to show (that) lonely house on
that lonely Road, I would indicate a super to the left of this

super: part of the (track.) There may be an instance where I wanted

Lonely St.   to contrast this video with video of that same house ten years
ago. Then next to the part of the track that talks about
the (lonely) house ten years ago, I would put a super that said

super: (that.) So, you ask, how does the director know when to insert

Lonely St.   these supers. He or she will know, because instead of giving

July, 1974 times to the producer to give to the director, as we do now,
we're starting a new system. As each photographer edits, he
will put circles around the words of the track where it would be
appropriate to insert those supers. When the piece is edited,
a copy of this package body will be given to the director,
with all the circles in place. The same will apply to sound bites
within your package body.

    ''The exact transcript of the sound bite will be typed out in its

super: entirety. So far this soundbite, which you will type in quotes,
has been covered with B-roll. But right (here) the head appears.

Dr. Bob King That's why the word head has been circled .   so the director

Heart Surgeon knows to wait to super the interview. Right (here) the head disappears
again, so put a second circle on the last word where the head is
still up. If there is no B-roll, don't circle anything. Include

Figure 3.18 Example of a variation of the scripting format required for the second part
of a television reporter package. Courtesy of KWTV, Oklahoma City, Oklahoma.

PAGE	SLUG/TAPE #/SOURCE			
	package body 2-2-2			
REP/PHT.	**DATE/PGM.**			
kab	7/9			

the total of the soundbite at the end.'' :40 (too long)

Chyrons

The same thing applies if you want the director to super

Full-screen

(full) screen chyrons, or add-on full-screen chyrons, live
on the air.

Add-on

(Type) the super next to the appropriate place on the
track. And the photographer should circle the ins and (outs)

super:
Michael John
(stand-up)

(STAND-UP) Indicate your stand-up ins, bridges, and
closes on your track, and write them out completely.
Also indicate your stand-up super to the left of the
script. And indicate the length of the standup. :12

If you do not have a stand-up in your piece, we will
continue to put your reporting super at the end.
Again, indicate that on your script. And please make
your outcues standard. If you include a location in

super:
Bryan reporting

your sig out, put that first. In Tulsa, I'm Tracy
Bryan, Newsline 9, late edition.

Figure 3.18 continued.

GNP 6/18 6a dh
PAT 0C/BOX GNP

A2

(PAT)

The nation's
economy didn't grow
as fast as first
thought during the
first three months
of the year.
          Revised
Commerce Department
figures show the
Gross National
Product rose
two-point-nine
percent during the
first quarter.
          Just a month
ago, the

(MORE)

change adda (money)

take adda full

vf:
Revised 1st
Quarter GNP
Up 2.9%

gnp cont.

vf:
Last month's
estimate:
Up 3.7%

A2a

government
estimated the G-N-P
had expanded
three-point-seven
percent from January
to March.

          #

Figure 3.19   Compare the first section of the script in Figure 3.13 to this example of an alternative copy format for establishing and then changing CG or ESS material within a story. Courtesy of Cable News Network, CNN.

Summary

This chapter has described and illustrated the basic types of radio and television news scripting formats. Essential copy page mechanics were covered, including page layout, margins, story slugs, and methods for timing news copy.

Basic radio news scripting formats were presented for readers, copy with actualities, voicers, wraps, live reports, and stories using natural sound. The principal television news scripting formats were described and illustrated for readers, copy with graphics, voice-overs, copy with soundbites, reporter packages, and on-set and live reports. Alternative scripting formats were also shown for scripting CG material and for package reports.

Once you know the scripting format and presentational options available for presenting the information that you have gathered, you can select the *best* scripting format to use to tell the story that you know.

Exercises

1. Monitor several local and network radio newscasts. Identify examples of the principal types of radio news copy formats described and illustrated in this chapter. Report your observations. Include comments about the number of occurrences of each kind of scripting format; the length of each story; the use of sound in voicers, wraps, live reports, and stories that include actualities; and the placement of each story in each newscast.

2. Follow the directions for Exercise 1, but monitor local and network television newscasts. Report the same observations as in Exercise 1, but instead of noting the use of sound, report the use of video in stories with graphics as well as stories written for voice-overs, soundbites, reporter packages, live reports, and on-set reports.

3. Record local or network radio news stories that illustrate several types of radio news copy formats described and illustrated in this chapter. Transcribe each story in the recommended format. If you are unsure about how to indicate a particular production technique, use your best judgment. Be consistent, and provide a brief explanation of your scripting notations on a separate piece of paper attached to each piece of copy typed.

4. Follow the directions for Exercise 3, but record and then transcribe several types of television news copy formats described and illustrated in this chapter.

5. Obtain samples of news scripts from one or more local radio or television stations. Compare the scripts with the examples in this chapter, and with one another. Indicate which scripting formats you prefer and analyze the reasons for your preferences.

Chapter 4

Leads

T his chapter and the next four chapters apply the broadcast writing style guidelines and news scripting formats described and illustrated in Chapters 2 and 3 to specific components of broadcast newswriting—leads, story structure, words, sentences, and rewriting. These five chapters form an integrated unit designed to help you write broadcast news stories more effectively. The suggestions and techniques offered apply to both radio and television news stories. Later chapters describe techniques that are uniquely suited to each medium. Chapters 4 and 5 work in tandem to provide the basic components for constructing a solid broadcast news story. Later chapters provide refinements that will enhance the quality of the stories you write.

With only a few exceptions, the news copy used in Chapters 4 through 8 has been recopied and shown *as received* from the various newsrooms. Copy format and style variations will occur.

This chapter examines leads—why they are used, how to choose what to include, types, and writing. Examples from a variety of newsrooms are used to better illustrate key points. After a summary, the chapter concludes with exercises designed to sharpen your ability to recognize and write effective leads for broadcast news stories.

Need for Leads

The lead is the beginning of a news story, a way to get into or to introduce the story. Start strong. Make the lead sentence your best. A good lead helps capture attention, prepare the audience for the story, and set the tone or mood of the news item that follows.

The broadcast audience often is distracted. An effective lead helps shake the consciousness of the audience and arouse their interest in what follows. The lead is the "hook," the brief bait designed to lure them into the story.

Remember that your story is competing for attention not only with other stories in a newscast, but with all of the other distractions that surround us every day—traffic, household duties, job responsibilities, and so forth. The lead should grab the ear or eye of the audience and say, in effect, "This is important! You really need to know about this! Pay attention!" Nancy Cope,

Executive Producer at KTRK-TV in Houston, puts it this way: "We try to stress that a good lead will sell the story to the viewers . . . that it's the responsibility of the writer to get the viewer's attention with his first line of copy."[1]

Here are leads that help capture attention:

Today's rain is creating some hazardous road conditions.

WTOP Newsradio 1500, Washington, DC

It was a massive display of nature's power. The storms swept through the southernmost counties of Illinois.

KFVS-TV, Carbondale, IL

Police call the murder scene particularly gruesome . . .

WTHR-TV, Indianapolis

Prepare the audience for the story. The lead should warm them up to the story and point directly to the nature of the story and how it will be told. Here are two examples:

The people who tow your car away when you're illegally parked or rescue your broken down vehicle on the road . . . want more money for their services. . . . So they're applying for a rate increase with the Public Service Commission. . . .

WOWK-TV, Huntington, WV

It wasn't your typical first day at school scenario: no mother crying at the bus stop, no Care Bears lunch box clutched in trembling hand. But then, the student in question was hardly typical. With all the princeliness befitting his title, Prince William made that first big step toward independence. He went to nursery school. And didn't cry . . .

Cable News Network

The lead helps set the mood of the story by announcing the general tone of the news item, as in the following examples:

Our top story . . . from Granite City . . . where the word tonight is fear. This time: a student from the Belleville College campus there terrorized by a shot-gun blast fired by a passing motorist.

KMOV-TV, St. Louis

Choosing the Lead

What do you include in a lead to arouse interest, capture attention, pave the way, and establish the mood or tone for the rest of the story? The best guidelines to suggest are the criteria described in Chapter 1 (see "News Judgment"). Try to determine which criteria or story angle can best be applied to the story you are writing.

Sometimes, a lead is based on *several* criteria, such as proximity, timeliness, human interest, and updating of previous reports:

```
Police in Prince George's County are searching for answers in
the murder of Deborah Ann Jones. The woman's 14-year-old son
found her body yesterday.
                              News Channel 8, Springfield, VA
```

Or perhaps the lead combines the criteria of proximity, impact, and timeliness:

```
Eastern Iowans are drying out tonight after getting about six
inches of rain over the past two days.
                         KGAN-TV, Cedar Rapids/Waterloo, Iowa
```

Most of the time, one criterion appears to be the key element in the lead. Examples will be provided for each of the major criteria described in Chapter 1.

Leads should stress the most newsworthy aspects of a story:

```
Police stormed into a kidnappers' hideout in Spain today and
rescued a five-year-old girl after a gun battle.
                                          Cable News Network

The Bay City Board of Education has given a resounding
endorsement of 5th year Superintendent Ray Keech. . . .
                              WSGW Radio, Saginaw, Michigan
```

Leads can highlight the *controversy* inherent in a story by updating or exposing issues in dispute:

```
A hazardous chemical leak at the Mallinckrodt Chemical Plant
is the third leak at the plant in the past two months.
                                          KMOV-TV, St. Louis

Legislation dealing with the "AIDS" problem has passed the
House of Delegates.
                                    METRONEWS, West Virginia
```

Leads can stress the *impact* of a news item by indicating the direct effect of the event or story on members of the audience. The more direct and universal the impact, the more effective the lead:

```
It's estimated that within just three years, two-thirds of all
the children five or younger in this country will be in some
form of day care.
                                        KUSA-TV, Denver

Another helping of gloom for the economy . . . wholesale
prices jumped 6 tenths [of a percent] last month . . . a surge
that's almost sure to fuel the jitters on financial markets.
                                        NBC Radio News
```

People tend to be more interested in what affects them most directly close to home. Here are some leads that tend to stress *proximity:*

```
An accident last night sent a Bozeman area woman to the
hospital.
                                KBMN, Bozeman, Montana

Emergency crews say it's a miracle tonight that four
Indianapolis residents are alive after a fiery crash on I-65.
                                WTHR-TV, Indianapolis
```

Leads should include *timely* or current information . . . the *latest* development in a story. If a traffic accident story was reported at the end of the day, contact hospital and police officials the next morning to get updates on injury conditions and possible filing of charges. If the governor levels charges against a city council member, get a response from that elected local official. Immediacy is one of the advantages of broadcast news:

```
With only five days to go until the election, both city council
candidates will spend long days on the campaign trail.

Hijackers are in control of Kuwaiti Airlines flight 422 . . .
on the ground in Iran, but reporter Michael Johns says
apparently not for much longer. . . .
                                        NBC Radio News
```

Leads can center on the notoriety and *prominence* as well as the power of those in the news:

```
The brother of West Virginia State Senator Truman Chafin could
spend time behind bars. . . .
                                WOWK-TV, Huntington, WV
```

Generally, you should avoid beginning a news story with an unknown or unfamiliar name, but there are exceptions. On some occasions a name that is normally unfamiliar may, for a brief time while the name is heard or seen in newscasts, actually become *very* familiar and, thus, could be used in the lead sentence of a news story. Notice the effectiveness of the simplicity of this Cable News Network lead used for one of the final stories about a little girl who captured international attention after she was trapped in an abandoned well in Midland, Texas, for several days:

```
Jessica McClure is back home.
```

Leads can accentuate the oddity or *uniqueness* of stories that are often light feature items:

```
Gone are the days when burglars donned stockings on their
heads. A would-be burglar in Milwaukee wore a loincloth. He
prowled in a crawl space between the roof and a suspended
ceiling over a food store. The ceiling FELL through . . . and
the man dropped between the onions and the watermelons, and
screamed. So did the startled produce manager who was getting
ready for the day. He wrestled the Tarzan-like intruder, and
called the police. He was charged with burglary and will appear
in court next week . . . presumably with his clothes on.
                                       Cable News Network
```

Leads may provide catharsis for the audience by emphasizing the *emotion* associated with a story:

```
The rotunda at the state capitol today was filled with the
worried faces of Medicaid recipients who feared their monthly
checks would be discontinued.
```

Leads may highlight the *human interest* angle of a story. People are curious about other people—whether prominent, not so prominent, or potentially prominent. This is how KBOZ began one of its stories about Montana's weekly lottery:

```
Donald Zarr of Belgrade will have to wait till Saturday to find
out if he's one and a quarter million dollars richer. . . .
                                    KBOZ, Bozeman, Montana
```

But the human interest angle can extend to events as well:

`Smokers are giving their lungs a break today in observance of`
`the Great American Smoke-Out.`

The lead may be molded around *available picture and sound* to help draw the audience into the story more effectively:

`With daylight running out and little hope of negotiating an end`
`to the stand off, state police made their move . . .`
`nat sot`
`firing vollies of tear gas and stun grenades into the suspect's`
`home`
`more nat sot . . .`
`Minutes later, 41-year-old John Rhom appeared at his back door`
`. . . The 9 hour siege over . . .`
`sot . . .`

`WTHR-TV, Indianapolis`

If you can determine what story precedes the one you are writing, maybe you can create a segue or bridge to help connect the end of one story to the beginning of the next related story. After a story on declining home sales in most areas of the country, a national business news reporting service began the next business story with the lead:

`Although home sales may be declining, national retail sales`
`are increasing dramatically.`

This lead helped connect or join the two stories into a seamless report— declining home sales are countered by increasing retail sales.

Types of Leads

Before writing a story, most experienced reporters do not pause and then consciously identify or select a particular type of lead to be used. They simply write the best lead for the story that needs to be told. But to help you get started writing effective leads for various kinds of stories, it may be helpful to identify, describe, and illustrate the broad categories into which most broadcast leads fall. These classifications are presented only for the purposes of illustration; the labels assigned may vary in different newsrooms.

Hard Leads

A *hard lead* goes right to the heart of the story, presents the most important piece of information, and stresses the immediacy of the story. This lead, also called a *summary* or *main point* lead, is the most common kind of lead used in broadcast news. Some examples follow.

AP Network News material being prepared. Photo courtesy of Associated Press Broadcast Services.

Four members of a family have been found stabbed to death in a
mobile home in San Antonio.

NBC Radio News

The county administrator and supervisors may be thrown in jail
for not following a judge's order.

KGO Radio, San Francisco

The Minnesota House Rules Committee voted today to send the
state lottery bill to the full House.

WCCO Radio, Minneapolis

Soft Leads

A *soft lead* adds perspective that might otherwise be overlooked or lost in a
hard lead. Such a lead adds meaning to a story by indicating the general nature
and impact of the events:

Early detection is considered the key to preventing deaths
from heart disease. That's why a new technique being used to
identify people with heart problems is so important.

Cable News Network

The earth moved in northern California last night. Authorities
say the quake, which measured 4.4 on the Richter Scale, knocked
pictures off walls, but caused no reported damage or injuries.
The quake was centered near Livermore, southeast of San
Francisco.

Texas State Network

Do not overuse soft leads. If every story in a newscast began with a soft lead, valuable time would be wasted, and stories would begin to sound pretentious.

The *throwaway lead* often resembles a newspaper headline in tone and structure. A short sentence or, more commonly, a sentence fragment or phrase introduces the story:

```
Tax Day. The government wants to hear from us by midnight . . .
```
                                                NBC Radio News

In most cases, you can eliminate or ''throw away'' this lead without weakening the essential meaning and structure of the story. Information in the throwaway lead is incorporated in the body of the story. A hard lead sentence often follows a throwaway lead:

```
Execution in Virginia . . . Earl Clanton was put to death in
the electric chair at the state prison in Richmond . . . for
strangling a neighbor during a robbery 8 years ago.
```
                                                NBC Radio News

Umbrella leads highlight two or more points in a story, or combine two or more related stories into *one* lead. They are also called *round-up, comprehensive,* and *shotgun* leads because they scatter attention for a moment to several different, but related, items. Umbrella leads help to combine, but should also simplify, the various aspects of a story. Here is an example:

```
Many folks have begun their Easter weekend . . . but members of
the Minneapolis council have a busy day ahead: their agenda
includes the controversial Nicollet Mall development . . . a
bill aimed at reducing the risk of AIDS . . . and proposed
increases in taxi fares and license fees.
```
                                                WCCO Radio, Minneapolis

When writing an umbrella lead, find the common thread that links the items or that forms a clear contrast between points of view, and then join them naturally. Do not try to force these tie-ins or links.

A *delay* or *suspense lead* saves the main point or punch line until the end of the story. It is often used to tell a story chronologically, add a touch of drama, and help build suspense:

Orlando, Florida Police considered the drawing of a nude model
and artist too obscene to auction with other confiscated
evidence. So they were going to burn it with some pornography.
Until a city official salvaged it because he liked the frame.
And finally noticed the signature. It's a Picasso. A limited
edition.

Cable News Network

Although it provides a pleasant break from the way most news stories begin, the delay or suspense lead should be used sparingly for greatest effect. This type of lead works well for stories with humorous endings; it will not be appropriate for most stories. The broadcast audience is accustomed to getting the news quickly and directly—much faster than is possible using the delay or suspense lead.

Humor Leads

Without straining credibility, be alert to words and situations that could provide, on occasion, a humorous angle or approach to a story. *Humor leads* should evolve naturally from the events and situations reported. They should never be used to belittle, insult, or offend the heritage, race, or disabilities of people. Humor leads should never be used when reporting tragedies, disasters, serious crimes, accidents, and obituaries. Here is a typical example of an appropriate use of humor as a *kicker* or final story in a newscast:

Police in Southern California are following the scent of a bank
robber. They say his *M.O.* . . . is *B.O.* The guy has held up 11
banks. But witnesses say there's no evidence he's spent any of
the loot, on soap or deodorant.

Mutual Broadcasting System

Question Leads

Some consider the *question lead* a lazy way to begin a story. The contention is that the audience wants answers, not questions, when listening to newscasts. Rhetorical questions may be confused with commercials, which often begin with a question.

However, if used carefully and thoughtfully, a question lead can help reflect questions that may be on the minds of viewers and listeners. If used *sparingly,* this lead can increase interest and clearly announce the nature of the story to follow:

Ever wonder what big sports stars do when it's time to retire
from football, baseball, basketball . . . whatever? Well
. . . the smart ones start thinking about it long before they
give up their game.

KXAS-TV, Dallas-Fort Worth

Do not use a question at the beginning of every story! To be effective, the question lead must be brief, have substance, and increase audience interest in a story. A question lead is only *one* way to do that.

Statement Leads

Sometimes you can make an effective lead from a particularly powerful, unusually compelling statement or quotation read aloud or presented as an actuality in radio or as a soundbite in television. *Sometimes!*

```
He told his mother early this morning, ''Don't feel bad . . . I
deserve this.'' Then, the lethal chemical injected into
Charles Bass took effect. . . .
                                        Cable News Network
```

This type of lead could temporarily confuse the audience, which is accustomed to hearing clear, attributable comments, not confusing or startling statements. Provide attribution as soon as possible after a statement lead is used.

Combination Leads

As indicated earlier, experienced broadcast newswriters try to provide the best possible lead for every story, no matter what label is attached to the type of lead used. Sometimes newswriters incorporate the characteristics of several types of leads into *one* lead sentence to form a *combination lead.*

To begin a story about a downtown parking survey, KXL Radio stressed the immediate impact on downtown meter-watchers by using what could be labeled a soft/throwaway lead. With a little rewriting, the story *could* have started with the *second* sentence.

```
Starting today, those who park in downtown Portland may find a
postcard on their windshield. The city's transportation
department is conducting a survey with these cards. . . .
```

To report two similar deaths in the same day, KSL-TV used a hard/umbrella lead to emphasize the proximity of the story (''local authorities . . .''):

```
Local authorities are investigating two stabbing-deaths in
the Salt Lake Valley . . .
```

The morning after an earthquake shook southern Oregon, a national network radio newscast began with a question and then a statement from an unidentified eyewitness:

```
What's it like to survive an earthquake?
```

[''The room was shaking. Dishes were falling off the wall. It was scary.'']

Writing the Lead

It might be helpful to capsulize some of the principles examined thus far in this chapter and, at the same time, provide a checklist that could be used to write effective broadcast news story leads.

Select the Type of Lead to Use

The type of lead you use depends on the *nature* of the story and the *manner* in which you want to tell that story. Ask yourself: What is this story about? Why is it important? What's *new* about this story? How can I tell this story most effectively? As you have seen, you can tell the same story in many ways. You will want to select the *best* way to tell the story so that you reflect the special emphasis and include the specific information needed. You begin with the lead.

Select the Best Story Angle

The lead must aim in the direction of the main point of the story. It must never *mislead*. The story must conform to the approach that is announced or represented in the lead; that is, the body of the story must support the lead:

```
What Argentina couldn't do on the battlefield in 19-82 . . . it
accomplished on the soccer field yesterday. Argentina is
celebrating a two-to-one victory over Britain in the World Cup
Soccer quarterfinals. It was the first sports competition
between the two countries since Britain defeated Argentina in
the Falklands war.
                                          Cable News Network
```

But how do you determine the best story angle to use? Review the criteria described and illustrated earlier (see "Choosing the Lead"). Remember that these criteria often overlap. Digest the facts of the story; determine what is most newsworthy, what will provide the most interesting, intriguing, enticing lead; and then start unraveling the story.

Let's consider the significant facts about two stories, analyze the alternatives, and then see the lead a particular newsroom used.

Story 1

- A woman says another motorist fired a shotgun at her car while she was driving along Naneoki Road near I-270 today.

- She was not injured.

- Police believe shotgun pellets may have lodged into a nearby house.

- This is the fifth reported incident of this type on the east side of town.

- Since the spree began almost two and a half weeks ago, one person has died and another was injured.

- Police do not believe all five attacks are related, but in two cases the shots were reportedly fired from a green car.

The lead needs to stress that this is not an isolated incident and that motorists face a serious threat of injury if they drive on the east side of town. People also want to know that steps are being taken to solve the problem. Consider the following alternatives.

Weak

```
For the fifth time in almost two and a half weeks, shots have
been fired along Naneoki Road on the eastside as police look
for a green car.
```

Better

```
Yet another sniper attack on an eastside motorist today . . .
as Illinois State Police step up their search for a suspect.
                                            KMOV-TV, St. Louis
```

Story 2

- Beginning at midnight tomorrow, 330 employees at two Consolidated Coal Company mines in West Virginia will be laid off.

- The Ireland Mine in Marshall County will lay off 220 employees.

- The Pursglove Mine in Monongalia County will lay off 110 employees.

- Consolidated Coal Company is based in Pittsburgh.

- Paul Kvederis, spokesman for Consolidated, says the coal market is to blame for the layoffs.

- Kvederis says the layoffs amount to about half the workforce at the Pursglove Mine.

- There's no word from the company on when the miners might be recalled.

- Consolidated is the largest coal company in the region.

This announcement affects practically everyone in West Virginia: Jobs will be lost, and lives will be changed. Save the comments from the company spokesman for later. Write the lead to emphasize the serious impact of this development.

The following examples are *not* the best leads available:

Weak

```
Three-hundred and thirty employees at two Consolidated Coal
Company mines are being laid off. . . .
```

```
More jobs are lost in West Virginia coal mines. . . .
```

Here is how METRONEWS wrote the story for one of the 39 newscasts fed to its radio affiliates spread throughout West Virginia:

Better

```
It's a dark day for several hundred West Virginia coal miners.
Consolidated Coal is laying off 220 miners at its Ireland Mine
in Marshall County and another 110 miners at the Pursglove Mine
in Monongalia County. Consol spokesman Paul Kvederis says
there's no word on when or if the miners will be recalled. . . .
```

The soft lead used by METRONEWS sets the tone and creates interest in the story.

Set Up the Story

The lead should set the tone and *prepare* the audience for the rest of the story. It must be coupled *to* the story, not serve as a complete story in itself.

Ease into the story. If a story is complex, or if a specific decision or point of view is important to note, put that in the lead and then peel away the layers of information as you reveal the important points about the story. Note how this is done in the following example:

```
A federal appeals court says the Illinois Central Gulf
Railroad is guilty of discrimination. The court ruled the
railroad discriminated against blacks applying for jobs. More
than 4-hundred blacks filed the class action suit. An East St.
Louis judge ruled in favor of the railroad . . . but the
appeals court says it is a clear case of discrimination. The
court will hold a hearing on damages the railroad must
pay. . . . They could run into millions of dollars.
```
KMOV-TV, St. Louis

Save the Details

Essential facts may be given in the lead, but *all* of the essential facts (who, what, when, where, why, and how) should *not* be crammed into the lead. If you include too many facts, the audience becomes confused and disinterested. Keep the lead simple and easy to understand. Create momentum, and generate interest in the story.

The name and location have been changed in this lead, which was actually used on the air:

Weak

```
Sixteen-year-old Billy Davenport of Central City has pleaded
guilty to three counts of murder in connection with the
shooting deaths of three Central City residents last November.
```

Too much information is jammed into the lead sentence. Save the details! Here is a suggested rewrite:

Better

```
A Central City teenager has pleaded guilty to three counts of
murder. He is 16-year-old Billy Davenport who was charged last
November with the shooting deaths of three Central City
residents. . . .
```

The first sentence captures the essence of the story; the second sentence starts filling in the details.

Here is the first version of a lead written in the KTRK-TV newsroom in Houston that squeezes the who, where, and what of the story into one sentence:

Weak

```
Gulf Coast fishermen along the San Luis Pass area of Galveston
Island are in a battle for squatters' rights.
```

Here is the rewrite that simplifies the lead and creates interest in the story by featuring only the what and the where of the story:

Better

```
A battle over squatters' rights is brewing these days on
Galveston Island. . . .
```

Most names, especially unfamiliar names, should not be used in the lead. The audience may miss the name, which may not be repeated later in the story. It is better to substitute a person's title or job or relationship to the story. Simplify the reference and *then* use the name:

```
China has a new man in charge. . . . Premier Zhao Ziyang today
was elected chief of China's Communist Party. . . .
                                          KMOV-TV, St. Louis
```

Another technique is to use the name at the *end* of the sentence, *after* the name means something:

```
Teacher of the Year honors will be presented at the White House
to 37-year-old Terry Weeks of Murfreesboro, Tennessee.
                                               NBC Radio News
```

Prominent names, especially prominent *local* names familiar to a majority of listeners or viewers, can be included in the lead to attract attention and spark interest in a story. Amid the controversy surrounding expenditures by the president of a major local university, WCCO Radio used this lead:

```
University of Minnesota President Kenneth Keller last night
ended weeks of speculation and announced he is stepping down.
```

Avoid using specific numbers and statistics in the lead. This would include ages, addresses, precise times, and exact dollar amounts. These tend to clutter the lead. On some occasions, however, numbers *should* be used, for example, the final score in a basketball game. An alternative is to use specific numbers at the *end* of the lead or in the *next* sentence:

```
The state unemployment rate in Kansas went up a little bit in
October compared with September . . . from four-percent to
four-point-three percent. . . .
```

```
A fire has taken the life of a Wichita man. The fire occurred at
28-40 East Harry around 11 Monday night. . . .
                                        KFDI Radio, Wichita, Kansas
```

Polish the Lead

Every word in a lead is important. Every word must be the *right* word, and every word must be there for a reason. That reason is to entice and motivate the audience to become interested in the story. The lead must be written in a compelling, engaging manner, and it must convey a clear and concise message to the audience. The lead has got to shine! It should highlight what is special, different, or newsworthy about an event or situation and make the story stand apart from the ordinary.

Intensify the immediacy of the story by using present and future tense verbs:

```
The Kuwaiti airliner hijackers make more demands for fuel
. . . saying they are ready to die . . . saying the 747 is wired
with explosives.
                                                    NBC Radio News
```

```
Twelve hours from now . . . we should know if the Twin Cities
will be in the international competition . . . to host the
summer Olympics. . . .
                                        WCCO Radio, Minneapolis
```

Short leads work best. An incomplete phrase or a short sentence is easy to read, understand, and remember:

```
The Minnesota Vikings are returning to WCCO Radio.
                                        WCCO Radio, Minneapolis
```

Use active rather than passive voice. (This is described in Chapter 6, ''Words.'') Change ''A law has been passed by the state legislature that . . .'' to ''The state legislature has passed a law that. . . .''

Avoid negative leads. Change ''The Governor says she will not sign the tax bill . . .'' to ''The Governor says she will veto the tax bill. . . .'' Positive leads are stronger.

Recording broadcast news reports. Photo courtesy of Associated Press Broadcast Services.

You can make routine stories interesting without sensationalizing their content:

```
This is the time of year store merchants look forward to, and
dread, all at the same time. The crowds that bring shoppers
spending money are the same crowds that bring shoplifters
stealing merchandise. . . .
                                        KFDI, Wichita, Kansas
```

Summary

The lead is the beginning of a news story. It is used to capture attention, prepare the audience for the story, and set the tone or mood of the story.

Identify the key element(s) of a story that can be used to write an effective lead—overall newsworthiness, controversy, impact, proximity, timeliness, prominence, uniqueness, emotion, human interest, available sound or picture.

Learn to use the various types of broadcast leads—hard, soft, throwaway, umbrella, delay or suspense, humor, question, statement, combination.

When writing the lead, select the type of lead that works best for a particular story, use the best story angle, set up the story, save the details, and polish the lead until it shines!

Exercises

1. Write your *best* broadcast lead for each of the following stories, based on the facts provided.

Note: All of the information for stories (a) and (b) is from local sources who tend to give rather informal comments to the local news media.

a. • Source of Information—Lt. Allen Peterson of your local police department.
- Man robbed the 13th & O Streets location of First National Bank about 4:04 P.M. today.
- About $2500–$3500 taken.
- Suspect is about 35, tall, in his 30s, dark graying hair with a thin moustache (''rather handsome'' one teller told police), was wearing a brown plaid shirt and jeans that were slightly torn in the knees, although you would never notice the tears much.
- Suspect came in, pulled a pistol, demanded the money, smiled at the camera above the teller's window, and stuffed the money before leaving the location yelling anti-Nazi and pro-American slogans, mostly in German.
- This bozo is still available in this local area.
- Police have interviewed and then released a few suspects who were found loitering around the bank.
- Same guy may have also robbed about three other area banks, a video store and two restaurants, all in the last two weeks . . . THAT suspect had the same M.O., but police say that he was wearing a red motorcycle helmet when he did those jobs. He also yelled something in Italian about the local university's football team as he left one of the restaurants. The restaurant heist was just after a big local fall football victory.

b. • Harold Stetson, 47, of this town crashed into a 40-inch wide, 60-foot deep hole yesterday afternoon at 1:59 P.M. at the Henry Doorly Zoo (located about 40 miles away from your local town).
- Stetson is in serious condition now at St. Joseph's Hospital in your town. No one knows the injuries Stetson sustained or the troubles he has seen.
- Stetson has worked for Peter Sullivan Construction Inc. for four years as a welder.
- Stetson had one wife and two children (Chad, 2; and Melonie, 4). Stetson lived at 3131 Southview Road locally.
- All questions about the accident are being referred to the safety director at the Zoo. She was not available for comment as we went to press with this story.
- All available information now comes from an unidentified local police officer.
- Occupational Safety and Health Administration officials would not say if safety precautions had been taken to cover the hole.

2. Convert these Associated Press *newspaper* leads into effective *broadcast* leads.

a. Indianapolis—A military jet fighter crashed just short of the Indianapolis Airport runway this morning, hitting a hotel and causing numerous injuries, state police said.

b. Chicago—Lab technicians and clerks frequently changed doctors' orders for diagnostic tests and actually cut down on inappropriate testing in some cases, says a report on practices at two hospitals.

c. Houston—A 7-year-old boy who had been kept virtually a prisoner in a bathroom, possibly for several years, was being treated for malnutrition after he escaped through a window, authorities said.

d. Honolulu—A Marine helicopter with three people aboard crashed off the island of Oahu . . . while on a flight to check maintenance done on its rotor blades, a Marine spokesman said. There were no reports of survivors.

e. Washington—Teams of elected officials from a Democratic Party group plan to campaign in coming months for a voluntary program that would link federal education, housing, and job training aid to participation in civilian or military service.

3. See if you can improve the leads used in the following stories taken from the Associated Press broadcast wire.

    a. The hostage ordeal for a Portland, Oregon police officer ended abruptly this morning when the officer escaped. Police report shots were heard from the motel room where the officer was being held by two suspects in a supermarket holdup. At least one of the suspects is said to be wounded. But the officer was unhurt as he made his getaway. The two gunmen are still holed up.

    b. Energy prices recorded a dramatic surge in April—while food prices rose modestly. Overall, wholesale costs rose four-tenths of a percent last month. However, wholesale prices minus food and energy were up far less than in March—and economists say that's a more accurate reflection of inflation pressures.

    c. There's word that an attempted coup in Guatemala has been quashed. Military sources say officers and soldiers in two military bases tried to overthrow the civilian government. The Defense Ministry confirms the coup attempt, but has given no details.

    d. Israel's ambassador in Cyprus says he believes his embassy may have been the target of a car bombing this morning. It may never be known for sure. The explosives-packed car blew up 200 yards from the embassy—but police say the car was moving away at the time. Two people were killed and several were injured.

4. Write one broadcast lead for each of five major world-national news stories printed in today's edition of a daily newspaper. Monitor a network radio or television newscast in which most of these stories are reported. Provide the following material for *each* story.

    a. The newspaper article
    b. *Your* broadcast news story lead
    c. The network's news story lead

5. Follow the directions for Exercise 4, but use a *local* newspaper and a *local* radio or television newscast for five *local* news items.

6. Follow the directions for either Exercise 4 or 5. Then identify each *type* of *broadcast* lead used.

7. Follow the directions for either Exercise 4 or 5. Now *rewrite your* lead so that a *different* type of lead, and thus approach, is used for each story.

8. Find a story with a standard hard news lead from a current daily newspaper. See how many *different* types of broadcast leads you can write for that *same* story without distorting the facts. Which lead is best? Why?

9. Rewrite each lead you wrote for Exercise 1. Is the *second* lead better than the first lead you wrote? Why? What process did you follow when you wrote each lead?

Note

1. Reprinted by permission of Nancy Cope.

Chapter 5

Story Structure

A few of the principles described and illustrated in Chapter 4, "Leads" are important to recall: (1) An effective lead generates interest and prepares the audience for a news story by pointing directly to the manner in which the story will be told; (2) story structure is coupled to and influenced by the lead; (3) the lead is determined by the special emphasis or angle the reporter intends to use to unravel the essential facts of a news story in a clear, direct, orderly, and interesting fashion.

Leads provide only the essential "foundation," or beginning, for a news story. The "girders" of the story are supplied by story structure—that is, how the story is organized and presented. Words and sentences (see Chapters 6 and 7) help furnish the "mortar" and "dress" needed to complete the structure.

You can structure a news story in as many ways as there are people to tell you about their impressions of last night's sporting event on television. Some story structure patterns tend to work better than others for certain kinds of routine stories. But *each* story deserves its own unique identity and development in terms of information selection and placement, organizational form and pattern, use of transitions and story endings, pace, rhythm, and flow. These news story components are the main topics in this chapter. Later chapters describe additional techniques for designing effective story structures.

Process

You can write a broadcast news story in many ways. Once you have written stories for a while, your personal preferences, as well as factors such as how much time you have and the nature of the stories that you write will shape the process that you use.

Take a few moments to think about the opening and closing of your story and to decide on a few main points you plan to include. At least outline your story *before* you begin writing your story.

Here is a simple four-step story writing process that requires less than one minute and that works for most news writers. *Relax:* Take a deep breath and try to clear your mind of other distractions. *Think:* Focus only on the story you are trying to organize and write. *Write:* Start with the anchor intro and the lead and then construct the story you have designed on paper or the computer screen. Finally, *edit:* Examine what you have written and sharpen the wording and structure of your story.

Phil Witt, News Anchor/Senior Reporter at WDAF-TV in Kansas City, recommends the following story writing process:

> Gather all your facts . . . , but then decide what the major story points are. Jot them down in descending order. Group the ones that are so co-dependent they can't possibly make sense without each other. Then write your story. When you've reached your time limit, either re-write what you've already put down to make it more concise so you can fit another element or two into your story or discard what you have not been able to include.[1]

Next is a suggested process for developing, writing, and structuring the first version of a news story. This process expands the basic steps just suggested and provides a thorough set of guidelines for story preparation. Following this more detailed and elaborate process might be best until you feel comfortable with broadcast news story writing needs and can devise your own modified writing process. You can use the same steps to *revise* a story (see Chapter 8, ''Rewriting Copy''):

1. Read the original source material carefully and thoughtfully.
2. Underline or highlight the main points or facts in the original source material.
3. Understand the *heart* of the story.
4. Answer key questions the audience might have asked. (This is discussed further later).
5. Tell the story informally to a friend, fellow newsroom reporter, or your keyboard.
6. Determine how the story can be told or structured *most* effectively on the air.
7. Select the type of lead that will be used.
8. Identify the organizational pattern to be followed.
9. Know how the story will end *before* you begin writing it.
10. Put away the original source material.
11. Write the lead and then stop!
12. *Remember* your plan of attack (lead, structure pattern, ending, etc.).
13. Write the rest of the story.
14. Now check your copy against the original source material to ensure accuracy, balance, and objectivity.
15. Read your copy *aloud, NOT* in your mind.
16. Improve word choices, sentence structure, story organization as well as flow, rhythm, and pace.
17. ''Tighten'' your copy. When you think you have written the best

possible story, eliminate five words from your copy. Then eliminate five more words. Capture the essence of the story without eliminating the heart and color of the information.

18. Check your copy for clarity. Ask yourself if the story develops only one idea at a time. Have you only referred to a key idea that is not developed in the story? Have you clarified points that may be confusing?

19. Read your copy aloud *again*.

20. Rewrite your rewrite (if you have time)!

The more stories you write, the faster and more efficiently you will work, and the easier it will be to follow this or a more compressed version of this suggested process. Let's examine several phases of this process more closely.

Information Selection and Placement

The same criteria used to identify potentially newsworthy stories and to place essential facts into an effective lead are also used to select and place information in the *rest* of the story.

When you write a news story you are *creating* the pieces of an informational puzzle. You connect, separate, shape, hone, and rejoin bits of information, trying to find the *best* way to arrange and present the facts and comments that you have gathered. In the end, you create a pattern, weave a fabric, devise a scheme, a "story line," a way to tell the story. You have created a *structure* for the news story. Several techniques may help you to select and place information in a news story.

Develop informed judgment.   Stay informed. Even your casual reading of newspapers and newsmagazines will come to your aid when you least expect it. Once you identify what is especially newsworthy, you can arrange these facts and comments to place what you know and understand within the context of current events and convey it in a clear, effective, and meaningful way.

A reporter *must* understand the information gathered before making any attempt to organize these facts and comments into a news story. If you do not understand the information, how can you possibly expect the audience to understand the story?

Talk through the story.   A news story must be a *progression* of information that answers key questions the audience may have formulated based on natural curiosity as well as specific interests and needs. One fact or comment should lead naturally and logically into another and then another until the story ends, for now (until further developments).

As you write a news story, try to pose and then answer obvious questions the audience is likely to ask. Each question that you ask should lead to a specific answer that you then work into the news story. Story details fill the "informational holes" created by your questions. Each answer that you provide should suggest another logical question and its corresponding answer. This process should continue for the entire story. In the end, you will have created a thread, a pattern, a story structure that guides the audience through the story easily, clearly, and informatively. Always try to answer the most obvious questions in *each* story (who, what, when, where, how, and why).

To illustrate the process just described, obvious questions that might occur to the audience and to the newswriter have been inserted between the lines of this news copy from KUSA-TV, Denver:

An accident at the Coors Brewery in Golden tonight. . . .
(*Was anyone injured?*)

26 employees were treated for nausea and skin irritations
(*How did it happen?*)

when a strong soap spilled or leaked.
(*Where did this happen?*)

It happened in the warehouse where carbonation and alcohol levels are checked before the beer is shipped out.
(*Any of the injuries serious?*)

It appears none of the injuries is serious. . . .
(*I hesitate to ask this, but is it still safe to drink the beer?*)

None of the beer was contaminated.

Here is another example from WTOP Newsradio 1500 in Washington, DC. Notice how questions help place the information into a story structure pattern that is typical for serious highway accidents.

A truck driver and two Fairfax County firefighters were taken to Fairfax Hospital, following this afternoon's head-on crash on Beulah Street.
(*How serious are the injuries?*)

One firefighter had to be medivacked with a fractured leg after
(*How did this accident happen?*)

the ambulance he was in collided with a truck. Fairfax County fire officials say the ambulance was en route to a call,
(*Where?*)

when the accident occurred on Beulah Street at Telegraph Road.
(*How long did it take to get the injured to the hospital?*)

The firefighters were trapped in the wreckage for about 30 minutes.

(*What's their condition now?*)

`Conditions of the injured are not immediately available.`

Several factors influence the number and specificity of the questions posed and the answers provided by the newswriter, including the following:

Market size—Even a minor fire in a small town receives extensive on-air coverage on a local newscast. But unless that fire involves a death or extensive property damage, details about that fire probably will not be heard in newscasts from other towns, large or small. As noted in Chapter 1, market size does influence news *judgment* and, thus, the news *value* and *content* of each story.

In the WTOP traffic accident story you just read, notice that the names of the firefighters and the driver were not used. Although identities were still being verified and relatives probably had not yet been notified, the names probably would not be used even in a later story. In a large metropolitan area, such as the District of Columbia, major traffic accidents are routine. The same story, used in a smaller market, would likely include the specific names if they had been verified and could be released.

Target audience—The questions that you ask help to define more precisely those in the audience who would be especially interested in certain aspects of a particular story. Remember to select and use only the information that will be particularly meaningful for your specific broadcast news audience. For example, when selecting information to report a cost-of-living increase, a reporter at a news or talk-based radio station would report the monthly percentage increase and its impact on measurements such as national productivity and the balance of trade; a news/talk radio listener would understand and expect this level of intense financial information. The same story, reported on a music-based station, probably would be short and relate the specific impact of this cost-of-living increase on the average listener; for example,

`It'll cost you almost two cents a loaf more for bread this week.`
`The cost-of-living this month rose . . . etc.`

See Chapter 8, ''Rewriting Copy,'' for more illustrations about customizing your copy to fit your target audience.

News Hole—The less airtime you have, the more crucial should be the information that you select to include in each news story. A brief news report should use less complex presentation formats and at least summarize the important story developments. Generally, if more time is available, stories can be longer and include soundbites and reporter packages. The news hole on National Public Radio (NPR) is usually larger than the news hole on commercial radio network newscasts. Notice the obvious differences in story length and presentation formats.

Limit the information included.   In each story, develop only two or three of the most important and compelling points. Use only enough information to make the story clear, understandable, and memorable. Select only facts and comments that will capture the essence of the story and that will be meaningful and significant to a majority in your audience.

Mutual Broadcasting System newswriter and anchor Frank Gentry puts it this way:

> You can't cram in every little detail like middle names, exact titles and specific dollar amounts. Concentrate, instead, on the bottom line of the story and tell that as concisely as possible. The story is *not* that "County Commissioners met last night," the story is what the Commissioners did or didn't do.
>
> Know your audience—find out who listens to your station. What do they care about? What do they do for a living? What stories do they *want* you to tell them?[2]

Emphasize the importance and impact of the story.   For example, a state budget story should indicate the funds allocated to specific state programs and projects and not the fact that the budget document was 659 pages long.

Remember that the type of lead used influences information selection and placement and, ultimately, story structure.   Examine these WCCO Radio news copy excerpts related to a murder trial:

```
''A loving and caring person.'' That's how a relative today
described a 16-year-old Caulder* boy charged in the stabbing
death of an 86-year-old man. . . . A brother-in-law of the
defendant testified this morning that he and the boy had a
''father-son'' relationship after the teenager moved in with
his family. . . .
```

```
Expert witnesses disagreed today on whether a teenager could
be successfully treated following the slaying of an elderly
Caulder* man. Dr. Tim Beloit* testified for the defense he is
confident 16-year-old Bobby Leets* could be successfully
treated for a conduct disorder by the time he is 19. But
```

---

*These names have been changed.

```
testifying for the state, Dr. Benita Jamin* said she didn't
feel it was likely Leets could be treated within two and one-
half years to protect public safety. . . .
```

Notice how information selection and story structure are tied directly to the kind of lead sentence used. In the first excerpt, the statement lead prompts additional comments about the character of the youth accused of the crime. In the second excerpt, the hard lead sets up the presentation of contrasting viewpoints by the expert witnesses mentioned briefly in the first sentence.

Form

Like any story, a news story must have a beginning, a middle, and an end. The sequence or progression of ideas must be interesting and logical. This approach makes it easier for the storyteller to organize and present the story and for the listener to understand and remember it.

```
Tractors sit in machine sheds as farmers wait patiently for
their fields to dry out so they can begin Spring planting.
Eleven counties will receive federal disaster assistance
following last month's floods. A state ag supervisor says that
low-interest emergency loans will be made based on estimated
losses on buildings and crops.
```

Techniques for beginning a news story were illustrated in Chapter 4. Let's examine now the structural requirements for the rest of a broadcast news story, especially transitions and endings.

Interrelationships

The parts of the *entire* broadcast news story must be intertwined. The lead previews and interlocks with the rest of the story, but the rest of the story also explains and develops the theme, tone, and direction presented in the lead. The entire story must be structured tightly, with no apparent gaps in information. The organizational patterns used to accomplish this objective are explained later in this chapter.

The "promise" made in the lead must be fulfilled as quickly as possible in each succeeding sentence as the body of the story develops. No obstructions, delays, deviations, or breaks should occur between sentences. Otherwise a tear in the fabric or structure of the story could create informational gaps, holes, and loose ends rather than smooth-flowing, informative, meaningful news copy.

Verify that *each* sentence reinforces, explains, or relates directly a specific aspect or part of the story introduced in the lead. Some newswriters find

---

*This name has been changed.

it helpful to reread the lead after writing the first few sentences and again as each successive group of sentences is added to the story.

After the lead sparks audience interest and begins to tell the story, the writer begins peeling away the layers of information and revealing facts and comments to create an interesting, steady stream of information for the audience.

Various kinds of transitional devices can help guide the audience and keep **Transitions** them on the trail of a news story. These connectors or guideposts can be single words, phrases, and even audio and video material.

Transitions can be used *between* stories in a newscast to help the audience recognize and understand the relationship between seemingly separate items. But they are also needed *within* stories to make ideas easier to understand; to enhance the connection, flow, and progression of ideas within a story; and to avoid sudden, unexplained shifts in story direction.

Use transitions judiciously. The connection between story parts should be obvious and natural. Insert transitions only when they help make the story easier to understand. Transitions must be clear and brief.

Each transitional word or phrase conveys a specific meaning, serves as a specific kind of informational guidepost, and thus must be used precisely. Here are some of the ways you can use transitions effectively *within* a news story.

For related ideas or events occurring simultaneously:

. . . Every firefighter in the city was at the scene, *while* county firefighters manned the city stations.
                                        KFRU Radio, Columbia, Missouri

Other possibilities include *meanwhile, as, and, at the same time, but.*

For noting elapsed time:

. . . Last month, this Orem plant was shut down after inspectors found salmonella bacteria in nutrien and vitalite products.

Now, after extensive chemical tests, the state has ordered the company to stop production of the same products at a new, remodeled facility.
                                        KSL-TV, Salt Lake City

Other possibilities include *thus,* or a specific time reference such as *last month, several years ago,* and *at the beginning of this decade.*

For indicating a change in location:

After describing the assessment by one U.S. senator from Montana of current overseas sales of American wheat, KBOZ used an interesting transition to bridge into information about Montana's other U.S. senator:

. . . Not far from the room where Melcher was testifying before the Senate Agricultural Committee, Senator Max Baucus is ready to introduce his plan to require tougher action. . . .

KBOZ, Bozeman, Montana

Other possibilities include *nearby, elsewhere,* or simply *in [location].* Time tags (see Chapter 6, "Words") are often added to such transitions (e.g., . . . *Further along the river bank this morning. . .*).

For bridging into additional information:

The Pennsylvania Crime Commission says organized crime is getting more violent. . . . *And* though the Commission warns of a coming power struggle between Black and Jamaican mobsters, the head of the Philadelphia Police Organized Crime Unit says don't write off the mafia yet. . . .

WCAU-AM, Philadelphia

Other possibilities include, *also, by the way, along with, in addition, plus, incidentally,* and *turning to.*

For noting comparisons:

To provide perspective about the improved fatality rate on Minnesota highways, WCCO-TV used this midstory transition sentence:

. . . An estimated 537 highway deaths may not seem like much . . . but when you consider there were just three less fatalities 25 years ago, you can understand the accomplishment.

Other possibilities include *on the other hand* and *just as.*

For indicating contrast or contradiction:

. . . *But* anti-nuclear activist Terry Gabriell's push to shut the Limerick-Two plant failed . . . as stockholders voted to keep going . . . *despite* a billion-dollar cost overrun.

WCAU-AM, Philadelphia

Other possibilities include *however, instead, besides,* and *on the contrary.*

Every good story should begin well but also must end well. The story ending must be clear, sharp, strong, and definite. The audience should have no doubt that the story is finished. Story endings need to relate back to the story angle presented in the lead, producing a "full circle" effect. The end of a *news* story must also tie together the facts that have been presented since the lead. Many newswriters think about how they are going to construct the *end* of the story before they write the *lead* for the story. This approach acknowledges the importance of planning story structure.

One of the most common ways to end a news story effectively is to *provide significant additional information,* facts or a final statement from a central newsmaker. A news story about governmental restrictions on a local nursing home could end with a note about when a review of nursing home conditions is expected. A story about the death of a local police officer could conclude with a summary of funeral arrangements or a note about the number of local police deaths in the last year or two. A story about the possible dismissal of a police officer ended this way:

```
Esposito's* lawyer says he will file a federal civil lawsuit
against the Miami Police Department if his client is fired from
the force.
                                      WTVJ-TV, Miami
```

A story about the restart of a nearby nuclear reactor ended with this sentence:

```
. . . The reactor has been closed since January.
                                      KIRO-TV, Seattle
```

One of the most effective ways to end a news story is to *indicate the expected impact of the story:*

```
. . . The cause of the fire is still being investigated . . .
but the bigger question for 62 students is how they'll cope the
rest of the semester.
                                      WTHR-TV, Indianapolis
```

Another effective ending is to *restate what the story is all about and indicate what the story really means or should mean:*

```
. . . Maryland's environmental department says it has
diverted most of the leak -- and expects the effect on the bay
to be negligible.
                                      Cable News Network
```

---

*This name has been changed.

To provide some measure of balance and perspective in a news story, the entire story, including the ending, could *offer opposing viewpoints or contrasting information:*

```
Some say yes. Others say no. And the world still waits for
conclusive evidence.

Has the Angel of Death been found?

If you ask Brazilian forensic experts, yes, he has. They
exhumed the remains from a grave in Embu last week. And they say
Josef Mengele's dental records match the bones uncovered.

But if you ask the man who performed the autopsy on the remains
back in 1979, no, Mengele has not been found. The Brazilian
coroner says the man he examined then . . . was too young to
have been the famed Nazi war criminal.
                                        Cable News Network
```

If a delay or suspense lead opens a story, *the ending can deliver the "punch line" of the story,* which generally has been told chronologically:

```
A man making a delivery in San Francisco found more than he
bargained for in one home. He heard cries from the house,
climbed up a drainpipe, and found an 89-year-old man who'd been
stuck in his bathtub for a day. The man was not seriously hurt --
though apparently very clean -- and asked for a shot of whiskey.
                                        Cable News Network
```

Timing considerations may also affect the way you end a news story. Here is a three-sentence medical story:

```
Waiters and bartenders are getting up to six-times the
secondhand smoke of office workers, according to a study in the
A-M-A Journal. The author calls it a "life and death issue"
for bar and restaurant workers -- and says smoking in those
places ought to be banned. A separate study finds food service
workers are one-and-a-half-times MORE likely than the general
public to develop lung cancer.
                                    Mutual Broadcasting System
```

The first two sentences form a complete story. The third is optional. Thus, the end of the story is "collapsible." It could end after sentence two, or after sentence three. Mutual Broadcasting System anchor Frank Gentry explains that "this technique is valuable for anyone who has an exact time cue to hit—such as a local newscaster who talks up to the hourly network join [newscast]."[3]

Notice that attribution is used *last* in the first sentence of the three-sentence story. Gentry makes this observation about this writing technique:

> I tend to disagree with the dominant belief that attribution *always* precedes the comment made. Sometimes, I feel it's more effective to do it the other way around (as in this story), putting the attribution right behind the comment. Otherwise, you'd have:

`A study in the A-M-A Journal says waiters and bartenders are getting up to six-times the smoke of office workers.`

> In this case, I don't think there's any harm in making listeners wait (literally) four seconds to get the attribution.[4]

Consider adding this technique to those suggested under ''Attribution'' in Chapter 2.

Patterns

You can arrange the basic beginning-middle-end story form recommended earlier in a variety of different shapes or patterns. Use the scheme, framework, or story structure that organizes story details logically and tells the story most effectively. News stories often use a combination of organizational patterns, but to help you gain a better understanding of the variety available, the following sections isolate and illustrate the principal patterns.

Chronological

Presenting a *sequence* of events or statements helps an audience understand and remember what happened; it is a natural pattern for storytelling. After the lead sentence, the chronology begins—the earliest event, then the next significant event, the next, and so forth, until the last major occurrence of the story is noted. The chronological approach works especially well for reporting accidents, robberies, and shootings; breaking the chronology in such stories could confuse the audience.

The chronological story pattern is often used after a summary lead or after a delay/suspense lead in which the climax, or punch line, of the story is revealed at the end of the chronology of events. Here is an example of a soft lead followed by the chronology of the story:

`Included in any day's mail . . . are the usual supermarket weekly specials . . . credit card applications . . . and a card from Advo-systems. One side has some kind of ad or coupon . . . the flip-side, a picture of a child reported as missing by the National Center for Missing and Exploited Children.`

`Five-year-old Amanda Lemons got the mail and immediately recognized the picture on it as one of her classmates in her suburban Fort Worth kindergarten class. Amanda's mother was`

skeptical . . . then remembered her daughter had been talking
about Joshua Olson since the first day of school . . . as if she
had a crush on him. Donna Lemons called the phone number on the
ad . . . and then the school, who notified police.

Five-year-old Amanda WAS right . . . and Joshua was reunited
with his father who caught a flight from their Chicago-area
home. He had been granted custody . . . but Joshua disappeared
9-months ago along with his mother.

Texas State Network

Topical

People can understand and remember ideas more easily when they are grouped
or clustered into topics or subject headings. An umbrella lead is often used
with a topical story arrangement. Key story ideas are introduced in the lead
and then developed in the rest of the story. As noted earlier, transitions help
guide the audience from one topic to another.

Notice how the lead ''announces'' the topics in this WCCO Radio news
story—first generally (''. . . considers taxi-cab resolutions . . .'') and then
specifically (''. . . increase fares for passengers . . . and increase what
owners pay for license fees.'') The copy then develops each topic in the order
of its appearance in the lead.

The Minneapolis City Council today considers taxi-cab
resolutions . . . which would increase fares for passengers
. . . and increase what owners pay for license fees. Owners say
they need a fare increase . . . to cope with rising expenses.
They say their liability insurance now averages 42-hundred
dollars a year. But they oppose increases in their license
fees.

WCCO Radio, Minneapolis

Opposing Viewpoints

Arrangement around opposing viewpoints is similar to the topical structure
just described, but the topics are more specific: They are the opposing viewpoints that often surround a controversial issue. Consider the following
example:

Parents who are upset about the Denver public school's
attendance policy . . . complained to the Denver School Board
tonight . . . in a public hearing.

The policy is: if students miss 12 to 18 classes . . . they
flunk the course . . . even if their absences are excused.

Some parents say it encourages students to drop out.

But one parent spoke in favor of the policy. . . . He says it
teaches students responsibility (a soundbite from the parent
was then used).

Opponents of the policy want the school board to give a student
a chance to make-up missed work . . . and earn a grade based on
his work, not on his absences. What, if any, action will be
taken isn't known.

KUSA-TV, Denver

Notice how the lead in the KUSA-TV copy focuses on the parents and their
comments. After a brief explanation of the controversial policy, so that the
audience is "up to speed" with the current story, the opposing viewpoints are
presented.

Here is a variation of this opposing viewpoints story structure:

The Fraternal Order of Police and City of Wichita can't agree
on a contract. . . . Pay raises are not the center of
disagreement.

The F-O-P says it's willing to accept the city's offer of
raises on a sliding scale of up to five percent. But it won't
take the city's changes in what's called a personal business
day. The city wants to change it to a well day that an officer
can use if he or she goes a certain time without using sick
leave.

This morning, the council said it's willing to extend the
contract into next year. F-O-P officials say they'll file an
unfair labor practice complaint with the state's Public
Employee Relations Board.

KFDI Radio, Wichita, Kansas

This KFDI story structure creates almost a Ping-Pong effect. Each side in this
labor dispute is featured alternately *throughout* the story as specific contract
issues are discussed.

Combination

As noted earlier, a *combination* of organizational patterns can be used. Use
the *best* story pattern, no matter what arbitrary label is attached.

Here is an example of a combination of standard story patterns used in
one news story. A chronological arrangement is combined with a traditional
opposing viewpoints structure.

Charges of racism and discrimination were brought against the
New Iberia Mayor by one of his city councilmen at last night's
council meeting. Following the 5-2 vote to appoint Anne
Mathews* as the City's new prosecuting attorney, Councilman
Arthur Breaux* attacked the racial records of Mayor J. Henry

---

*These names have been changed.

Hebert's* administration, claiming Hebert has kept blacks from advancing in the administration during Hebert's 24 years in office. [an actuality from Breaux was then used].

Hebert defended his record following Breaux's statements, and lashed out at Breaux's voting record, saying he had failed to represent the white constituency in his district. [an actuality from Hebert was then used].

After that verbal exchange, several black members of the audience stood up and marched out of the meeting. Despite the uproar, Mathews was appointed the City's new prosecuting attorney.

KDEA Radio, New Iberia, Louisiana

Pace, Rhythm, Flow

Despite their brevity, well-written broadcast news stories should have a noticeable texture and a unique kind of beauty and precision. The criteria for evaluating newswriting are similar to the aesthetic considerations often used to evaluate creative efforts in music, dance, poetry, other arts, the manufacturing process, and even sports! Your appreciation of the effective use of language hinges on your background, training, education, interests, and sensitivity to the language usage that surrounds you each day.

The next two chapters develop more fully the structural elements of pace, rhythm, and flow in terms of words and sentences. The examples of full story copy used earlier in this chapter illustrate some of the principles described briefly now.

Pace relates to the apparent rate, speed, progress, movement, and development of ideas. A faster pace generally makes it more difficult to absorb ideas, but a slow pace causes a listener to become disinterested.

Rhythm creates a pattern of movement, a cadence, a regularity, a steady progression of ideas. Word selection and placement certainly influence the apparent rhythm in a story, but varying the length and structure of sentences also has an effect.

Flow relates to the motion, fluidity, and ease of movement through a series of ideas. Create and maintain momentum. In each story, proceed from idea to related idea. Be certain that your copy is free of stumbling blocks such as technical terms, complicated attribution, and difficult phrases. Stumbling blocks cause a story to lose direction and encourage the audience to lose interest and become distracted.

Good broadcast writers go beyond the mechanics of language and story structure. They cultivate a love for the power of words and the challenge of organizing and presenting ideas effectively. Figure 5.1 illustrates many of the principles of news story structure discussed in this chapter.

---

*This name has been changed.

```
PAGE 12A                              P-FAILURE
TALENT-SHEILA
SONY SOT
6/9/93

CHYRON-JEANETTE
                                      SHORTLY AFTER MIDNIGHT, NEIGHBORS
                                      ON 14TH STREET RUSHED OUT TO SEE THIS
                                      HOUSE IN FLAMES . . . AND 26 YEAR OLD
                                      CHARLES BOWYER CRYING OUT FOR HELP.

SONY SOT
CHYRON-HILARY MATTHEWS/NEIGHBOR
IN Q-TAPE #1 9:35:55
                                      ((THERE WAS A GUY ON TOP OF THE ROOF.
                                      FIRE WAS COMIN' OUT ALL OUT THE
                                      WINDOWS, ALL OUT THE BOTTOM PART.
                                      AND HE WAS SCREAMING FOR PEOPLE TO
                                      HELP HIM AND HE WAS TRYING TO GET HIS
                                      WIFE OUT))

RUNS-:09
SONY SOT
CHYRON-SHEILA HYLAND/STANDUP

IN Q-TAPE #1 9:49:34
                                      ((NEIGHBORS SAY THE MOTHER WAS
                                      LEANING OUT OF THIS WINDOW SCREAMING
                                      AT HER HUSBAND FOR HELP. BUT BY THE
                                      TIME EMERGENCY CREWS ARRIVED IT WAS
                                      ALREADY TOO LATE.

RUNS-:09                              DEAD IN AN UPSTAIRS BEDROOM WERE
                                      CHARLES BOWYER'S 25 YEAR OLD WIFE,
                                      MARY, AND THEIR TWO CHILDREN . . . 3
                                      YEAR OLD JASON AND 7 MONTH OLD JOHN.
                                      NEIGHBORS HELPED CHARLES BOWYER
                                      DOUSE THE FLAMES WITH BUCKETS OF
                                      WATER AND HOSES, BUT IN MINUTES, THE
                                      HOUSE WAS ENGULFED.

SONY SOT
CHYRON-JONI TILLMAN/NEIGHBOR
IN Q-TAPE #1 9:39:35
                                      ((I SET THERE AND HELD HIM IN MY
                                      ARMS. HE KEPT BEGGIN' ME TO LET HIM
                                      GO TO GET HIS KIDS. I SAID YOU CAN'T
                                      GET IN THERE . . . THERE'S NO WAY HE
                                      COULD GET IN THAT HOUSE))
```

Figure 5.1 Fire story television script. Courtesy of Sheila Hyland and WTAE-TV, Pittsburgh.

```
RUNS-.08
                                BY THE TIME THE LANDLORD ARRIVED IN
                                THE MORNING TO BOARD UP THE CHARRED
                                HOUSE, FIRE INVESTIGATORS HAD
                                ALREADY LABELED THE BLAZE
                                ''SUSPICIOUS'', BUT WEREN'T SAYING
                                MUCH MORE . . . AND NEIGHBORS WERE
                                POINTING FINGERS AT 9-1-1 AND
                                EMERGENCY CREWS, SAYING THEY TOOK
                                TOO LONG TO RESPOND.

SONY SOT
CHYRON-
IN Q-TAPE #1 9:43:30
                                ((I DIALED 9-1-1 AND THEY WOULDN'T
                                ANSWER))
IN Q-TAPE #1 9:36:
                                ((THEY SAY THEY RESPONDED IN 4
                                MINUTES . . . THEY'RE LYING. NO
                                WAY))
RUNS-:03
                                JEANETTE POLICE CHIEF PHIL ROWLINGS
                                SAYS 9-1-1 LOGS SHOW EMERGENCY CALLS
                                WERE ANSWERED WITHIN 5 SECONDS AND
                                CREWS RESPONDED TO THE SCENE WITHIN
                                4 MINUTES.

SONY SOT
CHYRON-CHIEF PHIL ROWLINGS/
JEANETTE POLICE
IN Q-TAPE #1 9:53:24
                                ((IN EVERY FIRE PEOPLE ALWAYS THINK
                                YOU TAKE LONG WHETHER IT'S A
                                RESPONSE FROM POLICE, FIRE,
                                AMBULANCE))
RUNS-:05
                                EMERGENCY CREWS SAY IT MUST HAVE
                                SEEMED ESPECIALLY LONG TO NEIGHBORS
                                WHO WAITED . . . AND WATCHED --
                                HORRIFIED -- AS MARY BOWYER AND HER
                                TWO CHILDREN DIED BEFORE THEY COULD
                                BE RESCUED. SHEILA HYLAND WTAE FOUR
                                NEWS.
```

Figure 5.1 continued.

Summary

This chapter began by suggesting a process you can follow to make news story structure more effective and then analyzed portions of that process more closely.

Several techniques help to select and place information in news stories: develop informed judgment; talk through the story by answering questions the audience is likely to ask; limit what you use; emphasize the impact of the story on your audience; tie the lead to the rest of the story structure.

Like any story, a broadcast story must be complete. The beginning must draw you into the story; transitions help bridge between key ideas; endings help complete the informational process. Various organizational patterns can help form this basic story structure, among them the chronological pattern, the topical pattern, and the pattern of opposing viewpoints. Sometimes a combination of patterns is used.

Become more sensitive to the pace, rhythm, and flow evident in effective broadcast news stories. Generate enthusiasm for each opportunity to digest various facts and comments, then devise the best possible way to organize and present that information in an interesting and compelling manner that will make a difference in someone's life. Learn to become a good storyteller.

Exercises

1. Do *each* of the following after selecting *one* of the following sets of story notes:

a. Using the *same* fact sheet, write at least *two* versions of the story to be read by either a radio or television anchor at noon and one P.M. today.

b. At the bottom of each report, identify the story structure patterns used and indicate *why* each pattern is effective.

c. Between the lines of copy for each version of the story you have written, write the questions you asked yourself to help select and arrange the information into an effective story structure. (This process was illustrated in this chapter.)

d. All of the following information was provided by local officials late this morning.

Notes for Story 1

(All comments are from FBI Spokesman Larry Edgeholm who is based in your town.)

- Federal and state officials raided 20 pharmacies across the state this morning around 9am central time.
- Possible Medicaid fraud is involved.
- Edgeholm said a task force of officers executed 20 search warrants on pharmacies.
- Warrants were served by federal agents and state troopers to locations in Pressburg, Glenville, Barton, Elgin, Dunbar, Kirkland, and Compton. These are all small communities within a ten-to-fifteen mile radius of your location.
- Edgeholm said no charges have yet been filed, and he did not expect any arrests today.
- Search warrants sought records and information relating to Medicaid payments and prescription sales.
- Federal law requires drug stores to charge the lowest price possible for prescription drugs. Some of these stores have been accused of inflating prices on prescription drugs within the last three months.
- Nine federal and state agencies were involved, including the Food and Drug Administration, Drug Enforcement

Administration, Health and Human Services, FBI, and U.S. Attorney's Office.

- Pharmacists served with warrants expressed confusion about why such drastic steps had to be taken to get access to pharmacy records.

Notes for Story 2

(All of the following information is from Lisa Boyd, local spokesperson for Amtrak.)

- Train-truck collision about 7:45am this morning.
- It happened two miles south of Interstate 80, about ten miles east of Lincoln, NE.
- Amtrak train collided with a tracker-trailer rig.
- Rig was carrying hydrochloric acid and the chemical Xylene.
- 23 people hospitalized, most with respiratory problems.
- No serious injuries reported so far.
- Train was eastbound. Rig stopped on tracks for some unknown reason.

- On impact, rig was split in two sections and burst into flames.
- Approx. one-square mile around the accident site remained evacuated and blocked off for about one hour after the incident occurred.
- A gray, misty cloud rose from the crash site.
- Firefighters doused the scene with chemicals to kill the fire and to avoid further damage and an explosion.
- Environmental groups have begun to express alarm at the potential danger of the situation.
- 162 people were aboard the train, 12 were Amtrak employees.
- Driver of the rig was identified as Shelton Joseph Matthews, 26, of Denton, NE. A passerby pulled Matthews from the rig. Matthews was not seriously injured and refused treatment on the scene.
- Investigation is continuing.
- Matthews was charged with failure to stop at a railroad crossing.

Notes

1. Reprinted by permission of Phil Witt.

2. Reprinted by permission of Frank Gentry.

3. Ibid.

4. Ibid.

Chapter 6

Words

This chapter describes and illustrates essential concepts about the smallest language unit, words. Chapter 7 concerns the *placement* of carefully chosen words and phrases in effective sentences. Why, you might ask, is so much attention given to such relatively small, unobtrusive units of language as words and sentences?

Words and sentences are the smallest components of the stories that you will write. That does not, however, mean they are unimportant. Instead, it means that they prepare and establish the basis for everything you do in writing—for broadcast news stories or for anything else. No matter how startling and impressive the sounds and pictures that you may gather and use in your stories, if you do not surround them effectively with words and sentences that give them context and meaning, they will ultimately be ineffective.

The quality of your writing and reporting is based on details, the specifics of how you use words, sounds, and pictures to tell brief stories about a particular incident or event that has occurred on a particular day at a particular time. Good writing will always be an essential part of what you do. Your words and sentences deserve constant refinement and attention each time you write a broadcast news story.

Essentials

Broadcast news copy presents a special challenge to the writer. The words used must be easily heard by a partially deaf 90-year-old great-grandmother, readily understood by a 13-year-old whose vocabulary has not developed extensively and whose mind is easily distracted, but still provoke the interest of a 45-year-old business executive who is well educated, well informed, and short on time.

The challenge is to find a way to use words to mean what you want to say and to say what you mean. The broadcast audience gets only one chance at each story, so your copy must be clear, precise, concise, concrete, conversational, and readable when heard for the first and probably only time. A word that is out of place or doesn't mean exactly what it should, an awkward phrase, even wordiness will confuse and distract an audience or a newscaster.

Clear

Choose simple, but not simplistic, words. Do not belittle your audience's intelligence. Never use a long word when a short word works as well or better. Avoid using abstractions; choose words that make ideas easier to understand and remember.

Prefer the familiar to the unfamiliar and obscure. Ask yourself what a difficult word means in simple terms, and determine how you can rephrase such words so that others will understand.

Here are examples of words and phrases that often appear in news copy and that could be simplified to improve clarity.[1]

Original	More Simplified/Familiar
Board of Election Commissioners	Election Board
Board of Education	School Board
Secretary of Labor	Labor Secretary
Board of Police Commissioners	Police Board
Director of Health and Hospitals	Health and Hospital Director
remuneration or compensation	pay
objective	aim or goal
residence	home
laceration	cut
contusion	bruise
physician	doctor
attorney	lawyer
pact	contract/treaty/agreement
youth	teenager
vehicle	car, truck, van, etc.
conflagration	fire
altercation	argument, fight, dispute
spurious	false
of no use	useless, ineffective
on the rise	increasing
great amount of	extensive
initiate/commence/go into effect on	start or begin
begin again	resume
look into	examine
give consideration to	consider
do a study of	study
modify/alter	change
make changes in	adjust
plummet	fall
reside	live
encourage	urge
tells of	suggests
is opposed to	opposes
in favor of	favors

spoke in favor of/was in support of/put its support behind	supported
voted to allow for	approved
in need of	needs
acquire	get or gain
utilize	use
hurl	throw
take action	act
transpire	happen
is able to	can
cognizant	aware
never forget	remember
is of the opinion that	believes
just found out that	learned
get rid of	eliminate, delete
endeavor/venture	try
vie	compete
in charge of	handles
was the recipient of	received
kept up	maintained
shut down	closed
terminate	end
due to the fact that	because
along the lines of/in the nature of	like
from the point of view of	for
inasmuch as/on the grounds that/for the reason that	since, because
in favor of/for the purpose of	for, to
in accordance with	by, under
in the case of/in the event that	if
in terms of	in, for (or leave out of copy)
on the basis of	by
prior to	before
in the neighborhood of/having to do with/in regards to	about
with reference to/with regard to	about (or leave out of copy)
with the result that	so that
that is to say	in other words
subsequent to/as the result of	after
accordingly/consequently/for this reason/hence	so
furthermore	then
in addition (to)	besides, also
indeed	in fact
likewise	and, also

more specifically	for instance, for example
nevertheless	but, however
with the exception that (or of)	except
at this point in time	now
moreover	now, next
in the near future	soon

Avoid using words that tend to confuse an audience. Written words that are improperly placed in a sentence also can communicate an unusual meaning when read aloud.

Weak

The cost of *living alone* should not be the only factor used to determine teacher salary raises.

Better

Cost of living should not be the only factor used to determine teacher salary raises.

If you use unfamiliar words or expressions, jargon, technical or scientific terms, explain them in common, ordinary terms that will be understood by most people. Sometimes words creep into stories that are perfectly clear to those working regularly in news but may not be so clear to viewers and listeners. Here is how KMOV-TV in St. Louis suggests improving the clarity of typical news story fragments.[2]

Weak

Police apprehended and subdued the suspect and affected an arrest after the suspect flourished (or displayed) a weapon.

Better

Police caught and arrested the suspect after he pulled a pistol (or threatened the teller with a pistol).

You will soon discover that many other professions have their own precise language that makes sense to members of that profession but is meaningless to the average listener or viewer: government ("The city council will use the powers of *eminent domain* to acquire the land"); law ("The attorney general will file a *writ of habeas corpus* . . . "); economics ("The lower *prime interest rate* is being used by *the Fed* to control the *money supply*"); medicine ("The victim has *second-degree* burns and is listed in *guarded condition*").

When you encounter terminology that may cause confusion, ask yourself the following questions: (1) Can I explain this term in simple language? (2) Is this particular term *essential* to a *clear*, complete understanding of this story? (3) Would this story still be clear if this term or expression was dropped from the copy, or if a brief explanation was placed adjacent to the term in the copy, or if just the explanation was used?

Here are a few script fragments to illustrate how to work terminology into a story and add clarity to what is written:

`Cellulite bothers many female college students. Cellulite is the fatty build-up in the thighs, hips, and buttocks.`

`The new law allows adults to prepare a living will—a legal document saying ''Yes'' or ''No'' to medical treatment BEFORE patients become too ill to express their wishes.`

`The city will merge five downtown improvement districts into one. An improvement district uses money collected from businesses to maintain buildings, promote the area, and increase sales activity.`

`A warming trend for inflation . . . consumer prices, what we pay for things at retail, shot up by one half of one percent last March.`

What you write must not only be clear, it must also be precise. Use words **Precise** carefully to provide specific meanings and to avoid double entendres and exaggerations. Say what you mean to say!

Carelessness often causes imprecision. Bob Priddy, past Chairman of RTNDA and News Director of the Missouri Network, offers these examples:

> ''The price was *under* $50.'' If someone put the price tag beneath a stack of 50 one-dollar coins, that would be ''under $50.'' Otherwise, the price is LESS THAN $50.
>
> How often do we see (or say) that a victim was ''beaten *about* the head and the face.'' Boy, that's a relief. If the person had been beaten ON the head and face, the victim could have been hurt. But being beaten ''about'' means the assailant never laid a glove on him.[3]

Select and use **verbs** carefully.

Weak

`The system will provide several functions.`

Better

`The system will provide several services. or`

`The system will perform several functions.`

Weak

`The First National Bank suffered an armed robbery around noon today.`

Better

The First National Bank *was robbed* around noon today. *or*

There was a robbery at the First National Bank around noon
today.

Nouns must also be selected and used precisely.

Weak

The new admissions *proposal* starts today.

Better

The new admissions *policy* starts today.

Weak

The *seminar* will *decide* issues on food exports to Mexico,
Canada, and Japan.

Better

Seminar participants will *discuss* food exports to Mexico,
Canada, and Japan.

Double entendres also hamper precision. These are words or expressions that can be interpreted in more than one way; one interpretation is often risqué. Always read your copy aloud to see whether it has a meaning you did not intend.

KMOV-TV in St. Louis provides these examples of double entendres taken from newsroom copy:

Dr. Ramirez has had a hand in several birth control devices.

Actress Cynthia Wood is in great shape after her mastectomy.

The body of Major Ed Raymond is on the last leg of its journey
home.

Plans are being made to turn the building into elderly
apartments.

A man wielding a pistol and a woman held up a southside bank
today.[4]

If used sparingly and carefully, superlatives can help communicate the special significance surrounding a news story. But use caution with words like *smallest, largest, first, last, most, least,* and so forth. Maintain objectivity; avoid distortions and exaggerations. Be precise! When in doubt, leave superlatives out of your copy.

Every word in a broadcast news story must not only be clear and precise in meaning; it must have a purpose, a reason to be there. Airtime is too valuable to waste. Write as if you had a small quota of words to use each day—don't waste them.

You will need to distinguish between *repetition* (i.e., saying something more than once to make certain it is understood) and *redundancy* (i.e., using more words than needed to say something). You must write concisely, but what you write must remain clear and lively. Conciseness is valuable only if it aids clarity. A longer phrase may add extra color, emphasize or explain a point, or improve the pacing or rhythm of a sentence.

Two techniques will help eliminate redundancies and improve conciseness: (1) Follow the advice offered in Chapter 5 ("Story Structure")—tighten your copy by eliminating less important facts, opinions, and unnecessary transitions; (2) replace a series of words or a phrase with one word that means the same. For example, *once a month* could be written as *monthly; give testimony* becomes *testify; more than a few* is simply *many; close in proximity to* is simply *near.* You often can provide a positive spin to a sentence when you rewrite.

Weak

```
The new law is a major defeat for the President who wanted to
drop the bar against letting AIDS-infected people into the
country.
```

Better

```
The law is a major defeat for the President who wanted to allow
AIDS-infected people into the country.
```

Weak

```
Janet Bankston talked about people getting help and
controlling the bacteria opposed to people who ignore the
symptoms.
```

Better

```
Janet Bankston says people should get help to control the
bacteria rather than ignore the symptoms.
```

Here are some phrases in which the first (underlined) word should be the *only* word necessary: *appointed to the position; killed dead* or *killed instantly; close down; shooting incident; reason why; thunderstorm activity.*

In the following phrases, use only the *last* word: *auction sale; most unique; rather unique; new construction; different locations; advance preparation; final verdict; local neighborhood; major disaster; completely destroyed; formally charged; future plans; very first; little baby; true fact;*

definite proof; in order/in an effort/with a view to; end result; first introduced.

Concrete

Choose words that elicit tangible images and that relate directly to common experiences in the lives of most of the audience. Avoid abstraction. Convey meaning, and underscore the impact of the story. Here are some examples:

```
The bill would make it illegal for anyone under 21 to drive with
a blood alcohol concentration of point-zero-one-percent or
higher. That is about two beers for the average person.


. . . A wall of mud, four-and-a-half feet high, roared through
town . . . 60 people had to evacuate.
                              Mutual Broadcasting System
```

Another way to convey the meaning and impact of a story is to use positive rather than negative statements. For example, *The governor decided not to sign the bill today as expected* could be written more effectively: *The governor vetoed the bill.*

In the following example, the positively phrased sentences emphasize the story's immediacy, power, drama, and impact:

```
Hijackers hold a Kuwaiti Airways 747 at the airport in the
Iranian city of Mashhad. 114 people aboard. The hijackers
threaten to blow up the plane if anyone tries to approach it.
                                          NBC Radio News
```

Conversational

You are advised to write the way you speak because you are *speaking* to people not *reading* to them. But you don't write exactly as you speak. And you don't speak exactly as you write. As a broadcast newswriter, you are constantly balancing the two approaches.

Your copy needs to be *structured* like a conversation and placed into a conversational *framework,* but your copy should not be *exactly* like a regular conversation; conversations tend to be verbose, redundant, imprecise, rambling, and incomplete. How can you make word choices more natural, informal, and conversational?

Try using contractions. They sound more natural and familiar. They are easier to read aloud and tend to increase the momentum of a story.

But contractions must be used carefully. They should not be used when you want to emphasize an important point or clarify a crucial fact: *The governor does not support the bill.* However, you could write: *The governor won't be taking a long vacation this year.* Avoid using contractions with noun-verb combinations (e.g., *The governor'll go to New York tomorrow.*).

Avoid slang. Terms change very rapidly and often mean different things to different groups of people. It is difficult to use slang without making the copy sound obsolete, frivolous, affected, or offensive.

But when you target your newscasts to a younger, more contemporary audience, as done by the ABC Contemporary Network, *prudent* use of slang can make news copy livelier, more vibrant, and more colorful:

```
G-men call the people rounded-up today among the
deadliest. . . . Law enforcement agencies pooled their talent
and nabbed more than 200 people in 13 states and the District of
Columbia!
                                    ABC Contemporary Network
```

Clichés dull news stories. A combination of words that has been used too much loses effectiveness and meaning. Here is a helpful guideline: A word or expression that comes to mind readily is probably a cliché; avoid it.

Clichés are everywhere. Avoid prefabricated phrases like these that often appear in broadcast news copy:

only time will tell
remains to be seen
in no uncertain terms
goes without saying
in the final analysis
wants to get all its ducks in a row
huddled behind closed doors
clean bill of health
sitting down at the bargaining table
storm of protest
that's the word from
grew by leaps and bounds
for heaven's sake
it'll probably get worse before it gets better

When tempted to use a cliché, find an original image, make word lists, or free-associate.

Providing a list of clichés is less important than convincing you to become sensitized to their misuse. And that is a point to remember: Do not assume that *all* familiar expressions are clichés. In the right context, an obvious cliché can make an effective ending to a story:

```
In Bunol, Spain . . . they can what they can. . . . And what
they can't . . . they use to throw at the world's biggest food
fight. They grow a lot of tomatoes in this western town of
5-thousand. This year's surplus is 80-thousand pounds . . .
and going fast. What a way to paint the town red.
                                        Cable News Network
```

Idiomatic expressions provide familiar phrases that have definite meanings:

Diplomatic sources say the U-S embassy in Bahrain in the Persian Gulf was suggesting Americans *keep their heads low* after the U-S attack on Iranian oil installations.

ABC Contemporary Network

. . . The House Judiciary Committee today voted for a seven-month extension of the program, but *there are more hurdles ahead.*

KTRK-TV, Houston

. . . but for Glen Coleman* of Missoula, an appearance on the program ''America's Most Wanted '' *blew his cover.*

KBOZ Radio, Bozeman, Montana

Avoid using idiomatic expressions unless such usage is accurate, grammatically correct, widely understood, and adds needed color to your news copy.

Readable

Review the techniques and suggestions offered in Chapter 2, ''Broadcast Newswriting Style.'' Avoid using language that inhibits the smoothness, the readability of the news copy.

Plosives cause a popping sound in a microphone—*The Pontiff pushed past the bystanders.* Sibilants cause a hissing sound—*There should be some sunshine soon in the south.* Avoid writing alliterations (*threatening throngs . . .*), tongue twisters (*are already . . . the sixth such incident*), and awkward word combinations (*was seeking, bank card*). These can make news copy difficult to read and thus difficult to understand and remember.

Hear what you *write.* Tell each story to your keyboard. Read your copy aloud.

Meanings

Some linguists contend that less than 50 percent of the words we use actually convey meaning. The rest, they maintain, are added for style, flair, or to satisfy accepted standards of usage.

---

*This name has been changed.

Ted Koppel, ABC News "Nightline." Copyright Capital Cities/ABC, Inc.

Use "dense" words that cram a lot of meaning into a small space. Frank Gentry, Mutual Broadcasting System anchor, explains the concept this way:

> Forget about nouns, verbs, and adverbs for the moment. For our purposes only two types of words REALLY count in broadcast writing:
>
> - Informational Words
> - Grammatical Words
>
> The secret to good broadcast writing is to include as many informational words as necessary, while using as few grammatical words as possible.
>
> This sample sentence:
> "The QUICK BROWN FOX JUMPED OVER the LAZY DOG'S BACK."
> is a well-constructed container of information (even though it's doggerel). All but two words ("The" "the") convey information. The result is lean and clean. . . . With the words (and time) saved you can put in more facts, or get more stories into your 'casts.[5]

Broadcast news tends to be colorful naturally because of its informal, conversational writing style. But broadcast news cannot casually adopt the poor grammar, imprecise terms, inaccuracies, and so forth that are often accepted in casual conversation.

Adding Color

Extract the essence of natural, human conversation. Incorporate some of what you see, hear, smell, taste, touch, feel, experience, and sense into the words that you write. Invigorate your copy, but maintain accuracy and objectivity. Add color that flows naturally from the facts and comments surrounding each story.

Here are a few ways to add color to broadcast news copy:

- Use "dense" words, especially for nouns and adjectives.

- Use active voice (described later).

- Use strong verbs that describe as well as indicate action.

- Use positive rather than negative statements.

Look for ways to make your copy colorful and still avoid repetition of trite words:

```
Fire investigators say fireworks sparked this morning's
blaze.
                          KFRU Radio, Columbia, Missouri

The Minnesota Twins have the Detroit Tigers by the tail.
                                  The Associated Press
```

Color should not be added when doing so would simply confuse or distract the audience, add biased viewpoints, and not improve your copy. Think for a moment about the word *said*, which is probably the verb used most often in conversations and in news stories. It is not colorful, but it is clean, simple, precise, and neutral in meaning. Think about the subtle meanings conveyed by this sampling of alternatives: *warned, declared, added, vowed, charged, stated, asserted, noted, disclosed, revealed, promised, reported, told, spoke, remarked, expressed, related, announced, contended, maintained, notified, identified, ordered, characterized, portrayed, depicted.* These alternatives to *said* do help add variety and color to your copy, but they must be used wisely.

Generally, do not add color to stories involving especially personal and sensitive matters, such as death and disasters. As with most suggestions, however, some exceptions occur. Notice the vivid word choices filtered into the closing sentences of this Texas State Network story about the final efforts to rescue an 18-month-old girl:

```
The breakthroughs today sent a surge of optimism and
anticipation through the volunteers working at the site. The
volunteers punctured the well cavity shortly after five
o'clock this morning . . . 43 hours after the rescue efforts
began.
```

Expressing Opinions

The journalist's role and responsibility as a fair, objective, unbiased observer is weakened when adding color to copy also causes personal attitudes and viewpoints to be expressed. A reporter's opinions, beliefs, and value judgments must never be used in factual news stories. Use *only* the facts.

A fine line occurs between providing additional perspective or meaning and offering personal viewpoints and opinions. In a story about efforts to save lives in a fire, it would *not* be appropriate to write:

Weak

```
Rising hope turned into sorrowful frustration when
firefighters made tireless efforts to squelch the flames.
```

Better

```
Despite their best efforts, firefighters could not contain the
fire.
```

The second sentence in the following fragment should have been deleted:

```
The life of Paul Brewster* was spared by a Preston* County jury
today. That was more benevolent than Brewster was when he hired
a gunman to murder his wife. The Caldwell* man was convicted
Tuesday night of aggravated first-degree murder.
```

In the next example, the final sentence from a story about multiple law enforcement agency arrests of about 200 people in several states does express a point of view, but its intent is to provide perspective, not opinion, for the listener:

```
The law estimates there are a thousand members of these vicious
gangs, so today's arrests made a dent.
                               ABC Contemporary Network
```

Showdown is a highly charged word with strong implications, but KTRK-TV in Houston added precision and insight to its story by *not* using a more neutral, but routine, word like *meeting, conference,* or *session.*

```
After a showdown with her board of directors in Hartford* last
night, Dr. Helen Garbalz* will rewrite and resubmit her
resignation, effective March fourth. She will be in Houston as
health director on Monday, but leaves her former post with
mixed reviews.
```

Do not exaggerate or overstate an issue or situation by inserting inaccurate, inappropriate, or emotional langauge into factual news accounts. Let the audience form opinions based on the facts and comments from newsmakers that you present and attribute.

---

*These names have been changed.

Reporters can express opinions inadvertently in ''straight'' news stories, those in which the audience would, and should, expect to receive a reasonably objective viewpoint. Indeed, unless you announce otherwise, your audience should expect and receive only factual material in news stories.

Maintaining Objectivity

Avoid using words that can erode the objectivity of what you report. The words that you use to tell your stories reflect on the quality of your professionalism and the strength of your dedication to fair and objective reporting.

Avoid identifying people by race when such a reference is not a crucial part of the story. For example, knowing that a particular person charged with a specific crime is a member of a certain race is not crucial. Racial identity may be helpful when law enforcement officials include racial identification for a suspect still at large.

Replace sexist references with nonsexist words (*councilman/councilmember, chairman/presiding officer, waiter or waitress/server, workmen/workers,* and *newsman/reporter* or *journalist,* etc.). Sexist references can cause distortion and present biased viewpoints as acceptable.

Remember: Words do influence the way people think. Accuracy and fairness require that you monitor the words you choose when adding color and relaying opinions so that you do not abandon objectivity.

Usage

A thorough knowledge of basic English grammar and language usage will make you a better broadcast newswriter. A comprehensive review of this essential information is beyond the scope of this book. But a brief review of contemporary, conversational language usage, as applied to effective broadcast newswriting, *is* within the scope of this book. You must have a firm grasp of basic rules and practices. Broadcast newswriting must evolve from this essential language foundation.

Nouns and Pronouns

Both nouns and pronouns help identify people, places, and things. Use a pronoun only when its antecedent (the noun) clearly gives the pronoun its meaning. A pronoun used more than a few words away from its antecedent will tend to be confusing.

It is easy to use a singular noun and then incorrectly use a plural pronoun in a later reference.

Weak

The Citizens Coalition for Better Transportation is working to make *their* message clear.

Better

The Citizens Coalition for Better Transportation is working to make *its* message clear.

Collective nouns describe an entity made up of separate parts. Examples: family, jury, committee. Be alert to questions of subject-verb agreement and pronoun-antecedent agreement when using collective nouns.

Weak

`A local family was honored for `*`their`*` contribution to the Y-W-C-A.`

Better

`A local family was honored for `*`its`*` contribution to the Y-W-C-A.`

Better

`Members of a local family`` were honored for `*`their contributions`*` to the Y-W-C-A.`

If you use a singular noun, such as *university, grocery store,* or *city council,* either use the singular *it* or make the referent word plural (by writing *university administrators, grocery store owners,* or *city council members*).

In the following story fragment, whether *he* represents the mayor or the police chief is not clear:

Weak

`The mayor and the police chief battled about the budget today. He is expected to . . .`

If there is any chance that the pronoun reference will be confusing, repeat the noun in some form:

Better

`The mayor and the police chief battled about the budget today. Mayor Randall is expected to . . .`

A story of any length offers numerous opportunities for natural, unobtrusive reinforcement of nouns for the sake of clarity. Reinforcement can be given for locations, such as countries, towns, or streets, as well as for names and titles. For example, *the city's worst fire* can become *Littleton's worst fire,* and *police* can be written *Middleton Police.*

Provide a consistent point of view when using pronouns. Some newsrooms argue that the judicious use of first- and second-person references, for example, *I, you, we, us,* and *our,* helps to make news stories more personal and direct, intensifies attention, and creates more interest and involvement in the audience:

It'll be some time before "Scoop" Jackson is forgotten in
Washington State. For forty years, he represented *us* in
Congress. . . . Todd Smith has that story from *our* D-C Bureau.
KIRO-TV, Seattle

Other equally reputable news operations insist that only third-person references, for example, *she, he, it,* and *they,* be used because to do otherwise
jeopardizes the objective and more uniform presentation of the news. As suggested earlier, determine the preference of the newsroom in which you work
and follow it.

Verbs

One of your challenges associated with broadcast newswriting is to provide
copy that reflects contemporary, conversational langauge without breaking
completely the standard rules of grammar and usage. For instance, we know
that verbs express action or help to make a statement. But in broadcast copy,
verbs are sometimes dropped, especially in lead sentences (e.g., *A major earthquake in Peru today*). Also, nouns are often converted into verbs (e.g., *chaired
the meeting, headquartered at the hotel, heads up the committee, hosted the
reception* and even *sprinklered,* which was used in a story to indicate that a
particular building did have sprinklers). Besides these interesting, contemporary uses of verbs, other common concerns arise when verbs are used in
news copy.

Know which "voice" is speaking.   If the subject of the verb receives the
action, the verb is in the *passive voice—The suspect was booked this morning
by police.* If the subject of the verb performs the action, the verb is in the
active voice—Police booked the suspect this morning.
       Passive voice is useful when you want to emphasize the object of the
action—*The Pope was escorted to the White House by an honor guard.* Sometimes passive voice is clearer and simply sounds better than active voice—
Today's investor is caught between rising inflation and interest rates.
       Active voice is used most often in broadcast news copy:

The City of Philadelphia will have to free three-hundred
prisoners on bail today under a Federal court order.
Philadelphia prisons are overcrowded. . . .
Mutual Broadcasting System

Weak

The new construction of a department store and new mall shops
has been recommended for conditional approval.

Better

City officials granted conditional approval for the
construction of a department store and shops in the mall.

In the preceding examples, notice how using active voice produces copy that is lively, interesting, understandable, and concise. Active voice also conforms to the natural rhythms of *spoken* English.

Phil Witt, News Anchor and Senior Reporter at WDAF-TV in Kansas City, offers this advice:

> Use active verbs and sentence structure. Nothing bogs down a report worse than passive writing. It's dull. It's lengthy. It's a crutch. Go after active writing. It may take awhile to get to the point where it becomes natural. Don't get frustrated or lazy. Keep at it. Active verbs make people much better writers.[6]

Be conscious of verb tenses. As you move further away from the future and present verb tenses and allow the past and past perfect tenses to dominate, immediacy and impact decrease and meanings and implications shift. Compare the impact of each sentence as the verb tense changes:

Senators

   (will vote) [*future*]
     (will have voted [*future perfect*]
       (are voting) [*present*]
         (have voted) [*present perfect*]
           (voted) [*past*]
             (had voted) [*past perfect*] on the bill.

The present tense indicates statements or conditions that are still true when the story is used on the air. The present perfect tense reflects that actions have ended but are not far removed from the present time. The past and past perfect tenses are best used for one-time events that occurred at some indefinite time. Notice how time references shift appropriately in this sentence:

The House *has passed* [present perfect] a proposed law that *will close* [future] all election polls in the nation at the same time. . . .

                                        Texas State Network

Use future and present verb tenses whenever possible, but do not use them when doing so would mislead or confuse the audience. Use the verb tense that is the most logical for the story being written. Notice the power and impact this use of the simple past tense generates:

Spanish Police *stormed* an apartment building this morning and *shot it out* with suspected kidnappers to free a little girl held for ransom.

                                        Cable News Network

Sometimes a *mixture* of verb tenses works best:

```
In Butte, bids for the port of Montana's 5.6 million dollar
transportation hub have been awarded [present perfect]. The
first phase involves [present] clearing the hub site at Silver
Bow. Then road work and construction of the huge
transportation hub will get underway [future].
```
                                KBOZ Radio, Bozeman, Montana

Notice how the verb tenses seem logical and appropriate for each of the preceding items. The use of present and future tense verbs emphasizes immediacy, while each story is placed in the proper time frame by the honest use of other verb tenses.

No matter which verb tense you choose, you can add freshness and urgency to a developing story by adding time references or *time tags:*

```
Local police have made a breakthrough in the hit-and-run case
reported last Tuesday.

At this hour -- the San Francisco Port Commission is getting
ready to talk about . . .
```
                               KGO Newstalk Radio, San Francisco

```
A State Senate Committee is to decide within minutes whether it
will approve a controversial bill . . .
```
                                    Georgia Radio News Service

Use time tags sparingly; otherwise, the audience will become less sensitive to their use. Correct use of the present or present perfect tense is sometimes better than overusing time tags like *today, earlier this afternoon,* and so forth.

Keep compound verb forms together:

```
Two American military men have been killed in the crash of a
helicopter near Stuttgart, West Germany.
```
                                                NBC Radio News

```
A 35-year-old Saginaw man has been arrested for possession
with intent to deliver.
```
                                    WSGW Radio, Saginaw, Michigan

Lack of space prevents the discussion of other problems associated with the use of verbs. These include irregular verbs, infinitives, noun-verb agreement and verbals. Curl up with one of the English grammar books suggested in the bibliography (see Appendix C) to learn this useful information.

Whenever possible, use strong verbs instead of adjectives and adverbs. Although adjectives and adverbs may add color and variety to your copy, and might clarify or explain an action or comment, they also occupy valuable time on the air. Use "dense" words. Follow the advice given earlier by Frank Gentry (see "Meanings"). In the examples that he provides, notice the clarity and fullness of meaning that are possible *without* excessive use of adjectives and adverbs.

Adjectives and Adverbs

Avoid repeating the same word unnecessarily in the same piece of news copy. For example:

Synonyms and Homophones

`The city council will review the `*`proposal`*` this morning. The `*`proposal`*` would eliminate the need for prior approval of new subdivisions. If this `*`proposal`*` is like most city council `*`proposals,`*` a heated session should be expected.`

Good synonyms for *proposal* are *plan, project, idea, program, proposition,* and *suggestion*. When you find yourself stumped for a synonym to use to avoid distracting repetition, consult a thesaurus or a dictionary, or ask a colleague for suggestions. But remember that synonyms are sometimes *not* helpful; sometimes it is best to repeat a key word in a story to ensure clarity and accuracy (see the preceding discussion of *said* on page 118).

Avoid using homophones—words that sound alike but have different meanings (e.g., *site/cite/sight; rain/rein/reign; great/grate; bare/bear; peak/peek*.) Also be alert for words that look all right on paper but convey a different meaning than intended when read aloud (e.g., *a tax/attacks; and effects/and defects*).

Analogies can help explain difficult subjects by comparing complex things to relatively familiar things. A well-chosen analogy can help enliven as well as enlighten:

Analogies, Metaphors, and Personifications

`. . . The impact of the [budget] cuts was expected to be brutal. One lawmaker said the cuts would hit government like ''somebody dropped a toaster in the bathtub.''`

`                                        Cable News Network`

Be certain that each analogy is an accurate comparison and is necessary to make an uncommon word or phrase more understandable.

In a metaphor, a word or phrase denoting one kind of object, idea, or action is used in place of another to suggest a likeness between them:

`The Seattle school system is faced with an unexpected new `*`wave of red ink`*` . . .`

`                                        KIRO-TV, Seattle`

Watch for overused metaphors such as *cream of the crop, dog tired, came out smelling like a rose, comb a neighborhood, near death's door* and mixed metaphors, for instance *Even his opponents claim that the mayor's deep and soothing voice is a feather in his cap.* Well-chosen metaphors can help clarify ideas and add sparkle and color to your copy, but use them sparingly and carefully.

Personification assigns human characteristics to inhuman objects and situations—*Mother Earth* and *Grim Reaper.* Be alert to keep personifications like the following from creeping into your copy:

Weak

```
A Finger Lake police car suffered extensive damage to its
windshield when it was smashed last night.
```

Better

```
The windshield on a Finger Lake police car was damaged last
night.
```

You should never use words derived from the verb "to say" when referring to reports, proposals, and other inanimate objects; they cannot "speak."

Weak

```
The federal report says that record harvests are expected this
year.
```

Better

```
The federal report [predicts] [indicates] [shows] that record
harvests are expected this year.
```

Summary

This chapter has described and illustrated how to select and use words more effectively in broadcast news copy.

Choose words that clarify ideas, making them easy to understand and remember. Each word or phrase must have a specific meaning to avoid double entendres and exaggerations. Be concise. Write as if you had a small quota of words to use each day. Words should help convey the meaning and underscore the impact of a story, and they should elicit tangible images and experiences shared by most of the audience. Extract and use the essence of natural conversation. Avoid using slang, clichés and idiomatic expressions. Hear what you write; choose words that enhance the smoothness and readability of your news copy.

The meaning of each word is important. Add color and vitality to your copy, but do not lose objectivity by expressing personal opinions and attitudes.

Apply the standard rules of grammar to the special requirements of broadcast newswriting. When you use pronouns, be certain that their antecedents are clear and that a consistent point of view is evident. Active voice should be used most often. Use the verb tense that is the most logical for the story being written; generally, try to stay with the present, present perfect, and future tenses. Sometimes a mixture of tenses is appropriate. Time tags can help add immediacy to stories, but watch where you place such time references in each sentence. Avoid using adjectives, adverbs, and homophones. Use synonyms, analogies, and metaphors carefully.

Exercises

Use the principles explained and illustrated in this chapter to improve the following sentences.

a. Before terminating its gathering, the board members of central states utilities were the recipients of contract offers for future building and construction projects in the neighborhood of about $1.2 million. The board wants to get all of its ducks in a row before awarding the binding agreements.

b. The legislative group emphasized in no uncertain terms that the dam construction license was issued at this point in time due to the fact that rampant environmental oversights and contingencies were anticipated by the group.

c. (For use at the end of a news story about a celebrity milking contest at the local state fair.) The dignitaries look forward to a new first—some hands-on experience with the dairy industry.

d. At the present time, the lower prime interest rate is being used by the Fed to control the country's money supply.

e. The Pontiff pushed past the pedestrians in St. Peter's Square prompting people to speculate about the Pope's concern for safety.

f. The fire was squashed by firemen this afternoon.

g. The board of education has hopefully decided to fire the superintendent of education tonight.

h. The mayor this morning promises to peak in at the city council meeting when consideration is given to a tax on the mayor's cite for a new shopping center.

i. A Dodge County sheriff's car had its windshield smashed in advance of as many as 20 other standing vehicles last night.

Notes

1. Many of these suggestions for simplifying news copy are taken from *Channel 4 (KMOV-TV, St. Louis) Newsroom Standards* (St. Louis: KMOV-TV, n.d.), 7, 12.

2. KMOV-TV, *Newsroom Standards,* 13.

3. Bob Priddy, "Don't Get Lost," in *Newstips* (Jefferson City, MO: Missouri Network, n.d.).

4. KMOV-TV, *Newsroom Standards,* 17.

5. Reprinted by permission of F. Gifford, a.k.a. "Frank Gentry."

6. Reprinted by permission of Phil Witt, WDAF-TV, Kansas City, Missouri.

Chapter 7

Sentences

This chapter shifts your attention from words alone or words in small groups to words working together in larger units of meaning and impact. The care and attention used to select words and phrases now must be extended to constructing sentences that will provide even larger units of information. Sentences should provide the most direct route to the meaning of a news story. Eventually, several carefully formed sentences will be molded into a finished news story. This chapter can help you to select words carefully and to place them into sentences that will make what you write clear, interesting, well organized, and memorable.

Several key concepts about sentences will be examined: structure; clarity; and pace, rhythm, and flow. The simplicity and conciseness of what you write help determine the clarity of your sentences. Sentence structure—the order of the words and the relationships between them—can influence the clarity, the meaning, and the emphasis of the sentence. Two parts of this chapter, "Phrases and Clauses" and "Misplaced Modifiers," look briefly at the relationships between parts of sentences, at ways of signaling those relationships, and at problems that can creep in when the relationships are not kept clearly in mind at all times. The final section of this chapter examines ways to achieve effective pace, rhythm, and flow in your sentences, as well as problems that can slow the pace, disrupt the rhythm, and halt the flow of information in the news stories that you write.

Structure

Simplify sentence structure. Write short declarative sentences: *subject* followed by *verb* followed by *object*—*The Governor vetoed the bill.* This kind of sentence structure may not be considered creative or innovative, but such an arrangement replicates conversation and makes it easier for the audience to understand and remember the facts and comments presented.

Keep these three essential sentence elements (subject/verb/object) as close together as possible, as in the following examples:

The search for a Norfolk couple continues this morning.

Medical evidence confirms secondhand smoke is dangerous.

Oilers owner Bud Adams is ready to sign a lease with the Houston Sports Association. The required number of luxury skyboxes have been sold. . . . County Judge Jon Lindsey says plans are running ahead of schedule.

KTRH NewsRadio, Houston

Use *parallel sentence construction* to emphasize a relationship between ideas. When you write a compound predicate that includes two or more items in the last part of a sentence, pair a noun with a noun, an infinitive (*to* + a verb) with an infinitive, a phrase with a phrase, an adjective with an adjective, and so forth.

Weak

The Governor says her new appointment is a dedicated public servant who has integrity, a conscience, and *caring*.

Better

The Governor says her new appointment is a dedicated public servant who has integrity, a conscience, and *compassion*.
               [noun]   [noun]   [noun]

Notice the faulty parallelism in the following sentence when a compound predicate is used after the verb *will recommend:*

Weak

The final document, expected later this month, *will recommend to expand treatment and home care* and *better monitoring of blood supplies.*

Notice how this rewrite by Frank Gentry improves the logical flow of ideas in the predicate:

Better

The final document, expected later this month, will recommend expanded treatment and home care -- and better monitoring of blood supplies.

Mutual Broadcasting System

Repeating the word that begins each parallel idea helps to make the meaning clear in the predicate of a sentence:

To date more than 30-thousand acres have been seeded *where*
timber was cut or *where* fires struck.

KBOZ Radio, Bozeman, Montana

Other kinds of parallelism add rhythm and create a smooth and logical
flow of ideas in sentences:

A couple of weeks ago, Fred Lehman couldn't give away some
nice, cheap boiler fuel. . . . Now, he can't meet the demand.

KXL Radio, Portland

Instead of complete sentences (subject/verb/object), broadcast writers
often use incomplete sentences or sentence fragments to enhance the conversational tone of broadcast copy, save words, and add punch and variety:

Another encouraging sign for interest rates today. . . .

KMOV-TV, St. Louis

Use incomplete sentences only when they sound natural or conversational and when their use will help improve clarity. *All* sentences, whether
incomplete or complete in the traditional grammatical sense, must be clear
and understandable:

Several bombings this morning in South Africa -- one killed
four Blacks at the start of a Black general strike.

Mutual Broadcasting System

Place words that need emphasis at the *end* of a sentence. Your writing
will gain strength and clarity.

Spectators found it ironic that the accident happened where it
did . . . right under a sign saying *drive carefully.*

KXLY-TV, Spokane

If you use time tags (see Chapter 6, ''Words'') place them as close to
the verb as possible. Time references should surround the verb in a natural
position, either *before* the verb, as in the following example,

NASA *today* introduced the first crew member assigned to the
space station.

KTRK-TV, Houston

or in the more common position—*after* the verb:

Matt Schwartz gathers
information from a NewsStar
computer terminal in the
WOWT, Omaha newsroom.

A Webster County judge will decide *today* whether to dismiss
murder charges against a Des Moines man.

> KIMT-TV, Mason City, Iowa

Time references may sometimes appear *both* before and after verbs in the same
sentence to help clarify updated information. But notice how the most *recent*
time reference (*tonight*) is placed *first* in such sentences:

U-S Air officials *tonight* confirm that a fired employee—and
his former boss—were aboard P-S-A Flight 17-71 that crashed
into a California hillside *yesterday.*

> KXAS-TV, Dallas

Time tags can also help place a sequence of events into a logical, progressive order:

Weak

Smith was being questioned at the jail *at about nine this
morning* when he fled from custody.

Better

Smith was being questioned at the jail when he escaped *about
nine this morning.*

Word placement in sentences is important for *every* word, not just for
time tags. Notice the difference the placement of ''only'' can make in the
meaning and emphasis of each sentence:

1. *Only* blood pressure pills work if you take them.
2. Blood pressure pills *only* work if you take them.
3. Blood pressure pills work *only* if you take them.
4. Blood pressure pills work if *only* you take them.
5. Blood pressure pills work if you *only* take them.
6. Blood pressure pills work if you take *only* them.
7. Blood pressure pills work if you take them *only*.

The best position for "only" is near and in front of the word or phrase it modifies. In this case, sentence 3 is the most effective.

Clarity

Several common practices interfere with the clarity that is essential in sentence construction. One of the best ways to avoid problems with clarity is to follow the advice given earlier: Read your copy aloud. To make sense to the mind, a sentence must first sound right to the ear!

Simplicity

If a complex idea or term needs clarification, inserrt the term as soon as possible in the sentence.

Weak

The robbery of a Crestview bank at 12-05 P-M today has left police searching for a suspect to arrest as soon as possible.

Better

Police are looking for a suspect who robbed a Crestview bank around noon today.

If a complex idea or term needs clarification, insert the explanation as soon as possible in the sentence.

Western Alaska has the highest rate of meningitis in the world. . . . Meningitis is an inflammation of the membranes and a thickening of the fluid around the brain and spinal cord. . . . It could cause disorders from retardation to blindness.

KTUU-TV, Anchorage, Alaska

Conciseness

Include only essential information in each sentence and in each story. Use only enough words to make ideas clear. Although you should avoid long sentences, remember that using only short sentences does not necessarily ensure clarity of expression and ease of understanding. Vary sentence length for better control of pace, rhythm, and flow.

Several problems arise when long sentences of at least 17 to 22 words or more are used too often: The copy becomes more difficult to read because the on-air talent runs out of breath; ideas become difficult for the audience to understand; the rhythm and pace of the copy become sluggish; time is wasted because key ideas that are crammed into long sentences eventually must be repeated in a story to ensure understanding.

Remember: The audience can absorb a limited amount of information in each sentence. Lengthy or complicated information should be broken down into shorter sentences. Shorter sentences permit the audience to understand and absorb ideas more easily. Develop only *one* important idea or thought in *one* sentence. Communicating fewer ideas well is better than trying to cram too many ideas into sentences that soon become long, complex, and plodding. Sometimes, clarity is just a matter of writing leanly.

Phil Witt, News Anchor and Senior Reporter at WDAF-TV in Kansas City, offers this advice:

> Keep the sentences short, simple and to the point. This is especially important if you are writing for an anchor or reporter other than yourself. You can probably struggle through your own lengthy, clumsy sentences, but don't punish someone else with it. That's one of the fastest ways for a mistake in reading to get on the air. . . . Always keep in mind, the shorter the sentence, the better. Listeners and viewers have a hard enough time comprehending what we report on radio and TV without us making it more difficult by making the copy convoluted.[1]

Instead of writing a sentence like the first one that follows, notice how you can add vivid imagery and strong impact to your copy by using short sentences that include smaller amounts of information to digest, as in the second example:

Weak

The tornado caused major problems around the area including knocked-down power lines, traffic hazards and delays, as well as housing shortages.

Better

Power lines were knocked down. Power went out. Traffic came to a halt in some areas. . . . Cars had to maneuver their way through debris scattered across roads. . . . Some cars never made it. Several families were left homeless.
                                                    KWTV, Oklahoma City

Eliminating *all* long sentences does not always ensure clarity. The real yardstick for sentence length is not how many words you use in sentences, but whether you make your sentences easily understood *no matter how many words they include*. It *is* possible to use a sentence that would be considered long by general *broadcast* newswriting standards but not by writers working in the print media. The clarity, style, and solid structure of the following items are not eroded because of the length of each sentence:

The legislative committee meets for the first time tomorrow to recommend ways the state's mental hospitals and out-patient treatment system can be improved.

A nine-year-old girl on her way to a Girl Scout meeting at Cooper Elementary says she was almost abducted around six this evening.

KFDI, Wichita, Kansas

Surrogate parenting and right of privacy are two issues Iowa lawmakers are likely to debate again next year.

KRNT, Des Moines, Iowa

Many broadcast newswriters insist that using *only* short sentences will solve potential clarity problems. Short or even incomplete sentences tend to carry greater punch and power than longer sentences. They can also help to highlight key ideas and to build a story to a climax, or "punch line":

Bad luck for Dale Ames.*. . . No, he didn't invest in the stock market. . . . He was caught by the police in Madison, Wisconsin . . . caught siphoning gasoline from someone's car . . . to put in his car . . . a stolen car. . . . He said he didn't know that . . . and was in a race to Canada. . . . If he won he'd get a million pesos and a new car. . . . He's in the clink anyway.

ABC Contemporary News

Sentence fragments and short descriptive phrases can add impact, power, and immediacy to sentences in news copy:

A blow to the native sovereignty movement. The Alaska Supreme Court today . . .

KTUU-TV, Anchorage

Since the big southern California earthquake October first, there have been 30 aftershocks measuring a three or greater on the Richter Scale . . . the 30th late last night. . . . Nobody hurt. . . . No damage.

ABC Contemporary News

---

*This name has been changed.

Avoid using *only* short sentences or sentence fragments; too many short, consecutive "bursts" of information cause the copy to sound "choppy," abrupt, disjointed, and monotonous.

So, how long should your sentences be? Generally, you should *vary sentence length.* Use *both* long and short sentences as well as sentence fragments. This will add variety, increase interest, and improve the pace, rhythm, and flow of your copy:

```
Nearly six inches of rain has fallen on our area in the last two
days. Cedar Rapids is saturated. Sewers are full to
overflowing.
```
KGAN-TV, Cedar Rapids/Waterloo, Iowa

```
The hijacking of Kuwait Airways flight 422 ended early this
morning in Algiers. . . . There is no deal. No indication what
it entails. 31 hostages released say their captors who
murdered 2 passengers did mistreat them. The hijackers
reportedly have left Algiers . . . no indication where they
are going.
```
NBC Radio News

Your efforts at writing more concise copy will be rewarded when you discover that you have cleared room for more key ideas in all of your stories and left airtime to write even more stories for other newscasts. Writing concise copy also allows you greater flexibility as you determine how to begin a story and how to structure the details within each sentence of each story.

Phrases and Clauses

If you are to improve sentence structure and clarity, you must monitor what you include in each sentence. Keep the fabric of each sentence simple— subject/verb/object. Insert phrases and clauses in sentences carefully.

Here is a brief review of terms related to sentences. A *phrase* is a group of words used as a single part of speech and not containing a verb and its subject. Here are some examples: *The coach made the remarks <u>after the game</u>; The suspect stood along the wall <u>at the back of the room</u>; Testimony continues <u>throughout the morning</u>.*

A *clause* is a group of words containing a subject and predicate, but it is not a complete sentence. A *main,* or *independent, clause* expresses a completed thought and could be a sentence by itself. A *subordinate,* or *dependent, clause* does not express a complete thought and must always be attached to a main clause. In the sentence *After the weather cleared, the military exercise continued,* the main clause is *The military exercise continued,* and the subordinate clause is *after the weather cleared.*

Use the correct word when beginning a phrase or a clause that refers to a person or thing. *Who* should be used to refer to people only; *which* should be used to refer to things only. *That* may be used to refer to both people and things.

Confusion over whether to use *which* or *that* often causes problems. If a clause is essential for a full understanding of a sentence, use *that*. If the clause can be set off with a comma, and you can mentally put it in a parentheses, use *which*. Use *that* to provide restrictive, specific, essential, "limiting" information in a sentence; use *which* to describe more completely, or to add a bit of supplementary information in a sentence. Notice the difference in these examples:

The tax bill *that* is now in Congress is expected to pass.

> (*Meaning:* There are several tax bills. Only the tax bill now before Congress is expected to pass.)

The tax bill, *which* is now in Congress, is expected to pass.

> (*Meaning:* There is only one tax bill; it is now before Congress and is expected to pass.)

The word that begins a clause or phrase is often dropped from broadcast news copy to shorten sentences, simplify ideas, and improve clarity. But consider using such words occasionally to improve readability and to add variety to your copy.

Sentences often contain one main, or independent, clause followed by one subordinate, or dependent, clause. But notice how the emphasis changes and the progression of events becomes more logical when the dependent clause *precedes* the independent clause:

Once federal funds are received, renovation should be completed in five years.

After major renovations to Sherman Field, the capacity should increase to almost five-thousand seats.

Clarity is ensured when you write *simple* sentences that contain one main clause and *no* subordinate clauses. Following this advice too closely, however, produces stories composed only of very short sentences that will create a choppy delivery pattern. Pace, rhythm, and flow are affected.

You might be tempted to use long clauses or phrases to *begin* or *end* sentences to squeeze just that much more information into the short reports that you must write. However, doing so often makes it harder for the audience to absorb the extra information and disrupts the easy flow, pace, and rhythm in a sentence. The result is impaired sentence structure and clarity.

But sometimes adding an extra idea at the beginning or end of a sentence supplies extra power and meaning:

The terrorists who held the Kuwait Airways 747 for 16 days may be headed for Beirut. *Nothing definite,* but sources in Algiers say the hijackers probably will end up there.

NBC Radio News

The budget balancing act began at Portland City Hall yesterday
. . . *without Mayor Bud Clark.*

KXL Radio, Portland

If you judge them to be important, try to convert such "add-on" phrases and clauses into complete sentences. Compare the following:

Weak

Learning that the governor had vetoed the bill, Senator
Gillette announced that he would introduce the legislation
again.

Better

Senator Gillette says that he will introduce the legislation
again. He made the announcement after learning the governor
had vetoed the bill.

Do not add clutter to the *interior* of sentences by wedging subordinate or dependent clauses between the subject and the verb; this can create sentences that are long or confusing. Here is an example heard on a national network:

Weak

Baby Paul . . . the youngest-ever heart transplant patient,
who had the operation hours after birth . . . has been upgraded
from critical to serious but stable condition.

Here is a suggested rewrite that simplifies sentence structure and improves clarity:

Better

The youngest-ever heart transplant patient is now in serious
but stable condition. Baby Paul had the operation hours after
birth.

Sometimes, if a *short* phrase or clause helps clarify an idea or an identity, adding that phrase or clause to the *interior* of the sentence may be effective. Place it next to a noun or a pronoun:

Weak

Rural patients who pay the same amount for premiums for health
care services should get the same level of health care that
patients in urban areas get who are paying the same amount.

Better

Rural patients, who pay the same fees as urban patients, should
get the same level of health care.

Misplaced Modifiers

Words, phrases, and clauses that modify or refer to other words in a sentence should be placed as close together as possible. Otherwise, the meaning of the sentence could change and clarity could become impaired.

Examine this sentence: *A Korean Airlines plane has crashed into the Atlantic Ocean with 150 people aboard.* The phrase *with 150 people aboard* refers to the plane, not to the ocean. Place this phrase adjacent to the noun that it modifies: *A Korean Airlines plane with 150 people aboard has crashed into the Atlantic Ocean.*

Here is another example: *The Vice President emphasized that the country's security was not in danger during the news conference.* In its present position, the phrase *during the news conference* implies that *only* during the news conference was the country's security not in danger. Improve the clarity of this sentence by relocating the troublesome phrase: *The Vice President emphasized during the news conference that the country's security was not in danger.*

Pace, Rhythm, and Flow

The sentences used in broadcast news copy must not only be structured effectively and present information clearly, they must also arrange ideas into a smooth-flowing, regular pattern that creates momentum and adds interest to a story. (See Chapter 5, "Story Structure," for definitions of pace, rhythm, and flow.)

Varying the length and structure of your sentences creates variety in your copy and allows your ideas to flow smoothly and regularly in a natural rhythm or cadence. The newscaster will find such copy easier to read, and the audience will find it more pleasant, organized, and enriching to hear.

```
A 12-million dollar lawsuit against Putnam* Oil is in the
courts of Boyton,* Kentucky. The suit was brought by two former
executives who claim they were illegally fired. The men say
they were let go after speaking out against alleged illegal
bribes to foreign officials. Putnam Oil flatly denies the
charges.
                              WOWK-TV, Huntington, West Virginia
```

Vary sentence *length.* Long, rambling sentences can pose problems. However, even a long sentence can be clear and powerful when subject and verb make meanings clear early in a sentence. Here is a reporter's original copy for a drug bust story:

Weak

```
The Internal Affairs Division of the Houston Police Department
is conducting an investigation into some officers with the
```

---

*These names have been changed.

Tactical Response Unit of the Northeast Substation. A
Sunnyside family claims they were the victims of a bogus raid
on their home late yesterday . . . a raid that left family
members, including a 15-year-old retarded girl,
terrified. . . .

Notice how a producer's rewrite eliminates lengthy, plodding sentences and improves the vividness of the story:

Better

Houston Police officers say they thought they were pursuing a
drug transaction when they entered the home of a Sunnyside
family. What they found, instead, last night was a frightened
81-year-old-woman, a retarded 15-year-old girl . . . and
several other equally frightened family members. The police
had made a mistake. And now top police brass want to know how
such a mix-up could have happened.

KTRK-TV, Houston

Also vary sentence *structure.* Use a compound sentence from time to time for variety. Occasionally, start a sentence with a connective (transitional) word or phrase like *but* or *and* to connect ideas in a story.

The number of prison pre-release centers proposed for the
Houston area has prompted the mayor to form a committee to draw
up a new ordinance. *And* committee members plan to get started
on the measure this weekend.

KTRH NewsRadio, Houston

But do not sacrifice clarity and ease of delivery by linking material that would be better placed in separate sentences. Insert a clause or a phrase sometimes, but do not begin consecutive sentences with dependent clauses, as done in this lengthy copy that, unfortunately, made it on the air:

Weak

*Despite a breakthrough that led to the end of the hostage
crisis in Louisiana,* officials aren't expecting freedom soon
for 90 hostages held by riotous Cuban inmates in Atlanta.
*Although participation by a Roman Catholic Archbishop helped
end the Louisiana standoff,* a Justice Department spokesman is
ruling out any immediate invitation for the prelate to assist
in the Atlanta negotiations.

Better

Ninety hostages held by Cuban inmates in Atlanta are not
expected to be released right away. Although a Roman Catholic

Archbishop helped end the hostage crisis in Louisiana, the
Justice Department does not expect to receive additional help
in the negotiations that continue in Atlanta.

Use words judiciously. Place words carefully in your sentences. As illustrated in this chapter and in Chapter 6, the *placement* of words is just as important as the *selection* of words.

Go beyond minimum language usage requirements. Fine-tune the words that you use and the sentences that you construct, so that what you write is not only clear and logical but also engaging and meaningful to your audience.

Summary

Sentence construction and clarity are important components that affect the pace, rhythm, and flow of broadcast news copy. This chapter reviewed concepts and techniques associated with writing effective sentences.

Simplify sentence structure. Use short declarative sentences (subject/verb/object). Maintain parallel sentence construction. Avoid inserting material that causes confusion and unnecessary length. Use time references carefully. Place material to be emphasized at the end of a sentence. For variety, use incomplete sentences, sentence fragments and, occasionally, a long sentence.

Several techniques can help you to improve the clarity of your sentences: Keep ideas simple; limit the information included; use only one idea in each sentence; add phrases and clauses to sentences cautiously; keep words and phrases that relate to each other close together.

Pace, rhythm, and flow improve when sentence structure is simple and clarity of expression is maintained. Allow ideas to flow smoothly, easily, and regularly in a natural rhythm. Vary the length and structure of sentences, and use words prudently.

Exercises

Write a short (:10–:20) anchor reader story for either radio or television based on *one* of the following abbreviated fact sheets.

a. *Stabbing*
- FBI today arrested Hugo Muffalato, 32 (local resident).
- He is charged with manslaughter in brutal stabbing death of Winnebago Indian Henry Two Feathers.

- Stabbing done around 1 A.M. last Thursday on Winnebago Indian Reservation about 50 miles from here in Carter County.
- Muffalato held by U.S. Magistrate Ronald R. Swanson without bail until the next court appearance (four weeks from today).

b. *Shooting*
- A local woman, Roz Roy, 32, was arrested this morning at her family home in the southeast part of your town.

- Charge of murder was filed by District Attorney Frank Rodriguez.
- She's accused of killing her husband in the chest with gunshot wounds.
- The husband, Jim Roy, 34, was pronounced dead at the scene of the crime where a pistol was found yesterday morning.

c. *Robbery*
- Conoco station at 17th and A robbed late last night.
- Gas station attendant (Phil Moore) says supposed robber (about 24, blond, wearing sandals) bought chewing gum and then demanded money without a weapon.
- Robber took attendant's envelope containing cash and fled around the corner.
- Local police have no suspects in the case . . . but they are still looking for a blue recent model automobile seen nearby.

Notes

1. Reprinted by permission of Phil Witt.

Chapter 8

Rewriting Copy

Y ou can always write a lead, structure a story, choose words, and construct sentences in a better way to make a news story more effective. But other reasons exist for rewriting, besides simply improving news copy. You might, for example, want to provide a different perspective on a story or to view it from another angle. You might want to emphasize key elements more strongly, or you might want to focus on different elements in a story. You might wish to change the mood or the tone of the story—to make it livelier or more somber, for example. Rewrites can also be used to update continuing stories, follow up on earlier reports, customize news copy, and provide a local angle to a distant story.

A rewrite should provide a noticeable, substantial change in the original structure, focus, and content of a news story. Rewriting is polishing the polish, making a marginal story acceptable, making a good story even better.

This chapter focuses on the processes and techniques used to rewrite news stories. In particular this chapter will help you to consider stories from different angles, to update stories and to follow up on them, and to customize the news copy that you write and rewrite. In addition, this chapter suggests a number of situations in which rewriting might be necessary, and it provides examples of how you might handle copy in those situations. After a summary of main points, this chapter concludes with suggested exercises to help you practice rewriting techniques.

Basic Rewriting Techniques

Review the steps in the process suggested in Chapter 5, "Story Structure," for writing a news story. The same process can be used when *rewriting* stories.

All rewrites should stress immediacy—the latest developments in a story—and should always retain the main point, the essence, of the story. This can be accomplished in a variety of ways, and the techniques used generally coincide with the reasons for rewriting news copy.

Find a New Angle

Rewrites can add variety and breathe new life into a story. Even if story facts do not change, the news copy *must* change from newscast to newscast to keep the story attractive and interesting to the audience. Offer something distinctive that will make your story stand apart from those of competitors, who often rely on the same initial news sources that you use.

You can find a new story angle in several ways. You could identify an equally valid approach to a story, perhaps hidden in the original source material or used near the end in the original version of the story. You could "dress up" this story angle, make it the lead in your rewrite, and still not distort the essence of the story. Or you might discover that the *best* angle was not used to write the story in the first place.

Here are the opening lines of copy for two versions of the same story, each focusing on a different point of view or angle:

```
One man received minor injuries when he lost control of his
pickup and crashed into a garage near Westdale and Zoo
Boulevard Sunday night. Wichita police officer Russell Smith
says witnesses saw the truck leave the roadway, cross back over
Westdale, run through a cedar fence, and run into the backside
of a residential garage. . . .

Residents of a house that backs up to Westdale just off Zoo
Boulevard got quite a surprise Sunday evening when a pickup
truck crashed into their garage. . . .
                              KFDI Radio, Wichita, Kansas
```

Some beginning journalists tend to follow a set pattern in developing a news story: Gather the facts and comments needed, consider the length and structure of the story, and finally write and produce the *one* good story they know they can provide. They find it difficult to think of more than one way to tell a news story.

However, you need to remember that some stories are used in more than one newscast. Thus, you need to provide several versions of a story so that the audience has fresh ways to hear the facts and opinions associated with a single news story.

When a story is complex or several legitimate angles exist that cannot *all* be featured in a *single* story, writing multiple stories for a single news event may be necessary. Each story in this package of reports could focus on one key aspect but still incorporate the essential information needed to understand what happened. (See the preceding KFDI Radio copy.)

An efficient way to accomplish this is to write several versions of the same story while the facts are still fresh in your mind. Each version could vary in length, content, and perspective. For example, you could write a brief story for a headline newscast, a longer story for expanded newscasts, another with one or two tape excerpts from different news sources, another for use the next day or overnight, and so forth.

Provide Multiple Angles for the Same Story

Here are the first segments from multiple stories that were broadcast on KOTA Radio, Rapid City, South Dakota, on Memorial Day observances:

Rows and rows of white grave markers . . . a line of bright red, white and blue flags blowing in the breeze. Hundreds of people from all over the country paying respects at Black Hills National Cemetery this Memorial Day.

(CART..NATURAL SOUND . . . 2 blasts)
Memorial Day services were held in Hally Park to honor war dead. A circle of flags carried by representatives of area veterans groups . . .

Nearly 300 people attended a special Memorial Day ceremony at Black Hills National Cemetery. . . . The service, done in Lakota, honored Indians who had lost their lives as American GI's. . . .

Some newsrooms *require* multiple reports for each story covered. A typical set of such multiple reports might include two long versions, two short versions, and two tape excerpt or soundbite versions. Such a policy ensures that rewrites will be available to provide fresh news copy. If story details change after the rewrites are prepared, the multiple versions of the story can be tossed and new copy written. This technique is especially helpful for overnight copy, which is discussed later in this chapter.

Update Breaking Stories

Stories often take new twists and turns as they continue to develop. The initial report of a plane crash or major fire can be updated once fatalities, injuries, circumstances, and damage estimates become known. Monitor story developments and use the *latest,* most up-to-date information in your rewrite.

Here is how KOTA Radio began its first report about an early morning fire:

A rural Piedmont family escaped from their burning home this morning with the clothes on their backs and not much more. Lightning struck the Jack Sherman log home and started a fire. . . .

KOTA used this update in its rewrite the *next* day:

A fund has been set up to help a Piedmont family who lost their home to a fire. . . . The Jack Sherman family escaped injury but lost everything early yesterday morning when lightning struck their home. . . . The fund has been started at Norwest Bank.

In Chapter 10, KFDI Radio News Director Dan Dillon guides you through his station's continuing coverage of protests and violence at Wichita, Kansas, abortion clinics. KFDI provided an interesting set of reports that helped update and provide local perspectives for this important breaking story.

Locate *new* facts that relate to an earlier report. Once an initial story is written, assess the information on hand, determine what's missing, find it, and then place this new material into the fabric of the story when you rewrite.

Follow Up on Earlier Reports

WTAE-TV in Pittsburgh used voice-over copy for its first story on a local love triangle trial verdict:

(SCOTT/VO)

VO

CHYRON-COUNTY COURTHOUSE/DOWNTOWN

McKeesport businessman Brent Tenneco* and his friend, Alice McRoy*, were found guilty today in Allegheny County Common Pleas Court in a twisted murder-for-hire case.

They each faced four separate counts for trying to hire a hitman to kill the woman who was dating McRoy's old boyfriend.

Judge Stanley Benton* found them guilty on two counts each including criminal solicitation to commit murder.

TALENT-SCOTT

(SCOTT)

They're free on bond until they're sentenced in February.

A later story on the same verdict reviewed essential story facts but added a soundbite from the intended victim. This helped to follow up on the earlier report and to add another dimension to the story:

(SCOTT)

QUANTEL: LOVE TRIANGLE TRIAL

The ''love triangle'' trial almost seemed more like a novel than real life: McKeesport businessman Brent Tenneco* and his friend, Alice McRoy*, accused of trying to hire a hit man to kill the woman who was dating her old boyfriend.

VO

---

*These names have been changed.

```
(VO)

CHYRON-COURTHOUSE/DOWNTOWN

 This morning Judge Stanley Benton* found them both guilty on
two of four counts, including criminal solicitation to commit
criminal homicide.

 Benton* is allowing them to go free on bond until their
sentencing. Their intended victim told our Patricia Donneley*
she doesn't like that.

  SOT

(SOT)

RUNS-:13

OUTCUE-I don't know

CHYRON-Kathie Blair*/Intended Victim

((Are you confident she'll leave you alone. No. What do you
think she'll do? I don't know.))

  TALENT-SCOTT

(SCOTT)

QUANTEL: LOVE TRIANGLE TRIAL

Tenneco* and McRoy* will be sentenced on February 18th.
```

Tie Back to the Original Story	Rewrites should "tie back" to the original news event. You want your rewrite to sound fresh, but remember that your audience may have no previous exposure to the story. Provide enough information in the rewrite so that the story can stand on its own and not depend on the audience's memory of previous reports. Early in your rewrite, briefly refer back to the original news event so that the audience understands the relationship of the rewrite to the earlier story.

In the WTAE-TV Love Triangle Trial rewrite you just examined, notice that a reference to the original news event is made using voice-over copy that begins: "This morning Judge Stanley Benton* . . .," and ends: " . . . on bond until their sentencing."

In this next example, notice how KSL-TV ties back to the original story in this rewrite:

```
An Orem man who sold a purported miracle cure now faces
criminal charges . . . and authorities say the elixir could be
```

---

*These names have been changed.

fatal. Yesterday, police raided a warehouse owned by 63-
year-old Ned Crailey* and confiscated gallons of tonic called
"super oxide." Crailey reportedly sold the mixture of
bottled water and hydrogen peroxide under the name "Healthy,
Wealthy, and Wise . . ."

KSL-TV, Salt Lake City

Customize News Copy

Rewrites allow a newsroom to tailor or customize news copy to special writing styles that are unique to a particular news operation or newscaster. This is especially important in radio, where news copy often must appeal to a specific target audience that finds certain writing styles particularly attractive.

Here's how Ed Gullo, an anchor at Unistar Radio Networks, rewrote a wire story to make it more attractive for a younger, more contemporary audience:

David Rubio of San Antonio cast his vote yesterday . . . and
gave the government permission for a 10 million dollar bond
issue. His wasn't the deciding vote. . . . It was the only
vote. Rubio . . . who lives alone in a wooded subdivision . . .
voted yes . . . on improving roads in the area . . . 15 miles
north of downtown San Anton.

Oh yes, in addition to [casting] the only vote in that election
district . . . he also manned the voting booth at his mobile
home.

Use caution when customizing news copy. Any generally competent newscaster should be able to read an effective rewrite. If you write and broadcast your own copy, or if the newsroom stresses a particular writing style, use discretion. Customized copy can be a hindrance if not used properly.

Localize Distant Stories

Rewrites can highlight local angles in distant stories. Your rewrite can begin with the name of the local resident killed in a plane crash in another state, or you can indicate the local impact of a federal tax increase. Other aspects of localizing national and international news stories are illustrated later in this chapter.

Applications

These essential rewriting techniques and objectives can be applied to several kinds of rewriting situations: rewriting your own copy; rewriting the copy of others (reporters, wire services, and news releases and announcements); rewriting overnight and same day copy; and providing local angles to distant stories.

---

*This name has been changed.

Rewriting Your Own Copy

Bob Priddy, News Director of the Missouri Network and former Chairman of the Radio-Television News Directors Association, once wrote that "the art of writing lies in rewriting what you've rewritten."[1] It's good advice. Always look for ways to improve what you have written. Never be satisfied with less than your best effort; polish and rewrite until the copy shines!

Examples of rewriting your own copy have already been provided in this chapter; see KFDI Radio's pickup truck accident reports and KOTA Radio's Memorial Day stories.

Rewriting Others' Copy

Having another set of eyes review what you have written is always a good idea, not only for style but also for content. Some newsrooms assign a producer or editor to review copy before it reaches the air. Rewrites are usually done for reporters' copy, wire stories, and news releases and announcements.

Reporters

Here is the original version of a story a writer at CNN submitted:

Weak

    The Air Force grounded its entire fleet of new B-1-B bombers
    yesterday. The emergency escape systems will be checked. Once
    completed, each aircraft will return to flying status. The
    grounding comes after the B-1-B crash ten days ago that killed
    three crewmen. The bomber has been plagued with problems since
    the start. . . . However, the Air Force will buy one hundred of
    the jets in total.

The use of *yesterday* lacks immediacy. The importance of the story and the relationship of this development to earlier reports ("tie back") should be noted earlier in the story. A rewrite could combine the second and third sentences and abbreviate the idea expressed. The story flows well and presents a cause-effect relationship between earlier problems and the current grounding, but the sentences could be tightened and the ideas expressed more clearly. The dangling phrase *in total* is clumsy.

Here is the rewritten, on-air version of the same story:

Better

    The Air Force has grounded its entire fleet of B-1-B bombers,
    following a crash that killed three crewmembers last week. The
    Air Force says the emergency escape systems of every plane will
    be checked. During the crash, three men were able to parachute
    to safety; the other three never ejected. The bomber has been
    plagued with problems since the start. The Air Force is buying
    a total of one hundred of them.

Here is the original version of the lead-in to a KTRK-TV reporter's package, followed by the producer's rewrite that made it on-the-air in Houston:

Weak

```
A Galveston restaurant owner and two associates were part of an
international round-up of suspected heroin dealers—all part
of what the F-B-I says was a major drug trafficking ring tied to
the Silician Mafia. The arrests came today as the Justice
Department began a new assault against drug networks . . .
Deborah Wrigley reports . . .
```

Better

```
A Galveston restaurant owner and two associates are behind
bars tonight . . . charged in an international heroin
smuggling ring. The F-B-I says the three are tied to the
Sicilian Mafia. And as Deborah Wrigley reports, today's
arrests mark the beginning of a new Justice Department assault
on drug networks. . . .
```

The stories are about the same length, but notice how crisp, clear, and immediate the copy has become in the rewrite. The lead is shorter, more direct. The reporter's package is linked directly to the story by the last sentence, which integrates the name of the reporter and provides momentum for the beginning of the report.

Wire Services

It is best to rewrite wire copy, even *broadcast* wire copy. Wire services lack the time and personnel to focus carefully on broadcast writing style, and they have no opportunity to localize news items for specific kinds of broadcast news audiences. An item that may be especially newsworthy for your local audiences may be "buried" in a lengthy wire report.

Newsrooms prefer to use several wires when rewriting news copy. Broadcast wire copy is often written from print wire reports, which tend to provide more details than broadcast wire copy. Wires are discussed fully in Chapter 9.

Rewriting wire copy involves the same techniques described earlier—digest the basic facts, identify the significant information, and then write a brief broadcast story that captures the essence of the event.

Figure 8.1 shows an Associated Press story "captured" by KSL-TV's computer system.

Here is how KSL-TV rewrote this story for their newscast:

```
A 19-year-old inmate from the State Prison's young adult
facility was stabbed today. Brett Olsen of Richfield is in
stable condition. A prison spokesman says Olsen was stabbed in
```

```
                    KSL-TV NEWS — SALT LAKE CITY, UTAH
   02/07    20:14 gm 0:80 #1+11..v9089


   v9089    Out--r n AP-PrisonStabbing     02-07 0133  AP-PRISON STABBING



   (POINT OF THE MOUNTAIN, Utah) _ utah state prison officials say A
19-year-old resident of the young adult facility is listed in serious but
stable condition at a Salt Lake City hospital tonight after he was stabbed in
the abdomen.

   prison spokesman Juan Benavidez says Brett Olsen of Richfield entered the
control room of the prison's Young Adult Correctional Facility about 3 p-m
today with a stab wound to his lower right abdomen.

   He was airlifted to the University of Utah Health Sciences Center, where
he'll remain several days to make certain there are no internal complications.

   Olsen was referred to the facility by the courts November 25th after he was
arrested for aggravated assault.

   benavidez says the stabbing is being investigated.

AP-NY-02-07    2236EST
```

Figure 8.1 Copy of an Associated Press broadcast wire story on a prison stabbing.
Courtesy of Associated Press Broadcast Services.

```
the stomach about 3 o'clock. He went into the control room of
the prison and showed guards that he'd been hurt. He was
airlifted to the hospital. The incident is under
investigation.
```

KSL-TV shortened the lead as well as the rest of the copy. Several details were deleted: the reference to Utah, since the prison mentioned should be obvious to Salt Lake City viewers; the name of the prison spokesman; the inmate's specific wounds; the length of the inmate's hospital stay; and his criminal convictions. The rewrite is more direct and much more effective.

Figure 8.2 shows the wire copy for a story about a construction accident. Here is how WCAU-AM in Philadelphia rewrote the copy shown in the figure for an early morning newscast the day *after* the incident happened:

```
Two Burlington County construction workers died when a trench
they were in caved in on them. The two men were laying a gas pipe
in the Parklands Landfill . . . a pipe to draw off methane from
decomposing garbage. The sides of the trench gave way . . .
burying the two workers.
```

Notice how the key story points are included in the rewrite and how phrases were added to convey the essential information in an easy-to-understand, conversational writing style.

Chapter 9, "Identifying and Organizing News Sources," offers several suggestions for *handling or processing* news releases, announcements, and handouts. Here are suggestions for *writing* stories based on these materials:

News Releases and Announcements

a. Quickly scan or read the *entire* news release or announcement.
b. Identify the most promising news angle, if there is one.
c. Eliminate material that is self-serving and emphasizes special interest points of view. Often such material exaggerates a particular situation or development.
d. Condense, distill, refine the material until you have only the crucial facts.
e. Look for ways to personalize and localize the material received.
f. If you have questions, contact the person whose name appears on the handout or news release.
g. If facts look suspicious, contact additional sources to verify the original information supplied and to obtain additional points of view. Once broadcast, such a story becomes *your* newsroom's story.
h. Contact other sources and obtain additional information that may be more pertinent to your audience and perhaps more newsworthy than the original material.

NTOWN TOWNSHIP) -- police in bordentown
township say Two workers died wednesday
when a trench in which they were
working collapsed on them.

    police sergeant Brian Dumont says
The collapse occurred about 2:30 p-m at
the Parklands Landfill, which accepts
garbage from all Burlington County
municipalities.

    a spokesman for the state Department
of Environmental Protection says the
victims, whose identities were not
immediately known, were working in a
trench about eight to ten feet deep.

    d-e-p spokesman Jim staples says
that At the time of the accident, a gas
ventilation pipe was being installed to
draw away methane gas which builds up
as garbage in the landfill decomposes.

    staples says The sides of the trench
gave way and buried the workers.

    police say there were no other
casualties.

    AP-NY-04-13   1736EDT

Figure 8.2 Copy of an Associated Press broadcast wire story on a construction accident. Courtesy of Associated Press Broadcast Services.

Early morning newscasts must not only report what happened while we slept, they must also provide a fresh perspective on stories that are *still* newsworthy but have not changed much over the last few hours (see the preceding WCAU-AM rewrite). As suggested already, the late-night news staff can do such rewrites.

Be cautious when writing these ''holdover'' or ''second-day'' stories. Select items that are likely to be newsworthy the next morning. Write stories that indicate what is scheduled to happen or develop early the next day. Be sure to get your time references correct. Avoid ''yesterday'' references by using future, present, and present perfect verb tenses.

Several kinds of stories can be developed into excellent overnight rewrites: an important evening speech or presentation; a major fire that is brought under control shortly before your last nighttime newscast (see the KOTA Radio reports on an early morning fire shown earlier in this chapter); an early morning report on a late-afternoon construction or automobile accident the previous day (see the WCAU-AM story earlier in this chapter). If an important local conference or seminar is scheduled over the next three days, an overnight rewrite could summarize conference activities up to that point and then preview what is scheduled that day. The same kind of story could be written overnight for each day of the conference.

Rewriting Overnight Copy

Same day copy deserves the same care and attention as overnight reports. The audience must always be convinced that in subsequent newscasts it is getting a complete and current report on major stories. This is especially important in radio, where hourly newscasts require constant rewriting.

Rewrites are the only way to stay on top of a major developing story that causes a continual flow of new facts, new information, and new comments. As noted earlier, rewrites must incorporate the new developments into the fabric of the basic story, especially in the lead.

Major accidents or natural disasters require constant monitoring and updating as new information flows into the newsroom. Nan Siemer was working in the WTOP Radio newsroom in Washington, DC, one late September day when a traffic accident was reported. Nan describes the situation:

Rewriting Same Day Copy

> It started with a little rain and a report of a head-on accident involving an ambulance. The rain had just started to fall, and that accident was followed by many more . . . prompting this to become the big story of the afternoon drive period. . . . The story moved from a single accident to reaction about a rash of accidents in our area.[2]

Here is the initial WTOP accident report.

`Fairfax County fire officials say two firefighters are trapped`
`in the wreckage of an accident. Authorities say an ambulance`
`and truck collided head-on at about one-thirty near the`

intersection of Beulah Street and Telegraph Road. Two
firefighters are trapped in the ambulance, and a helicopter is
on the way to the scene. Stay tuned to WTOP for further
information on this developing story.

A subsequent story was analyzed in Chapter 5 to illustrate effective story
structure. Let's look at that report again, but this time as a rewrite and an
update of a same-day traffic accident story.

A truck driver and two Fairfax County firefighters were taken
to Fairfax Hospital, following this afternoon's head-on crash
on Beulah Street. One firefighter had to be medivacked with a
fractured leg after the ambulance he was in collided with a
truck. Fairfax County fire officials say the ambulance was en
route to a call, when the accident occurred on Beulah Street at
Telegraph Road. The firefighters were trapped in the wreckage
for about 30 minutes. Conditions of the injured are not
immediately available.

Later WTOP stories incorporated soundbites from state police and transportation department spokespersons. They reminded listeners about safe driving
techniques while WTOP updated accident statistics, lane closings, and so forth
for that afternoon's drive time.

Notice the flow of updated story developments on a major Indianapolis
plane crash in these excerpts heard on the ABC Contemporary Network:

An Air Force jet slammed into the lobby of the Ramada Inn Hotel
near the airport at Indianapolis today. At least nine people
were killed. . . . Air Force Colonel William Johnson says the
pilot's in a hospital now. They're searching the Ramada Inn
room-by-room for possible victims.

It was some sight this morning when an Air Force supersonic jet
fighter making an emergency landing fell short of the runway
and plowed 20-feet into the lobby of the Ramada Inn at the
airport in Indianapolis. . . . At least nine people were
killed! Airport Operations Chief Jim McCue says the pilot
tried to steer the plane to an open field. . . . The pilot
bailed out before the crash. He's O-K. . . .

The essence of the story is told in each ABC/C rewrite. Actualities from
eyewitnesses (not shown here) provided additional, vivid accounts. The copy
has been customized to appeal more directly to the ABC Contemporary Network's primary target audience—listeners in the 18 to 25-year-old range.[3]

Viewers and listeners tend to be more interested in important local stories: items that affect them directly, at home. A good journalist constantly searches for a local perspective that will "bring home" the importance, impact, and meaning of every story. This approach helps the audience relate to news wherever it happens; it helps them understand why a particular event is important and relates the consequences a particular story may have for the local community.

Identify your local audience's interests, needs, expectations, and even knowledge about current issues and developments. Learn the economic, political, and social structure and activities that surround you and your audience. Become "tuned in" to your community, whatever its size. Every town is different. The strong labor and manufacturing activities in a northeastern city are not especially interesting to farmers in a small community in Iowa. But then, the agricultural concerns of Midwestern towns hold little interest for audiences in sparsely populated ranching areas or in the logging and fishing areas along the Pacific Coast. Local concerns about inadequate day-care facilities may not be shared by a community only a few miles down the highway. The basic principle is simple—know your *local* audience! Keep their concerns in mind when writing news stories. Figure 8.3 shows how KFVS-TV generated a local angle for an issue that continues to interest communities around the country.

While it is important to *know* your local community, it is equally important to *find* the local angle that you want to provide. You may need to do some additional research and make a few extra telephone calls to local experts or authorities, especially at local universities and research centers, in order to add local "reference points" to your copy. Chapters 9 and 10 suggest ways to identify, locate, and handle local news sources.

Here are examples of national and international stories, local contacts that could be made, and suggested local angles to pursue:

- *A significant U.S. Supreme Court decision*—state or local bar association president, your state attorney general, or a local law professor (the impact of the decision on local community affairs); if the court decision involves a controversial issue, contact local social action groups for reaction statements that point to the local impact.

- *Announcement of sweeping federal budget cuts*—governor, mayor, state and local fiscal representatives (local projects and programs affected by these cuts).

- *A new leader comes to power in a foreign country*—local residents born in that country, a local political science professor who specializes in international affairs, local business representatives (effect on foreign nationals from that country living in your town, impact on U.S. foreign relations, loss of income by local businesses supplying goods and services to that country).

It's a debate that is officially thirty years old. Should prayer be allowed in public schools? Today is the anniversary of the Supreme Court's ruling to ban prayer from public school. As Ben Hall reports, religious groups in the Heartland are joining those across the country to ask that prayer be put back in schools.

The same scene is taking place across the country. Religious groups are preparing for rallies . . . where they expect big crowds. Their message—put prayer back in public schools.

[BITE JAN SMITH CO-ORGANIZER: "I just think the people should be permitted to do it." (:03)]

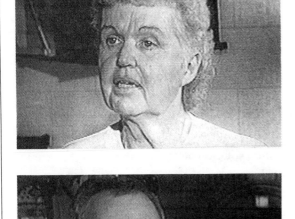

[BITE #1 FRED STARKWEATHER CO-ORGANIZER: "Give an opportunity for those who wish to participate and acknowledge that there is a god and to acknowledge a dependency on him to help them through the day." (:08)]

Figure 8.3 Local perspectives on a national story anniversary. Courtesy of Ben Hall and KFVS-TV, Cape Girardeau, MO and Carbondale, IL. For instructional purposes, a photoboard and transcripts of soundbites have been added to the original KFVS-TV news copy.

Religious leaders say when prayer was taken out of public schools a moral decline began. They point to statistics showing an increase in teenage violence and pregnancies and say prayer would help turn the tide.

[BITE #2 FRED STARKWEATHER CO-ORGANIZER: ''Educators are having to deal with much more serious issues like violence in schools, even a shooting—you know, [like the one] we had a few months ago here in our area—as compared with things like in the 1950's of chewing gum in school and throwing wastepaper on the floor instead of in the wastebasket.'' (:18)]

But others say you can't blame those changes on the lack of prayer in public schools. They say allowing prayer in schools would put peer pressure on students to conform to a certain religion.

Figure 8.3 continued.

[BITE CAL MYERS, AMERICAN CIVIL LIBERTIES
UNION: "A teacher may say: well, you
don't <u>have</u> to pray. Well, you know
children as well as I do, even adult
children that I teach . . . They're
afraid to be different from the rest. And
I'm sure it's going to frustrate them and
their parents." (:11)]

The organizers of this rally are
optimistic that eventually prayer will be
allowed back in public schools. They say
one way to make that happen is with public
rallies like this. In Marion, Ben Hall,
Heartland News.

TRT-1:29

Figure 8.3 continued.

- *A new round of foreign terrorist activities*—local travel agents and travelers at a nearby international airport (impact on local reservations for foreign travel and hesitations expressed by travelers headed to that country).

- *Revised federal guidelines on health coverage*—local health agency representatives and clients (budgets and services lost or diminished).

You can localize stories on two levels: getting a local person to comment about a national or international issue or event, and actually showing the local connection to a national or international story. Let's say that the United States has joined United Nations peace-keeping forces providing food and medical supplies to a war-torn nation. The first level would involve comments from a local political scientist or international business expert who might assess the value or danger of the overseas operation. The second level would involve comments from a local business representative who would trace the process used to manufacture some of the materials going overseas. The *same* story would be covered in each instance, but two different kinds or levels of local angles would have been provided.

Localizing news copy requires that you be vigilant to identify local story angles, creative to find local comments, and innovative to provide a natural local angle that gives a unique perspective on what otherwise might be a routine story from a distant location.

Anniversaries of national and international events are also opportunities to localize a story and provide local comments and recollections about a significant event that touches a community directly.

Summary

This chapter has described and illustrated basic rewriting techniques and shown their application to typical rewriting situations. Essential rewriting techniques include finding a new angle; providing multiple angles for the same story; updating breaking stories; following up on earlier reports; tying back to the original story; customizing news copy; and localizing distant stories. These techniques can be applied to rewriting your own copy; other copy (from reporters, wire services, and news releases and announcements); overnight copy; same day copy; and distant stories to provide local angles.

Exercises

1. From a daily newspaper, collect at least three national or international wire stories. Do *one* of the following:

a. Convert each wire story into an effective radio or television news report. Turn in the original newspaper stories and your rewrites. Briefly indicate *why* your rewrites are effective.

b. Contact at least two *local* sources to develop a *local* angle to *one* of the wire stories collected.

2. Provide *another* rewrite for the wire copy in either Figure 8.1 or 8.2.

3. From a local governmental agency, obtain the following: a recent news release about a significant issue or project, and the agenda for an upcoming meeting associated with this agency. Provide a 20-second radio or television story by doing *one* of the following:

a. Rewrite the news release.

b. Write a ''future'' story that can be broadcast *before* the meeting occurs. This story should preview the important topics to be considered at the meeting.

c. Write a story based on the agenda and your notes made while attending the meeting.

d. Collect newspaper accounts of the meeting and then rewrite them.

e. Develop a follow-up report on an important issue discussed at the meeting.

4. Select *one* of the abbreviated lists of facts provided in Chapter 4, Exercise 1, and provide a brief (less than 20 seconds) but complete story based on the facts presented.

5. Provide a *full* rewrite of one of the *complete* stories used as illustrations in Chapter 5. The rewrite must use a story structure pattern that is *different* from the one in the illustration.

Notes

1. Bob Priddy, in *Newstips* (Missouri Network, n.d.).

2. Reprinted by permission of Nan Siemer.

3. Reprinted by permission of Merrilee Cox.

Part Two

Sources

Identifying and Organizing News Sources

U p to this point in this book, the emphasis has been on writing effective broadcast news stories in proper form. Essentially we have focused on putting words on the screen or on paper in a consistent and effective manner. However, no matter how well you write, you need something to say—information to use for your news stories. It is important, then, to help you to identify, organize, and develop key sources of information to use as you write your broadcast news stories.

Some of the sources you will routinely use in developing your stories are rather clearly defined and well known. Others, though less well known, are available with only a little work in identifying them. And other sources are the kind that will call on your investigative skills. They will make you work diligently to identify and find them, but they will solidify your stories in a way that other sources cannot.

Reputable newswriting and reporting is not based on unconfirmed rumors from unidentified sources or unfounded assumptions made by careless reporters. It is based on accurate reports of information that can be confirmed from a variety of reliable, reputable news sources.

Professional news organizations establish enviable reputations for accuracy, objectivity, reliability, and completeness by basing news reports on facts and information gathered through objective observation and through research or investigation. Some information is gathered firsthand by reporters. Other information is obtained secondhand from people involved directly in an event or situation who report what they saw and heard. Records and documents can also help verify facts and comments and provide background material that often can enrich a reporter's final version of a story. More often than not, reporters do not witness the events they report. Even when they do, they need help to understand these events fully—to explain what happened, why, and with what probable results.

The time constraints in broadcast newsgathering and reporting are severe. You should not expect to have the time or opportunity to use every information source discussed in this chapter for every story that you cover. Know what is available, and then use a limited number of key sources for each story to meet or exceed the informational needs of the broadcast audience.

Chapters 9 and 10 are companion chapters. Chapter 9 describes basic sources of news and information, which have been divided into three general categories (public, private, and internal or from within the newsroom) to better identify the essential origin of each source. The second part of the chapter suggests techniques for organizing news sources and determining what you need to know, where to find it, and how to handle what you uncover. Chapter 10 describes and illustrates how to better *develop* the news sources you have identified and organized.

Public Sources

Broadcast newsrooms can also use several resources that are available to the general public. These include standard reference works; government records, documents, and reports; and public safety communications.

Standard Reference Works

Several kinds of standard reference works are available. Some, such as dictionaries and thesauruses, concern words. Others, such as encyclopedias, atlases, and almanacs, provide statistics and general background information. Still others concern people; examples include biographical dictionaries, official telephone directories for cities and towns within a station's coverage area (so that you can check local names and addresses as well as emergency services, governmental offices at all levels, human services agencies, and even maps of the city), and city directories that offer telephone and street references for households and businesses as well as alphabetical listings of most local residents.

Many of these reference works are found in the broadcast newsroom. All of them can be found at large local libraries that also keep a variety of periodicals such as newspapers and magazines on their shelves or make them available on microfilm or microfiche or from other libraries via interlibrary loan. On occasion, you may need information from special kinds of archives. These might include local and state museums and historical societies; local newspaper "morgues"; or files of clippings of previously published stories.

Government Records, Documents, and Reports

A variety of governmental records, documents, and reports often go unused either because broadcast reporters are not aware that they exist or because time constraints prevent regular use of such resources. You need to know the kinds of written material available from governmental agencies and to be aware of recommendations and precautions associated with their use.

Government agencies at all levels provide two kinds of written material. *Records and documents* are essentially statistics and unmanipulated data. *Reports* are written by people in governmental agencies and generally are based on specific records and documents. Governmental records, documents, and reports range from single-page flyers to multivolume tomes on almost any subject imaginable. Reporters regularly use single records and reports such as police reports and court dockets listing the schedule for specific court activities, but a variety of other kinds of written material can be used.

Kinds of Written Material Available

Vital statistics can be obtained from several sources. City and state agencies record births, deaths, divorces, and so forth. Several publications provide statistics that may be useful. These include booklets that provide data from city, county, and state government agencies. The *Statistical Abstract of the United States* provides useful statistics and profiles the industrial, social, political, and economic organization of the United States.

Police reports indicate the name and known address of the person(s) accused of a specific offense as well as the time and place of arrest.

Depending on local, state, and federal laws that control access, court documents can supply information about civil and criminal cases as well as those involving probate cases (wills, estates, and trusts), bankruptcies, and even military affairs as with the U.S. Court of Military Appeals. The clerk of the court involved has access to a variety of information, including names and addresses of plaintiffs and defendants as well as the lawyers representing both sides; the nature of the charge (if a criminal case); and transcripts of trials, preliminary hearings, and other courtroom appearances.[1] The Administrative Office of the U.S. Courts in Washington issues an annual report that outlines electronic surveillance activity by law enforcement agencies across the nation. Chapter 19 describes the laws concerning access to court documents and records.

Regulatory governmental agencies leave a paper trail that could be useful to a broadcast reporter. The results of a labor dispute could be found in a report from the National Labor Relations Board. The cause of a local private airplane crash eventually will be officially identified in a written report by the Federal Aviation Administration. Various boards and agencies at all governmental levels regulate, license, and certify many professions and businesses, including engineers, barbers, nurses, and even liquor stores. Local building codes are enforced when construction permits as well as citations of violations are issued. Safety codes are enforced when public elevators are inspected.

Fiscal documents are also available. Property tax assessments come from the local assessor or the state tax commissioner. Both must provide written records of their determinations. Some business or corporate records are available because every state requires that articles of incorporation be filed if a company makes its headquarters in that state. Such records list principal owners and officers as well as major stockholders and financial holdings. Publicly traded companies, in which stock can be purchased by individuals, are required to file regular reports on their activities with the Securities and Exchange Commission (SEC). Want to know the financial status of your bank or savings and loan? Quarterly financial reports are available on federally insured banks. Indicate the city and state of the bank you are inquiring about when you write: Federal Deposit Insurance Corporation, Attn: Disclosure Group, 500 17th St., N.W., Washington, DC 20429.

Politics can be covered using available government documents and records. The election commissioner in some states allows reporters access to lists of eligible voters that indicate voting participation as well as the address provided by each person registered to vote. A reporter could determine the truth of a charge that a candidate did not vote until becoming a candidate or that a particular candidate votes in one precinct but receives low property tax assessments on a home in a different precinct. Most states now require that candidates indicate where they get large campaign contributions and how they spend them. Unfortunately, the review of these documents is not easy; the information is not usually organized into easily recognizable patterns such as alphabetically or according to zip code.

Recommendations and Precautions

Using government reports and documents for broadcast news stories should be considered for several reasons. When combined with reporters' personal observations as well as the results of interviews with knowledgeable sources, the review of such written material can provide more complete details, fresh approaches, and different perspectives about a specific story. Such material helps reporters to understand the people with whom they are dealing and to confirm story details provided by other sources. It may also provide clues to other details needed for a particular story—clues that might come in handy when preparing for a particularly difficult interview.

Also remember these precautions. Be certain to contact the appropriate governmental agency for the information that you need. For example, the Environmental Protection Agency handles environmental information but does not handle the same issues and concerns as the Department of Health and Human Services. Determine whether you have access to the information that you need. Always double-check the accuracy of the information you gather. Remember that no piece of information is true merely because it is in writing, even if it is on the letterhead of a governmental agency.

Public Safety Communications

By using special audio receivers, most newsrooms regularly monitor the activities of local and area law enforcement agencies as well as fire units and rescue squads. Some newsrooms also monitor the activities of ambulance services, civil defense units, citizens-band emergency channel 9 for traffic and road condition reports, and even the two-way transmissions of competing broadcast news operations! In large cities, a teletype service often supplements these audio transmissions.

Each newsroom audio receiver can monitor several different frequencies. Each receiver scans these frequencies until a transmission begins. Then the scanning process stops, and the receiver reproduces the transmission over a newsroom speaker. When the transmission ends, scanning resumes until the next transmission occurs on one of the frequencies being scanned.

Public safety agencies generally issue transmissions in special numbered codes that indicate the nature and severity of various activities. These codes vary in each locality. Each public safety agency tends to use multiple sets of frequencies, which requires the use of several newsroom receivers.

These transmissions are only preliminary reports and must be verified by phone or in person before they can be used on a news broadcast. Specific FCC regulations prohibit the rebroadcast of items from police, fire, and FAA agencies as well as from other broadcast stations without prior authorization from the public agency or broadcast station involved *and* from the Federal Communications Commission (FCC). Newsrooms generally obtain prior authorization from each public agency monitored. Such agencies tend to be cooperative because news broadcasts help them to disseminate information that they want to reach the general public. Permission to rebroadcast material already used on broadcast stations or networks is negotiated individually (see the ''Copyright'' section in Chapter 19). Reports from ham and CB stations may be rebroadcast without special permission.

Many reporters are surprised by the depth and diversity of information they can uncover simply by using readily available, public sources of information. If you have reasonable investigative skills and lots of curiosity, you will be pleasantly surprised about the quality of what you can find in public records, documents, and reports, as well as in standard reference works. Use your limited time and resources to explore the key information sources needed for a particular story.

Private Sources

A wide array of private news sources is also available. These range from people and organizations to electronic information systems and publications.

People

People are one of the best sources a reporter can use. Practically nothing can match the intensity of the reaction by an eyewitness who saw a private plane crash into her neighbor's home, killing all aboard but sparing the lives of those on the ground. Authenticity increases when an environmental expert explains the impact of a nuclear dump site on a small community in your coverage area.

Interviews and comments from people make a broadcast news report come alive as the pieces of a story are unraveled by the reporter. Listeners and viewers can share experiences, look for prejudices, and determine points of view in an effort to get a complete and accurate picture of what happened and why.

Groups and Associations

A reporter can often contact as news sources representatives of professional, civic, political, and special interest groups and associations. Members of these organizations have developed contacts and materials as well as proposals and programs through their special interests, concerns, and community involvement. Local chapters of these organizations generally are eager to be consulted for information on their activities.

Be aware that many of these organizations serve as lobbyists who try to influence public officials toward actions these groups or organizations would regard as favorable. Special interest groups such as the American Civil Liberties Union, the John Birch Society, the National Organization for Women, and the Anti-Defamation League of B'nai B'rith recognize, as every reporter should, that having a formal organization and working to accomplish specific goals improves the likelihood of media coverage.

News Releases or Handouts

In many cases, potential news stories come to the broadcast newsroom instead of vice versa. The news department is on mailing lists to receive agendas, monthly publications, feature items, reference material, and so forth from various public service organizations and governmental agencies as well as special interest groups, citizens committees, and even the public relations offices of private businesses.

Handouts may take the form of news copy only or they may include audio or video material prepared by someone outside of the broadcast newsroom. Handouts may be individual items or complete programs offered for station use. On occasion, newsrooms receive calls offering live or recorded comments from elected officials or even from representatives of potential on-air interview guests usually associated with commercial enterprises who, you discover, will be "in your area next week" and prepared to talk about subjects ranging from weight loss programs to motivational success strategies.

Here are several suggestions to keep in mind when handling *any* handout material:

a. You have no obligation to use any handout, in whole or in part.
b. Reserve the right to edit handout material that you use.
c. Always identify the source of such material when and if it is used on-the-air. Good journalistic practice is to identify the source of *all* information.
d. Scan the contents of every handout received. You never know when an interesting story might be hidden between the lines of an otherwise dull news release.
e. Handle each handout only once. Either discard it or decide to use it by placing the item in the future file (described later in this chapter) or starting your newsroom's local follow-up to that story.

f. Work with the source of the handout material to check essential facts, provide additional background information, or schedule contacts for follow-up reports. Watch for news release "embargoes," which involve holding the release of information until an agreed upon or specified time.

Audio and Video News Releases

Professional associations, corporations, nonprofit organizations, and governmental and public relations agencies provide regular preproduced news stories to radio and television newsrooms around the country. Paper and audio or videotape news releases, sent by mail or delivery service, have been replaced with written material that is faxed to the newsroom. Fax messages are also often news releases or agendas for upcoming events, but fax messages can be used to indicate satellite coordinates to receive updated or expanded information. Standard paper news releases are readily available from the local office of civic or charitable organizations as well as governmental agencies.

Video news releases (VNRs) have virtually replaced more traditional delivery forms for news releases. The satellite-fed VNR material generally provides a traditional-looking video or audio story, but it will also often include such material as additional footage and soundbites, names and titles of people who appear in the electronic news release, suggested news copy for the newscaster or anchor to read both before and after the prepared news release, and additional information surrounding the story. If interactive satellite sessions are arranged, local reporters can participate in distant news conferences along with reporters in attendance.

The increasing use of VNRs by broadcast newsrooms reflects a growing interdependency between television news and public relations. Offers of additional background information, interviews with local and national or international experts on specific subjects, and other specialized news-related activities often accompany VNRs. As staff cutbacks force newsrooms to face the realities of reduced staff sizes, VNRs present a tempting source of information for broadcast news personnel. Editorial judgment must accompany use of *all* news releases, including VNRs.

Research Organizations

People are curious about other people—what they say, do, and even what they wear. People also want to know what other people think about themselves and the world around them.

Broadcast news stories occasionally cite the results of polls and surveys conducted by well-known national research companies like Louis Harris and Associates, Roper, and Gallup. A few local stations conduct their own research projects using the resources of either national research companies that market their services to local stations or major universities and research centers that develop research projects in conjunction with local stations.

Be cautious and skeptical when reviewing and reporting the results of surveys and polls. Remember that they are only one of many information tools available to a reporter. Here is the advice of ABC News:

> Whenever major poll results are reported on the air, we should include the pertinent facts about who did it, when it was done, the size of the sample and margin of error. The [research] question should be phrased accurately (exactly is always best) immediately preceding the results. Occasions obviously arise where it may be unnecessary or cumbersome to include all of the information about a particular poll. . . . But when the poll itself is the story, we should err on the side of providing too much rather than not enough information about its specific characteristics.[2]

Determining the method used to gather the information and the individual or organization who commissioned or paid for the research project is also advisable. People can easily interpret the results of any survey or poll to their advantage. Learn to analyze these kinds of results and to form conclusions that are reported in a fair, impartial manner. Courses in statistics will better prepare you to deal with questions about polling procedures and statistical error.

Newspapers

Although many broadcasting executives consider newspapers as advertising competitors, most broadcast newsrooms continue to subscribe to local as well as area newspapers from within their station's coverage area. In addition, subscriptions are recommended for newspapers with statewide circulation that are generally considered to be opinion leaders; national publications like *U.S.A. Today, The New York Times,* and *The Wall Street Journal,* along with periodicals like *Time* and *Newsweek*; and special types of publications that will enhance regular coverage of areas like health and medicine, business, and the environment.

Broadcast newsrooms continue their newspaper subscriptions for several reasons:

a. Newspapers often provide tips on recent stories that can be developed by a broadcast news reporter.
b. Newspapers are a consistent source for future file items (see "Internal Sources" later in this chapter).
c. Newspapers can be used to check the spelling of names used in a story.
d. Newspaper accounts can be a helpful source of background information for a new reporter just starting to cover a particular story or news beat.
e. Newspapers can add depth and background to a story, which may not be available from broadcast reporters, wire services, or other sources.

However, several *disadvantages* also are associated with the use of newspaper stories for broadcast reports:

a. Newspapers should be considered only as *sources* of information. Thus, if an entire broadcast story is rewritten from a newspaper (which is *not* recommended), credit must be given to that newspaper just as for any other source.

b. Use of newspaper reports may be considered an infringement of copyright laws. Most publications copyright each edition that they publish.

c. Verify the essential information found in a newspaper story before it is used on-the-air. If a newspaper publishes a libelous statement and a broadcast station repeats the statement without attempting to verify it, both the newspaper and the broadcast station could be held responsible for libel charges (see Chapter 19).

d. Newspaper accounts need to be rewritten in standard broadcast style to avoid style problems such as long sentences and attributions placed at the ends of sentences.

e. Each newspaper must at least be scanned on a daily basis to be of any consistent value.

f. Newspaper delivery is not always reliable. The paper may arrive wet, torn, or late—or it may not arrive at all.

Databases and Bulletin Boards

Once computers are introduced into a broadcast newsroom, newswriters can start using databases and electronic bulletin boards to gather and exchange information. *Databases* are computerized information retrieval systems accessed via telephone lines or other methods of interconnection. *Electronic bulletin boards* link computer users over an extensive electronic hookup. Once a modem links a computer terminal or a personal computer to a telephone line, even a one-person newsroom can have access to enormous electronic libraries or databases as well as personal insights offered on electronic bulletin boards. You will need to spend time to learn how to use these sources efficiently and effectively.

Since the mid-1980s, broadcast journalists have been using computer-assisted, on-line information retrieval systems. Database searches can be useful to do the following: help generate ideas for new stories; locate background information for stories and interviews already under way; identify experts to interview; keep ahead of your competition; and even retrieve audio or videotape material from your newsroom archives.

Nexis and Dialog are two of the largest commercial full-text database services used by over 50 percent of broadcast newsrooms around the country. Nexis, part of Lexis/Nexus, is used extensively by both print and broadcast newspeople. Nexis can provide access to more than 800 sources of full-text news from regional, national, and international newspapers; magazines; news letters; and worldwide wire services. Abstract or abbreviated information from more than 1,000 information sources is also available, in addition to the complete texts of all ABC and CNN television news and public affairs programs. Dialog, owned by Knight-Ridder, carries the complete text of approximately 50 newspapers, including all of those owned by Knight-Ridder, plus articles published in *The Washington Post, The Los Angeles Times, The Chicago Tribune,* and *The Chicago Sun-Times.*

Searching databases offers many advantages. It is *fast,* often requiring less than five minutes. It is *complete.* Names and concepts can be combined to retrieve precisely what you want. Articles in major as well as some specialized publications are indexed and summarized. Specific information that you designate can also be retrieved from wire services, news syndicates, encyclopedias, and even ''electronic mailboxes,'' where messages can be exchanged over electronic bulletin boards. It is *current.* Using database memory capabilities makes it possible to receive regular reports about specific topics or towns in your coverage area. It is relatively *inexpensive.* Some database services require sign-up fees; most do not. Most require monthly fees ranging from 10 to 50 dollars. The on-line costs per hour are under 150 dollars; most are under 60 dollars.

Use databases to update information and provide background material for a story that you develop locally. Databases can also help fill in story information that you cannot obtain locally. In addition, they can help confirm conflicting comments or facts you may have gathered.

Using databases too heavily or exclusively can also lead to problems. Databases can cause journalists to: go to database sources automatically and routinely, rather than pursue worthwhile local information sources; neglect local sources because national and international sources appear to be more attractive and credible; and perpetuate errors stored in databases.

A growing number of print and broadcast journalists as well as citizens interested in more extensive information sources are tapping into electronic bulletin boards as well as databases. Most subscribe to mainstream systems such as CompuServe and Prodigy.[3]

All of the electronic bulletin boards are linked by Internet, the primary electronic highway for E-mail, which is a kind of high-tech postal service as well as a two-way mobile electronic mail service. More than 22,000 separate computer networks and up to 30 million people worldwide use Internet to access graphics, photographs, and audio and video material. Internet is truly a network of networks. Access is available via cellular telephones, modems, or other standard interfacing connecting systems. Internet provides fast, efficient, versatile, and relatively inexpensive access to an exciting worldwide array of materials that will be useful for the radio and television journalist.

The Wires

A large share of the news stories heard on newscasts come from domestic wire services, especially the Associated Press, which provides news to roughly half of the nation's commercial stations. Although still referred to as *the wires,* a variety of wire services feed their reports to broadcast newsrooms via satellite into high-speed printers using continuous rolls of fan-fold paper or into newsroom computers so that local news personnel can edit the material. Networks and syndicated information services have begun offering news and information that once was considered the exclusive domain of traditional wire services. Before you begin to use the wires as news sources, you should know how they operate, what they offer, and how to handle the wire service copy that you receive.

Each domestic wire service operates a 24-hour-a-day national broadcast service from a central location. A regular schedule is established for the transmission of world and national news items and packaged reports or summaries that can be used as newscasts. Bulletins and other emergency or important news items interrupt this schedule as needed.

How They Operate

Approximately 30 minutes after most hours, state and regional news items are sent to member or subscribing stations from bureaus strategically placed throughout the country. Stations can share their stories with other stations in their area by contacting the wire service bureau.

Wire copy can be selected or customized to meet the needs of individual broadcast newsrooms. Copy can now be "dumped" into newsroom computers equipped with modems without the need to print the copy on continuous rolls of paper. Many broadcast newsrooms continue to receive wire copy on printers that operate at 1,200 words per minute.

Domestic wire services offer a wide variety of services to the broadcasting and cable industries. These include the *radio wire,* which provides newscasts or summaries of the current top world and national news stories as well as sportscasts, features, and special reports on business, agriculture, and entertainment; the *TV wire,* which combines radio wire and newspaper wire material with items prepared specifically for television; *an audio network* (AP Network News and UPI Audio), which offers a full range of network services, including hourly newscasts, regular sports programs, business and agriculture reports, feature material, and regular feeds of actualities, voicers, and wraps billboarded in advance on the wire for affiliated stations to use in locally produced newscasts; *photographic services,* which deliver to television stations each month pictures of people and places in the news as well as topical maps and graphics that can be added to a basic set of graphics material already on hand; a full-service selectable wire providing *in-depth coverage* for heavy news and information stations; *high-speed services* covering top stories in Spanish-speaking countries; *computer software programs* to help newsrooms manage news and information resources; and *interactive information systems* to exchange requests, concerns, and information.

What They Offer

Increased competition has led wire services and networks to launch news packages tailored to fit narrow radio station programming formats as well as stations with limited news budgets or news needs. AP DriveTime, CBS Zapnews, and the ABC News Wire are examples of wire services and networks customizing news and information to better satisfy contemporary needs in the cable and broadcasting industries. Stations can decide exactly what they want by selecting specific items from these menu-driven services.

Here are the broad categories of news and information items available on domestic broadcast wires: state news (individual stories; news summaries; agriculture news; sports scores and stories from the region served by the specific wire service bureau); national and international news (individual stories from overseas, around the country, and especially Washington, DC); newscast scripts prepared as one-minute hourly headlines or three- and five-minute summaries or newscasts; business stories and summaries; agriculture stories; features of various kinds; national sports scores and summaries; audio network billboards and advisories; state and national weather forecasts, radar summaries, temperatures, and weather advisories.[4]

How to Work with Wire Copy

You need to know how to identify specific kinds of notations in a wire service report and also what to do with the wire copy you select. Each piece of copy contains notations that help identify the nature of the wire item as well as the time it was sent to broadcast newsrooms. A one- to three-word copy or story slug appears at the beginning of each item; for example, COLLEGE BASKETBALL, WEATHER, or NEWS SUMMARY. The date and time the item was sent to stations are noted at the end of each item. For example,

11-10-98 1904 EST

This wire item was sent on November 10, 1998, at 7:04 P.M. Eastern Standard Time. A 24-hour clock and eastern time zone references are used for most wire copy. If a story is updated, or if a news summary is sent in multiple feeds, or "takes," the same slug will be used. The date and time references allow you to find the latest information about a particular story or the location of the rest of a news summary. Each item also displays computer storage and retrieval information that some newsrooms may find useful. Individual wire stories also indicate the dateline or location of that story. News summaries generally note the wire editor who supervised the preparation of that material.

The wire copy received can be used in several ways. Here are the basic alternatives:

1. *Use the wire copy as received.* "Rip-and-read" newscasts may cut costs by eliminating the need for news personnel, but this approach also provides no opportunity to localize the copy or check the accuracy and writing style of wire copy that is generally prepared hurriedly and in large volumes. Also, these kinds of newscasts will sound the same as all of the other stations that "rip-and-read" the same wire copy because the words will be identical.

2. *Review and then use the wire copy.* This approach is essentially the same as the one just described, but at least an effort is made to check spelling, punctuation, and garbled or unreadable wire copy, and to pencil-edit a few lines before determining the order in which stories will be used in the newscast.
3. *Rewrite the wire copy* (see Chapter 8).
4. *Use the wire copy only as tips or leads.* Many broadcast newsrooms consider a wire service only as a *source* of information and never use wire copy as received. Instead, local reporters follow up wire stories and provide fresh angles and updates that make the story more meaningful to a local broadcast audience.

No matter which approach is used, wire copy is stored in newsroom computer systems or printed as received and then placed in slots or in/out boxes, hung on hooks, or spiked on metal pegs in the newsroom. Each newsroom determines its own system for handling the flow of wire copy.

Other wire services supply broadcast newsrooms with specialized information. The National Weather Service wire is found in most newsrooms. Domestic wire services compile their weather information from the NWS wire, which provides national and area forecasts as well as current weather observations and hazardous weather warnings. Some newsrooms monitor one of the seven NOAA (National Oceanic and Atmospheric Administration) Weather Radio frequencies. These 24-hour-a-day audio transmissions cover approximately 90 percent of the country and provide continuous updates on local and national weather patterns, one- to three-day forecasts, agricultural weather forecasts, road conditions, and even a few weather statistics such as sunrise and sunset times, high and low temperatures, and amount of precipitation received.

Other Kinds of Wire Services

Large-market and network newsrooms generally subscribe to the ''A'' wire, which provides longer stories for use in morning and afternoon newspapers. Although the ''A'' wire provides a wider variety of stories written in more depth than the broadcast wire, ''A'' wire material must be rewritten if used on-the-air. Reuters is another internationally acclaimed news service often available in larger broadcast news operations.

The CQI SportsTicker from Western Union provides detailed coverage of major sports events. Other specialized wire services offer detailed reports, summaries, and stories about business and finance as well as agricultural interests.

Local wires in large cities provide coverage of local events that generally are beyond the coverage capabilities of any single news organization. This might involve covering a lengthy criminal trial or a weeklong visit by an important foreign dignitary. This kind of wire is also used to alert newsrooms about upcoming events such as news conferences, speeches, rallies, and marches in case a station's reporter needs to be assigned. The copy provided by local wires is written for local newspapers and must be rewritten for on-air use.

The ideal situation is to have available as many sources of information as possible, including wire services, so that key facts and alternative story angles can be reviewed. However, high costs and lack of available personnel prevent most newsrooms from having so many resources.

Other News Services
Commercial news services as well as networks and other broadcast stations are additional sources of news material. They offer additional choices for newsrooms that find it increasingly difficult to satisfy the audience's demands for high-quality information from a variety of sources.

Commercial news suppliers, such as Conus Communications and CNN Television, offer raw (unedited) newsfeeds as well as preproduced feature packages, weather, sports, and graphics story packages. These are almost turnkey news package services for national and international information.

Conus operates one of the largest member station cooperatives. Stations can join or form a membership cooperative that uses mobile uplink vans to relay coverage from the site of a news story to a satellite and back down to a central distribution point or directly to member station newsrooms. Such co-operatives own or lease transponders (receive/send channels) on satellites and can coordinate joint news coverage efforts to produce national news reports for individual member stations.

Network-affiliated stations can also receive via satellite (several times each day) network-produced newscasts and sports reports, various special in-terest and feature programs, special events coverage of news and sports events, and other audio or video material for use in locally produced newscasts. Tel-evision networks offer affiliates soundbites, reporter packages, and graphics, and even late feeds of breaking stories that can be used near the beginning of the local station's last regularly scheduled newscast. National networks use supplemental, satellite-fed channels to provide live special events coverage, and regional bureaus to ferret out stories from local stations that can be shared by affiliates within the same region. Several statewide audio networks provide similar services to affiliated stations. Network-produced material should be integrated into local news coverage to form a total news package for a station.

Other broadcast station news operations can also supply news material. Some stations establish regular exchanges of news reports with stations in other areas of a state or region. Even without such an arrangement, stations may call another station in the area of an important news event and request coverage. The cooperating station expects reciprocity. This kind of coverage is helpful when a local resident is involved in an incident outside the station's coverage area. For example, if a prominent local business executive is charged with embezzlement of bank funds in a neighboring state, the local station can satisfy local curiosity and interest by using a preliminary report from a station where those charges were filed.

Pooling news coverage is another alternative. Instead of each broadcast news operation covering a particular story or incident with its own news personnel, a smaller news crew can cover the event and offer the audio and/or video material to other broadcast newsrooms. Sometimes pool coverage is the only way to get a particular story, for example, sensitive military operations or restricted state supreme court proceedings, because of limited access or limited facilities. In other circumstances, pool coverage is more efficient and cost-effective. One of the major problems with pool coverage is that all newsrooms receive the same information. Fresh angles and perspectives are needed for stories based on pool coverage.

Internal Sources

Several sources of news and information operate from within most broadcast newsrooms. These include future files; other newsroom files and records; and the reporters, correspondents, and stringers who cover stories the local newsroom assigns.

Future Files

One of the most difficult tasks in managing a newsroom is to keep track of future news events that your local news staff needs to cover. One answer to the problem is what most newsrooms call a *future file* or a *suspense file*.

Future files contain information about newsworthy events that will occur sometime in the future. Several kinds of items are placed in a newsroom's future file by assigned personnel, usually the assignment editor or the news director. These include notices and/or agendas for meetings; news releases that relate to some future event; clippings from newspapers and magazines; personal notes and reminders from newsroom personnel about upcoming events; news copy of previous stories used on-the-air; and reporters' ''story notes,'' follow-up suggestions for a story already covered that mention an upcoming event.

Newsrooms use several systems to maintain future files. A giant desk or wall calendar with large blocks for each date could be used to note the items needing coverage. Inexpensive computer software can accomplish the same task as a desk or wall calendar and also provide additional systems to manage newsroom personnel and facilities more efficiently. Some newsrooms use one of these two systems and then arrange the available written material into file folders organized either by news beat or topic area, for example, city council, schools, and courts, or by calendar dates. This last system is the one used most often for future files.

Basically the calendar system involves the use of three sets of file folders: one set numbered 1 to 31; another set labeled for each month of the year; and a third set labeled for each of the next five to ten years. As a future news item is called to the attention of newsroom personnel, a written notice is placed in the appropriate file folder. A particular news item works its way through the file folders until news assignments are made for a particular day.

Let's take an example. Suppose that on 22 October your local chamber of commerce sends your news department a news release indicating that an international track meet will be held in your city next June. This news release would be placed in the file folder for next year. When the new year starts, you would go through the file folder marked with that year's date, take this news release and place it in the file folder marked *June*. Any subsequent items relating to this track meet would also be filed under *June*. At the beginning of June, you would sort through that file folder and place the news release in one of the folders numbered 1 to 31, selecting the numbered file folder that matches the date of the track meet. Coverage of the track meet would be determined on the basis of staff availability and news priorities.

Future, or suspense, files are valuable for several reasons. They help newsroom personnel plan each day's news coverage. They provide useful background information for story coverage. On weekend newscasts, they can be used to preview the upcoming week's events.

Other Newsroom Files and Records

Broadcast newsrooms maintain other kinds of files and records that help generate story ideas and locate useful background information.

Rotary or index file cards can be used as *call sheets* to contact individuals who supply newsworthy items on a regular basis.

Local news copy is saved in files, boxes, or bundles usually by the date and time each local story was used. One news director (whose identity, unfortunately, I do not recall) devised another system in which a number was assigned to each *type* of story that was covered regularly, for example, *1* for city council stories, *2* for school board meetings, *3* for local traffic fatalities. Using his system, each story written locally was assigned a number that matched a category. At the end of each day, each piece of copy was placed in the appropriate, numbered file in chronological order. At the end of the year, the contents of each numbered file were bundled and placed into storage or transferred to a background file for each story category. This kind of filing system helps prepare year-in-review programs and quickly orients a reporter just beginning to cover a particularly complex news beat.

Some broadcast newsrooms also catalogue the audio or video material used in local stories. A computerized database program or a simple index card system can be used to log each item. Each entry could include a brief summary of the contents of the taped material along with the date and time of each newscast in which the material was used. Retrieval of this material is useful when a future story requires file footage or a recorded comment or when the newsroom faces legal or ethical accusations or charges about a local story already broadcast.

Reporters, Correspondents, Stringers, and Tipsters

A local broadcast station that has a wide coverage area or an overabundance of stories to cover will often hire correspondents and stringers to supply news stories to supplement coverage by full-time reporters. Correspondents and stringers could be based in strategic locations within the coverage area. They may operate out of bureaus established by the station or simply work as free-lancers out of their homes or businesses. They are paid a retainer each month or a fee for each story used on-the-air, or a combination of a monthly retainer and a per-story fee.

Correspondents and stringers are valuable to a broadcast news operation only if they can do the following:

  a. Write and report *broadcast* news.
  b. Understand and follow directions about newscast times and the acceptable times for filing stories.
  c. Develop, on their own, news contacts that will be beneficial to general news coverage.
  d. Always represent the best interests of the station.

Every station has its share of *tipsters*—people who call a newsroom to tell someone about a particular event they observed or rumor they heard that they believe is especially newsworthy. Always remember that these are un-official and unsolicited reports that must be investigated and verified by full-time news personnel before they can be used on-the-air. Tips simply *begin* the reporting process.

Always follow these steps when a news tip is received: Verify the name, address, and telephone number of the tipster; ask the tipster specific questions about the story; verify the accuracy and completeness of essential story details with all possible sources *before* anything is broadcast; and never assure a tipster that the tip will be used automatically. *Never* broadcast a tip without verifying the information!

Organizing News Sources

Once you know the key sources of news and information used in broadcast newsrooms, you must learn how to apply that knowledge to each reporting situation. Remember the following steps:

  1. Determine what you need to know.
  2. Identify where to find what you need.
  3. Handle what you find.

We will examine this three-step process with the understanding that it is difficult for most broadcast news personnel to follow these recommenda-tions to the extent that they would like; news events develop so fast and facts change so rapidly that lack of time often prevents thorough, thoughtful, and extensive use of these guidelines. However, no matter how compressed the process, these are the three phases of organizing news sources.

Determine What You Need to Know

As you cover a story, ask yourself these questions: What's missing? What should I know more about to make this a more complete, newsworthy story? What are the information needs of my listeners or viewers?

Be specific! Exactly what do you need to know? Do you want to know the latest tax assessment for a local elected official's home? Do you want to know if there was a recent inspection of the elevators in that apartment building that was leveled by fire overnight? Do you want to know how serious crime on campus has become—Which crimes? Over what time period?

Be inquisitive and curious. These two traits will distinguish you among your fellow newsroom workers and often lead to some noteworthy stories. The more you know, the more you should *want* to know.

Identify Where to Find What You Need

Review the primary types of news sources profiled earlier in this chapter. Should you tap public sources like reference works or maybe government documents and records? Would private sources like personal interviews, newspaper clippings, or the results of a poll or survey provide better information? Can another reporter in the newsroom give you some advice, or were similar stories covered in earlier newscasts now filed away?

Be aware of the variety of viable news sources available. Look for knowledgeable, reliable, primary sources of information. Become enterprising in identifying and then exploring different kinds of news sources. Your time to work on a story is limited in broadcast news operations. Approach a limited number of *key* sources.

If you have identified precisely what you need to know, locating a news source to provide that information will be considerably easier. For example, if you want to know the taxes paid on a particular piece of property, remember that tax assessments are filed locally with the tax commissioner or assessor and at the state level with the state assessor or tax commissioner. Most states consider this kind of information open to the public, or a matter of *public record.*

Another example: If you want to know the inspection schedule for the elevators in that apartment building that burned, check with the local code authority or regulatory agency that handles elevator inspections. If the building was due for an inspection when it burned, you might have a story! Maybe a reporter in your newsroom who stays in regular contact with the fire department or whose beat is city hall can tell you who to contact for a follow-up to the fire story.

As a final example, if you want to go beyond the surface facts about a recent burglary on campus, you might provide a more complete story about crime on campus if you interview police officers who have investigated burglaries and other recent campus crimes, prosecuting and defense attorneys involved in recent campus crime cases, sociologists and criminologists who can identify criminal activity trends, and city or state officials who might be concerned about the campus crime situation and could be considering legislation to correct the problem. Do some research: Examine previous newspaper clippings, stories retrieved from an on-line database, or national statistics offered in a reputable almanac or a recent poll or survey.

Learn where to go and who to ask for the information that you need. Be persistent. Never stop looking for useful news sources.

After you obtain what you think you need for a story, handle what you have found by completing the following steps:

Handle What You Find

1. *Verify.* Consult more than one source for complex or sensitive information. You might need to talk to more sources and search more documents before proceeding.
2. *Evaluate.* Collate the opinions and information obtained from various sources. Determine what is newsworthy and what is not, what demands closer scrutiny and what does not.
3. *Organize.* Step back from the story, if only for a few moments. Put away your notes. Turn off the equipment. In two or three sentences, tell yourself the essential facts of the story. If you cannot do this, you are not ready to write the story. Remember the principles described and illustrated in Chapters 4 and 5 on leads and story structure.
4. *Interpret.* In simple terms, tell viewers or listeners what is important to know about a particular story and what it means to them, in a personal way. This may mean simplifying technical jargon. It always means selecting the key pieces of information to tell the basic facts of a story.
5. *Report.* Now write the story with the assurance that you have taken steps to organize and use available news sources.

Summary

This chapter concerned the identification and organization of key sources of news and information.

News sources comprise three principal types. *Public sources* include reference works; government records, documents, and reports; and public safety communications. *Private sources* include people; various groups and organizations; audio and video news releases; surveys and polls; newspapers; databases and bulletin boards; broadcast and specialized news wires; commercial news services; and other broadcast news operations, stations and networks. *Internal sources* originating within the newsroom include future files; other newsroom files and records (call sheets, previous stories and tape material); and correspondents, stringers, and tipsters.

Organizing news sources involves a three-step process: determine what you need to know; identify where to find what you need; and handle what you find.

Do not expect to use every news source discussed in this chapter for every story that you cover. Review the range of sources available. Then use a limited number of sources allowed by time restrictions to produce the story that you need.

Chapter 10 explores techniques for *developing* news sources through observation, interviewing, and news beats. It also examines how to handle reluctant news sources and how to enterprise news stories.

Exercises

1. Obtain access to at least two national or international news reports or publications. This could be newspapers, magazines, wire services, transcripts of network news broadcasts, or other database-originated material. Use a service such as Lexis/Nexus or standard library printed sources. Using at least these two sources, summarize the contents of and reactions to a recent legislative initiative by the president of the United States. The legislative initiative or issue might be a national health plan or budget reduction proposal, a foreign policy statement on a current hot spot in the world, or other topics that reflect current concerns within the United States. Now contact at least one local or area source connected in some way to this same national or international news story. Write a 40-second radio or television reader report that summarizes what these *three* specific sources said about this *one* specific presidential initiative. In your story, be sure to cite each of the three sources.

2. List three regulatory governmental agencies with local or statewide jurisdiction. Contact one of them and obtain a copy of a recent report issued by the agency. Write a 30- to 45-second radio or television news story based on your summary of this written report.

3. From one of the three regulatory governmental agencies listed but not used in Exercise 3, obtain copies of several recent news releases issued by this agency. Write a 10- to 20-second radio or television news story based on the contents of one of these news releases. Attach a copy of the original news release to your story.

4. The following news items lack essential information. Rewrite each item in *broadcast* style. Below each rewrite, list the questions left unanswered in the audience's mind and where you would find the missing information.

    a. Randall R. Taylor, 35, of 3435 Q St., died about 4 P.M. today after a five-story fall from a scaffold on the Stuart Building, which he was painting. The cable on his safety line broke, according to local police officials and a spokesman at Memorial Hospital, where Taylor was taken after his fall.

    b. The city council yesterday hiked next year's tax rate 30 cents per $100 assessed valuation to an all-time high, according to City Councilwoman Meredith Price. Earlier, the council approved a $24,564,398 budget, which represents a 4.78 percent increase over last year's spending. The increased tax is expected to provide $2,121,789 more income than the city has available during the current year.

Notes

1. The American Bar Association offers a 40-minute videotape presentation entitled "Following the Paper Trail: A Journalist's Guide to Locating Legal Documents." The program provides an overview of research techniques that apply to all types of news stories. Covered are explanations of where to find and how to interpret records such as: property documents; campaign finance reports filed by candidates and political action committees; court records from civil and criminal cases; and government contracts at the city, county, state, and federal levels. It is the second in a series of materials for journalists produced by the ABA. For additional information or to order a copy of the videotape, write: Commission on Public Understanding about the Law, 750 North Lake Shore Drive, Chicago, IL 60611.

2. *ABC News Policy Book* (n.p., n.d.), p. II.20.

3. For an overview of how databases and electronic bulletin boards are used in broadcast newsrooms, see Penny Williams, "Database Downside," *Communicator* 47, No. 6 (June 1993): 14, 16–17.

4. Contact your nearest AP or UPI bureau to obtain a list of current wire service material offered to broadcast newsrooms.

Developing News Sources

C hapter 9 identified basic sources of news and information and then suggested techniques for organizing those sources. Chapter 10 describes
and illustrates approaches, strategies, methods, and techniques for developing
and cultivating news sources.

Specifically, Chapter 10 focuses on three key methods of digging stories
out of routine daily events: observation, interviews, and news beats. Then it
offers suggestions for handling reluctant news sources or people who want to
protect their identity. Finally, approaches and techniques for ''enterprising,''
or generating, news stories are discussed and illustrated.

The suggestions offered in this chapter apply to general broadcast news
coverage. Subsequent chapters (specifically Chapters 14 through 17) explore
further how to identify and develop news sources associated with live reports,
coverage of other routine newsgathering situations, specialized reporting assignments, and feature stories.

Observing

A good reporter is an efficient and careful observer. A reporter's observations
can add color, dimension, vividness, impact, and strength to a story. You need
to learn what to observe, how to observe, and how to select what to report
from your observations, so that the images and comments you gather as a
reporter can help the audience understand the story better and appreciate more
fully its news value. Not every story requires a reporter to insert such specific
observations, but many do, and many more stories could be improved if such
observations were used to give them depth and dimension. In the rush of
collecting information, reporters often neglect this obvious, but very useful,
reporting tool.

Concentrate on your work. Avoid distractions. Look for significant, interesting story details. You cannot go back and observe a news scene once
you have left it.

Become sensitive to your surroundings. Scan what's available—sights,
sounds, smells, impressions. Determine a hierarchy of things to observe. Then

observe the ''pieces.'' For example, if you were covering a speech, look around the room. Notice the sign on the speaker's podium. Evaluate the speaker's gestures and manner of speech. Make note of the tone of the speech and the environment surrounding the speaker (congested, relaxed, intense, confused, etc.).

Look beyond the obvious.   Train yourself to look for details that would ordinarily be missed. Go beyond the essential facts. For example, if you were covering a major traffic accident, you would, of course, report the essential details of the story such as who was killed, how, and when. But if the accident occurred in a remote area, another interesting story might be a feature on the rescue capabilities of remote emergency teams or the nurse who pilots the helicopter that goes on these kinds of calls.

Observe from the audience's viewpoint.   Observe those things associated with the story that the audience might like to know. That is the most honest and worthwhile point of view to maintain. For example, what was it like to survive a devastating hurricane or a major earthquake? How violently did the ground shake? What was it like to see parts of buildings flying by?

Filter what you observe.   Recognize what is important to observe and discard the rest. Remember the pain shown on the face of the rescue workers who failed to save the coal miner trapped in a mine for over three days. Do not focus exclusively on the number of oxygen tanks standing by or the array of mining company officials ready to make comments about mine safety.

Observe objectively.   Some distortion is inevitable when making personal observations. An experienced reporter will be alert to this problem and try to keep it under control by remembering to be as objective as humanly possible. Some reporters identify what they *expect* to find when approaching a story situation. Then they guard against these predispositions as much as possible but are ready to use observations that correspond to a particular predisposition if it provides an honest assessment of the story situation.

Keep your emotions in check.   Reporters are human. They have feelings and priorities based on prior experiences. At times tragic stories will touch you emotionally, but do not allow your personal biases to interfere with the objectivity and quality of your reporting.

Check your observations with others.   Look for alternate points of view to verify what you observe. In the case of the speech story mentioned earlier, ask others who attended whether they agree with your estimates of crowd size, your impressions about the level of noise encountered by the speaker, or your assessment that the speaker gave a wry smile when asked about a particularly sensitive issue.

Report your observations with as much precision as your abilities permit. As appropriate, use your observations to paint a backdrop for the story to flesh in details that may make the story more meaningful.

Interviewing

The interview is an important tool for the reporter. Interviews help nail down facts and gather opinions. They also allow the audience to hear the voice of the newsmaker or to see facial expressions and body language, adding meaning to the words heard.

The following sections cover several facets of interviewing: deciding when and if to interview; preparing for the interview; conducting the interview in person or over the telephone; and handling details after the interview. This discussion focuses only on interviews done for spot or breaking news stories, not on extended interviews done for on-air interview or talk programs. However, many of the suggestions offered apply to both situations. Chapters 12, 13, and 17 provide other suggestions about equipment usage and personnel positioning when conducting interviews for radio and television news stories and features.

Deciding to Interview

Interview when you need opinions as well as information. You might get facts more quickly and reliably somewhere else, for example from documents and previous stories. Use interviews to explore, discover, reconfirm, investigate, and understand the facts surrounding a story. Use interviews to get the opinions of those most directly affected by the story or those whose special knowledge and position qualify them to have worthwhile opinions about the facts you may already know from other sources.

Interview the obvious source but also talk to those most directly affected by the story. Talk to the fire chief about the overnight warehouse fire that caused considerable damage but also visit with the firefighter who rescued the overnight security guard from the blaze. Talk to the head of the street department, but don't neglect the group of homeowners soon to be displaced by a street-widening project.

Preparing to Interview

Organize yourself and then organize your interview approach. Reread the suggestions in Chapter 9: Determine what you need to know; identify who can tell you what you need to know; handle what you find.

Be prepared. Before the interview, find out as much as you can about the person, issues, and interview situation. Careful preparation helps frame significant questions, catch inconsistencies and vague comments, and recognize newsworthy comments when they come along.

Unfortunately, the broadcast reporter has little time and often limited resources available for such preparation. "Preparation" may mean only reading a news release previewing an event or a few words scribbled on the back of a used envelope by the assignment editor or news director. If you're rushed to get to a last-minute interview, maybe you have a moment to review the wire copy or a morning newspaper story related to the interview. Once you're on your way to the interview, if you have a cellular phone, contact a specialist in the field that you will discuss. Maybe talk briefly with another station reporter who has interviewed this same source or handled a similar story.

Plan your strategy.   Determine what you want to accomplish in an interview and how best to accomplish it, but be ready to adjust your approach as the interview unfolds. Have a clear idea of why you are talking to this particular person and know what you expect him or her to say. Even experienced interviewers find that rehearsing a short sequence of critical questions that they want to be sure to ask is helpful.

For breaking stories, the best interviews may be those done on the run, without prior notice. Catching a source off guard or unprepared may produce better comments. While the source may be unprepared, as a reporter, you must be prepared with questions for the eyewitness to a tragedy or the political candidate accused of wrongdoing cornered in a hallway by reporters.

For less urgent stories, make an interview appointment. Be persistent. You often have to sell the story and your ability to handle it. Convince the potential interviewee that his or her comments are vital for a comprehensive, accurate, balanced account. Once you have an interview appointment, show up on time, dress appropriately for the occasion, and come prepared.

No matter how you decide to conduct an interview, always identify yourself and indicate the specific information you need.

Conducting the Interview

The type of story you are covering will determine who you interview, the approach you use, the questions you ask, and the techniques you use to ensure that you get and maintain cooperation and stay in control of the interview situation. The hurried interview of an accused robbery suspect in the hallway of a municipal building just after a court appearance is significantly different from the more-relaxed, less-congested setting for an interview with the new director of the state roads department.

Approaches

Interviews can be conducted in person or over the telephone. In-person interviews are preferable. They allow you to establish rapport, pace the conversation, determine the attitude and mood of the interviewee by observing facial expressions and body movements, and handle more carefully issues that are complex and personally or politically sensitive.

Time constraints and deadlines often require that interviews be done on the phone. The telephone is an essential, powerful tool. People will interrupt almost anything to answer a ringing telephone. Although telephone interviews are no substitute for being on the scene, they are a quick way to fill holes in stories, get usable comments from a variety of sources on a number of stories, and pursue more efficiently news tips and local angles to national stories. Some reporters find they get better cooperation because people are used to talking on the phone. A telephone call, even without a full interview, is a quick way to check the spelling or pronunciation of names used in stories.

Here are *suggestions for conducting telephone interviews to gather information for news stories:*

a. Make certain the equipment works properly *before* you call.
b. Your time on the phone is limited, so *briefly* introduce yourself and explain why you are calling and what you want to know.
c. Have specific questions ready.
d. Stress the importance of getting the newsmaker's comments.
e. Remember to indicate that you want to record the comments. Be casual and reassuring. Something like this should work: ''I'd like to record our conversation and maybe use some of it on the air. Okay?'' Once the tape is rolling, it's a good idea to repeat this request to get the interviewee's agreement on tape. This provides additional legal protection.
f. If the interviewee objects to being recorded, try to overcome the objections. If that fails, ask to continue recording with the understanding that the tape will be used only to verify information.
g. Get the best recording possible. If there is extraneous noise on either end of the phone, or if there is static on the line, call back from a quieter location. If you plan to use the recorded comments on the air, tape quality is as important as content.

The key to a good broadcast interview is asking the right question of the right person at the right time to obtain the necessary information or opinion, and recording it on tape if at all possible. How you phrase a question depends on the purpose of the interview and how you plan to use the comments. ***Techniques***

Here are *suggestions for asking worthwhile questions in any interview situation:*

a. Identify worthwhile topics needing comment by briefing yourself *in advance* about the person to be interviewed and the issues to be discussed.
b. Instead of an ''interview,'' try to have a conversation. Interact with the interviewee. Show interest in the answers given.
c. *Listen* to the answers. Check for clarity and completeness. Listen to what is said but also to what is left *unsaid*. This provides clues about follow-up questions to ask.
d. If the interview is done in person, observe word choices and body language to better gauge emotions, attitudes, perspectives, priorities, and points of view. Use these observations to probe related topics and issues.
e. Resist the urge to provide vocal encouragement to your source. Avoid saying ''yes'' or ''uh-huh'' to everything said. You might

get the source to say more when you do this, but you may also ruin a good soundbite possibility.

f. Do not be afraid of silence. Be quiet after an especially startling comment. Most sources will try to fill the void by restating a comment in clearer form or adding comments on a point that you hadn't thought to raise.

g. *Conduct* the interview. Set the tone and pace. Control the questions asked, and guide the interview so that you accomplish your purpose and obtain the comments that you want.

h. Pace the interview by asking questions that get the interviewee talking. If possible, save tough questions for later in the interview. You may have to ask sensitive questions immediately if you face time constraints or pressurized interview situations. This could happen if you are trying to get opposing attorneys to comment after a stormy court appearance or labor negotiators to give you a comment after lengthy union bargaining sessions.

i. If questions are controversial, ask less controversial, easier-to-answer questions for a while before returning to sensitive topics.

j. Pursue your news source. Rephrase a question that is avoided or not answered fully. Be tactful, but also be persistent.

k. Be compassionate in some situations. Many people interviewed for news stories have never faced a microphone or camera. Understand their perspective and help them with their comments. This should not be necessary for those interviewed regularly by reporters.

l. Practice asking embarrassing, personal questions. If you verbalize such questions a couple of times *before* the interview, you will usually ask your interview source the question in a strong, confident, forthright manner during the interview. This practice will make the interview less uncomfortable and difficult for you and your source.

m. If your source hesitates or hedges on a question, take a moment to explain the importance and usefulness of the information and comment, or for a while cover information that can be easily discussed or released by the source. For example, if a local police officer shoots a citizen and you try to get an official comment about that particular shooting incident, you might encounter hesitation or resistance from a police source. You could try asking about the continuum of actions police use in similar situations (physical presence, then physical force, and finally deadly force). This information relates to the shooting incident you are trying to cover, allows you to assess how this particular situation was handled under current police department policies and provides excellent background information that could be used in later stories. In all interview situations, obtain and use the best information that you can.

n. Do not answer your own questions. Avoid loaded questions in which the answer is presupposed. Let the interviewee supply the answers.

o. Ask questions that are brief and specific. Do not ask overlong questions. Ask one question at a time. Avoid double-barreled questions in which two actions are equated. For example, do not ask, *Should the governor sign the bill and pursue a policy of noninvolvement in local affairs?*

p. Ask questions that require specific, short answers. If you encounter simple *yes/no* responses, ask for a restatement, clarification, or qualification of the comment or simply ask, *Why do you feel that way?* Generally, restated answers provide responses that are shorter, to the point, and more usable on the air.

q. Ask for clear explanations of technical terms and jargon. Ask that your source provide an example or describe an event or situation that will help you understand.

r. At the end of the interview ask, *Is there anything else I should know or that you want to add?* The comments that follow may provide useful insights.

s. At the end of a television interview, ask the photographer or videographer, *Any questions you'd like to ask?* You can always reject the questions suggested, but at least you have another perspective to consider that you may have overlooked. Also, this technique demonstrates your efforts to involve others working on the story with you.

Interviews need to be recorded. A combination of written notes and recordings works best. Have your equipment ready before the interview. Get permission to record interviews. During the interview, make written notations about potentially usable comments. Note the counter number on your recorder and a brief phrase about what was said. Later you can review your notes and the tape and decide which comments to use. This technique works best if you "zero" the tape counter at the start of the interview and use a different note page for each interview topic. Even when the interview is recorded, take a few notes to indicate you are interested in what's being said. Do not rely on your memory!

When you interview a news source, you need to get and keep cooperation and to stay in control of the situation. Here are suggestions for strategies to use: **Strategies**

a. Demonstrate that you have done your homework, that you have taken steps to brief yourself about the interview situation, the news source, and the issues involved. Project the image of a professional journalist trying to understand an event or situation.

b. Project an image of a human being, not just a journalist who is informed, intelligent, reasonably friendly and compassionate, and anxious to get comments for a story.

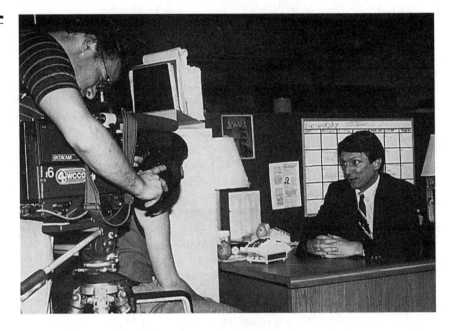

Often interviews are done in the newsroom rather than in the field.

c. Take steps to make the source feel at ease—about your equipment, the interview setting, the questions to be asked, and about you as a reporter.

d. Build rapport. Establish a cooperative, harmonious relationship between you and the news source. If time permits, *briefly* talk about things that are of strong personal interest to your source or activities that you both share that may relate to the story being covered. Try to understand your news source's perspective. Get the source to share your interest and enthusiasm for the story— why the story is important, what you need to know, et cetera. Avoid arguing. It restricts the comments you will be able to get and may preclude worthwhile future contacts. In most situations, avoid hostility and suspicion.

e. Remain neutral. During in-person interviews, watch your body language and facial expressions as well as your vocal inflections and the words you use. They reveal your attitudes and expectations. Do not offer your opinions, and do not respond to the interviewee's expressions of opinions.

Handling Details after the Interview

After the interview, you will need to do the following:

a. Make certain that you have a good recording and comments on key questions you wanted to ask. Do not leave an interview situation until you have what you need to write the story!

b. Review the recording of the interview and your notes to determine the recorded comments you will use. Labeling the interview tape and keeping it for a few days is a good idea.

c. If time permits, verify the accuracy of the comments made by checking with other sources, or checking back with your interviewee. Some reporters record, on tape, the name, title, and telephone number of the interview source in case further clarification is needed or a question arises about whether permission had been granted for the interview to be recorded.

d. Write the story incorporating excerpts from the interview. Determine how the story will be "packaged." Will you need to prepare a reader, soundbite, or wrap story? While the interview details are still fresh in your mind prepare multiple versions of the story for use in later newscasts. As you write your stories, be sure to retain the tone, spirit, and accuracy of the original interview comments.

The Beats

Some newsrooms develop news sources by using general assignment reporters who are assigned on a random basis to cover preplanned events or breaking stories. Other newsrooms assign reporters to *beats* so that specific news sources are contacted regularly. Each newsroom decides how it will handle reporter assignments on the basis of staff and market size, news priorities, and preferences of the news management team. If you work under a beat system, you should know the types of beat systems commonly used and how to organize and develop contacts on your beat.

Types of Beats

Two beat systems are in common use: regular, or assigned, beats; and special beats. The precision with which the beats are identified and the specific beats used in each newsroom will vary according to the factors mentioned above. Some beats will be added and others deleted; sometimes a combination of the two systems is used.

Regular, or assigned, beats include several traditional categories, for example, government; courts; police and crime news; business; labor; education; health and medicine; environment; youth; entertainment; transportation; minority concerns; religion. Some newsrooms use broader beat categories, for example, careers (jobs, training, self-improvement, legislation affecting careers); recreation and leisure time; relationships and companionship (social issues, the elderly, etc.).

Special beats are generally temporary assignments lasting only for the duration of special news coverage. Examples include a two-day visit by an important group of foreign investors to local manufacturing plants, the three-week trial of a suspect in an extraordinary local murder case, or the election campaign of a particular gubernatorial candidate.

Organizing Beats

The efforts of individual reporters as well as the newsroom help organize regular or assigned beats. Most reporters keep personal "black books" or card files for worthwhile contacts on their beats. Newsrooms and individual reporters check news sources by using *call sheets*.

Call sheets list individuals and agencies to call on a regular basis, often several times each day. These call sheets generally list who to call, when it is best to call, for example, just before the shift change at the local police department, and phone numbers to use (office *and* home). These beat calls help reporters to check story details, fish for potential stories, and keep track of developing stories.

Here are some guidelines to help you use call sheets effectively to develop news sources:

a. Brief yourself about current developments *before* you call. Check recent stories. Examine newsroom files or talk to the reporter previously assigned to a particular beat.
b. Call sources regularly, even when you do not have a specific story in mind. The day you don't call is the day you'll miss an important story.
c. Make occasional in-person visits. This helps reinforce your visibility and remind news sources that you are always anxious to hear about potential news items. It's also a good way to get acquainted with additional sources on your beat.

Developing Beats

Although call sheets provide quick access to news sources on a beat, there is no substitute for personal contact. Developing sources requires persistence as well as tact and ingenuity. Once a regular beat is assigned, identify who to cultivate as sources and plan how you will cultivate or develop them.

Who to Cultivate as Sources

Once you get acquainted with your assigned beat, you can better identify the people to develop as news sources. Check with the reporter who previously had the beat. Review previous stories related to your beat. Visit with your news director about the parameters and expectations of your beat. Look at documents that provide background about the people and issues you might encounter. Talk to those now out of the limelight; this might include former officials, those representing minority viewpoints, and lobbyists. Most of this kind of work will be done on your own time, at home, nights and weekends.

Learn the "politics" of your beat. Determine who really wields the most clout. Differentiate between how various agencies on your beat are supposed to operate and how they actually operate.

Get to know the people on your beat who handle day-to-day business— police dispatchers, secretaries, clerks, midlevel civil servants. They can help identify the politics of your beat and often are the sources for many of your beat stories.

Talk to obvious key people on your beat. If you are covering transportation, talk with the managers of the local airport and mass transit system. If you are covering the police beat, visit with the heads of local and area law enforcement agencies. Know who they are, what they do, what they like and dislike, and how they expect to be treated by the media. Find out their interests, concerns, and priorities. Let them fill gaps that may exist in background information you have reviewed.

Identify those on your beat who will readily tip you off about a story and can supply information quickly, accurately, and in detail.

Handle logistics. If you are covering courts, determine where court documents are kept. If you are covering city government, find out who the current officeholders are and where they hold meetings.

How to Cultivate Sources

Establish strong personal but professional relationships with key sources. Project an image of a responsible journalist trying to gather worthwhile information.

Talk about your beat. Get sources to share your interest and enthusiasm for informing the public about important events. Stress the need to report accurately, fairly, and completely.

Come prepared! Anticipate stories from your beat. Have the necessary reporting tools such as equipment, notepad, et cetera.

Be ready for some ''small talk'' on your beat. People like to feel that you are interested in them not only as news sources but also as human beings. Many reporters keep track of birthdays, anniversaries, and so forth and remember to mention these events as they occur. Allow enough time to cover your beat effectively.

If you have a business card, leave it with your sources. It might remind them to call you when something of interest develops.

Always be ''on the job.'' If you encounter a potential news source who plays on your amateur basketball team, get a name and telephone number. If a member of your church is also the head of the highway patrol, make a note about that. If you need their input on future stories, you will have a ready list of sources to consult.

Avoid being ''cultivated.'' You are ultimately obliged to serve your audience, not your news sources. Avoid being used as a way for news sources to obtain personal gratification, to grind axes, attack enemies, or promote pet projects. Establish friendly, comfortable relationships on your beat, but avoid cronyism. Do not allow the demands of friendships to interfere with your news judgment. Be aware of this danger and learn to cope with it. Neither affection nor fear should be allowed to influence a reporter's work. Chapter 20 examines conflicts of interest in more detail.

Handling News Sources

Reporters often encounter sources during interviews or on their beats who are reluctant to comment or who agree to comment but also ask for confidentiality or anonymity. You should know the ground rules as well as how to handle these kinds of situations.

Most news sources will cooperate with you, *if* you approach them in a way that makes them feel comfortable about what they are doing. However, you need to be prepared to handle objections from sources when they arise. This section suggests a number of techniques that can be useful in situations like this.

Reluctance

Sources may be reluctant to talk to reporters for several reasons. They may fear retribution from their superiors or the loss of their jobs. They may want you to contact an official spokesperson. Another reporter may have treated them badly on a previous story in which they willingly cooperated. Some sources, who do not routinely talk to reporters, may think that their comments are not that newsworthy.

Several strategies may help overcome a source's reluctance. The police department dispatcher on duty can be asked to simply confirm what you already know from monitoring the newsroom scanners. The supervisory nurse on duty can at least confirm the condition report of an accident victim. If the dispatcher says you will have to contact the duty sergeant who is out in the field, stress that you have a deadline and that you will make efforts to contact the sergeant but that you need the dispatcher's perspective and information as well. If the nurse says only the attending physician can release condition reports, stress that you will call the physician but that you need the condition report now to complete your story for the next newscast. Never let a source off the hook so easily!

If you are asking for confirmation of information you already know, you might attribute your question to another person. For example, you might say to the dispatcher, "The store clerk I just talked to says the suspect drove off in a blue car. Is that what you have?" To the nurse, you could say, "The ambulance driver I just talked with said the accident victim was injured seriously. Is that the current listing of her condition?"

If people like the dispatcher or the nurse indicate that they were treated shabbily by another reporter, be sure to say that you are sorry they had that kind of experience, but quickly add that you are not that reporter and that you make special efforts to report the facts as accurately and completely as humanly possible. Emphasize your commitment to ethical reporting and fair treatment of news sources.

If sources hesitate to comment because they feel their comments are not especially newsworthy, convince them that they have insights and information that are newsworthy and that no one else has. A little persuasiveness on your part will help an eyewitness to a robbery or a plane crash give you what you need. Generally, once they start talking, it is difficult to stop them.

Confidentiality and Anonymity

Remember that if you have clearly identified yourself as a reporter, everything a newsmaker says to you can be used in a story unless the newsmaker indicates *in advance* that the comments are confidential or that anonymity is requested.

You should know the ground rules associated with such requests and how to handle them.

These requests can occur at any point during your contact with a news source—at the beginning of a conversation on your beat, even in the middle of an interview. Be alert to these requests, and be sure that both you and your source understand the implications of such requests.

Unfortunately, several phrases are used interchangeably to request various levels of confidentiality and anonymity. The words *not for attribution, background,* or *background briefing* generally indicate that the newsmaker's comments can be used but not attributed directly to that source. Thus we hear phrases like these in stories: *A source close to the mayor . . . ,* or *According to an informed source in the governor's office, . . . ,* or *A spokesperson at the military installation. . . .* On the other hand, the words *off the record* and *deep background* generally indicate that you cannot use in *any* way in a story the information a source provides. The comments are strictly for the reporter's background information. They might help prepare more comprehensive reports in the future or confirm comments obtained with attribution elsewhere.

When faced with these requests, reporters have several alternatives:

a. Reconfirm what the request means for both parties and abide by the requirements of the request.
b. Try to convince the source to stay ''on the record'' so you can use the comments in your story.
c. Refuse the request and leave the source immediately with the clear indication that you do not want your ''hands tied'' and will try to get the comments needed from someone who will go ''on the record.'' Sometimes, sources will then withdraw such requests and stay ''on the record.'' Some reporters contend that if they readily accept such requests, the audience cannot evaluate the importance or credibility of a source or identify a source's ulterior motives.

If you do abide by such requests, be aware that there are inherent dangers. If you are able to obtain the information you need from another source that does permit attribution, the original ''off the record'' source may think that you have broken your trust. This attitude may shut you out from worthwhile future contact. Get the source back ''on the record'' as soon as possible so you will have attributable information with which to write your story.

Play fair with your sources. Cutting corners on confidentiality produces empty victories followed by regrets and eventually penalties. If you abuse agreements for confidentiality and anonymity, you will get the reputation of being a reporter who backstabs sources. Soon you won't have any more sources.

Chapters 19 and 20 offer additional considerations and concerns associated with confidentiality, anonymity, and the privacy rights of news sources.

Enterprising Stories

Developing news sources effectively to produce meaningful stories depends on the individual reporter's commitment and efforts to observe carefully, manage interviews well, and stay in close touch with news sources. It comes down to enterprise—ferreting out worthwhile stories and adding impact, meaning, color, and dimension to otherwise routine story details. Enterprising a story often involves the use of nontraditional approaches and scarce resources. *Enterprising* means pursuing a unique story opportunity often under severe deadline pressure to gather material and make it work on-the-air. Enterprise is the watchword for successful investigative reporters.

Methods

A reporter may cultivate an enterprising spirit in several ways. Some newsrooms require specific kinds of information from reporters that help in the effort. Generally, the individual reporter's initiative is what fosters a healthy spirit of enterprise.

Some newsrooms require reporters to file "story notes" about each story covered. Story notes help provide a summary of the story filed. They also indicate contacts made while covering the story and suggestions for follow-up stories. Each reporter compiles such records and then keeps them in personal beat files or gives them to the assignment editor or executive producer who can then post them or merge them with other reporters' material into one consolidated report or into the electronic assignment system in the newsroom. Other newsrooms require reporters to suggest story ideas and contacts based on the reporter's personal readings of wire copy and publications, contacts and comments on beats, and previous coverage by that newsroom or competing newsrooms. The success of either system depends on each reporter's alertness, aggressiveness, news sense, experience, and professional commitment.

In large metropolitan areas, newsrooms often maintain a current list of the numbers and locations of pay phones that ring areas where news events routinely occur. For example, in Washington, D.C., such a list would provide ready access to eyewitnesses at a protest rally or memorial service near one of the national monuments. Reporters who use this technique find that after momentary hesitation, most people cannot resist picking up the phone and at least finding out who is calling. Once contact is made, your telephone interview techniques will be challenged to the fullest.

Sometimes, reporters go "around" an obvious source who absolutely will not comment. For example, on a Sunday morning, if you need information about a suspect arrested for D.W.I. (driving while intoxicated) the night before, you might contact the booking officer at the jail where the suspect is held or the nurse on duty at the detoxification center if you learn the suspect might have been placed there. Your approach might be to say, "I want to make sure I have the correct spelling of the name of the suspect brought in around midnight. Do you have that handy?" It is best not to overuse this tactic. Save it for when you need it. Also, be prepared to have your "bluff" found out.

Look beyond the obvious. If on Monday morning, when you review the arrests made over the weekend, you discover that the suspect arrested for D.W.I. has the same last name and address as the local mayor, you might have a story!

To better illustrate how to enterprise news stories, we will trace the efforts and stories of a radio newsroom and a television newsroom. The story situations are different—in the medium used, as well as in the nature of the story and the approaches used by the reporters—but they show the kind of work broadcast news reporters, especially investigative reporters, can do.

Examples

When this investigative report won an Edward R. Murrow Award in Television, the Radio-Television News Directors Association (RTNDA) judges said that this WCCO-TV investigation "was broadcast journalism at its best." Judges were struck not only by the thorough research but also by "the responsible use of a video sting operation leading to chilling admissions from a pardoned child molester that he was abusing children again. The investigation disclosed improper behavior by high state officials, resulted in immediate changes in the law, and—most importantly—revealed the victimization of innocent Minnesotans by pardoned criminals.[1]

WCCO-TV's "Secret Crimes" Series

Investigative reporter Steve Eckert described his three-part series of reports:

> Imagine someone secretly erasing convictions for serious crimes, including rape, kidnapping and murder. Imagine someone secretly sealing all court records about the crimes—even removing them from state and federal crime computers.
>
> In Minnesota, it wasn't imaginary; it was real. . . . The WCCO Television I-Team began a series which revealed that the records of hundreds of convicted criminals had been secretly erased by the Minnesota Board of Pardons. The response was swift . . . and dramatic. Within three days, the Minnesota House voted—131-to-nothing—to abolish the secret pardon system.
>
> In order to document the story, the WCCO Television I-Team fought in court to force the state to open Pardon Board files. Then, the I-Team painstakingly reviewed more than 400 Pardon Board cases. And, finally, the I-Team documented how some criminals—armed with their pardons—were committing new crimes.
>
> We believe the I-Team's "Secret Crimes" is an example of investigative reporting at its best.[2]

Figure 10.1 is a transcript of a portion of the first report.

DIS to St. Peter

(short nat ..)

David Fritz was committed to the State Hospital in St. Peter. Doctors said he suffered from pedophila—an extreme sexual interest in children.

(O'Malley/t26 .. 00:09:56)
"that's a very scary situation .."

Jack O'Malley heads a federal strike force that investigates child pornography. He says pedophiles often repeat their crimes—even after treatment.

(O'Malley/t26 .. 00:10:10)
"We must know who these people are, and they must be kept track of."

DIS to Fritz
mug shot ..

David Fritz was kept at the state hospital for nearly 7 years.

DIS to paper

But in 1985—just one year after his release—Fritz sent this application to the Board of Pardons .. asking that all of his criminal convictions be erased.

XCU on words

He wrote: "I was sexually involved with kids . . ." But, he continued, "Now I know better!!"

Others weren't so sure about David Fritz ..

DIS to EFX

In this letter, a county prosecutor opposed the pardon, saying Fritz was still potentially "dangerous." He said officials at St. Peter had wanted to keep Fritz even longer because he still had "a strong potential" for abusing children.

stand-up

(stand-up ..)
But on February 26, 1986—2 years and 42 days after David Fritz had been released from the state hospital—all 3 members of the Board of Pardons voted to issue this Pardon Extraordinary .. a pardon which said David Fritz was of "good character and reputation."

EFX

As with all such pardons .. the Court records about David Fritz's crimes were sealed.

Figure 10.1 A transcript of a portion of the first in a three-part series entitled "Secret Crimes." Courtesy of WCCO-TV, Minneapolis.

jail ..	
	As with all such pardons .. David Fritz was given the right to say he'd never been sent to jail.
computer room	
	And .. as with all such pardons .. David Fritz's crimes were erased from the state's centralized crime computer.
computer	
	(short nat .. at computer)
	From now on, if a police officer would ask if David Fritz had a criminal history .. the computer would answer "no record exists."
DIS to Fritz	
	In effect, David Fritz had become an invisible criminal .. invisible to police .. invisible to the communities where he lived .. invisible to everyone but his victims.
DIS to locations	
	(short nat ..)
	Since his pardon, David Fritz has lived near the Twin Cities .. near Grand Rapids .. near Hibbing.
	He was even allowed to host a high school foreign exchange student.
	In every town he's lived, the I-Team found boys who met David Fritz ..
DIS to interview (pixilated)	
	(pix int/t54 .. 00:42:25) "Every position you could think of, they had the kid doing it with an adult."
	This boy says he went to Fritz's house 3 years after the pardon, and saw pornographic photos of children—even video tapes.
	(Pix int/t54 .. 00:42:30) "they were home-made videos of him with kids."
eckert stand-up	
	(stand-up . . .) The I-Team has learned that, in the years since his pardon, police in several communities have received new tips about David Fritz and young kids.
	But the police did not know about his past. And, because of the pardon, they couldn't find out.
	(boy1/t52 .. 00:14:07) "I think about it now and it's like he did it to me, you now, and who else is he doing it to?" We wondered too . . .

Figure 10.1 continued.

Confrontations between advocates and opponents of abortion clinics continue to receive extensive news coverage. Such stories require enterprise, sensitivity, and patience for reporters to provide reasonably complete and balanced stories.

KFDI Radio News Director Dan Dillon guides us through his station's coverage of such a case. Transcripts of each soundbite and voicer report were drawn from an audiotape of each story supplied by KFDI Radio:[3]

The 1991 Operation Rescue coverage was the most difficult story I've ever been involved with. I've never been involved with such an emotional issue. Each time we aired something, either pro-choice or anti-abortion, people would call complaining about our coverage. Whenever Operation Rescue blockaded a clinic in Wichita, they did so with no warning. Every morning we would do assignments, and then have to juggle them because Operation Rescue was at it again. Many of our listeners grew weary of hearing about the arrests each day, and the rhetoric. Our coverage was segmented. . . . Much of it was live. . . .

The memory of that '91 coverage came back when Dr. George Tiller was wounded [in August 1993]. Connie Weber was the first reporter at the scene. She was three blocks away covering a near drowning. [This is one story she filed the next morning.]

> Dr. George Tiller is home from the hospital after he was shot outside his abortion clinic in the 51-hundred block of East Kellogg.
> Wichita Police Captain Jack Leon says Tiller was driving out of the lot around 7:15 last night when a woman pulled out a gun.
>
> CART/12 LEON :15 Q . . . LOCATION
>
> [''She actually walked up to the doctor as he was in his vehicle. She fired the shot that actually went through the driver's side window. He then continued to drive on . . . drove away from the scene, went around the block and came back to this location.'']
> Several clinic employees chased the woman south down Bleckley, but she got away.

Ken Vandruff covered the preliminary hearing for Shelley [Rochelle] Shannon . . . the woman charged with the shooting.

> The woman accused of shooting Dr. George Tiller is headed back to Wichita. Police Lieutenant Ken Landwehr says 37-year-old Rochelle Shannon apparently rented a National Rental car at Will Rogers Airport in Oklahoma City early Thursday. She was at the clinic several times,

```
the last at about seven p-m when she allegedly shot
Tiller. . . . Landwehr says Shannon was arrested at about
12:30 this morning, after turning the car back in at the
airport rental desk.

CART 24/LANDWEHR    :13   Q . . . TO WICHITA.

[''It is my understanding that she has waived
extradition, or has made a motion to waive extradition.
Details will have to be worked out with the district
attorney here and there to facilitate her return to
Wichita.'']
```

There's an interesting "aside" to this story. After the Shannon woman was arrested in Oklahoma City, she was scheduled for a first appearance in court in Wichita Monday . . . three days after the shooting. When I arrived, a friend of mine who works for Judge Paul Clark told me confidentially [that] the Judge had already conducted the first appearance for the woman in a different courtroom, and an hour early because he was worried about protestors jamming his courtroom, and possible trouble from radicals on both sides. . . . Reporters from newspapers in Oregon (where the woman is from) and others locally were outraged to learn they couldn't get a photo of the woman in court. All were very angry a "public hearing" was done in secret. Afterwards, most ran to the Administrative Judge of the 18th Judicial District complaining about the actions of Judge Clark. I didn't leave the Judge's outer chambers. After 45 minutes he walked out, said hello, and said "I bet you're wondering why I moved Shannon's first appearance." I said, "Yes, but I don't want to know unless you tell me on the record." He proceeded to explain his reasoning . . . along with his attempt to get some of the attention focused on him instead of Ms. Shannon. He said it was his attempt to provide her with a fair trial. The preliminary hearing that Ken [Vandruff] handled . . . was handled by a different judge. The explanation from the Judge was the only one he gave. KFDI's call letters were included in stories across the country.

The bottom line is: You can get more stories with honey than you can with vinegar. I do my best to get along with potential newsmakers. Whenever I'm in the courthouse, I try to get in to just say hello to the judges, the District Attorney, and the Sheriff. It pays off down the road. This incident is a good example. Judge Clark has said over the years, "You can trust Dan Dillon and the rest of the reporters at KFDI."

```
Concern over safety caused a Sedgwick County District
Court Judge to move a woman charged with shooting Dr.
George Tiller into another courtroom. (KFDI's Dan Dillon
has the story.)
```

CART 34/DILLON VOX :35 TAG OUT

[''Judge Paul Clark says if the shooting Saturday night of
an abortion doctor is connected to the battle over
abortion rights . . . then that's a possible indication
some groups are using terror as a political tool. Clark
says safety for the people in his courtroom and a fair
trial for Rachel Shannon are the reasons he moved her
first appearance into Judge Karl Friedel's courtroom an
hour early. Shannon was charged with attempted first
degree murder. Her bond is one-million dollars. She'll be
in court again September seventh for a preliminary
hearing. This is Dan Dillon.'']

Summary

This chapter has suggested approaches and techniques for better development of news sources once they have been identified and tentatively organized.

A reporter's observations can add special insights to a story. Specific suggestions were made about what to observe, how to observe, and how to select from your observations those images and comments that can enhance the meaning of a story.

Reporters must decide not only when to interview sources but also whether an interview is the most efficient way to gather facts and opinions. Several techniques were suggested for conducting interviews on the telephone as well as in person and for handling reporting details once an interview is completed.

Personal observations and interviews with news sources are used by general assignment reporters as well as reporters assigned to regular or special beats. Developing an assigned beat requires that you identify those who will provide worthwhile information on a regular basis. Several suggestions were offered for cultivating news sources on a beat.

Reporters need to exercise special care when handling news sources who are reluctant to comment or who request confidentiality or anonymity before any comments are made.

The techniques and strategies suggested in this chapter for developing news sources are best illustrated in stories that reporters enterprise. The insights that result from the initiative and energetic efforts of reporters produce stories that are more meaningful and have greater impact than those produced by reporters who have not developed an enterprising spirit.

Exercises

1. For several of the following news story situations, indicate the specific sources you would contact and the specific details you would gather through observation and interviews.

   a. You arrive on the scene of a chemical spill of toxic materials. Several fatalities and serious injuries have been reported.

   b. You approach the picket line at a local manufacturing plant at which local police are present to prevent the recurrence of recent violent incidents.

   c. You arrive at an isolated farmhouse that police have surrounded after receiving reports that shots have been fired and hostages are being held inside.

   d. You and area law enforcement officers are the first to arrive at the scene of a plane crash reported less than 30 minutes before.

2. Participate as the reporter or as the reluctant news source requesting confidentiality in one of the following role-playing interview situations that can be recorded and then critiqued.

   a. An eyewitness to a car-train crash

   b. A teacher dismissed today on sexual misconduct charges

   c. A city official charged today with mismanagement of public funds

   d. A clerk at a convenience store robbed just before closing

3. Take notes on a local news story either printed in a newspaper or broadcast on a radio or television station. Interview by phone at least two news sources associated with the original story (but not mentioned in the earlier report) who can provide more complete, updated information. If possible, record the entire telephone conversation with each of the two sources called. Provide the following material: your notes on the original story; your notes made during the telephone interviews; copy for a 30-second radio reader report; and your written critique of your telephone interview techniques based on suggestions offered in this chapter.

4. Select one of the following news beat assignments: courts; education; city government; health and medicine; law enforcement agencies; business and industry; public transportation; minority affairs and concerns; religion; environment. Do *one* of the following:

   a. Record an interview with a key source from the beat selected. Write a 30- to 45-second radio or television story based on your interview.

   b. For several weeks, collect and organize worthwhile news items from newspapers, magazines, appropriate groups and organizations, and radio and television broadcasts that relate to the beat selected. In a written presentation, indicate five specific stories suggested by the material collected that you deem worthy of news coverage by a local broadcast newsroom. Justify your story suggestions. Why is each story idea newsworthy?

   c. Follow the directions given in exercise 4(b); then develop and write one of the stories suggested.

5. Write a 30- to 45-second radio or television story based on comments made to you on tape during one of the following interview situations.

   a. A prominent local business representative discussing the economic initiatives and rewards possible when local governmental agencies and businesses work together to improve the financial health of your city

   b. A local hospital emergency room nurse discussing the results of motorcycle helmet and vehicle seat belt laws in your state

   c. The local election commissioner or coordinator commenting on the participation of young adults in recent elections

   d. A local fire department official discussing the problems associated with false alarms

   e. A local bar owner discussing the problem of selling alcohol to underage minors

6. Assemble a ten-item call sheet for sources to be contacted on a daily basis by local broadcast newsrooms.

7. Write a 15- to 30-second radio news story for your 6 P.M. newscast based on the following facts collected from city police officer Roxy Grieger (GREE-guhr):
· Philip Bartlett family involved in one-car accident.
· Happened at 4:10 P.M. today about two miles from Apple Street Beltway exit ramp.
· Killed was Mary Bartlett (no age given).
· Injured seriously was Philip Bartlett, 32, and both of his two children: John (age 2) and Brenda (age 7).
· Grieger says Philip was driving, had a blow-out, swerved to miss cars, lost control of his '95 Dodge Caravan wagon, rammed into a utility pole.
Now, indicate the sources you would contact to obtain missing or updated information to write a better story for the next morning's newscasts.

8. The senior member of your state's Congressional delegation will be in your town next week. You have been assigned to interview the senator. Trace your steps as you prepare for this exclusive 15-minute interview. What sources would you contact or consult? What information would you try to gather? How would you decide the topics or issues to use in the interview? Based on current political, economic, and diplomatic conditions, what ten specific questions would you ask?

Turn in a summary of the information you have gathered; a description of the process you used to prepare for the interview; and the ten questions you plan to ask.

Notes

1. Quoted in *Communicator*, October 1992, 41.

2. Reprinted by permission of WCCO-TV.

3. Reprinted by permission of Dan Dillon and KFDI Radio, Wichita, Kansas.

Part Three

Reporting

Chapter 11

Broadcast Newsroom Organization and Operation

Broadcast news stories begin and end in the newsroom, where decisions are made about the stories to be covered as well as how they will be written and prepared for broadcast. You need teamwork, coordination, and interaction inside as well as outside of the newsroom to get people and machines working together to produce an effective report of the day's important news events.

This chapter traces the broad outlines of broadcast newsroom organization and operation used in most newsrooms throughout the country. The first section outlines the organization and structure of the broadcast newsroom by describing typical jobs, responsibilities, and interactions among those who work together on a daily basis. The second section describes the operation of the newsroom by outlining the processes involved in developing news coverage.

Throughout this chapter, the focus is on the medium-size television newsroom. Generally, this is the size of newsroom encountered by most young journalists seeking their first jobs in broadcast news. Also, the structure and operation of such newsrooms provide a middle ground from which to consider more intricate organizational patterns in larger television and network newsrooms. In most cases, radio newsrooms use more compressed and abbreviated organizational structures and operational procedures than those described in this chapter.

Introduction

Market as well as staff size are important considerations when describing newsroom organization and operation. Generally, the larger the market and news staff, the more complex and specialized newsroom responsibilities and job titles become. Large newsrooms employ more people with more specialized responsibilities; smaller newsrooms demand more abilities from fewer people, who have to assume an increasing number of duties. Television newsrooms tend to be structurally and operationally more complex than radio newsrooms. However, a large metropolitan radio station that broadcasts news throughout the day tends to resemble in structure and operation a medium-size television newsroom. A radio station in a small community may have a news team of one-and-one-third people—one person who handles most of the news duties and is assisted by part-time help when additional news coverage is needed.

In a national survey, Vernon Stone, Radio-Television News Directors Association (RTNDA) research director and University of Missouri journalism professor emeritus, concluded that during the early 1990s, the broadcast news workforce had grown slightly in television but shrank in radio. In 1992 the typical television news operation had 22 full-time and three part-time staff members. The typical radio news staff had one full-time and one part-time employees. Between 1987 and 1992, the typical television newsroom staff increased about one-fourth, whereas the typical radio newsroom staff decreased about one-fourth. News operations were found in approximately 80 percent of the television and 87 percent of the radio stations participating in the survey.[1]

Although those in management agree that, generally, news produces good financial results, and a quality news operation enhances a station's image in a community, newsrooms now operate with fewer people who have a wider variety of skills that are used in a flexible and efficient manner to produce a quality news product. Newsroom duties have been consolidated, especially in television. Some radio and television operations have been combined to better coordinate newsroom efforts and improve the efficiency and quality of the product. In most cases, combo newsrooms provide a strong, competitive edge in the marketplace.

The one-person news machine has become more common in both large- and small-market television newsrooms. Reporters are often expected to operate cameras and recorders, edit videotape, and even transmit reports by satellite while still writing and reporting their stories. Today's reporter must be multitalented to handle these expanded demands effectively.

The existence of craft unions also influences newsroom organization and operation. In larger stations and at the networks, union contracts generally dictate that engineers and technicians (who belong to the International Brotherhood of Electrical Workers [IBEW] or the National Association of Broadcast Employees and Technicians [NABET]) operate the equipment, while reporters and on-air talent (who may belong to either the Writers Guild of America or the American Federation of Television and Radio Artists [AFTRA]) control the news content and present stories on-the-air. Reporters tend to face more restrictive union requirements in larger markets and in television. In small- and medium-size markets, reporters are expected to gather and report story details as well as operate the equipment used in developing each story. More-sophisticated video equipment is operated by engineers, who are often unionized. Current restraints that are often placed on news personnel to gather and report the news but not operate equipment may change with increased use of automation, improved miniaturization and computerization of equipment, and future union contracts that may lighten such restrictions.

Newsroom management teams often spend as much time handling union contracts and consultants' reports as organizing and supervising daily news coverage. On-air talent contract demands and negotiations often require inordinate amounts of time and patience to resolve. Managers face intense competition in their local markets and are anxious to increase the amount of revenue generated by a strong local news operation. Management and newsroom personnel often find it difficult to resolve matters such as the selection of a news consultant and the manner in which a consultant's report is activated in a local news operation.

Despite this gloomy report, be encouraged that local radio and television news will continue to be a valued experience for listeners and viewers, as it has since news broadcasts began in the 1920s. Your work as a broadcast journalist will continue to contribute to a better understanding of important issues and events in the community. No matter how a news operation is organized, or how consolidated its operation becomes, be confident that broadcast news will remain a vital part of the telecommunications industry.

To do well in this ever-evolving environment, you need to understand how newsrooms are organized and the variety of operational patterns used. This will help you better determine your place in the electronic media newsroom in the future. You also need to make your writing and reporting skills the best they can become, which will ensure your satisfaction as a broadcast journalist.

Many of the jobs and procedures described in this chapter are blended and overlap according to the preferences and practices of individual newsrooms. Each newsroom determines its own unique structure and operational patterns to fulfill specific news objectives and commitments. Additional steps and techniques used to gather, process, and report specific kinds of news items are described in subsequent chapters (see Chapters 14 through 18). To make it easier to understand the various components of the broadcast newsroom, duties, responsibilities, and procedures have been isolated as much as possible without causing inaccuracies. In spite of the changes just noted in newsroom structure and operation, the jobs and specific tasks to be done remain the same as they have been in the last several years.

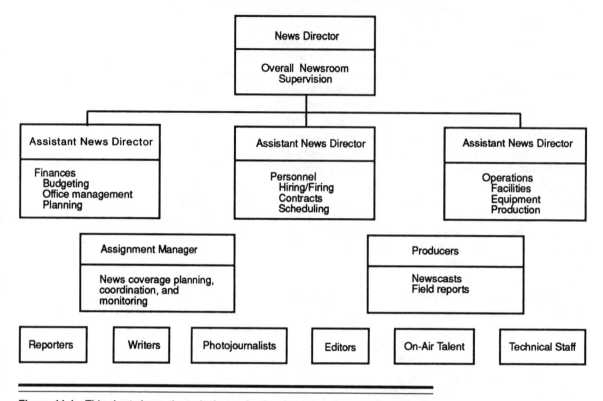

TYPICAL NEWSROOM ORGANIZATION AND STRUCTURE

News Director

Overall Newsroom Supervision

Assistant News Director

Finances
Budgeting
Office management
Planning

Assistant News Director

Personnel
Hiring/Firing
Contracts
Scheduling

Assistant News Director

Operations
Facilities
Equipment
Production

Assignment Manager

News coverage planning, coordination, and monitoring

Producers

Newscasts
Field reports

Reporters | Writers | Photojournalists | Editors | On-Air Talent | Technical Staff

Figure 11.1 This chart shows the typical organizational structure for a medium-sized television newsroom. Larger television newsrooms have more elaborate organizational structures. Smaller ones, and most radio newsrooms, use less complex structures. Lines indicating the chain of command are omitted because these arrangements vary greatly, depending on market size and managerial policies; this chart shows only the general levels of the hierarchy in most newsrooms.

Newsroom Organization

A broadcast newsroom is organized to facilitate the selection, coverage, processing, and broadcast of news stories. A chain of command helps to coordinate efforts (see Figure 11.1). Also, interaction among the newsroom staff should encourage the teamwork necessary to produce the final product—a news story. No matter how a newsroom is organized, all three components are necessary—*coordination, interaction, teamwork*. If any component is missing, newsroom efforts will falter. These three components are examined more closely later in this chapter.

News Director

The news director develops the structure of the newsroom and supervises the overall operation. He or she runs the entire newsroom and answers to the station manager or program director for the work of everyone on the news staff. In effect, the news director is responsible for what enters and leaves the news operation.

The news director handles personally or delegates to assistant or associate news directors the tasks necessary to hire, fire, and motivate newsroom personnel and to provide the money and equipment needed to cover the news.

To be effective, a news director needs special talents. Strong administrative and supervisory skills help mold and shape news philosophy and provide direction and motivation to the news staff. Extensive news experience helps cope with ever-changing news coverage situations. More than passing interest is needed in economics and business management; budgetary and personnel adjustments in the newsroom may be necessary. A news director must also be acquainted with the potential applications of new technology. A solid foundation in current communications law may help a news director to avoid potential legal entanglements.

Hiring, motivating, and keeping good news staff members require news directors to apply a special brand of leadership to a variety of situations. News directors build trust and confidence in their staff when they handle potential personal or newsroom problems early. They can also give staffers a sense of pride of ownership by providing some direction with room to mold and shape each story that they cover. This kind of nurturing attitude often produces fresh story ideas and even increased revenues for the news operation. Obviously, such nurturing by the news director needs to be reciprocated. You will probably not reciprocate this nurturing attitude when you encounter a news director who does not, in your opinion, meet or exceed these ideal standards. At least once in your career you'll probably work for a news director whom you cannot stand. Take it in stride. Learn what you can. Contribute what you know, and be a team player. Handle the personality quirks of newsroom personnel. It's part of any newsroom operation.

Assistant News Directors

The duties of the news director fall into three main categories—personnel, operations, and finances. If the news staff is large enough, an assistant or associate news director may be assigned to handle each area under the supervision of the news director. In some small and medium markets, an executive producer serves as an assistant news director *and* a supervisor of newscast producers.

Good people are a key to the success of a broadcast news operation. Their motivation and experience often make or break a news organization. Personnel responsibilities include hiring and firing members of the news staff; negotiating union contracts (if staff members are unionized); setting work schedules; adjusting job responsibilities to better match employee abilities, interests, and preferences; resolving employee disputes that may develop; and critiquing the quality of the work of each employee. Personnel matters, especially those dealing with on-air talent, must be managed carefully to handle legal, professional, and ethical concerns.

Assignment desk at KTVK-TV. Courtesy of KTVK-TV, Phoenix, Arizona.

Operational duties entail: purchase, maintenance, and repair of equipment and facilities; planning for future newsroom activities that rely on new technology developments or shifts in news coverage priorities; providing logistics, coordination, and scheduling to help make news coverage more efficient and productive; and monitoring the news production effort.

The most expensive part of a local station's operation is its broadcast newsroom. It takes money to equip and operate a quality newsroom, no matter how large or small the staff may be. The financial investment in the broadcast facility often determines the capabilities of a newsroom. Financial responsibilities include formulating news budgets (for people and equipment); monitoring news expenditures; recommending budget appropriations that make the news operation cost-effective; projecting future news expenditures; and handling office staff activities.

Assignment Manager

The principal job of the assignment manager is to assign, coordinate, and monitor news coverage. Instead of assignment *manager,* some newsrooms label this position assignment *editor* because this individual not only identifies potential stories but also controls or edits the coverage once it is under way.

The assignment desk is the hub of news coverage planning and execution. The assignment manager orchestrates news coverage logistics on a short-term as well as a long-term basis to handle both today's coverage and tomorrow's potential coverage. The assignment manager generally reports directly to one of the assistant news directors or to the news director.

In larger newsrooms, an assignment *manager* may be hired to identify, consider, and evaluate future stories and special events, while a news *planner* handles the scheduled, "predictable" news stories. The assignment manager would then be responsible for breaking stories and overall logistics for all daily news coverage. Larger newsrooms maintain a 24-hour assignment desk with assignment managers scheduled to handle overnight, dayside, and evening news coverage. If satellite news reports are a regular part of newsgathering efforts, a *satellite coordinator* may be employed to oversee these activities from the assignment desk.

In small newsrooms, the news director often handles the duties of an assignment manager or delegates them to a senior reporter. This system places extra burdens on the news judgment of young reporters and photojournalists who may not yet have developed the skills needed to cover their own stories and also plan the coverage of others.

The work of the assignment manager is complex and delicate. Most assignment managers begin their shifts after briefing themselves on news developments by reading newspapers and the wires, monitoring local radio and television newscasts, making calls to regular news contacts, and reviewing previous coverage by the newsroom as well as the future file and story tips supplied by reporters.

Once stories have been assigned at news staff meetings (discussed later in this chapter), the assignment manager continues to monitor the day's news developments and coverage by doing the following:

a. Watching the wires, listening to the newsroom scanners, and monitoring competing newsroom coverage for information updates as well as unplanned breaking stories.

b. Staying in touch with reporters in the field (often with paging devices and cellular phones) to assess the value of the stories assigned and either provide updated information about those stories and the way they will be "packaged" for upcoming newscasts or move crews to more worthwhile stories.

c. Keeping newscast producers informed about shifts in the day's news coverage. If "live" coverage is planned, the assignment manager works with field coordinators as well as technicians and producers to plan, prepare, coordinate, and monitor such field reports.

The assignment manager's shift is usually filled with constant pressure, instant decision making, unexpected frustration, and sometimes intense bickering among news staffers about such things as story assignments, equipment malfunctions, story placement in newscasts, and the mixture of temperaments of those assigned to work together.

The assignment manager must possess several important skills. Sound news judgment decisions must be made quickly, responsibly, and calmly. The ever-changing strengths/weaknesses, likes/dislikes, and personal relationships of each news staffer must be identified and monitored to team a reporter and photojournalist who work well together. There is a constant need to know what has already happened, what is happening, and to anticipate correctly what is going to happen in order to better plan and manage news coverage and production. Assignment managers must know local geography thoroughly and be able to rapidly organize the logistics necessary to get people and equipment to stories quickly and efficiently. A lot depends on the often hurried decisions made at the assignment desk! Working as an assignment manager prepares someone very well for the responsibilities of a reporter, photojournalist, or producer.

Some newsrooms find an alternative structure useful. Although less common than the arrangement just described, this alternative involves hiring a managing editor who coordinates a team of assignment managers who work at different times in a newsroom. Under this arrangement, an executive producer would be responsible for the individual producers and their specific newscasts, whereas the managing editor would handle newsroom budgeting, personnel, and operations matters just as a team of assistant news directors would. The executive producer and managing editor would report directly to the news director.

Reporters

In many ways, reporters are the ''foot soldiers'' of the newsroom—developing, writing, editing, and reporting stories assigned by the assignment desk. Reporters are expected to stay informed about news developments by reading newspapers, wire stories, and publications and monitoring competing news coverage.

Reporters participate in a limited way in story assignments. They can propose story ideas and make news production suggestions at daily news staff meetings, and they provide feedback to the assignment desk and producers once story coverage is under way and also when it is completed.

Once a story assignment has been made in a middle-market television news operation, the reporter is expected to do the following:

a. ''Research'' the story by reviewing all available information.
b. Plan coverage by calling contacts and sources to line up interviews and potential story angles and locations.
c. Gather the equipment and use the transportation scheduled to get to the story.
d. Work with the assigned photojournalist to mold and shape story content and visual treatment. (One-person story coverage is discussed in Chapter 13.)
e. Stay in touch with the newsroom throughout story coverage to receive informational updates and direction about story coverage and presentation.
f. Work with the assigned photojournalist as well as producers and editors to prepare each story for broadcast. In most cases, the reporter writes the story and then, with a tape editor or the photojournalist who covered the story, selects and edits the video portion of the report.

In small and medium-size radio newsrooms, reporters often go into the field and cover stories during a portion of their workday and then work as assignment managers and anchors during the rest of their workday. The smaller staff requires this kind of flexibility in newsroom duties.

Photojournalists

The photojournalist shoots and often edits the pictures and sounds used in the stories written by a reporter. The photojournalist's work requires knowledge and experience in handling electronic and video equipment. You'll need a solid but flexible background in video and sound recording, lighting techniques, and creative editing to mold and shape the story *with* the reporter. Chapter 13 describes the teamwork needed by both reporter and photojournalist to produce quality TV news reports.

Writers

Not many medium-market newsrooms have designated staffers who only write news copy, but some do. Except in larger news operations, newscasters, reporters, producers, managing editors, and even assignment managers write all of the copy that will be used on the air.

Some newsrooms use reporter/writer/tape editor *teams* to process and prepare each story. Together, all three scrutinize the content and "flow" of the story, consider alternatives for integrating tape with the reporter's narration, check news judgment, and ultimately mold and shape the story to provide an effective report that is acceptable to all three as well as to the newscast producer. The reporter provides essential story facts and details. The writer serves as a bridge, or liaison, between reporter and tape editor. The tape editor manipulates picture and sound to match decisions made by all three on the *presentation* of the story.

Producers

The producer organizes and supervises the overall content and production of each newscast. Newsrooms may employ several producers, each handling one or more newscasts or other newsroom duties.

The producer must be thoroughly familiar with the day's news events as well as the coverage planned by the newsroom. Thus, constant interaction occurs between each producer and the assignment manager who is in touch with news crews in the field. The producer monitors the raw material of the day's news coverage. Eventually, the producer must decide what stories to include in the newscast, in what order, and how to present each story with the most effective use of picture, sound, and graphics. Copy needs to be written and tape edited and approved.

The production of the newscast is also important. Deadlines must be established and enforced for all of the components of each story in the newscast (copy, tape, graphics). The presentation format for each story must be determined and communicated to all involved. The on-camera talent and the newscast director need preproduction information (illustrated in Chapter 18, "Newscasts"). The producer generally sits in the control room with the director, who puts the newscast on-the-air based on the material provided by the producer. Often, the producer must make last-minute changes in the newscast lineup as the program is on-the-air. Stories may not be ready, or live reports may last longer than expected or, worse, they may not get on-the-air at all because of a technical problem or a missed cue to a reporter in the field.

On weekends, news coverage is generally less intense; a producer will often handle the duties of the assignment manager as well as those of the on-air anchor or newscaster.

Larger news operations often hire a senior or executive news producer as well as assistant producers. As noted earlier, the senior or executive news producer generally reports to the news director or to one of the assistant news directors; duties include responsibility for the content and production of *all* newscasts as well as occasional special events coverage, such as election returns and special live field reports. Assistant producers may be assigned to each newscast producer to handle various routine duties. This could include: the preparation of newscast stories—copy, tape, and graphics; and the writing and production of regular and special newscast segments as well as news specials or live reports.

An effective producer must have many talents: a knowledge of the technical capabilities of the broadcast newsroom; the ability to apply those capabilities to specific news coverage and reporting situations; the ability to organize people and machines to accomplish specific tasks quickly, efficiently, and effectively; flexibility in responding to ever-changing news coverage and reporting situations in enough time to minimize on-air errors; confidence based on experience in making the right decision consistently; sound journalistic experience to assess story developments and to finalize story presentation; and the ability to communicate those decisions to the people involved in producing and presenting the newscast. The producer is a news manager and organizer familiar with logistics, technology, production, and writing who strives for the best possible news product quality and coordinates the efforts of the newsroom team to ensure that such quality is provided consistently.

Technical Staff

While reporters concentrate on high journalistic quality, engineers and technicians strive for the highest possible technical quality. The newscast director and other technical and production employees work together as a team to get news reports on-the-air and to make them technically effective. The technical staff may be permanently assigned to newsroom operations or scheduled as needed by a facility's engineering supervisor to install, maintain, and operate the necessary equipment.

On-Air Talent

Newscasters as well as various specialty on-air talent are the most visible and usually the best-paid members of the news team. Some write and edit their own copy and tape, depending on their abilities and preferences as well as the needs and requirements of each newsroom.

Newscast directors work closely with producers and the production crew at WCCO-TV, Minneapolis, Minnesota.

Positions in Larger Newsrooms

The availability of a larger news staff plus the scheduling of more extensive news coverage in large market and network newsrooms permit additional specialized jobs and responsibilities. Some of these have already been described.

Senior editors and producers can help refine news coverage and content by screening the video from reporters and archives or reviewing copy to coordinate the work of various reporting teams covering the same or similar stories.

A unit producer may be assigned to cover, with a reporter, a specific beat, such as entertainment, finance and business, health and medicine. Stories from that assigned beat may be developed for regular newscast segments or special reports.

Field producers oversee production of in-the-field news coverage. They scout locations, set up interviews, complete preliminary research and writing for stories, and may produce a finished package voiced later by a reporter. If a newsroom operates its own satellite-fed newsgathering unit, a field producer may be assigned to accompany the news crew when the satellite truck rolls out to cover a story.

Graphic artists and electronic titling operators generate television graphics. These individuals use their visual and technical talents to tap the electronic capabilities of today's sophisticated graphics equipment.

As indicated earlier, larger newsrooms often employ newswriters who work under the guidance of a copy editor, managing editor, or producer to log and then select available tape material; assemble and then write stories from

Reporter Tom Olson talks to an editor about the file video needed for a story. Photo courtesy of KTVK-TV, Phoenix, Arizona.

several sources, including wire copy, reporters' notes, and telephone interviews; work with reporters to shape the writing of a story; and write copy for live reports or newscast stories that use only an anchor or anchor with graphics. To be effective, a writer must know the technical capabilities and preferences of the newsroom as well as acceptable news copy formats.

Copy and tape editors may be available. They work with copywriters, reporters, and producers to rewrite wire copy; identify important story details for locally produced stories; select tape material and graphics to integrate into each story; and review copy for all stories included in newscasts. They are concerned about the ''flow'' or ''sense'' of copy and tape within each story.

Newsroom assistants are available to help the assignment manager or newscast producers. They answer the phones, handle wire copy, monitor the scanners, distribute newscast copy and memorandums, and handle various clerical chores.

Newsroom Operation

No matter how large or small a newsroom staff might be or how it is organized, people and machines must be set in motion to gather and report the news. The essential steps or phases involved in planning and coordinating news story coverage are shown in Figure 11.2. The typical medium-market television newsroom will be used again to describe the operational procedures generally followed. Larger newsrooms tend to follow more intricate procedures; radio newsrooms tend to follow more-compressed, accelerated processes than those outlined here.

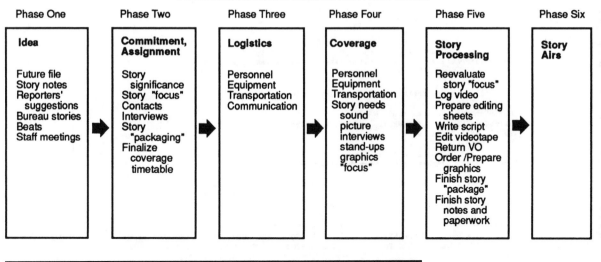

TYPICAL NEWS STORY PRODUCTION FLOW CHART

Phase One	Phase Two	Phase Three	Phase Four	Phase Five	Phase Six

Idea
 	
Future file
Story notes
Reporters'
  suggestions
Bureau stories
Beats
Staff meetings
	Commitment, Assignment
	
	Story
	  significance
	Story "focus"
	Contacts
	Interviews
	Story
	  "packaging"
	Finalize
	  coverage
	  timetable
		Logistics
		
		Personnel
		Equipment
		Transportation
		Communication
			Coverage
			
			Personnel
			Equipment
			Transportation
			Story needs
			  sound
			  picture
			  interviews
			  stand-ups
			  graphics
			  "focus"
				Story Processing
				
				Reevaluate
				  story "focus"
				Log video
				Prepare editing
				  sheets
				Write script
				Edit videotape
				Return VO
				Order /Prepare
				  graphics
				Finish story
				  "package"
				Finish story
				  notes and
				  paperwork
					Story Airs

Figure 11.2 Typical news story production flowchart.

Phase One

First, the newsroom staff must have a story idea. Although the assignment manager ultimately must determine the stories to cover, anyone on the news staff can suggest story ideas.

A story idea may come from any number of sources: the future file; reporters; the newsroom's bureaus in nearby towns or more distant locations; developments monitored from assigned beats; and daily news staff meetings. Some of the best stories are often suggested by those who work *outside* of the newsroom, for example, receptionists, custodians, sales personnel, and studio production crew members. The assignment manager draws the best ideas from these various sources to make worthwhile and viable news story assignments.

An *outlook* sheet (also called *insights, stacks,* or *skeds* in some newsrooms) is an effective way to keep track of both potential story ideas and available personnel. An example appears in Figure 11.3. Newsroom computers make such a system easier to use and maintain.

Daily news staff meetings help pull together people, ideas, and facilities to formulate the "game plan" of news coverage. Some newsrooms have the news director, assistant news directors, assignment manager, producers, and in some cases reporters and photojournalists come together around nine or ten o'clock each morning to review story ideas and finalize assignments. Then a brief meeting at about two or three o'clock that same day of the assignment manager, evening newscast producer, and principal on-camera newscasters updates the day's news coverage and begins the process of assembling the stories for upcoming newscasts. Smaller newsrooms tend to have fewer such meetings and follow a less formal process. Larger newsrooms tend to have

```
OUTLOOK      =THURSDAY, November 19          UPDATE=3:30
*********************************************************
SICK=
VACATION=Pratt
OFF=Callan, Matt, Porter, Wood, Hinckley,Taylor
CUTINS=O´leary
SUBS=Simon shoots sports.
NITESIDE=Van Brocklin, Harui, ABrown, Granfors, Burnside
PUBLIC AFFAIRS=Baxter
OUT OF TOWN=
NOTE=Rich Pauli will be in at 10am
*****************************************************
HFR
***********************************************************
SATELLITE  FROM:            TIME:          SATELLITE INFO:
=Washington, DC.            =TBA           =TBA
=                           =              =
***********************************************************
EE? -- TBA -- FERRY EXPANSION.  STATE FERRY FOLKS ARE SUPPOSED TO PROPOSE
ADDING AN EXTRA CAR DECK TO THE ISSY CLASS FERRIES.  IT WOULD INCREASE CAPACITY
30%, THE EQUIVILENT OF ADDING TWO MORE ISSY BOATS TO THE MIX.  THIS IS
HAPPENING AT A STATE DEPT. OF TRANSPORT MEETING THURSDAY, THOUGH THE LXR WOULD
HAVE TO GIVE FINAL APPROVAL.  IS THERE ALSO A SIDEBAR TO DO ON THE BOATS?

GRAPHIC OF WHAT THE ADDITION WOULD LOOK LIKE?

UN -- REMOTE -- CHRISTMAS TREE. The tree in Occidental Park will be lighted
Thursday night around 5:15. EGODS, A REMOTE.

UN -- TBA -- CONVENTION CENTER. Regular meeting of convention board. We might
want to do a story on the whole issue of private/public ownership/operation of
the center.

MF -- ON SET -- GREAT AMERICAN SMOKEOUT. Enuf Said. Micki will do the serious
side of cleaning up offices.  Suggest Larry might cover relay races, games
planned to go along with it.  GOOD IDEA.

UN -- TBA -- SOVIET JEWRY. Seattle Action for Soviet Jewry talks about
refuseniks at Seattle nc. NAH.

UN -- TBA -- SENIORS/APPLE CUP. Horizon House nursing home dresses up in purple
and gold and visited by the Husky mascot as residents prepare for Saturday´s
game.  CUTE VO.

UN -- TBA -- CAR SMASH. Students car smash in front of the HUB at 10:30am.
IS THIS FOR THE APPLE CUP, OR GENERAL PRINCIPAL?  SHOOT IF WE CAN.  IF LARRY
CAN´T TURN A SMOKEOUT PIECE, MAYBE HE SHOULD PUT ALL THESE APPLE CUP THINGS
TOGETHER.

UN -- TBA -- CITY COUNCIL. Second round of budget deliberations begins. 9am.
Might be good to folo up the Rainier story.

UN -- TBA -- MOUNTAIN GOATS. 7pm meeting to talk over fate of Olympic Mountain
Goats.

UN -- TBA -- RED WOLF RELEASE. Another Red Wolf release. These guys will be
sent to South Carolina Thursday.
```

Figure 11.3 Example of an outlook sheet, which suggests potential story ideas and indicates staff assignments for a particular day's news coverage. Courtesy of KIRO-TV, Seattle, Washington.

more meetings throughout the day, attended by fewer people, to handle news-room shift changes and adjustments in news coverage priorities.

Figure 11.4 shows how KMOV-TV in St. Louis handles its daily news staff meetings.

Phase Two

No matter how it is done or where it originates, the viability of each story idea must be determined. The assignment manager must be convinced that a story idea is worth the time and effort of the news staff. Each story idea must be evaluated for news value and significance. In daily staff meetings, assignment managers will often ask why a particular story idea has particular merit, how it might be developed, who might be contacted for interviews and taped state-ments, and why the station's identifiable audience would care particularly about this story. Testing the viability of a story idea at this stage saves valuable time and resources later. Each story must be weighed against the news value of every other potential story. A commitment is made to a story idea only after such a process of evaluation.

Commitment leads to assignment. The assignment manager must think through how the story will be handled. The main idea or angle of the story needs to be determined. Preliminary contact may be needed with news sources to better identify the focus of the story. The preliminary timetable and logistics of covering the story must be determined and coordinated with other stories the rest of the news staff is covering that same day. A preliminary determi-nation must be made about how the final news report will be packaged (live, anchor copy with graphics, a reporter package, etc.).

WMAR-TV in Baltimore has developed the News Assignment-Follow-Up Sheet shown in Figure 11.5 to make newsroom assignments and to provide a process for communicating potential follow-up story ideas. At WMAR-TV, the assignment manager fills out the top half of the form, which tells the reporter the date, time, location, and synopsis of the story together with how the story will be packaged, the newscast on which the story will appear, and the news crew assigned. The assignment desk also provides a list of contacts for the story and appropriate phone numbers. Such a sheet is given to each reporter when assignments are made each day. At the point when WMAR-TV reporters return from their assignments, they fill in the lower half of the sheet shown in Figure 11.5. This provides immediate story information to newscast producers, who can use the information to prepare short teasers for upcoming newscasts and follow-up information, including additional con-tacts and phone numbers, for the assignment desk. This kind of information sheet increases the efficiency of a newsgathering operation.

Phase Three

Newsroom staff must consider the logistics of story coverage throughout the planning process. Logistics are kept in mind as story ideas are evaluated and then confirmed. They are often adjusted once a story has been assigned.

Logistics involve identifying and then orchestrating the components needed to cover each story: People have to be assigned, equipment has to be

Daily Meeting Times:

7:30 AM - <u>Conference Call</u> - Assignment Manager conducts meeting
attended by News Director, Assistant News Director,
Operations Manager and Assignment Coordinator.

9:00 AM - <u>Staff News Meeting</u> - Assignment Manager conducts
meeting. This will be a brief session for reporters
and photographers to get story assignments and make
story suggestions.

11:00 AM - <u>Producers Meeting</u> - Assistant News Director conducts
meeting attended by Assignment Manager, 5:00 PM and
6:00 PM Producers. Daily coverage explanation followed
by program split.

1:30 PM - <u>Blocking Session</u> - Executive Producer runs meeting.
5:00 PM and 6:00 PM Producers distribute rough rundowns.
Attendees: Assistant News Director, Operations Manager,
Assignment Manager, Anchors and Directors, if available.

Between 2:30 PM and 3:00 PM - <u>Production Update</u> - Executive Producer
runs meeting with 5:00 PM and 6:00 PM
Producer and Directors, if possible.

Immediate after Production Update - <u>NIGHTSIDE Meeting</u> - Assistant
News Director runs meeting attended by
Operations Manager, Assignment Manager,
Night Assignment Coordinator, Night
Reporters and Night Photographers.

5:30 PM - <u>Planning Session</u> - Operations Manager conducts meeting with
News Director, Assistant News Director,
Executive Producer, working off prepared
story rundown for next day.

NOTE: Each news program followed by Executive Producer critique
session.

Figure 11.4 Example of a schedule of daily news staff meetings designed to plan and coordinate local news coverage. Courtesy of KMOV-TV, St. Louis, Missouri.

NEWSCENE 2 – Assignment/Follow-Up Sheet

Date:	Time:	Crew:

Location:	Story Form:

Story Slug:	Newscast Intended:

Story Synopsis:

Contacts:

Reporter Notes: (Brief summary of how story developed. List those people interviewed and any additional contacts you developed.)

Follow-Up: What:

When:

Where:

Who: Reporter _____

DESK COPY

Figure 11.5 Example of a story assignment/follow-up sheet used to assign local news story coverage and identify potential story ideas. Courtesy of WMAR-TV, Baltimore, Maryland.

secured, transportation has to be scheduled, communication links have to be established. These things must be done for each story covered. Logistical planning is done continuously throughout story coverage and is replicated for each story assigned.

Phase Four

Story coverage begins as soon as a story assignment is made. Last-minute phone calls may be needed to finalize coverage plans and interviews. The assignment may have to be crystallized and "fleshed in" by the assignment manager, reporter, and photojournalist.

The interaction between those in the newsroom and those in the field begins as the story is developed and explored. Reporters and photojournalists share ideas and concerns on the way to the story, during the story, and when the story is being organized for presentation. Ideas may be discarded and replaced because of comments or situations that were not anticipated when the story was first assigned. Conflicts may develop between field news crews and newsroom personnel over story coverage priorities as shifts are made in story assignment locations.

Story coverage also involves gathering the pieces of the story needed to prepare a report: Interviews must be completed, sources must be pursued or rescheduled, sound and picture must begin to make sense, potential graphics must be considered for later use on-the-air, the focus or point of the story must be remembered. In a broadcast newsroom, story coverage and logistical planning are evolving continually, for *each* story.

Despite everyone's efforts to make story coverage smooth and efficient, plans can go awry. On the way to cover a school board meeting, for example, a reporter could be diverted to a big fire that is leveling several buildings in a downtown area. Pulling reporters off assigned coverage and changing schedules and connections causes delays, frustration, and confusion when both the fire story *and* the school board meeting story are written and processed later the same day. But that's just the nature of broadcast news coverage. Plans change. Decisions must be made continually about the quality and value of each story covered. When an unexpected development creates an unanticipated story, assignments will change. It's all part of the reality of broadcast news coverage. It's also part of the reason journalists continue to work in broadcast news—they thrive on change.

Phase Five

Once coverage is completed, the story must be processed. All story elements must be evaluated to distinguish the important from the unimportant. Notes have to be reviewed. Last-minute phone calls may need to be made to check on a specific fact or comment. Tape material has to be reviewed and prepared for editing. The assignment manager and newscast producer as well as the news crew who covered the story must reassess the focus of the story. The reporter has to tell the newscast producer the essence of each story covered. Summarizing in a single sentence is best. This helps the producer assess the news value of each story, write anchor lead-in copy that is often needed, and place the story in the newscast along with the other stories covered that same day. Unfortunately, most producers do not have time to check each part of each story covered. Reporters must use their best judgment about the fine points of each story prepared.

A script has to be written that incorporates all essential details and presents visual material clearly and effectively. The timing and packaging of each story must be finalized. Story notes and routine paperwork must be completed. With the launch of regional cable news channels and networks around the country, many reporters are expected to develop, shoot, and possibly edit their stories while still in the field. Laptop computers and flexible video equipment provide a field-to-newsroom link that can keep a news team in the field to help save time and operating expenses and expand the number of stories covered.

At this point, newsroom activity often becomes a blur as details are handled and people and machines endure the crunch of unforgiving deadlines. This is an exhilarating time in the news day as the pieces begin to come together to produce the ultimate product—news stories.

Phase Six

With determination, careful planning, cooperation, and teamwork, and usually a little bit of luck, the story makes it on-the-air. The story visualized earlier in the day may be completely different by now. Untold amounts of time, energy, effort, sweat, and worry have been expended on this fragile product that has been shaped and formed by the efforts of people and machines.

To not only survive but to do well in this kind of pressure cooker environment requires those on the news staff to continually challenge themselves through their work, foster a spirit of commitment, and find satisfaction in a job well done. It is certainly a challenging and exhilarating opportunity!

Summary

This chapter has outlined the basic structure and operation of broadcast newsrooms. A broadcast newsroom is organized to provide the coordination, interaction, and teamwork needed to select, cover, process, and produce broadcast news stories.

The news director develops the structure and supervises the overall operation of the newsroom. Assistant news directors or managing editors and executive news producers may be hired to handle the three main responsibilities of the news director: personnel, operations, and finances.

The assignment desk is the hub of news coverage planning and execution. The assignment manager or editor assigns stories to be covered and then coordinates and monitors the coverage provided by the news staff, especially reporters and photojournalists.

The assignment manager works with producers, who are responsible for the overall content and production of each newscast. In larger newsrooms, producers may also handle other duties.

Engineers and technicians strive for the best possible technical quality in each news report. For the broadcast audience, on-air talent are the most visible component of a broadcast news operation. Technicians and on-air talent often belong to unions.

Large newsrooms are organized and managed so as to use the specialized talents of various people, such as field and unit producers, graphic artists, and copy and tape editors.

Six primary steps or phases are involved in planning and coordinating news coverage: First comes an idea for a story; second, a commitment to the story idea leads to a firm assignment for coverage; third, the logistics of coverage are developed; fourth, actual coverage takes place; fifth, the story is processed or shaped into finished form; and sixth, the story is on-the-air.

Exercises

(The following exercises can be completed as group field trips as well as individual projects.)

1. Consult with the news director or assignment manager for a local broadcast newsroom. Formulate an organizational flowchart for the structure and operation of this specific newsroom. Provide a brief written narrative in which you outline the "chain of command" as well as the responsibilities of each major division. Be certain to list typical staff duties and to indicate how various staff members interact to produce news coverage.

2. Obtain permission to observe a morning newsroom staff meeting at which the day's news coverage is discussed and assignments and duties finalized. Provide written comments from your observations about the interaction among those attending this meeting; how story ideas are generated, developed, and finalized; how final assignments are made; and how logistics are discussed and finalized.

3. Follow the directives in Exercise 2. Then obtain permission to accompany a reporter on a specific news assignment. Observe the process followed from the time the assignment is made until the time the story airs. Provide a written report on your observations about the reporting process followed.

4. Obtain permission to monitor (for the few hours approaching the broadcast of a local newscast) the activities of either the assignment manager or the newscast producer. Provide a written report about the newsroom activities and decision-making processes of the individual selected.

Note

1. Summary of a survey conducted by Vernon A. Stone, "TV News Work Force Grows, Declines Continue in Radio," *Communicator,* May 1993, 26–27.

Chapter 12

Radio Reporting

Sound is as important to radio as visual images are to television. Sound has a value and richness that must be recognized. In addition, sound provides the vibrancy and reality that makes radio news so effective. Listeners are placed directly into the scene when sound takes them there. Examples include the crack of thunder during a live severe weather report, the chants of rioters as a reporter tries to place into perspective a change in presidents in a faraway country, and a police officer's account of a heroic rescue.

The first part of this chapter focuses on the ways in which sound can be used to enhance radio news broadcasts. What sounds can be used, why they should be used, and how they can be incorporated into a news broadcast are keys to using sound effectively in radio reporting.

Other parts of this chapter describe the care and use of equipment to gather and record sound; the systems used to file, process, edit, and store audio material; and the creative ways sound can be fused with news copy to produce a news story that is better than if the sound were not used. Exercises at the end of this chapter will help you to apply what you learn to specific radio reporting situations.

The richness, variety, and creative use of sound in radio news reporting cannot be replicated on the pages of a textbook. Although some copy examples are provided for various kinds of audio uses, be alert and listen critically to the sound that you hear on radio newscasts.[1]

Importance and Value of Sound

Sound can take a listener far beyond the radio receiver. Bill Polish, News Director at KIRO Radio in Seattle, puts it this way: "In my mind, the purpose of radio is to take people where they can't go or bring that place to them—inside their car, inside their bathroom, inside their kitchen."[2]

Those who have worked extensively in radio news emphasize that sound can help listeners construct strong mental images. Bob Priddy, past Chairman of RTNDA, contends that "tape is radio's photograph. It's used as newspapers use pictures—to illustrate or emphasize a story. Newscasts can be more interesting and more effective when the listeners hear the event taking place or hear the voices of those making it happen."[3]

Scot Witt at WDCB in Glen Ellyn, Illinois, used a sound collage to paint a striking aural picture of the scene at the funeral of a police officer killed in the line of duty. Here is a transcript of a portion of that extended report to give you some idea of how sound was used to capture the moment:

```
TAPS ................................................:10
CROSS-FADE TO ORGAN MUSIC ...........................:06
ORGAN MUSIC UNDER
VOICE OVER P.A. SYSTEM:
```

[''I am convinced that officers in law enforcement, regardless of what agency, whether they are city, county, state, or country, have a common bond . . . and it's not written in a rule book. They share the same source of danger, stress and sorrows if one of their own falls from the ranks in the line of duty. Officers who have never met or even heard a fallen comrade's name hold the same reverence and respect, and share the same grief with the family of the deceased, as if they were an actual part of the grieving family. . . .'']

```
CROSS FADE TO WIND NOISE .............................:05
SOUNDBITE FROM AN UNIDENTIFIED PERSON:
```

[''It's the only send-off that we can give a fellow-officer. And that's why we come out . . . to give him that honor . . . and to let the family know, let the community know, that we care and his death will not be in vain.'']

```
BAGPIPES .............................................:11
AND THEN FADE OUT TO
SOUNDBITE FROM AN UNIDENTIFIED PERSON (voice shaky):
```

[''A sea of blue fl. . . . . . . A sea of blue flows forward for a fallen comrade . . . to pay tribute . . . '']

```
TAPS ................................................:12
```

Despite its obvious importance and value, sound must never replace good newswriting. Use sound whenever possible to make radio news stories more vivid, but continue to make your copy strong enough to stand alone, to tell the story, if necessary, only with the voice of the newscaster reading your copy. Good news copy is still important!

Uses of Sound in Radio News

Sound is used in several ways in radio news—actualities, natural or location sound, Q & A's (questions and answers), voicers, and wraparound reports. Each can be used in a different way to present information more effectively in radio news reports. How to write copy that best integrates each type of sound is explained later in this chapter. Chapter 14, "Live Reporting," covers how on-air talent can best use their voices to deliver news material more effectively.

Length is an important consideration, regardless of the kind of sound used in radio news. Long actualities break the flow of a story and eventually cause boredom. Bob Priddy describes it this way: "Longer tape cuts have a tendency to drift as far as topic is concerned, confusing the listener about the point being made. The longer the voice—probably unfamiliar to most of your listeners—keeps speaking, the greater chance your listeners will forget who this person is, or what the point of your story is."[4] But if such material is too short, the listener has difficulty adjusting to such rapid changes in sounds and voices and eventually becomes confused and disinterested.

Several factors should determine the length and use of any piece of audio material. These include the news value of the story containing audio material; the contribution that a particular piece of audio makes to the effectiveness of a story and/or a newscast; the length of the newscast in which the audio material would be used; the amount of air time available; the length and position of the other stories to be used.

Here are full story length guidelines that can be used: *Actualities* and *question & answer (Q & A)* segments should be as short as possible, but no longer than :15 or :20; for *natural or location sound* no specific length is suggested; *voicers,* :30 to :35; *wraparounds,* :30 to :45. The *best* guideline is to follow the requirements of the newsroom in which you work.

Actualities (also called *soundbites*) use the voices and sounds of the *actual* news event to help tell a story. Comments are recorded, edited into short statements, and then melded into the news copy.

Why an actuality is used is just as important as getting and recording the actuality. Actualities can offer additional information, but they can also provide emotional reactions to tragedies as well as triumphs such as the drowning of a close friend or relative, or the winning of the state lottery. In the middle of a story about mechanical problems at the Royal Gorge Bridge that stranded 60 tourists at the bottom of a canyon, causing them to climb about 770 feet, KRLN in Canyon City, Colorado, inserted this actuality:

`Les Bugia (BOO-guy) of Sequin, Texas, was one of those who made the climb. KRLN asked him what happened when the rail cars came to a stop.`

> ["Fear at first . . . And the fear continued, but the rapport with the group was very, very good. There was joking and laughing, even though it was serious. We were trying to figure out what was going to happen. . . . It was handled pretty well. It just took a long time."][5]

An actuality should not be used only because you have a comment on tape, the recording is good, or it took a long time to record and edit. Use the sounds of the people and settings involved that best tell the story to the radio listener.

Be certain that listeners will be able to hear the actuality. Actualities recorded in areas with more noise and activity *tend* to add even more color and impact to the words of the newsmaker. But if *you* cannot understand the words heard, assume that the listener (who gets only one chance) will not hear and understand the words either.

Your audiotape quality "test" needs a tolerance factor. Sometimes a piece of audio will not be good technically, but it will be especially striking, memorable, or important for the listener to hear. Audio might help a listener understand what happened and maybe determine why and how it happened. Here are some examples: the final words of a pilot before a crash landing; the sobbing comments from a survivor after a bridge collapses, killing a close friend. If you use audiotape that is difficult to hear and understand, keep the soundbite short, and alert the listener about the marginal sound quality. Let the newscaster say something like, "Officer Morgan says he almost died in the fire trying to save the two children. Listen carefully. . . ."

Natural or Location Sound

Many radio news reporters consider natural or location sound another type of actuality. These on-scene sounds help place the listener at the *actual* news scene and add nonverbal information about a news story. They are like an actuality without a voice—capturing the mood, color, meaning, and intensity of a news event, but without words.

```
[cold open top]
#85 SOUND . . . UP THEN UNDER. . . .
Protests in a West Bank village erupted in violence . . . as
some Jewish settlers attacked homes and cars owned by Arabs.
                                                  NBC Radio News
```

Other terms are also commonly used to describe the actual sounds or noises associated with a news story: *ambient, background, wild, raw,* and *nat sound.*

The listener should always be able to recognize the nat sound used. Do not use the sound of shuffling feet and expect listeners to understand how it relates to a story about a protest march unless you make a reference in the copy.

```
It was the largest of the recent demonstrations on U-S policy
in Central America . . . but it was also the most peaceful:
---------------------
in: Chanting . . . 05 sec . . . fade. . . .
---------------------
                                        WCCO Radio, Minneapolis
```

Stay alert for nat sound opportunities. Covering a fire? Step back and record just the sounds of trucks and fire-fighting crews working the fire. Doing a story on a holiday parade? Record a band selection and use some of the music to begin your report. Recording natural sound separately will make it easier to integrate the sound into the story at the proper volume level.

KVOO Radio news reporter Laurie Krueger depends on natural sound for stories that she covers in Tulsa:

> When I arrive on the scene of spot news, the first thing I do is start recording! Natural sound from the scene is a must. Because radio does not have the luxury of being able to show video of the scene, we must create the image of it through use of sound. A recent high rise fire in downtown Tulsa required help from 13 fire trucks. Fortunately, when I arrived at the building, many of the fire engines were still arriving as well. I immediately turned on my recorder and got sound of the engine sirens, one right after another.
>
> Keeping that tape rolling can prove valuable later. When I worked on my high rise fire voicer back at the station, I used the sirens as background. The consistency of the sirens re-created the urgency of the situation that night and helped our listeners picture what was happening at the time. . . . You'd be surprised what kind of natural sound you can gather just by keeping a tape rolling by your side while looking for the facts.[6]

Laurie Krueger's fire story is shown later in this chapter as a wraparound report example.

Integrating nat sound into a report takes time, but ambient sound can add dimension and imagery to radio news reports when used creatively. Do not take shortcuts. If natural sound from a fire scene is mixed under an interview about the fire that was recorded at a city hall news conference, you will have committed a breach in journalistic ethics. Do not mislead your listeners. Use sound in a natural, ethical manner, and do not distort reality.

Questions and Answers (Q & A's)

Two types of Q & A's are used regularly as actualities in radio news reporting. At networks and in larger newsrooms, a reporter could respond to questions from a newswriter or newscaster about a breaking story just covered or still under way. The ad-libbed answers are then edited and used as a Q & A. A more common Q & A form is a newsmaker responding to a reporter's questions. A portion of this recorded exchange can then be used in a radio news story.

Creative use of Q & A's can make a story more intriguing, compelling, and intense. Listeners not only can hear an event but also are able to feel and see an event through the audio pictures painted by on-the-scene comments and sounds. Here's a transcript of a Q and A exchange between reporter Nan Siemer, anchor Bruce Allen, and a riot participant heard during WTOP Radio's coverage of the Mount Pleasant riots. Bruce Allen's questioning added immeasurably to the award-winning coverage:

ALLEN: . . . Nan Siemer . . . was able to speak with someone who was actually involved in some of the violence. Nan?
SIEMER: Yes. O.K. I do have Angie with me right now, Bruce, and I'm going to let you talk to her.
ALLEN: Now, you were involved in some of the brick throwing and the bottle throwing . . . is that correct?
ANGIE: Yea . . .
ALLEN: How do you expect that that will help what you're trying to accomplish?
ANGIE: You know, maybe it won't mean anything to the cops and stuff, you know, but to us it will. For us to respect them, you know, they have to respect us.
ALLEN: What would you do if you were arrested tonight?
ANGIE: I dunno . . . I guess I'd be arrested.
ALLEN: What would you do if you hurt somebody with a brick or a bottle?
ANGIE: You know, we . . . we're not out here to hurt anybody, you know, we're just trying to get our point through, and we, you know, feel this is the only way, you know, that cops are listening to us, even if they're not talking.
ALLEN: Were you having fun?
ANGIE: Sort of . . . (laugh). I mean, it's the first time I('ve) actually done something like this, you know. I just came out to look, and then . . . you know, I ended up doing the crowd.
ALLEN: Well, don't you think it's kind of destructive excitement, and that it's about time it ought to stop? Don't you feel bad about what you've done?
ANGIE: No, not really . . . No, I mean, you know, we feel that we're getting our point through, sort of, you know, and . . . I don't know, when the cops are willing to listen, you know, we're willing to stop.
ALLEN: Well, you know, if it goes far enough, the mayor has told police they can shoot.
ANGIE: Yea . . . but we're not afraid.
ALLEN: Well, that's easy to say now, Angie. I hope that you don't have reason to be afraid. And thank you for talking to us. . . .[7]

Voicers

Voicers may be the next best thing to actualities. After a newscaster lead-in, only the reporter is heard giving the essential facts of a story. Voicers can help reporters meet deadlines quickly. And they can add variety to newscasts.

Voicers are especially effective when the reporter can provide special insights or perceptions, vivid descriptions, and informed observations that would not otherwise be available about a story that the reporter has covered.

To accomplish this, reporters often talk into their tape recorders using notes or speaking extemporaneously, trying to capture the color, texture, and feel of the news event as they witness it—what's it like at the scene of the story? What are the sights, sounds, smells, and feelings associated with this story? This could be a rather lengthy report, eventually ending when the reporter runs out of things to say, determines that the event has stabilized and no longer lends itself to such reporting, or simply runs out of audiotape. Networks and some larger newsrooms refer to these kinds of reports as *ROSRs* (pronounced ROSE-err) for *Radio On-Scene Report*. Other newsrooms call these *sceners,* since the reporter tells what it's like to be on the scene. Another obvious term used is *voice-ality* to indicate that the reporter is the only voice heard but that the content resembles an actuality, since the comments indicate firsthand, eyewitness information the reporter has gathered. These 15- to 25-second personalized reports might be useful when covering stories like fires, natural disasters (tornadoes, hurricanes, earthquakes, etc.), riots, election-night celebrations, and the visit of a pope to the United States:

The crowds the Pope is attracting may not be quite as big as expected, but ethnic groups are making up for the numbers with enthusiasm. Here in San Antonio, Hispanic Americans shouted long live the Pope in Spanish as the Pope's motorcade wound its way past the Alamo. The Pontiff also got a warm reception at a party thrown by the Polish community in Texas. Today the Pope will meet with Native Americans in Phoenix. I'm Craig Windham with the Pope in San Antonio.

Unistar Radio Networks

Here is a suggestion for doing effective voicer reports: Record natural sound whenever possible; later, close your eyes and describe what you see of the scene from memory and add voice-over copy. This will help re-create what listeners will see and feel. Do not pretend to be on the scene of a story if you are actually re-creating the scene back at the station with the use of natural sound. This is ethically incorrect. Be sure listeners know that you are not trying to make it appear as though you are live at the news story scene.

Wraparound Reports

Wraparound reports are also called *doughnuts* and are often abbreviated as *wraps* or *V/As* because they combine the characteristics of voicers and actualities in a single taped report the reporter prepares. An anchor introduces or leads in to the packaged report, and the reporter begins telling the story. Soon one or more actualities are heard before the reporter closes out the wrap.

Here is an example, written as a transcript from an off-air broadcast:

```
It took a brigade of firefighters nearly three hours to bring
under control a fire in a high rise building in downtown
Tulsa. . . . K-V-O-O's Laurie Krueger was there.
-------------------------------------------------
[NAT. SOUND OF FIRE TRUCKS RACING TO THE FIRE . . . UP FULL AND
THEN UNDER THROUGHOUT WRAPAROUND REPORT]
When the first fire engine pulled out of the station just five
blocks away from the Petroleum Club Building, they could
already tell the fire was going to be a big one. Flames were
curling from the 15th floor, engulfing the 16th floor, along
with thick black smoke.

Fire Captain Jim White says lack of a sprinkler system in the
building gave the fire a head start:
```

> ["There is no sprinkler system. This building, as I understand, was built around 1964. We did not start mandating sprinklers in high rises until 1975. Therefore, this is one of the buildings downtown that, unfortunately, is not sprinklered."]

```
It was a two-alarm fire requiring 13 fire units to be called,
and about 120 firefighters who worked in shifts. One fireman
was injured when he fell down some stairs inside the building.
He was taken to the hospital with a shoulder injury.

Laurie Krueger, K-V-O-O News . . .
[NAT. SOUND OF FIRE TRUCK SIRENS . . . UP FULL AND THEN OUT]
                                              KVOO Radio, Tulsa
```

Earlier in this chapter, Laurie Krueger stressed the importance of recording natural sound for radio news stories. That practice proved useful for this report.

Gathering and Recording Sound

This discussion is limited to the minimum equipment and basic techniques that a radio news reporter needs to record audio material in routine newsgathering situations. A more-sophisticated discussion of this phase of radio news reporting is beyond the scope of this book.[8]

Young radio reporters may be working with station-owned equipment, or they may need to purchase their own. If the station supplies the gear, concentrate on maintaining the equipment in good working condition. If you need to buy your own personal gear or if you will purchase gear for the newsroom, keep the following considerations in mind.

Determine the equipment you will need. This equipment list should be based
on how often you are out covering radio news stories that require equipment
and the types of stories that you cover regularly.

Keep all gear together, in one place. When a breaking story must be
covered, you won't have time to search for the equipment that you need. Use
a carrying bag or attaché case (with straps) that offers strength, durability, and
water protection!

Buy a high-quality microphone. You could use the microphone that
comes built into an audiocassette recorder, but the extra cost is worth the
increased sound quality you will achieve. Buy a decent dynamic-type microphone, preferably one with an omnidirectional pickup pattern.

A microcassette unit is satisfactory for a few situations, but *purchasing
a conventional audiocassette recorder is best.* Look for these desirable characteristics: reasonably good audiotape quality; small; compact; lightweight;
as portable as possible; reliable; and durable in adverse weather and human
handling situations.

Here are *additional features* many radio reporters prefer:

- three heads, giving you the ability to monitor tape as it is being
  recorded

- a choice of manual/limiter/ALC (automatic level control) record
  levels

- a line level input for recording news conferences from a mult box
  that provides various types of connections between a recorder and a
  PA system

- variable speed control to correct for dying batteries or speed
  differences between different machines

- a built-in speaker and microphone to use when you forget to bring
  your hand-held mic

- a pause control button with audible cuing in both FF (fast forward)
  and REW (rewind) positions to better prepare wraparound reports
  fed over the telephone

- dual-speed record/playback capabilities that allow you to record a
  two-hour meeting on a 60-minute cassette at half-speed ($1\frac{7}{8}$ inches
  per second [ips] instead of the normal cassette speed of $3\frac{3}{4}$ ips).
  Unfortunately, what you gain in tape length, you lose in signal
  quality.

Avoid ''bargain'' audiocassettes. Buy what you can reasonably afford
and still maintain audiotape quality.

Include other items as required: pen or pencil; notepad or notecards;
important telephone numbers such as the news director's home phone and

network newsroom phones; spare change for pay phones; extra audiocassettes, erased and rewound; extra audiocassette recorder if sound mixing is done in the field; various plugs, adapters and cables to handle *local* news coverage situations; earphones or earplugs for monitoring each recording; extra *fresh* batteries; microphone stand or clamp; microphone extension cord; electrical extension cord; AM/FM pocket radio to hear on-air cues for live reports; gaffer's or duct tape; pocketknife; small screwdriver set.

Here's a good rule: If you do not use a particular item within three months, take it out of your equipment bag! Do not continue to lug the item from story to story. Another good rule: When you think you have packed the necessary gear, walk around the block or the parking lot a few times. You will then know what toting this gear around with you for an entire day of news coverage will be like.

Most radio reporters still use conventional or analog audiocassette recorders, the type you probably have access to on a regular basis. Some radio newsrooms are also using digital audio tape (DAT) to manipulate, store, and reproduce audio material. DAT stores audio as digital impulses just as a computer does. Editing is easier with DAT because computer systems can be tied in to a DAT system for less than $2,000. Large newsrooms have integrated word processing, news wires, and digital audio functions. This allows a reporter to record actualities, write the stories, read the stories on the air, and run the actualities from the computer keyboard and monitor.

Radio reporters who have used DAT systems indicate the DAT recorders are less expensive and outperform conventional two-track and mono audiocassette recording machines. However, the possibility always exists that the computer may crash in a completely digital system. Despite such difficulties, perhaps one day, all radio reporters will be using DAT recorders.

Techniques

Perform regular maintenance on your gear. Unless you take care of your equipment, you will not have the reporting tools you need to do your job. Here are *maintenance checks to remember to keep your gear in good repair:*

a. Clean everything that comes into contact with the audiotape— erase and playback heads, guides, pinch roller, capstan. A cotton-tipped stick made for this purpose or a clean, soft cloth dipped in medicinal or denatured alcohol should be used until no red oxide shows on the cotton or cloth.

b. Get an engineer to demagnetize your recorder after every 25 to 30 hours of use to maintain the quality of your recordings.

c. Ask an engineer to check the alignment of the erase and record-playback heads as well as record bias and equalization on your portable tape recorder.

d. Check batteries regularly. If the batteries start to go dead, the tape will move slower than usual. Then when you try to edit the recording on house power or using new batteries, the tape will sound faster than normal; the machine will run at normal speed, but the recording, made at a slower speed, will sound too fast. Therefore, check and change or charge batteries.

e. Make certain audiocassettes are wound tightly and not ripped, warped, or full of splices.

Here is a checklist for the *weekly maintenance checks* most radio reporters and engineers recommend:

a. Break down your equipment bags.
b. Remove and test all batteries.
c. Clean all battery contacts and all recorder heads.
d. Recoil all extension, microphone, and adapter cords.
e. Rewind all cassettes to the beginning (but off the leader tape).
f. Be sure the pocket radio you carry for cues off-air is tuned to the correct frequency again.
g. Be sure your reporter's notebook is no more than half full.
h. Be sure you have enough gaffer's tape and parking meter and telephone change.
i. Be sure your press credentials and telephone charge cards are current.

Anticipate the recording situation. Be prepared for likely as well as unlikely contingencies. Think *quality* sound. Know the capabilities of the gear that you carry. Keep notes about specific recording situations encountered and refer to these notes when similar situations are imminent.

Get the microphone as close as possible to the source of the sound. For example, at a speech or news conference, tie in to the public address system (if used) by using a *splitter* or *mult box* that provides various types of connections between your recorder and the PA system.

To get a good recording *you might have to change locations or try to avoid certain situations:* for example, the "buzz" from fluorescent lights that often gets onto audio and videotape; the air rush noise that air conditioning outlets create; or wind noise when a wind screen or shield is not used over a microphone.

Make a test recording before beginning your critical recording to make sure your equipment works satisfactorily. Make it a habit to listen with earphones when recording. You need to hear what is being recorded onto tape to be able to adjust and obtain the best recording possible.

At the beginning and/or at the end of the audiocassette recording, *record the name and title of the person interviewed or the identity of the nat sound recorded.* This technique will prevent recording over material you want to save and will also help identify audio material later when editing tape and writing the story. Attach a label to the audiocassette with this same information noted.

Plan your recording strategy. Here's advice from Laurie Krueger at KVOO:

> The first people I approach after arriving on the scene of spot news are those who have witnessed the event. Citizens many times will tell you what they saw, that they heard, what they felt, what they were doing at the time, or what they may have done to help out . . . and they'll tell it like it happened without official jargon. . . . After I have gotten all of the sound and witness tape I want, I look for the officials who can give me some of the facts. This will most likely be a public information officer, a fire chief, or a lieutenant or sergeant from the police department.[9]

Filing, Processing, and Storing Audio Material

Audio material can be filed from the field or in the newsroom before it is processed for on-air use and eventually stored. Although each newsroom establishes its own system and procedures for each step, some common ways exist to handle these jobs.

Filing

Audio material fed to the newsroom from the field can be sent from a mobile unit or from a telephone. A mobile unit could use one of several methods to feed the signal directly to the newsroom, including the following: two-way radios using the newsroom as the *base station;* walkie-talkies, which are portable two-way systems with lower power and range; mobile telephones connecting the newsroom to a mobile unit; or cellular phones in which an area is divided into *cells,* allowing a signal from the mobile unit to be "handed" from one ground station to another as the mobile unit travels across the area.

The use of cellular phones is widespread. They offer advantages over other mobile unit systems: better audio quality; more mobility getting *to* the scene of the story; better reception in metropolitan areas. Disadvantages often noted include: Some cells are not particularly strong or may not even exist; signals are weak in suburban and rural areas; the nickel cadmium batteries used do not hold an electrical charge as long as some manufacturers suggest; and the standard cellular phone is not designed to be used with "alligator" telephone clips.

If the newsroom is configured for digital audio, combining the use of cellular telephones with other technology to process or file radio news stories is possible. Reporters can use a laptop computer with a microphone and a tape recorder connected to it. Audio material can be edited on the laptop computer screen, and the edited file of digital audio can be fed to the newsroom through a computer modem.

Various kinds of connections can be used to feed audio material to a newsroom from a conventional telephone. The details of each system are beyond the scope of this book. However, here is a simple system that works: Use a cord with a plug on one end and a pair of *alligator clips* (short metal clamps with small teeth) on the other end; plug the cord into the *earphone* or *monitor* outlet on the recorder; remove or cover the mouthpiece from the telephone and hook the alligator clips to the two prongs inside the handset. The mouthpiece from a telephone does not have to be removed to make this kind of connection. Instead of alligator clips, an acoustic or inductive coupler can be used to cover the mouthpiece on the telephone. Although both systems work well, most newsrooms no longer use them. Instead, reporters use cellular telephones or simply place the recorder next to the telephone mouthpiece to transfer the sound from one location to another.

Here are standard steps used to file (via mobile unit or telephone) field-produced stories that include audio material:

1. Cue up recorded material to be sent to newsroom.
2. Prepare equipment for transmission (as described previously).
3. Contact the newsroom: Indicate what you have and, to save time, provide a suggested lead-in and write-out for the story.
4. Provide an audio level test by feeding audio material and reading copy.
5. Once the newsroom is ready to record, count down each report (4 . . . 3 . . . 2 . . . (pause) . . . START FEEDING MATERIAL).
6. Feed voicers first to give newsroom personnel a general "feel" for the story. Then, if available, send actualities and wraps. During the feed, monitor the tape as it is playing. If you make a mistake, pause a moment, announce the next "take" number, and begin again. Repeat this process until your feed is completed and accepted by the newsroom.
7. After your feed, ask the newsroom contact to check the quality and usability of the material. Also determine what you are expected to do next and when the newsroom expects to hear from you again.

Processing

Back in the newsroom, audio material can be broadcast live or recorded for later use. Material can be recorded in studios, from mobile units, or over the telephone onto digital audio systems or quarter-inch audiotape, edited, and then transferred or dubbed onto cartridges or *carts* that are labeled, numbered, or color-coded according to newsroom practice.

Larger newsrooms use log sheets (sometimes called *actuality logs*) to note the date, cart number, length, contents, out-cue, and manner of presentation of audio material. Common abbreviations used include: A = actuality; NS or NATS = natural or ambient sound; Q & A = question and answer; V = voicer; W or V/A = wraparound.

Figure 3.5 shows a verbatim sheet, also used in larger newsrooms to process audio material, especially actualities. These sheets provide a transcript of a piece of audio material.

News Director Brian Barks edits audiotape at KKAR in Omaha.

Storing

Many stations save on audiocassette or reel-to-reel audiotape locally originated audio material that has been used on-the-air. Others simply retain an off-air copy of newscasts for a limited time period (generally 30–60 days). When newsroom computer systems are used, only floppy disks might be necessary to provide a useful tape or news copy morgue retrieval system for legal purposes as well as for future news coverage.

Editing Sound

The intricacies involved in editing sound creatively are, again, beyond the scope of this textbook. The best way to learn how to edit tape is to find someone with access to the necessary equipment and knowledge of editing; then edit different kinds of audio material as often as possible. You should at least be familiar with the basic processes used to edit audiotape.

Audio material can be edited in the field as well as in the newsroom. In the field, simply cue up the audio as needed; if you have the necessary connections and a second recorder, transfer (''dub'') audio material from one machine to another. In the newsroom, audio material can be recorded onto quarter-inch audiotape and physically spliced using editing blocks and splicing tape before being dubbed onto carts; you can also dub directly onto carts using electronic ''editing'' to bypass the usual stop tones and ''build'' audio material in sequence onto a cart.

Radio newsrooms are exploring the possibilities that digital audio editing systems offer. Cutting and splicing happens instantly, as fast as you can electronically cut out what you want and relocate it. Most digital audio editing systems allow you to place individual audio elements such as natural sound, soundbites, and transitions onto different tracks that a computer will later mix together into a finished recording. Separate left and right channel volume controls are usually available. Most digital systems provide a graphic display of

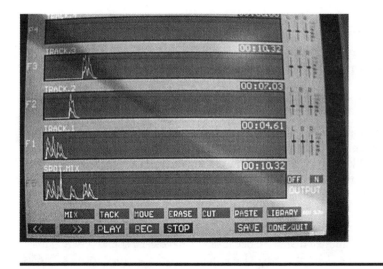

Figure 12.1 Screen from the Audio Prophet digital audio editing system.

the audio as each track is recorded and played. Editing is accomplished with a basic set of electronic ''splicing'' tools for moving, retrieving, positioning, recording, and playing audio material. (See Figure 12.1.)

Figure 12.1 shows a few screens from a soundbite edited on a digital audio editing system. Each track shows one sentence to be edited into the final version of the soundbite. F1 is the sentence: ''We're not sure this process will always work.'' F2 is the sentence: ''We're optimistic.'' And F3 is the sentence: ''We'll adjust as we go.'' F4 has been left blank. F5 is the edited soundbite in which the three sentences have been moved around to produce this sequence of sentences: ''We're optimistic. We're not sure this process will always work. We'll adjust as we go.''

Regardless of which editing system is used, here are editing suggestions to follow:

a. Never change or distort the meaning, intent, or integrity of a recorded comment that a newsmaker made on tape. Remain faithful to the sense of the remarks as a whole. Eliminate unnecessary material best summarized by the reporter or the anchor. These include repetitiveness and stalling, and lengthy explanations.

b. Leave natural breathing spaces between sentences edited together.

c. Retain natural speech rhythms and inflection patterns when editing. With rare exceptions, sentences should end with *down* inflections.

d. Be sure to dub onto cart only the ''good'' recording, so that you avoid false starts and miscues on-the-air.

Writing to Sound

Unless sound is used in a live report, eventually news copy must be written for the sound that has been recorded, edited, and processed. Integrating sound into news copy requires a review of the audio material and the use of various scripting techniques to get to and from the sound used.

Review Audio Material

Limit the subject matter. Include only one central idea. Cover only relevant and recent events and statements.

Let the newscaster do updates and establish time references. Protect the usability of recorded material by letting the newscaster's copy update information that is likely to change. This might include roads closed from floods, number of fatalities or strikers on a picket line, approximate damage estimate after a disaster, and so on. Avoid time references like *tonight, early this morning,* and so on in recorded material.

Be certain the sound adds something significant to the report. Your story should be *better,* not just different, because you have used sound in your story.

Maintain the flow of ideas. Use sound early in a story to make news copy progress more smoothly, logically, and vividly.

Consider the structure of the copy. A common practice is to select and edit the sound to be used and then build the copy around the recorded material into anchor-based copy or reporter-based copy (voicers and wraps). Notice how contrasting viewpoints are woven into the fabric of this story about a $750,000 addition to a local nursing home:

```
. . . James Hunt [a nearby resident] says the sewers in the
area won't handle the nursing home expansion.

cart 257 . . . runs :20 . . . and filth.

But Florence Home employee Vicki Simpeck says the project is a
necessity.

cart 257 . . . runs :15 . . . We can.
                                       KKAR, Omaha, Nebraska
```

Consider creative approaches to story structure. Here are a few possibilities:

    a. Start with an actuality or natural sound and then fade it under a voicer or the voicer portion of a wrap.

    b. Combine actualities with natural sound. You could use an actuality from a local labor leader talking about a current strike and then complete the wrap with voicer copy over ambient sound of picket line activity. For another approach, use ambient sound of the picket line under your introduction to the actuality from the union leader and then complete the wrap with ambient sound of the picket line in the background. The use of ambient sound in this manner could be considered radio's equivalent of *B-roll* (see Chapter 13, "Television Reporting").

c. Before reading your voicer copy, use a montage of actualities to create an "aural mosaic" of various voices commenting on an event or issue such as on-the-street interviews with ordinary people marking the day when a particularly startling event occurred—President Kennedy's assassination, landing of the first man on the moon, etc.

d. Consider using two audio inserts in the same story. To maintain continuity, a transition, or *bridge,* must be built into the copy. The bridge in the following example helps lead *out* of the first sound and lead *in* to the second sound.

Philadelphia City Councilman David Cohen sums it up . . . after a day of hearings on Mayor Goode's trash-to-steam proposal. . . .

> ["People today just aren't going to let anybody do something to them that makes them feel their lives and the health of their children and grandchildren are being jeopardized."][10]

About a hundred people made that clear as the mayor's representative . . . Marjorie Adler . . . tried to explain the planned trash-to-steam plant in south Philadelphia. . . .

> ["Right now, as a matter of fact, we are spending more on trash disposal than we are on recreation centers, libraries and parks combined . . . a sorry fact for the world-class city we all envision for Philadelphia."]

But the audience repeatedly jeered Adler . . . showing just how charged the city's growing waste problems have become.
                                                          WCAU-AM, Philadelphia

Although creative use of sound is interesting and challenging, to do it well requires time and opportunity. Both commodities are in short supply in most broadcast news operations. You should master basic or routine story structures *before* taking the liberties described above.

Both voicers and wraparounds usually end or "sign off" with an identification of the reporter. This *close-out* to the story also often notes the news affiliation and location of the reporter. Here are some examples: *Jack Reilly, 1210 W-C-A-U News; At city hall, Tim Fleck, K-T-R-H NewsRadio, 7-40 A-M; From Washington, Frank Gentry, Mutual News.*

The lead-in is the copy read just before a piece of audio is heard. It could be the newscaster's introduction to a reporter's voicer or wrap or the words of the anchor or reporter just before an actuality is heard. Various techniques can be used to accomplish what lead-ins are designed to do. In general, lead-ins should prepare the listener for the audio insert that follows.

Lead-Ins

Lead-ins should identify who is talking next. *Before a voicer or wrap* is heard, the lead-in could mention the reporter's name:

```
Before the day is over the House is expected to approve a major
health care package. Correspondent Dan Scanlan has a
preview. . . .
```
Mutual Broadcasting System

But the lead-in could also preview what the reporter will say in the voicer or wrap:

```
Voters in Wisconsin do not have to declare a party to cast
ballots in today's primary. Correspondent Bill Groody reports
from Milwaukee THAT probably will figure in the outcome. . . .
```
NBC Radio News

Or it could indicate the location of the reporter:

```
Alan Duke reports from the State Capitol. . . .
```
Georgia Radio News Service

It could also stress the intensity and immediacy of the story:

```
K-F-D-I's Theresa Yohn was on the scene as emergency crews
tried to revive the victim. . . .
```
KFDI Radio, Wichita, Kansas

For an actuality, sometimes you should simply indicate the job or role an individual or a group played in the development of a news story rather than try to get listeners to recognize a specific title and name before an actuality is heard. Identify someone only by their role or job when it is important to remember *what* was said rather than *who* specifically said it. For example, identify someone as the eyewitness to an accident, a police spokesperson who is about to describe a crime scene or a suspect, or a medical specialist who came to the aid of someone trapped in a car:

```
The paramedic who rescued the little girl described how he got
her out. . . .
```
KTRH NewsRadio, Houston

Perhaps you can use the specific name and title of an individual if a second reference is made in the same lead-in copy:

```
A spokesman for Interchurch Ministries of Nebraska is trying
to get more organizations involved in trying to assist farmers
with drought problems. Mel Loo-Chen says. . . .
```
KKAR, Omaha, Nebraska

Maybe indicating the agency or company that supplied the information would be best, as in this lead-in to a story that tried to update flood coverage that extended over several weeks:

Finally, some good news for the Midwestern flood zone. The National Weather service sees a break in the storms:

> ["Right now there are still some thunderstorms in extreme eastern Iowa, and western Illinois, but west of that through the remainder of Iowa, back into Nebraska, the Dakotas and Kansas it's dry right now and, it will remain dry for at least the next several days."][11]

That's Weather Service Meteorologist Bruce Terry. Levees are still holding in Kansas City, where both the Missouri and Kansas Rivers are cresting at record levels. Even if it STOPS raining now, and STAYS that way—flood problems will continue for weeks.

Mutual Broadcasting System

A lead-in should also set the scene of the story about to be told and help narrow the focus of the story for the listener. Notice how this lead-in provides a brief background on the issue before the actuality is heard:

The effects of widening a popular Sacramento County avenue are being discussed with county supervisors. The avenue in question is Howe, which is targeted to be expanded to help ease the flow of commuter traffic.

Jim Wray with the County's Public Works Department says some people are concerned about the possibility of adding two lanes. . . .

WRAY 1Q: OF CONCERN :15

KFBK, Sacramento, California

The lead-in should *noticeably* add something to the telling of the story, and it should continue the forward movement of the story, not stop the story "dead in its tracks." Notice how this lead-in helps create listener interest and continue the flow of the story despite the need to shift listener attention from the anchor to the reporter:

A South Bay judge is threatening to throw the county supervisors in jail . . . KGO's Gene Rusco reports they've got just a few days to prove their innocence:

The judge told the supervisors and the county administrator to start supplying more cells and beds for inmates at the Santa Clara County jail. . . .

KGO Radio, San Francisco

The *reporter* is best prepared to determine what needs to be or should be said in anchor lead-in and write-out copy and what is best said by use of audiotape from a newsmaker or a reporter.

Do not use *blind* lead-ins. For example, *The mayor was asked to comment on the new downtown development plan . . .* is better written as *The mayor thinks the new downtown development plan needs more study.* For another example, *We talked to Senator Jones today and he said . . .* or *Here's what Senator Jones thinks about the bill . . .* would be better written thus: *Senator Jones says he favors the bill.* Lead-ins should offer specific information about the story.

Avoid "parroting." Never introduce an actuality, voicer, or wrap with the same words or phrases that will be used at the beginning of that piece of audio. Paraphrase what is about to be heard. Start the recorded segment with the *second* sentence. Use the discarded sentence for the anchor or reporter lead-in. This technique helps create a flow of ideas and a conversational "fabric" for listeners. This makes it easier for listeners to understand the story and clearly link the soundbite to the words of the anchor or reporter.

In most situations, use more than one sentence to get from the anchor to a reporter or a newsmaker. This gives listeners time to adjust to a shift in the sound heard.

Use a *complete* sentence leading into an audio insert. Never lead in with a partial sentence (*But the governor adds . . . ; Mayor Bartholomew's reaction to the proposal . . .*). Invariably, the tape is not heard because of technical problems or slipups. Also, using a *complete* sentence provides a finished, completed thought for the listener.

Sometimes you can make a story more vivid for listeners by starting "cold" with an actuality, before any copy is read:

I am informing the board that I intend to resign and that they need to appoint an interim replacement.

Those were the words of Kenneth Keller last night as he announced his resignation from the presidency of the University of Minnesota. . . .

WCCO Radio, Minneapolis

But most experienced radio newswriters agree that constant use of "cold" actualities causes too much unnecessary confusion for the listener. A startling comment or crucial statement may be missed because the audience cannot remember who said it and what it means to the story that you are just starting to tell.

You can use a variety of *throw lines* or *tosses* in the lead-in to preview the soon-to-be-heard comments of the reporter and/or newsmaker. This technique helps continue the information flow going into a voicer, a wrap, or an actuality:

```
Thirty-six students from Portland's Lincoln High will be
heading for Washington D.C. this weekend. KXL's Bill Gallant
reports they'll be competing in the national bicentennial
competition on the Constitution and Bill of Rights.
                                    KXL Radio, Portland, Oregon
```

Q and A's present special problems since *both* reporter and newsmaker must be introduced in the lead-in. You could write something like this: *Senator Davis told News 11's Ray Jones he opposes the bill.* If the exchange is between an anchor and a reporter, something like this would work: *I asked Nan Siemer what it looked like on the street* or *Nan Siemer told me the situation was getting very serious.*

Write-Outs

The *write-out* is the copy read just after a piece of audio is heard. Other terms used include *tag* and *tag line*.

The write-out signals the listener that the story is over and that it is time to move to the next story. Since the write-out ends a story, the contents can be the same as suggested in Chapter 5 ("Story Structure") for the conclusion or ending of any news story. This would include additional information, expected impact, opposing viewpoints.

Write-outs are needed after actualities and Q & A's to underscore the importance of the audio insert used, reestablish the newscaster, and maintain the flow of information within a newscast.

```
Some sexually active people in college these days apparently
figure that AIDS is not gonna get them! Check this finding from
a survey Professor Jeff Fisher did of students at one big
school in the northeast:
```

> ["Only about 30% of the students surveyed always used condoms during sexual intercourse."][12]

```
Fisher says college students could well become the fuel for the
next possible explosion in the number of AIDS victims.
                                    ABC Contemporary Network
```

Write-outs are not as essential after voicers and wraps because the reporter provides an obvious conclusion, or close-out, to the story. A write-out is needed if new developments occur after a voicer or wrap is recorded but still used on-the-air.

Summary

This chapter has reviewed fundamental techniques and processes associated with the use of sound in radio news reporting. After noting the importance and value of sound in radio news, the various uses of sound were discussed: actualities; natural or location sound; question and answer (Q & A); voicers; and wraparounds, or wraps. The length and uses for each kind of sound were suggested. The basic equipment and techniques used to gather, record, file, process, store, and edit audio material were also discussed.

Review audio material to be used before writing lead-ins and write-outs. Various techniques were suggested for making these links to and from audio material smoother and more meaningful.

Exercises

1. Using the information contained in *one* of the following fact sheets, write *three* stories to be used in consecutive newscasts *tomorrow* morning, the day *after* these events would have occurred.

Story 1 will be a 20- to 30-second story for the newscaster that incorporates at least one actuality (see quotes and approximate timings in the fact sheet).

Story 2 will be a 20- to 35-second voicer report. No actualities are needed, but an anchor lead-in is needed. The use of nat sound could be suggested in the copy.

Story 3 will be a 30- to 45-second voicer wraparound that incorporates at least one actuality not already used in Story 1.

See Chapter 3 for recommended copy formats to use for each type of story to be filed. See Chapter 8 for suggestions for writing multiple stories based on the same news event.

Note: You can suggest the use of only a portion of an actuality. However, make these notations clear in the copy provided by noting the in-cue, out-cue and length of each actuality. Also, attach to each anchor lead-in a separate page that shows your copy used to record the voicer and wrap for Stories 2 and 3. Imposing deadlines for the writing of each story will make this exercise a realistic professional experience (e.g., 20 minutes for Story 1, and 30 minutes each for Stories 2 and 3).

a.
- Local members of Graphics Communications International Union Locals 221 and 520 and Machinists Lodge 31 settled their strike against Oakview's American Signature plant. Oakview is ten miles from your newsroom.

- American Signature in Oakview operates an eleven-press plant and prints 90 catalogs and magazines.

- The new two-year contract was ratified late last night on a close vote. No specific vote totals are available.

- Striking workers are expected back to work as early as Sunday with phased-in activity on an upgraded scale as the week progresses.

- Strike lasted 16 days.

- About 700 local workers had been on strike.

- About 70 replacement workers had been hired during the strike to keep the company operating.

- Contract terms include: a 3 percent annual wage increase beginning next month; health care premiums will be frozen for two years; a more equitable employees' work schedule provision; negotiation with union reps if new machinery is used and if job descriptions need to be changed; and "language union leaders wanted" concerning retaining seniority of union members.

- Ellery Jonas, President of the Local 221 union unit said: "We have agreed that striking workers will be brought back by seniority. We're meeting with the replacements who had taken our jobs during the strike. I don't think their situation will be totally resolved until maybe next week." (FOUR SECONDS FOR EACH SENTENCE ON TAPE)

- Jonathan R. Rafferty is Chairman and President of American Signature, which has plants in Oakview and three other cities.

- Rafferty said at a news conference after the vote: "We feel the settlement is an important step forward to assure American Signature's ability to retain business in an increasingly competitive national printing marketplace. This new contract will help us meet the quality and service needs of our customers while at the same time address the long-term concerns of our employees." (TEN SECONDS FOR EACH SENTENCE ON TAPE)

b.
- Big chemical plant explosion this afternoon!

- Happened about 3:45 P.M. at the Westlake Chemical Plant which is about one mile north of the village of Pinecrest on South 68th Street, but in Lancaster County. You are in Lancaster County.

- The explosion rattled windows ten miles away.

- Six people remain hospitalized; three are burned badly and remain in critical condition.

- About 50 others, including motorists, complained of respiratory problems; they were treated and released from Lincoln General Hospital.

- Frank Lothrop is Westlake Chemical Plant Manager. At a 5 P.M. news conference, Lothrop said: "A lot of structural steel is down and spread all over the place. We had a cylinder four or five stories high and about ten feet wide knocked to pieces. A lot of workers and people in the area had a tough time breathing." (RECORDED ON TAPE. FIVE SECONDS FOR EACH SENTENCE)

- Mary Wolverton told reporters that her husband, Reco, 23, a Westlake employee, was injured. Mary said on tape: "Reco was caught by falling debris inside the plant. He told me he was trapped in a small room. Dust kept falling on him, and into his eyes. They don't know if they can save his eyes." (RECORDED ON TAPE. THREE SECONDS FOR EACH SENTENCE)

- Cause of the blast is still undetermined.

- Blast happened in the processor where urea—a fertilizer—is made. A cloud of granular chemicals blew across 68th Street, across the fields, and into the south part of Lincoln, your base of operations.

- Ammonia leaked from pipelines making it difficult to breathe.

- Sheriff's deputies and the state patrol warned everyone to keep windows and ventilation systems closed.

- One state patrol trooper said it nearly blew his windows out, ten miles away from the blast.

- At 6:42 P.M. today, the ammonia was washed down and the pipes sealed. The all-clear signal was given.

2. This assignment involves enterprising a story (see Chapter 10). Record onto audiocassette several short segments of location or ambient sound at *one* of the following locations:

    a. a crowded restaurant

    b. a congested urban street corner

    c. an enthusiastic crowd at a sporting event or a political rally

    d. a busy railroad switching yard

    e. a noisy auto repair shop

    f. an active children's playground

    g. a local gun club, with the sound of guns being fired

    h. auctioneer at a large home or farm auction/sale

    i. horses leaving the starting gate at a racetrack

    j. a section of a busy interstate highway

    k. a busy checkout counter at a department or food store, with the sounds of cash registers or credit card machines operating

    l. police, fire, or ambulance sirens with vehicles en route to an emergency situation

Now enterprise a story related to that wild or raw sound so that in the end you provide a brief recorded report using only your voice and a portion of the natural or location sound you have recorded. For example, the recording of restaurant sounds could be used for a report on health standards in local restaurants. Downtown traffic sounds could tie in to a story about new construction or downtown development and planning.

Notes

1. For a modest fee, Radio-Television News Directors Association can provide a 60-minute audiotape entitled ''Sound Ideas for the '90s'' that demonstrates the effective use of sound to tell a news story. RTNDA Radio Board members provide commentary and critique. For a fee, RTNDA will also provide a set of the latest award-winning entries in the annual RTNDA Edward R. Murrow competition. For details, write to: Radio-Television News Directors Association, 1000 Connecticut Avenue, NW, Suite 615, Washington, DC, 20036. Or call: 202–659–6510.

2. Quotation from a recording of a personal interview with the author.

3. ''Use of Tape,'' *Newstips,* September 1986 (Jefferson City, MO: Missouri Network).

4. ''Use of Tape,'' *Newstips,* September 1986 (Jefferson City, MO: Missouri Network).

5. A transcript of this actuality was made from an audiocassette provided by KRLN Radio, Canyon City, Colorado.

6. Reprinted by permission of Laurie Krueger.

7. Sent to the author by Nan Siemer on July 15, 1993. Reprinted by permission.

8. An excellent source for in-depth information and clear illustrations is F. Gifford, *Tape: A Radio News Handbook,* 3d ed. (Englewood, CO: Morton Publishing, 1987).

9. Reprinted by permission of Laurie Krueger.

10. A transcript of each actuality in this WCAU-AM story was made from an audiocassette copy of the newscast provided by WCAU-AM, Philadelphia.

11. The transcript of this actuality was taken from the verbatim sheet supplied by MBS News.

12. The transcript of this actuality was taken from the verbatim sheet supplied by ABC News.

Chapter 13

Television Reporting

A lthough some reporting techniques and technical terms transfer readily from radio to television, many significant differences exist in the way reporters and photojournalists work together and use the tools of television production to gather, record, and edit picture and sound to provide quality television news stories.

To become acquainted with writing and presenting news for television, you must learn the equipment, the procedures, and the terminology associated with television news reporting. At first the equipment may seem incredibly intricate, the procedures extremely complex, and the terminology exceedingly confusing. Don't let any of this intimidate you. Remember that any piece of equipment is only as useful as the skills and knowledge of the operator. The more you know about how particular pieces of equipment operate, the easier you will find using this equipment to help you with your reporting tasks. The more fully you master the technology, and the more fully you understand the relationships among the various aspects of television reporting, the more effectively you can combine your skills in writing with sight and sound to produce clear, vivid, and effective television news stories.

This chapter provides only essential technical information because space is limited. Also, television reporters often rely on other news personnel to complete many of the technical steps required to get a story onto the screen. Several books listed in the bibliography in Appendix C provide more detail about the technical details surrounding television news production. The organization of this chapter parallels that used in Chapter 12, ''Radio Reporting.''[1]

Importance and Value of Video

Pictures give the journalist an additional tool with which to tell a news story. Television news can place the viewer at the scene of the news event in a very real sense. Pictures provide details, illustrations, and visual information that may be too complex to put into words or too emotional to capture effectively in news copy only.

A skillful photojournalist fuses sight and sound to produce a news story that has extra dimension and meaning. Video and audio blend and overlap to establish and reinforce the flow and continuity of a visual message. Television news reporting requires a complex blend of creative and technical skills to use pictures as well as sounds to tell a visual story well and more completely. Pictures can capture a moment, add a sense of time and place, and convey that experience to viewers. Television viewers become not only eyewitnesses but also vicarious participants. Through pictures and sound they gain insights into the larger meaning of news events and the issues they address.

Uses of Video in Television News

Remember that you can present a television news story in several ways. Let's look a little closer at several of these methods of presentation and add a few terms to your television news production vocabulary.

Graphics can help make stories easier to understand and more appealing visually. Many newsrooms interface computers and electronic design centers to create sophisticated graphics systems capable of integrating words and pictures in a creative, and informative manner. *Character generators (CGs)*, often called *electronic titling machines* in larger newsrooms, produce various lettering styles and sizes for on-screen identification, statistics, precise quotations, or English translations for foreign-speaking newsmakers. Electronic paint systems use an electronic tablet and a stylus or electronic pen to generate predetermined or free-form shapes and patterns often in animated sequences to illustrate complex information or to provide visuals for a story when none are readily available. *Electronic still storer (ESS)* systems load, retrieve, and display incoming video from a variety of sources such as satellites, VTRs, slides, and electronic paint systems and can provide photos, maps, charts, graphs, symbols, preproduced graphics material, and so forth. Composite graphics, in which several visual elements are creatively combined into one graphic, are popular in television news today. The procedure for designing and using graphics in television news stories is described later in this chapter.

Soundbites and Q & A's are parallel terms from radio news production. CG information generally is inserted (*supered,* or *keyed*) over *sound on tape (SOT)* segments to better identify who is seen speaking on-camera and to avoid providing unnecessary or redundant identifications in the news copy.

Voice-overs (VOs) consist of news copy that a newscaster or reporter reads while edited video is shown full-screen.

B-roll is a technique that can be used to enhance soundbites and voice-overs by providing better illustration of what is being said. B-roll also provides visual relief. During a B-roll the newsmaker or reporter continues to be heard, but the picture changes to scenes that illustrate what is being said.

Stand-ups in television resemble voicers in radio. The only picture is the reporter at the scene of an important, breaking story. Stand-up reports run less than 60 seconds and often are used when the story is important but no other pictures are available. Although *stand-up* may be the term used in the copy, reporters have been shown sitting, walking, squatting, or in positions other than standing. Short stand-up segments are used regularly in packages for transitions.

Packages in television resemble wraps in radio. After an anchor lead-in, a package provides a complete, self-contained report of a news event by using a combination of graphics, voice-overs, soundbites, and stand-ups. Packages average 1:30 to 2:00 in length and are a mainstay in television news. The structure of packages is examined later in this chapter.

Natural sound is used with virtually all on-the-scene television news shots. Nat sound adds intensity and enhances authenticity for the pictures seen and the words heard.

Gathering and Recording Video

Acquiring videotape to use in locally produced news stories requires familiarity with the equipment used, the personnel involved, and standard procedures and techniques followed. Some television newsrooms refer to this process as *ENG (Electronic News Gathering)* or *EFP (Electronic Field Production)* to distinguish today's videotape or electronic news production from the earlier use of motion picture film alone in news production.

Professional news photographers are not the only sources for video material. Seeing home or amateur video on the nightly news of a flood that devastated farmers or of a fire that destroyed a prominent business and involved heroic actions by firefighters is not unusual. Although home video has been accepted primarily for breaking stories, especially those that are weather-related, the use of amateur video is growing as news budgets decline, competitiveness intensifies, and speed becomes critical.

Equipment

Manufacturers are constantly improving cameras and videotape recorders. Television news material is gathered using three-quarter-inch videotape news-gathering equipment as well as new systems such as half-inch videotape units and erasable and reusable CD and video compression systems that allow a reporter to edit video at a computer terminal. The Hi-8 format is attractive because the equipment is inexpensive, compact, and operates in low-light situations. New systems are interfacing with existing systems to make television newsgathering equipment lightweight, compact, portable, flexible, sensitive to control, easy to use, stable, ultrarugged, durable, weatherproof, and energy-efficient.

Both picture and sound must be recorded. The videotape recorder captures video from the camera and sound from a microphone or other audio source and lays these onto a videotape for later editing, processing, and on-the-air use.

Equipment selection and use are an integral part of television news coverage. Know the capabilities of the gear you have available. Determine what you will need to cover the stories assigned. Make certain the equipment works *before* you leave the newsroom. Photojournalists are often expected to maintain and keep in an assigned vehicle a basic set of equipment the news department provides.

Personnel

Working together. Trusting each other. Communicating. Shaping the story with *both* picture and sound. Television news reporting is a collaborative effort between *all* members of the team. That's how *effective* television news stories are done.

Teamwork between the reporter and the photojournalist or videographer is particularly crucial. The bond between them must be professional, cooperative, and caring, a spirit without which much of the value of television news reporting is diminished. The reporter cannot operate simply as a reporter, even if a single person writes the television story *and* gathers the video material. Words and pictures must be brought together and firmly united; neither words nor pictures can operate in isolation. Working *together,* a reporter and a photojournalist can make a news story literally come alive for a viewer. The reporter *must* know the shots the photojournalist has taken or expects to take. The photojournalist *must* know what shots the reporter wants or expects, how the reporter ''sees'' the story, how the reporter ''visualizes'' the presentation of facts and opinions.

Most reporters agree that working *with* a photojournalist is the *best* way to shape a television news story. Jill Kelley, reporter/anchor at WKRC-TV in Cincinnati, advises not to overlook a photojournalist's input:

> One mistake some reporters make is not listening to the other half of their team while shooting a story. Some [photojournalists'] opinions deserve more respect than others, but I guarantee, you'll get a better result if you treat your partner in the trenches as you want to be treated.[2]

Merely *wanting* to get the advice and cooperation of your photographer may not be as simple as you think. Frankly, some photographers will balk at using the ''team'' approach to news coverage and will never want to share ideas. Others will welcome being on a team, sharing ideas, and cooperatively shaping a news story with picture and sound. Learn the personalities of those with whom you work and adjust your approach accordingly. If you encounter resistance, be patient. Work at establishing a friendly, professional relationship. Ask advice on critical stories. Getting help will be easier as time goes on.

Here are other *ways to improve reporter-photojournalist relationships:*

   a. Share ideas and information about story coverage *throughout* the reporting process.
   b. *Together* identify how the story should begin, what the middle of the story should be, and how to end the piece effectively.
   c. *Together* decide how to adapt story coverage techniques to each reporting situation; for example, initially leave the camera in the

Reporter Lynette Romero and Photographer Sandy Kowal prepare a 6:00 A.M. weather live shot for 9 News. Photo courtesy of Barb Simon and KUSA-TV, Denver.

news car for sensitive story coverage or split up at a fire when pictures are at one place and information is at another.

d. Openly share the experience of covering a story—difficult, emotional stories as well as tedious, routine stories.

e. Consider replacing the labels *reporter* and *photog.* with terms like *journalist* or perhaps *broadcast journalist, photojournalist,* or *electronic journalist. Videographer* is also a common term used to replace *photog.* Using a professional designation for your partner could help improve your professional attitudes toward each other.

f. Respect each other in what you say, how you behave, what you wear, and how you treat each other.[3]

Different jobs are assigned to reporters and photojournalists. In large newsrooms, reporters gather information and report the story. Photojournalists handle the sensitive equipment in the field and may also edit the videotape with the reporter if a video editor is not assigned. In Chapter 11, the section titled "Positions in Larger Newsrooms" provides a brief rundown of the personnel and processes involved in assembling television news stories in large-market and network newsrooms. In smaller newsrooms, the reporter is also the photojournalist as well as the video editor. Generally, the larger the newsroom, the narrower each person's job.

One-person news coverage has become common at all levels. Equipment has become relatively easy to operate, and one person costs less than two people. A person working in television news as a *one-person band* works simultaneously as a photographer and a reporter. This coverage system not only saves money, generally it is faster and more efficient than some traditional two-person reporting teams.

One-person coverage, however, is not without its challenges. You have to be very efficient with your time, attention, and energy. In addition, you

KXAS-TV Reporter/Weekend Anchor Jim Douglas and Photojournalist Linda Angelle shoot interviews for a story at Arlington Police headquarters. Photo courtesy of Dennis Lyon and KXAS-TV, Forth Worth.

have to be flexible and resourceful. For example, how do you shoot reporter cutaways that can be used when editing interviews? Usually this involves setting up a chair, turning the camera around to photograph the chair, and then running around to sit down while the camera rolls—all of this while the interview guest tries to make sense of this commotion! You soon discover that you have to save as many steps as possible while covering stories; this means watching for dangerous situations that may develop while shooting, and asking for help holding equipment or cue cards and notes, especially when shooting stand-ups. Stand-ups can still be shot even if you have to frame the shot using buildings, light posts, or pieces of paper to mark your place in the frame.

One-person coverage is certainly challenging and is becoming a common system for television news coverage. Learn how to handle *all* of the essential jobs needed to get a television news story on-the-air. Your efforts now could save your job in the future.

Procedures and Techniques

Whether working alone or as a member of a reporter-photojournalist team, you eventually develop ways to cover stories very efficiently. Although the process involved in gathering and recording video material is complex, three phases or steps can be identified: determine what you need; shoot what you need (and then some); and check what you get.

Determine What You Need

Each television news story is unique—not only in the contents of the copy, but also in the pictures and sounds needed to convey the meaning of that story as clearly and meaningfully as possible. As soon as a story assignment is made, a good reporter is *constantly* examining the structure, angle, and contents of that news story and *constantly* shaping and refining story details, shots needed, points of view to be expressed, and so forth.

The reporter must constantly deal with some persistent questions: How can I make this fact better understood? What shot should I use to tie this scene to the next scene? Will a viewer understand what I'm showing now? Are there places where the picture says it all? Ask yourself what types of people have been left out of previous coverage. How can you see and tell the story from a point of view different from your own? A good television reporter is constantly turning over in his or her mind the story being covered. It seems there is always a better way to cover and then report every story!

How do you determine what you need to gather while in the midst of covering a television news story? Here are a few suggestions:

a. *Assess quickly* the story being covered.
b. *Decide firmly* the *specific* story angle you are trying to tell. Try to deliver *only one* central message.
c. *Look carefully* for the pictures and sounds needed to tell *that* story by illustrating crucial story points such as time and place and by stressing newsworthiness; for example, emphasize prominence, impact, and conflict. Look to your visual sense to take something from the scene that will strengthen the visual progression and continuity of the story. Find pictures that illustrate clearly how the story affects people.
d. *Remain flexible* by *always* looking at each story from as many angles as possible. Consider your alternatives. This does not mean you should try to cover too much in one story. Stick with your main story focus, the one main message you are trying to deliver.

As suggested in earlier chapters, capture on videotape those sights and sounds that do not remain long at a news scene; this would include shots of ambulances, motorcades, eyewitnesses, and survivors. Get pictures *first* because they are fleeting. Get detailed information and facts later. If possible, to save time later, shoot scenes in the order in which they are *likely* to be used in the story. And *always* shoot more than enough cutaway footage. You usually need more than you think.

Shoot What You Need . . . and Then Some

Describe precisely the sights and sound needed to tell the story that you have identified. Although extensive discussion and illustration of video production techniques are beyond the scope of this book, several books listed in Appendix C provide a comprehensive review of these activities.

Here is **a video composition "short course"** that might help when you are shooting your own video or conferring with a photojournalist on a story:

a. *Shoot at eye-level.* Avoid exaggerated high- or low-angle camera positions except for special applications.
b. *Keep essential or important visual information in or near the center of the frame* to make certain most viewers will see it.

c. *Be conscious of the visual balance and emphasis in each shot.*

d. *Leave minimum headroom* (the space between the tops of heads and the top of the television screen) but enough space at the bottom of the picture to be able to insert CG material to clearly identify who is shown on-camera.

e. *Leave visual ''breathing room.''* Allow a little space in the portion of the picture into which a person looks or the direction in which the action appears to be moving. Most viewers need that space to avoid feeling visually confined.

f. *Watch for distracting backgrounds* such as lamps or plants growing out of heads, background colors blending into foreground shots, or too many details distracting viewers from the main feature of the shot. Change camera angles to avoid some of these problems.

g. *Be conscious of the visual perspective or point of view shown in each shot.* For example, shooting opponents from different angles can visually emphasize contrasting viewpoints.

h. *Avoid using pan or zoom shots.* Make certain that pans and zooms are motivated and that they are used only to follow action and to show spatial relationships within a scene. Thoughtful editing precludes the need for most pans and zooms. If you *must* use a pan or zoom, begin taping and, then, count to three slowly before beginning the move. At the end, count to three slowly again before stopping the camera. This procedure makes it easier to edit the move into the visual story.

i. *Maintain visual logic.* Remember the point of view or visual angle that previous camera shots established. Maintain spatial relationships between objects and people in the picture. This is especially important during interviews (discussed later), but also for parades, football games, and so forth. Once a spatial relationship has been established, the camera cannot cross over this ''imaginary line'' without disorienting the viewer. This happens when movement in one direction suddenly shifts to the opposite direction; for example, the parade is moving left to right in the picture but is suddenly shown going right to left because the next shot was taken from the opposite side of the street.

Several terms are used to describe the variety of shots commonly used in television news stories. We'll use a typical traffic accident story for visual references. An *establishing (cover)(long) shot* such as an overview of a traffic accident scene provides a wide visual orientation for the viewer and is often used at the beginning of a story to show where or when the story occurred as well as to introduce the general nature or major elements of the story. *Main action shots* such as closer shots of damaged vehicles and ambulances help emphasize important visual elements of the story. *Cut-ins* (sometimes called *inserts*) are smaller, more magnified portions of main action shots; they enhance visual unity and help place viewers even closer to specific visual information. In our traffic accident story, this might be a shot of a shattered front windshield. A *medium shot (MS)* is a shot closer to the action than an establishing shot. A *close-up (CU)* is a shot that is even closer to the action.

Although later editing can help, you need to get shots in the field that will help avoid *jump cuts*. These are shot changes that show an unnatural or illogical jump in the action. For example, a jump cut would result if a cover shot of a demolished car being pulled out of a ditch was followed immediately by a cover shot of the same car being towed on the highway. Visual continuity has been disrupted and must be corrected to avoid distracting viewers with vehicles that illogically leap forward in time!

You can avoid jump cuts in several ways. Here are a few:

a. Change the distance and/or the angle between the camera and the person or object. For example, after the cover shot of the demolished car being pulled out of a ditch, cut to a close-up of the winch on the wrecker taken from a slightly different camera angle.

b. Use *cutaways* to momentarily direct the viewer's attention away from the main action to show something mentioned in or related to the story. For example, you could show skid marks on the highway or a patrol officer directing traffic around the accident scene.

c. Use *reverse angle* shots taken from exactly opposite the perspective of the previous shot. For example, follow a shot of a car being lifted from the ditch with a reverse angle shot of bystanders watching the scene. The same camera *position* would be used, but the camera *angle* would be reversed, to show the bystanders as the car might "see" them.

Shot sheets or *logs* (also called *short cards, dope,* or *breakdown sheets*) help identify what is recorded. Printed forms, notecards, sheets of paper, or even backs of used envelopes can be used to keep track of the length, content, and location (on the videotape) of each shot. A little paperwork in the field saves valuable time when editing or preparing *live shots*. Even if you do not keep a complete log of the shots, whatever information you can capture on paper, on tape, or in your mind as you gather video material will help you process video material later when meeting deadlines is critical.

The interview is probably one of the most common television news-gathering situations used. The principles for shooting interviews on videotape are the same whether you are interviewing "on-the-run," in a group interview

Examples of three key shots needed for a television interview to be easily edited: (a) two-shots of both reporter and newsmaker; (b) H & S shot of the interviewee and newsmaker; (c) reverse angle shots of the reporter.

(a)

(b)

(c)

situation such as questioning an attorney on the steps of a courthouse after a verdict, or sitting in a controlled and comfortable studio environment.

Here are the *types of shots needed before you can start to edit television interviews:*

a. A few shots in which *both* reporter and newsmaker are shown speaking in natural conversation. These *two-shots* help establish spatial relationships for the viewer and can be recorded before or after the interview.

b. The full interview, shot over the reporter's shoulder with the interviewee shown in an *H&S shot* (from the shoulders to the head). Do not change camera angle or position during the interview.

c. A few reverse angle shots of the reporter (from the interviewee's viewpoint) asking key questions on camera. These can be used to add variety to the story and also to help avoid jump cuts.

d. Shots suggested or brought to mind during the interview. For example, after an interview with a zoning commission supervisor about the construction start for a major shopping center, go out to the site and record several shots showing the location. If the mayor complains about overcrowded jail conditions, get interior shots of the jail to use as B-roll. The B-roll would be used for cutaways.

Despite the addition of pictures, the principles of interviewing described in Chapter 10 remain the same. A few video-only suggestions might *make the television interview process smoother and more effective:*

a. Let the camera record the comments. Some reporters record the interview simultaneously on an audiocassette to help write and edit the story. This technique could also help protect the reporter from later accusations of misconstruing a story.

b. During the conversation, look at the interviewee and not at the camera or other equipment.

c. Keep the interview as natural as possible. For example, to avoid unnecessary distractions, the camera operator can gently touch the reporter on the shoulder when comments are ready to be recorded rather than yelling "Okay. We're rolling!!"

d. If various viewpoints will be expressed on an issue, consider establishing a *visual* point of view for each interviewee. For example, those favoring the issue could look screen left and those opposing the issue could look screen right.

Here are *suggestions to make television video newsgathering efficient, easy, and noticeably effective:*

a. Get "people" shots and comments. Viewers identify better with people than with buildings, cars, streets, rivers, and so forth.

b. Let the people closest to the story tell it. Save officials, observers, and experts for your own background information and possibly for your voice-over narration segments. Such people didn't experience the story; they're just talking about it.

c. Get as close as possible to the action of the story.

d. Use your video equipment efficiently. For example, after recording a short interview, keep the videotape recorder (VTR) running, and let interviewees pronounce and spell their names and perhaps give you their relationship to the story you are trying to tell (eyewitness, office supervisor of convicted murderer, etc.). Announce the take number and provide a countdown each time you rerecord an on-camera report; in addition, hold up the number of fingers that match the cut number; these shots are easy to find and save time when editing videotape.

e. At the beginning and again at the end of each shot, record a few seconds of extra video and audio to make editing easier.

f. Systematically label all videotapes used by indicating a particular story-related item or two—story slug or location, time of day, interviewee's name, and story segment such as B-roll or stand-up segments. Develop a labeling system that is easy to remember, efficient, and helpful for finding what you think you have when you edit.

g. Keep a shot log *during* shooting. Do not rely on your memory.

h. Use a generous but reasonable shooting radio (i.e., the proportion of footage shot to footage used); 4:1 or 6:1 is reasonable for most stories. Remember, the more you shoot, the more you log. Shoot enough to tell the story, but do not shoot 45 minutes of videotape for a routine 2-minute story!

i. Always record natural sound on one of the audio channels available on professional model videotape equipment.

j. Plan and then use your news story coverage time efficiently and productively.

Unfortunately, time pressures often preclude the use of many of these suggestions. With experience, however, you will develop your own methods for recording and using video in television news stories.

Check What You Get

In most cases, you cannot return to the scene to rerecord material needed for a story. The highway has been cleared after the accident; the presidential candidate has flown on to the next airport interview. Although you learn to know and trust machines and the people who operate them, you also need to remember Murphy's Law.

In broadcast news, not many second chances occur. Know what you need and want for every story, and then get it right . . . the first and probably the only time!

Before you leave a news scene, make certain you have what you need and everything that you came for. Quickly review your notes, and play back a short portion of the videotape recording.

Writing to Video

Many television reporters spend less time writing actual news copy and more time logging video already shot, ordering graphics that often get changed, supervising and worrying about videotape editing still to be completed, and making sure everything that is technical is ready for each story. But a television reporter must focus on delivering a story with *both* picture and sound, video and audio, meaningful shots as well as meaningful words. Remember what the story really means. Recapture the experience of the story for your audience. Show the details that sparked your own strong reaction to the story.

Chapter 3 illustrated the copy formats used in television news but did not explain the *processes* used to assemble a television news story, how visual continuity is established and maintained, how pictures can be used to tell a story effectively, and how to write effective copy for various types of television news stories. These points are covered now.

Processes

Each newsroom determines the specific steps to be followed to complete the preparation of each story. The processes that a particular newsroom prefers depend on several factors: budget, size and experience of the news staff, amount and quality of the equipment available, and simply the preference of the news director or newsroom supervisor.

Most newsrooms have similar processes that work well. We'll look at those and examine how a story using videotape is prepared for broadcast. Understand that the processes examined parallel those also used to prepare other kinds of video material such as CG and ESS items.

Most television news stories (like radio stories) are structured in the field—as the story is being covered. The reporter and photojournalist constantly examine what they have and what they need to tell a developing story clearly, effectively, and meaningfully. Some reporters start writing on the way to the story—anticipating what they will encounter, forming questions that they want to ask of people they want to be sure to contact. Then, during story coverage, they constantly scrutinize how the story is developing, what has been and what needs to be recorded or gathered. On the way back to the newsroom, rough drafts of the copy can be scribbled as notes are studied, basic questions asked, and video reviewed (generally in the viewfinder of the camera). Eventually, final news copy must be written and reviewed for length as well as effectiveness and use of available video. So, writing a television news story should be under way *constantly*—during *every* phase of story coverage.

After stories have been assigned and covered, here are *the steps used to assemble most television news stories involving videotape material:*

1. As time permits, look at the videotape available and verify the accuracy and completeness of shot sheets (described earlier). Even when you work with a photographer and an editor, always *look* at your video and *listen* to your sound *before* you write your story.

2. Determine the best arrangement of shots for telling the story. Limit what you include. Select only two or three critical pieces of information to use in a single story to support *one* main message. Save the rest for another story. You should already have identified the main ideas or story points, the story length needed, and the presentation format you will use.

3. Select the soundbites (if any) to be used and note the in-cue, out-cue, and length of each soundbite. Use soundbites to convey subjective information. Examples include reactions, emotions, or firsthand observations connected to the story.

4. Indicate on the news copy the videotape number or identification as well as the exact videotape counter numbers for each soundbite needed.

5. If not already done, write a rough draft of the script. Suggest graphics to use (if needed) and note on the script the *exact* times when the various kinds of video and audio material will be used in the story. Remember, graphics are usually inserted at the time the story runs on-the-air.

6. If used, record voice-over segments onto videotape directly or onto audiotape for later transfer to videotape.
7. Edit the videotape. Here are two approaches that work:

Approach 1

    a. First, all sound-on-tape (SOT) segments (soundbites and stand-ups).
    b. Second, all voice-over (VO) and natural sound segments as well as segments that will use music.
    c. Third, all videotape that will be needed to accompany the VO copy that has been written or that will be used as B-roll with SOT segments. Edit the entire sound track of the story before adding these supplementary (B-roll) shots.

Approach 2

    a. First, all natural sound segments, without soundbites.
    b. Second, all SOT segments.
    c. Third, all VO segments.
    d. Fourth, all B-roll shots used with VO segments.
    e. Fifth, additional soundbites (if needed).
8. If time permits, get producer approval for copy and videotape (content, presentation quality, length, etc.).

Another story assembly tactic that works, depending on the time available and the nature of the story involved, is to edit pictures *first,* and then surround what is shown with news copy, voice-over narration, soundbites, natural sound and music segments, and so on. This method allows the *video* to determine the natural structure of the news story. This method must be used judiciously by an experienced video editor.

An additional scripting step may be needed. Even with computerized scripting systems, reporters are often required to provide transcripts of soundbites for the teleprompter as well as closed-captioning transmissions. Closed-captioning helps hearing-impaired viewers as well as those situated in noisy locations or who might be a long way from the television set speaker. This is one more responsibility for the reporter, but it helps provide a very useful service.

Visual Continuity and Progression

As noted in Chapter 5, every story is different. You can tell a story in many ways. Regardless of how you tell a story, however, *all* stories must have a beginning, a middle, and an end. Television news stories are no exception. Like a lead sentence, the first shots of a television news story must capture attention and then engage and prepare the viewer for what follows. The middle of the story should explain more about what is happening and who is involved. The ending should provide a conclusion for the story.

Use pictures as well as sounds to provide the continuity the viewer needs to understand and then recognize the *visual* progression of the story. As you watch television news stories, think about the *progression* and *sequencing* of sound and picture that has been used to tell you a story. Evaluate how well each story is constructed and how well the various elements of the story are presented.

Map or outline the story *before* you start writing. List the elements you want to use—natural sound, soundbites, VO sequences—and place them in the order you will use them. This planning should help streamline the video and copyediting process.

To provide continuity, control both what is said *and* what is seen. Just as the newswriter thinks about the words used and how words form sentences that connect to other sentences to build blocks of ideas and information, so the television reporter must use this natural linking or flow of individual shots to form logical sequences that build effective segments for each television news story. Do not use pictures for their own sake—because they look good or were difficult to obtain. Use pictures because they help link and communicate the main points of the news story that you are trying to tell.

Guidelines for aural continuity in radio copy parallel those for visual continuity in television copy. Cramming too many facts into one story (just like changing shots too often in too short a time) causes confusion and consternation. Long sentences (like lengthy shots) tend to slow the pace of a story. Odd word choices (like unmotivated or poorly placed or poorly edited shots) distract and confuse the audience.

You must see clearly in your mind what the screen will look like for every line of news copy that you write. Picture *and* sound must blend together to give maximum emphasis and unity to both elements; yet they must provide the viewer with a *composite* viewpoint for a story, and tell a story that is particularly meaningful *because* both picture *and* sound are used.

Telling the Story

A balance and correlation must exist between what is heard and what is seen. News copy can relay facts and background information; pictures can best show actions and emotions.

In television news, the copy and sound are still important, but pictures and visuals tend to dominate and are what viewers most readily remember. Pictures, especially pictures of people in action, probably tell most television news stories best. People continue to be fascinated with other people—who they are, what they do, and how they think.

Copy and pictures need not be linked so closely that they *always* match exactly. The temptation is to write news copy for everything that is seen. The news copy should avoid redundancies as well as unnecessary and obvious visual references (*shown here* or *as you can see now in this footage*).

Television news copy is used most effectively when words are heard that emphasize a key point needing verbal repetition or that talk about the situation or events the pictures represent or suggest. Television news copy should place the viewer directly *in* the story:

```
At first it didn't seem too bad. Just a lot of smoke billowing
from a second story room where the pastor emeritus kept his
valuable book collection. Even firefighters thought they had
it under control. But the heat proved too intense. . . .
```
                                                            KWTV, Oklahoma City

At times, the picture is so strong, compelling, exciting, and even dramatic that words may get in the way. Sometimes only pictures and natural sound are needed or perhaps only limited news copy. Often a television news story improves noticeably after the writer simply gets out of the way of the story and lets it be told *visually*—by what viewers can see, understand, and evaluate for themselves.

A reporter sometimes faces the challenge of telling an important story that does not offer obvious or readily available pictures. For example, providing strong visual material for a financial or budget story that offers only predictable statistics and comments is difficult. A creative and thoughtful reporter thinks about the *heart* of each story and then asks: How can I best tell this story *visually?* Perhaps a simple stand-up or anchor reader report is the best visual presentation possible. But also consider the use of graphics, charts, maps, documents, file footage, an on-the-set interview or report—something to make the story *visually* better. Also talk to others in the newsroom; ask their advice.

Lead-Ins

Newscaster lead-ins for television news stories have essentially the same functions as lead-ins written for radio news stories—begin the process of telling a story, introduce the nature of the story, contribute worthwhile information, prepare the audience for what it is about to learn, and introduce the reporter or the newsmaker who will provide additional information and keep the story moving forward. An effective television story lead-in uses various kinds of graphics and video material to begin telling a visually enticing news story.

One of the most common, but important, television news story lead-ins to write involves soundbites. In such a lead-in, attention should begin to shift from the newscaster to the newsmaker and what he or she is about to say as the meaning and significance of the story is noted.

Notice how the 13-second VO track leading into the following soundbite identifies the apparent cause of the accident and prepares viewers for the on-camera comment by the police officer, Corporal Steven Kowa.

[DAVE TIGHT]
(DAVE)
MARYLAND UNIVERSITY POLICE HAVE IDENTIFIED THE THREE MEN
KILLED THIS MORNING IN A COLLEGE PARK SINGLE CAR CRASH.
[TAKE VO] {**VO**} [TRUNS :13]
[CG=2000=College Park] (College Park)
CAMPUS POLICE SAY THE ACCIDENT HAPPENED WHEN ARTHUR CLARK, 21,
A STUDENT AND RESIDENT OF BALTIMORE WAS DRIVING TWO OF HIS
FRIENDS DOWN PAINT BRANCH DRIVE. CLARK APPARENTLY LOST CONTROL
AND HIT A POLE AND A TREE.
[TAKE SOT] {**SOT**}
[CG=2010=Cpl. Steven Kowa—UMD POLICE] (Steven Kowa, UMD
Police)
[TRUNS=7]
''We do have witness statement that this vehicle was observed
traveling at a high rate of speed. So speed appears to be a
factor.''
[OUT: TO BE A FACTOR]
[KEEP VO] {**VO**}
(DAVE)
ALSO KILLED IN THE CRASH, 25-YEAR-OLD SHAWN EVANS OF ADELPHI
AND 21-YEAR-OLD DAVID CHISHOLM OF SILVER SPRING. POLICE SAY
BOTH EVANS AND CHISHOLM WERE WEARING SHOULDER BELTS, BUT NOT
LAP BELTS.

News Channel 8, Maryland/Virginia/Washington, DC

Review and time carefully the edited soundbite. Write brief VO copy
for the few seconds just before the soundbite begins. You could identify
someone indirectly by noting their association with the news story; for example, *"Firefighters had a difficult time getting to the family trapped inside."*
A CG insert could identify a specific person with a direct story connection;
this person would then be seen and heard when the CG material was shown.

	. . . A 3 month old baby girl
dissolve to	. . . Mrs. Hibbler's
sot coming	granddaughter . . . was saved by a
	firefighter who only wished he could
	have done more.
Dissolve vtr sot	
runs: 11	_____(sot) ____
s/Jeff Bridick	in: you lost two
Madison Firefighter	out: because of the flames

KMOV-TV, St. Louis

Some newsrooms (like KMOV-TV) use *two* videotape machines to ensure a smooth transition from an anchor VO to a soundbite. An extra few seconds of video is available on one videotape recording as the anchor reads VO copy, leading into the soundbite. The second VTR, containing only the soundbite and appropriate B-roll, is started as the anchor finishes reading the VO copy.

Two or more soundbites can be used back-to-back—generally with only CG identification added. Sometimes the anchor lead-in copy provides all of the essential identification information needed. Notice how this lead-in emphasizes what three eyewitnesses saw and experienced rather than simply their names, titles, or addresses. Verbatims of the soundbites are provided to help illustrate this point. This lead-in prepares or sets up the viewer for these three *MOS* (man-on-the-street) soundbites:

```
lead-in
```

```
. . . Before firemen arrived, neighbors and people who stopped
to help saved the lives of the children's parents and their
three-month-old nephew . . .
```

```
sot mos -45 -51 -59
```

```
[SOT MOS 1: ''And that woman was hollering, ''My babies! My
babies!'' And then she was laying up on the roof and there was
another guy standing there.'']
```

```
[SOT MOS 2: ''He finally picked up the baby and tossed the baby
down and I caught the baby and I was — you know — frantic and
scared, so I said: Someone take the baby.'']
```

```
[SOT MOS 3: ''He handed it to me and I held the baby. And he kept
hollerin' he had three more babies in there and nobody could do
anything.'']
```

```
vo track 1
```

```
Investigators say children playing with a lighter set fire to a
living room sofa.
```

```
sot from fire dept.
```

```
[SOT: ''Children frequently will run once they've done
something like this. They're afraid of it. They know it's bad
once it's happened. And we can only speculate that they ran to
the highest point and to possibly their room where they felt
safe.'']
```

vo track 2

The two family home didn't have any smoke alarms. Neighbors
claim it took firefighters too long to get here, but fire
officials say they arrived just one minute after getting the
call. . . .

WTHR-TV, Indianapolis

Notice how the three eyewitnesses provide a progressive narrative of the
rescue effort; each statement leads naturally and easily into the next statement
by another eyewitness. Notice also how the lead-in to the fire department
spokesperson's comment also serves as a bridge between segments that trace
the rescue effort and the cause of the fire. ''VO track 2'' helps bridge from a
comment about the cause of the fire to a comment about the response time of
the fire department. And so the story progresses. Each lead-in should help pull
together the pieces of the story and arrange facts and comments into a logical
stream of information.

Here is the typical structure of television news stories involving soundbites: The newscaster begins the story on camera—full-screen or often with a
''box'' filled with graphics placed over the shoulder of the anchor; VO copy
is read by the anchor leading to and introducing the soundbite; one or two
soundbites are used next with visual identification provided by the CG; the
newscaster finishes the story on camera—full-screen or reading VO copy over
additional visual material (edited videotape, ESS, CG, or other graphics material). See Figure 3.14 for an illustration of this copy format.

Here is good advice provided by KMOV-TV in St. Louis: ''If you've
put together a good story, it is a good story *without* the sound bite. The bite
just enhances it.''[4] The copy in Figure 13.1 follows this advice and also illustrates the typical structure of soundbite stories.

Write-Outs

The same general guidelines apply to television write-outs as to radio write-
outs: Most are not needed. Some newsrooms insist on using them to reestablish
newscasters on camera before moving to the next news story and possibly
another voice and face on camera. Write-outs, or *tags,* can be used to provide
additional or updated story information (see Figure 13.1).

Graphics

Television graphics provide a creative way for reporters to tell stories that are
often complex and visually dull. Maps, statistics, story and company logos,
photographs, quotations, and many other visual items can be used to help
identify people and locations, indicate dates or the use of video from various
sources, or any number of other pieces of information that help communicate
the news to the viewers. Banners, boxes, and animation (moving images) have
become part of a television reporter's vocabulary and have added another layer

COPS FIRED	(BRAD)	9
DVE FZ	THREE DALLAS POLICE OFFICERS WERE FIRED TODAY FOR THEIR INVOLVEMENT IN THE SHOOTING OF AN UNARMED 16-YEAR-OLD GIRL LAST MONTH.	
VTR VOSOT (COPS FIRED) KEY: DALLAS	VANESSA SMITH TONIGHT IS AT HOME RECUPERATING. SHE WAS SHOT IN THE LEG, OFFICERS EVA DECHOUDENS . . . LARRY POPE . . . AND RESERVE OFFICER M-L EDWARDS WERE FIRED FOR FALSIFYING REPORTS AND LYING TO INVESTIGATORS.	03 04 12
SOT FULL AT :12 TO :26 KEY: CHIEF BILLY PRINCE :12 - :16 DALLAS POLICE DEPARTMENT KEY: JOHN WILEY PRICE :19 - :23 DALLAS CO. COMMISSIONER (AT)	IN: IT WASN'T DONE . . . OUT: AND TO BE FAIR. RUNS TO: 26 IN: JUST BECAUSE . . . OUT: YOU HAVEN'T APPEASED US,	
TAG	THE GIRL'S FAMILY HAS HIRED AN ATTORNEY AND THEY ARE CONSIDERING A LAWSUIT AGAINST THE POLICE DEPARTMENT.	

Figure 13.1 This copy illustrates the typical structure of television soundbite news stories and the use of back-to-back soundbites. Courtesy of KXAS-TV, Forth Worth, Texas.

of options for presenting news stories. Although a complete discussion of television graphics is beyond the scope of this book, consideration of the following is useful: why graphics are used, common errors that occur, steps used to design graphics, and suggestions that might improve graphics that you use.

Why has the use of graphics in television news increased? Graphics can help a viewer grasp the essence of a story quickly. They can enhance the visual presentation of a story, especially when the video elements are weak or missing. A well-designed graphic can help make things clearer if a story is complex and difficult to explain with copy alone or with copy and videotape; for example, highlighted quotations might help emphasize key points in a lengthy governmental report or study.

Many newsrooms have adopted style guides to develop a strong, consistent sense of style. Though style is not a substitute for content, a graphic consistency communicates content more clearly than if consistency is absent. Consistent, attractive graphics set the tone and provide the familiar framework that builds strong station identification in the minds of the viewers. Consistency creates a sense of style. Style creates a sense of unity and a feeling of momentum within a news staff. *That* can add a competitive edge to a newsroom operation and pay long-term dividends in audience ratings and recognition.

What are some of the common errors associated with designing and using graphics in television news stories? Sometimes the graphics do not coincide with the flow and structure of the story *as established by the news copy*. News copy must guide, not follow, the graphics used! Graphic copy and script copy must match exactly. If they do not match, the listener gets distracted and then has to choose whether to read from the graphic or listen to the words the reporter or anchor reads. In most cases, the text in the graphic will override the reporter or anchor's narrative. You can be more assured that you have accurately communicated the story's content if you take the initiative to read and understand the story. If the graphic does not help a viewer understand information, it is not useful and should be discarded.

Each newsroom devises its own specific rules and guidelines for designing, processing, and using graphics in television news stories. Generally, a reporter collaborates with a graphic artist (sometimes called an *electronic titler*). Using standardized forms, the reporter suggests content and design ideas and expresses preferences about how the graphics could be used on the screen (full-screen, right or left of the anchor, over the shoulder, etc.). The graphics specialist contributes design suggestions and alternatives based on the capabilities of the available graphics system and the newsroom's graphics practices. The graphics used are limited only by newsroom resources and the imagination and creativity of the reporter and graphics artist.

KXAS-TV Graphics Coordinator Carla McMurray using the Chyron Infiniti character generator. Photo courtesy of Dennis Lyon and KXAS-TV, Forth Worth, Texas.

Very few reporters actually complete complex graphics designs on their own. Only a qualified graphics specialist has the necessary technical knowledge, skill, and training. But to get the most out of today's sophisticated graphics systems, reporters must know the capabilities of the graphics system available.

Before you decide to use graphics in a television news story, ask ''How will this help viewers understand the story better?'' Maybe another soundbite would be better. Or perhaps it would be better to provide additional information with the anchor or reporter speaking on-camera. Perhaps the news copy needs to be rewritten.

Know the time line used by your graphics department. The steps described earlier may not be the same or they may be compressed or lengthened.

Communicate with the graphics artist and the newscast producer. Interaction, pooling experiences, creativity ''bursts'' produce creative design solutions. Stay in touch once you have given your suggestions. If provided, use standardized guidelines, forms, and terms to provide written instructions and suggestions for each graphic design. Work as a team to design, build, store, and evaluate the graphics produced.

To be effective, graphics must be simple and clear to help communicate only one key point of the story at a time (see Figure 13.2). A minimum of copy on the screen can reinforce or illuminate the script copy, but too much writing in the graphic tends to clutter the screen and dilute the impact of the story.

Specific story graphics are more effective than generic graphics when a specific local story is involved. For example, a story graphic pulled from a frame of videotape showing a specific local area is better than a graphic with flames as the image and ''FIRE'' as the cutline, or caption.

Use animation for a reason, not just because it looks good or provides a clever transition to another graphic design.

Cutlines should be referenced to the first sentence in the copy. Viewers read words on the screen. When the cutline is referenced, viewers will not lose track of what is being said.

If you have a lot of copy points to cover, consider using more than one graphic or ask to animate the graphic to allow for changes and transitions as new information is presented in the copy.

Graphics can be used more than once in a single story as long as each graphic helps clarify, enhance, or highlight a key story point.

Critique graphics that you use. Identify specific techniques that work best in a variety of situations. Here are a few questions to ask:

Does the graphic capture the essence of the story? Does it illustrate the key element of the story? Does it make sense?

Does the photograph or drawing or sketch used obscure or clarify the information in the story?

```
┌─────────────────────┐                          ((BETSY        ))        ┌──────────────┐
│  ELECTION DAY       │   BETSY/ELEC. XDAY         DON'T FORGET,           │ PG.          │
│ SLUG                │                      TOMORROW IS ELECTION DAY.     │      26      │
│ AE   XX 11/2    6   │                           VOTERS IN ST. LOUIS      └──────────────┘
│ WRITER  DATE   PGM  │              FS/ESS    CITY AND COUNTY CAN GO
└─────────────────────┘                      TO THE POLLS FROM SIX
                                             IN THE MORNING UNTIL
ELECTION DAY                                 SEVEN IN THE EVENING.
POLLS OPEN 6 AM                                   DON'T FORGET TO
POLLS CLOSE 7 PM                             BRING YOUR NEW VOTER
                                             IDENTIFICATION CARD...
                                             YOU MUST HAVE YOUR
                              FS/ESS         NEW I.D. CARD, OR SOME
ELECTION DAY                                 IDENTIFICATION WITH YOUR
BRING NEW VOTER REGISTRATION CARD            SIGNATURE  IN ORDER TO
                                             VOTE.
                                                  IF YOU HAVE NOT
                                             RECEIVED YOUR VOTER I.D.
                                             CARD, BE SURE TO VOTE AT
                                             YOUR REGULAR POLLING
                                             PLACE, AND BRING ANOTHER
                                             FORM OF I.D.
```

Figure 13.2 This copy illustrates effective use of graphics in television news stories. Courtesy of KMOV-TV, St. Louis, Missouri.

Do the words and symbols, pictures, logos, sketches, and so on, work *together* to create a single, clear message?

Does the graphic distort the data or quotes or information used in the story?

Is the graphic used at the right time in the story? Is the graphic integrated smoothly into the story structure guided by the news copy?

What other options should I consider for the design and utilization of this graphic?

Should I use a graphic at all? What are the other alternatives I should consider?

Narration and Voice-Overs

Writing narration and voice-over copy (sometimes called *tracks*) poses special problems for the newswriter. Picture and sound should coincide, but if the words heard always exactly match the pictures seen, the viewer could become bored with the tedious and redundant matching of audio and video. Use narration to convey objective information. This might include statistics, locations involved, the background or history of the story, facts, and so forth.

In some stories, picture and sound should match directly to emphasize important information and to ensure precision. But in other stories, narration can provide supplemental, background information to complement what is seen:

. . . It was called the crash heard round the world. A plane carrying humorist Will Rogers and Aviator Wiley Post crashed near Barrow . . . killing them both. This is rare film when the two landed in Juneau on their way to Barrow. Post was headed to the Soviet Union to explore a possible air route between Russia and the U.S. Rogers was along because he wanted to meet Charles Brower . . . who operated a trading post in Barrow. After leaving Fairbanks . . . Post and Rogers ran into fog. . . .

KTUU, Anchorage, Alaska

Narration can also add clarity and meaning or provide additional perspectives, by telling how or why what is seen relates to what is *not* being shown.

Often, story structure and news copy style must respond to available video. The television newswriter is constantly juggling video and audio to produce the best possible television news story.

Experience will help guide the writing of effective narration and voice-over copy. Here are a few suggestions that have proved to be helpful:

a. The words heard need to be associated in some way with the pictures shown.
b. Let viewers make the connection and establish the significance of most picture and sound matchups.

c. Tell viewers something related to but not obvious from viewing a particular shot or scene.

d. Make the copy sparse. Use only enough words to supply the information that available pictures cannot show. Voice-over copy can help link various story parts.

e. Let pictures breathe. Allow time for the viewer to think about the words heard and to digest the pictures shown. Use short musical segments or let natural sound carry some of the burden of telling the story. Sometimes using SOT segments as ''natural sound'' (even when a foreign language is being used) helps the viewer absorb what is shown.

f. Determine the speed of the person reading so that the pictures shown are only slightly longer than the copy written.

g. The copy should begin to tell a new part of the story as a new scene begins. Thus, when a new shot begins, a new sentence and a new idea should also begin.

h. Use contrasting narration carefully. If the screen is showing one scene, and the narration is offering a different viewpoint, the viewer could become confused.

Stand-Ups

A television news stand-up features the reporter at the news scene relaying only one or two key facts associated with the story. A stand-up often is the only way to report from the news scene as quickly as possible, before more complete reports can be developed, or to cover story information for which pictures are weak or nonexistent.

Good stand-ups advance a story and give it perspective. They let the viewer connect with the storyteller. They can help the storyteller describe things, confide in the viewer, or make a specific point.

A creative reporter can identify and devise a number of different alternatives for each story. If you know the physical elements or environment of the story well, you can develop a stand-up that connects the surroundings to the content and flow of the story. These are often labeled *involvement stand-ups*.

A television story about the shooting of a police officer will help illustrate the various types of ''involvement stand-ups.'' In a *reference stand-up* the reporter may gesture toward a building with a head nod, shoulder turn, or verbal reference; in our shooting story this may involve shooting a stand-up in front of the hospital where the officer was taken to show a location used early in the story. A *reveal stand-up* involves moving from one location to another to show the connection of two elements in the story; for example, to help show what happened at the hospital after the shooting, the reporter could start in the emergency room, explain that the officer was brought there for initial treatment, and then indicate that the officer was moved to an operating room as the camera moves down the hospital corridor. Another possibility is to walk out of one frame and into the next frame or location. A *prop stand-up* involves holding a prop or item to give viewers a visual cue about a particular aspect of the story; for example, the reporter could hold up the flak vest used by the officer who was shot. The prop stand-up could lead to a *demonstration stand-up* in which the reporter adopts a show-and-tell attitude and pulls on the flak vest. An *effects stand-up* involves using video effects systems such as dissolves, split-screens, and graphics to help clarify complex story details; in our shooting example, maybe a map of the area where the officer was shot and where the suspect was arrested would help viewers recognize the location or setting for the story.[5]

Stand-ups must fit into the natural flow of information; they must not look contrived. These qualities are ensured when reporter and photojournalist work together to use the time and resources available to make stand-ups an effective part of a story. Practice and care are key ingredients for success.

Most often a brief stand-up is inserted in the *middle* of a package when a transition or bridge is needed between locations or time frames, or to present a new or contrasting idea or issue associated with the story. The stand-up helps reestablish the reporter's presence at the scene of the story and can also help the viewer understand or interpret facts and ideas more easily, especially when the reporter demonstrates or shows something connected to the story.

This stand-up, used in the *middle* of a package report, is short and informative and *shows* a fact connected to the story being told:

vo

. . . Seven inches of rain dropped from the sky in just two hours. Mike Oliver watched in disbelief as his liquor store and home filled with water . . .

sot you just kept thinking. . . . and deeper :07

[''You just kept thinking it's going to quit raining. And it never quit. Then it came in from the south there, and it just kept getting deeper and deeper.'']

stand up

[''The water kept rising until it was more than chest-deep. There's the water line to prove it.'']

[GESTURES TO A MARK ON THE SIDE OF THE BUILDING]

vo

. . . The floodwaters rose faster than many residents could run.

Stand-ups can also be done at the *beginning* of a package report to introduce or begin the story and at the *end* to review important story points, add new information, or provide perspective about the story.

The term *stand-up* may be misleading and restrictive. Reporters often label as a "stand-up" on-camera comments they make while sitting in a car, lying on a bed, suspended under a parachute canopy, and so forth. You do not have to be literally standing up to do a stand-up!

Provide the best stand-up material possible. Develop brief stand-up segments that present one or two key facts in a clear and interesting manner. Record several *takes* and variations of stand-ups for possible use in different parts of the finished report. Developing *short* stand-up segments will allow you to quickly memorize what you want to say or, if necessary, to use notes or cue cards.

The skills needed to do an effective stand-up involve many of the skills associated with live reporting. "Handling On-Air Performance" is the last major topic discussed in Chapter 14, "Live Reporting."

Packages

Reporter packages have become the workhorses of television news. They are the preferred presentation format for most stories.

Here is the typical or traditional structure of a package report: anchor lead-in; reporter open to the story usually told VO, but occasionally in a stand-up; a SOT segment; reporter bridge or transition usually done in a stand-up, but sometimes as a VO; a second SOT segment or additional VO by the reporter; reporter close-out to the story; an optional anchor write-out. Refer to Chapter 3, Figures 3.15 through 3.18 for copy format examples.

Get to the first soundbite as soon as possible. Stand-up and SOT segments should carry most of the storytelling responsibilities in a package. Here is how one package report began:

```
WIPE TO VCR/SOC :00 (SOC UP FULL)

SOC UNDER :07 (ENDS '' . . . flat ground.'')

[''We were glad to help out . . . but it's great to be back
again on flat ground.'']

WEST BRANCH

Three Federal Park Service rangers based at West Branch are
happy to be home tonight after fighting Western forest
fires . . .
                        KGAN-TV, Cedar Rapids-Waterloo, Iowa
```

The same kind of information used at the end of radio wraps can be provided during the reporter's close-out at the end of television packages. During the reporter's closing comments, on-screen identification is usually provided; this generally includes the reporter's name, story location, and news organization logo.

Sheila Hyland, WTAE-TV reporter/anchor, cautions to avoid trying to cover too much in a package report:

> Keep in mind—the average length of a package is a minute, 30 seconds. You must decide which details are absolutely essential to the story. Then, find an angle—and focus your story. That's when you can really let the soundbites and the pictures say what you can't, or don't have time for. People can read all the details in the paper. You need to show and tell them what they can't find in the newspaper.[6]

As illustrated earlier, two or more soundbites can be used back-to-back.

Natural sound can also be emphasized at the beginning, in the middle and at the end of a package report or a voice-over segment.

Using Natural Sound

Meaningful and appropriate natural sound adds substance and texture to a story that words alone cannot provide. Nat sound helps both reporter and photojournalist to communicate a visual news story more powerfully. Although pictures can carry a large share of the storytelling burden, natural sound helps fill in the spaces and complete the viewer's perception of the news scene while interest in the story increases. Be sure that the natural sound used does not detract from but rather enhances the story being told.

Most photojournalists use microphones built in to videotape cameras to record natural sound routinely on one of the two available audio channels. The nat sound can be isolated when editing videotape.

Editing Video

Editing can give clarity, meaning, direction, coordination, and form to the information gathered, but only if the person editing the videotape knows the specific story to be told. As discussed earlier, news stories are structured and mentally edited throughout the newsgathering process. Videotape editing is simply one of the final steps used to help answer constant questions like the following: What is this story about, really? How can I *best* show or explain what is happening and who is involved? How should picture and sound work together to tell the story I know? Editing helps link and coordinate picture and sound to tell the visual story in the best way possible.

An examination of the specific steps, procedures, and techniques involved in actually editing television news videotape is beyond the scope of this book. Several books listed in the bibliography in Appendix C provide more complete and illustrated discussions of the videotape editing process. However, you must know the essential equipment involved and the techniques reporters use when videotape is edited.

Videotape editing systems include several essential items: playback and record machines to see and hear what you have captured on videotape; a control panel or unit that allows the editor to select where edits begin and end and also what is transferred from one machine to another (picture and sound, picture only, sound only); other audio sources (a microphone for recording voice-over segments, audiotape or cartridge playback/record units, etc.); additional video sources such as CG, ESS outputs; other equipment to enhance picture and sound quality such as time base corrector (or TBC), audio limiters, and so on.

Cuts are generally used to go from shot to shot as one picture instantly changes to the next picture. Cuts help maintain the visual pace and progression of a news story and are also the quickest and easiest transition for the editing equipment to make.

Chief Photographer Mike Plews edits last-minute video material for a noon newscast on Chronicle Broadcasting station WOWT, Omaha.

Other kinds of visual transitions are available when larger, more complex videotape editing systems are used. These systems can add the speed, accuracy, and efficiency of specialized computers to the video editing process. Edit points can be selected and then stored in computer memory for later use when the editing process is completed. Engineers generally handle these sophisticated editing systems.

Eventually video assembly will require little more than selecting from among dozens of tiny freeze-frame icons on a video terminal, clicking a mouse, and then highlighting the portion of the script each scene is to match. Nonlinear editing systems may end many of the frustrations and delays of traditional videotape editing. With nonlinear systems, editors can locate specific shots without reviewing unneeded video. Editors also have a constant overview of their work to help maintain visual continuity. Multiple versions of edits and duplication of material can be accomplished without video quality deterioration. Many special effects, once reserved for sophisticated and expensive editing systems, can be accomplished easily on the emerging nonlinear editing systems.

Some newsrooms are using nonlinear systems for special purposes such as investigative reports, multiple-part miniseries, magazine programs, and promos. Traditional videotape editing techniques would be used for day-to-day breaking news coverage.

Most newsrooms save only locally originated news material—news copy, videotape, still-frame pictures, and graphics. News copy can be kept as paper in boxes or file cabinets, or on disks if newsroom computer systems are used. Edited videotape can be stored on videocassette by dates or newscast times or as individual stories or entire on-the-air newscasts. Still-frame and graphics items can be stored on ESS disks.

Filing, Storing, and Retrieving Video Material

Most newsrooms have access to news services that provide video material for national and international stories and thus do not retain such material. Unfortunately, many newsrooms overlook these resources. They contend that if they didn't go out and shoot the footage themselves with their own cameras in their own town, then the video is not usable.

If retained at all, video material at a local station is often kept for only a short time (usually less than two years), unless legal action requires retention of such material for a longer time period.

Local archival video material is often overlooked. The material is available and simply has to be identified as "file footage" on the screen to avoid legal hassles. Video file material can be used to not only clarify but also improve stories. For example, file tape of a crime scene can make a story about a suspect's trial more compelling. However, to be used, the material must be filed and identified.

A well-organized, efficient morgue system can help a newsroom report future stories with a depth, clarity, and completeness that would not be possible otherwise. But for such a system to be useful, procedures must be established and regular cataloging must be completed before efficient retrieval is possible.

Summary

Always try to write the "perfect" news story. Make sure the anchor lead-in sets the scene for the viewers and whets their appetite for the story that follows. Be sure the copy is compelling, that it grabs viewer attention, interest, and concern. Write with absolute clarity; remember, viewers cannot go back and reread what was said or shown. The pacing of the video and narration should be brisk, but not too fast. The soundbites should be short. The closing of the story should be memorable. A good television news story should touch a viewer's emotions. It should inform, but not bore. It should inspire, but not condescend. It should be oriented to people, not faceless businesses, agencies, or commissions.

Figure 8.3 helps illustrate effective television news story structure and visualization techniques. The photoboard in the left column in Figure 8.3 is made from key scenes taken from the edited videotape of the story.

This chapter has examined the special reporting strategies, techniques, routines, requirements, and skills that the television reporter needs.

The effectiveness of television news stories relies on the creative fusion of picture and sound to tell a story in a meaningful, visual manner. Various methods of presentation are available: graphics, soundbites, voice-overs, stand-ups, natural sound, and packages (the most complete form used).

Gathering and recording videotape material require familiarity with the equipment used, coordination of the personnel involved, and consistent use of procedures and techniques for determining what you need before you shoot any videotape and for checking what you get. Special attention should be given to interviews, which constitute a large share of television newsgathering activity.

The processes or steps used to prepare television news stories were traced. Suggestions were offered for establishing and maintaining visual continuity as well as for using pictures to tell effective stories. News copy was used to illustrate how to write various components and types of television news stories.

The equipment involved and the techniques used to edit videotape were briefly explained. Filing, storing, and retrieving television news material were also discussed.

Exercises

1. From a daily newspaper, select one news story that includes several quotations and that is at least one full column long. Rewrite this story into one of the following:

   a. A :20 to :30 anchor reader story using at least one graphic

   b. A :20 to :30 anchor voice-over story

   c. A :30 to :40 story using an anchor voice-over and one soundbite

   d. A 1:10 to 1:20 package story

(*Note:* Anchor lead-in and write-out copy is needed for the package story, assume that videotape of key story points is available as needed; read quotations aloud to estimate the length of soundbites that can be "edited" from the written account of the story; use copy formats illustrated in Chapter 3 unless instructed otherwise.)

Provide: the original newspaper story (indicate the date and name of the publication); and your news copy.

2. Select one of the following outlined stories. Each story contains the following information: story slug; the copy format to use (VO, VO/SOT, or reporter package); story facts; shot log or sheet. Any shot can be shortened, but none can be made longer. Shots would be edited to match the news copy you write.

Story 1

   STORY SLUG: Iowa Train Crash

   COPY FORMAT TO USE: Anchor Voice-Over (VO) . . . maximum length :40

STORY FACTS

[All information comes from Anthony Bacino, Operations Manager of the Iowa Division of Disaster Services.]

- Head-on crash of two freight trains, both operated by Union Pacific.
- Accident occurred on a single track about one-half mile northeast of Altoona, Iowa (a suburb northeast of Des Moines).

- Two crew members killed . . . four others seriously injured. Identities withheld until relatives contacted. Bodies of dead still not recovered.
- Both deaths were train engineers aboard a westbound freight train. The eastbound crew managed to jump clear before the collision.
- About 1,000 people around the site were evacuated for fear of explosions and fires.
- 9,000 people at a theme park two miles away were allowed to continue riding attractions.
- Accident happened around 10:30 A.M. this morning.
- 10 of the 86 cars derailed when the two trains collided.
- Bacino said that fumes from raw denatured alcohol are toxic and explosive but smoke from burning alcohol is not.
- Bacino says one of the tank cars that derailed contained denatured alcohol. He said [on tape]: "It could go. It's not liquid petroleum. It's just alcohol. You don't know how it's going to react."
- Too early to know why the trains were on a collision course. The National Transportation Safety Board investigator was due to arrive in Des Moines tomorrow.

SHOT LOG OR SHEET

00:00 Helicopter shot of derailment scene

00:07 CU shots of injured crew receiving medical help

00:11 MS of people being evacuated

00:16 CU of front of both train engines

00:22 SOT of Bacino [SEE TRANSCRIPT OF SOUNDBITE ABOVE]

00:30 MS of alcohol containers being removed

00:36 Helicopter shot of derailment scene

00:42 BLACK

Story 2

STORY SLUG: Oliver Home Explosion

COPY FORMAT TO USE: VO/SOT . . . maximum length :60

STORY FACTS

[All information comes from City Fire Inspector Larry Cole.]

- Explosion and fire at 5:30 A.M. today . . . 6664 Knox St. locally.
- Only injury was Dan Oliver, 19 . . . lived with his parents (Mr. & Mrs. Glen Oliver) and his sister, Barbara, 15.
- Dan is listed in critical condition now at the local General Hospital . . . first- and second-degree burns over 60 percent of his body.
- Natural gas explosion ripped through southwest section of the home just before sunrise this morning.
- Here's Cole's account [recorded on tape][each sentence lasts approximately five seconds] ''The gas leak was outside the house, between the main line and the meter in the basement. Rain and heavy snow 'sealed' the ground causing fumes to seep into the house through the wall or hole where the gas entered the basement. The explosion blew out the southwest portion of the house and this may have prevented other injuries and saved some lives. Fire damage was confined to the basement . . . the rest of the three-bedroom frame house sustained only heat damage. We haven't had a chance to complete a damage estimate at this time.''
- The Olivers smelled gas around 10:30 last night and again at 3:00 A.M. today, but could not find the source of the gas smell each time.
- Dan returned home around 4:00 A.M. . . . was asleep when explosion happened.

SHOT LOG OR SHEET

00:00 Cover shot of the fire/explosion scene

00:06 CU of firefighter dousing portions of house

00:11 MS of neighbors watching fire-fighting units

00:15 SOT of Cole [SEE TRANSCRIPT OF SOUNDBITE ABOVE]

00:40 CU shots of southwest portion of the house

00:46 LS of house and fire units

00:50 BLACK

Notes

1. Additional television reporting techniques are illustrated by the winners in a reputable international news competition. For a modest fee, the Radio-Television News Directors Association will provide a set of the latest award-winning television news entries in the annual RTNDA Edward R. Murrow competition. For details, write to: Radio-Television News Directors Association, 1000 Connecticut Avenue, NW, Suite 615, Washington, DC, 20036: Or call: 202–659–6510.

2. Reprinted by permission of Jill Kelley.

3. Dave Hammer (WOWT, Omaha); summary of his comments at a session of the Nebraska Associated Press Broadcasters Association meeting in Grand Island, Nebraska, 25 April 1987.

4. KMOV-TV, *Channel 4 (KMOV-TV) Newsroom Standards.* (St. Louis: KMOV-TV, n.d.), 3.

5. Summarized from ''Producer's Corner,'' *Communicator* 45, no. 10 (November 1991): 35–36.

6. Reprinted by permission of Sheila Hyland.

Chapter 14

Live Reporting

Live reporting is one of the most difficult assignments for the broadcast journalist. Logistical obstacles and ethical concerns must be resolved. Both the reporter and the audience find themselves in an interesting situation—witnessing the process as well as the result of newsgathering *as it happens!*

Listeners and viewers expect to "experience" a story. They want to see, firsthand, the story as it develops. They want the latest information about an event. They want to know the facts and what they mean to their family and community. *They* want to decide what is important and what is not. *They* want to be assured that what they see and hear is happening *now*. The immediacy and completeness that live reporting provides cannot be duplicated. Despite its difficulty, live reporting has developed as a routine way to present ongoing, developing news stories.

Live broadcasts (especially interviews) are done regularly for different reasons and under many different circumstances. This chapter explains how to prepare live reports from the scene of breaking hard news stories. After an assessment of the value of live reporting, a review of the types of live reports commonly filed is presented. Next the planning, coordination, and production of live reports are considered. Finally, the chapter offers suggestions on how to assess and improve your on-the-air performance in the field as well as in the studio.

Value of Live Reports

Live reporting becomes especially valuable during times of emergency. If a snowstorm buries your town under several feet of snow, or if homes are threatened by rising waters from a nearby river, live reports can give viewers vital information that may save lives and help avoid more difficult circumstances.

A live report from the scene of even a minor news story can stimulate the audience's interest in the outcome of a story still under way or just completed. But not every story deserves a live report. Many routine stories are covered live in a promotional effort to boost ratings and increase the popularity of local newscasts. A well-marked news vehicle provides strong promotional value and visibility on the scene during a live report. The decision to "go live" should be based on the specific conditions surrounding each news event as well as the capabilities and priorities of each newsroom.

The suspense, immediacy, and challenge that live reporting adds to news coverage must be balanced against the loss of editorial control and the potential lack of perspective that may result. During an intense breaking news story journalists have little time to assess thoroughly events and developments that are seen or heard *live,* witnessed by the audience firsthand, as they occur, with no editing and no chance to evaluate what is aired.

The portability and flexibility of field reporting equipment, especially cellular telephones for radio and ENG units for television, have increased the feasibility, desirability, and effectiveness of live reports.

Types of Live Reports

Providing useful guidelines for structuring every live report is difficult. Just as each news story is unique in its content and structure so the circumstances surrounding each live shot vary. This causes reports to be shaped in the field using the best structure possible—often a *combination* of the reporting and scripting formats illustrated in previous chapters.

Here are a few ways to structure a live report:

   a. *Reporter only* (voicer in radio; stand-up in television)
   b. *Reporter with someone else* (interview with newsmaker; Q & A with newsmaker and/or newscaster; combination of interview and Q & A)
   c. *Reporter with recorded material* (actuality or wrap in radio; VO, VO/SOT, or package report in television)
   d. *Combinations* (e.g., stand-up, VO bridge to VO/SOT package, and live interview of a newsmaker with the anchor, *or* an interview with a newsmaker followed by a prepared report like a wrap for radio or package for television)

A typical structure used for a television live report is as follows: The newscaster leads in and cues to the live reporter; the reporter begins with a brief stand-up to place the reporter at the scene; a specific cue given by the reporter bridges to a package report, recapping what is happening now and what happened earlier; the reporter uses standard write-outs to end the report from the scene. A brief Q & A between newscasters and on-the-scene sources (reporter, newsmaker, or both) may conclude the live report. Some live reports begin with a *news sounder,* or brief musical introduction, followed by the reporter, who gives his or her name and location and begins telling the story.

Handling Live Interviews

Live interviews are often included in live shots and pose special challenges for the reporter as well as the person interviewed. Only one or two worthwhile questions can be asked to elicit meaningful responses in a short time, generally 20 to 60 seconds. As in *any* interview, pace and content must be controlled.

The interview must conclude smoothly within the allotted time. Both reporter and newsmaker must respond to the pressures that a live interview poses; retakes and edits are not possible.

In addition to the general suggestions already offered in Chapter 10 for handling interviews, here are some techniques that can help make *live* interviews easier to do and provide more worthwhile information:

a. Be conscious of the physical setting of the live interview. How a guest looks and sounds during an interview often determine attitudes toward you and the news organization for which you work. This may also influence your success as an interviewer.

b. Place yourself next to the interview guest to establish an open, interested attitude and to give the guest the quality of attention needed. Interviewers often stand closer to interviewees on-camera than they would off-camera. The reason for this is that the camera magnifies the distance between the persons in front of it, and this spacing often makes them look awkward or uncomfortable. So, to eliminate the spacing problem, interviewer and interviewee often stand shoulder-to-shoulder in two-shots, and the interviewer backs away as the camera zooms in to the interviewee. Once questioning starts, the interviewer stands almost face-to-face with the interviewee. The camera shoots over the shoulder of the interviewer. This technique often needs to be explained to interviewees unaccustomed to appearing on-camera.

c. Make microphone or camera placement as unobtrusive as possible.

d. Avoid distractions. Just before going live, turn around or shut off the television set used for cues. Nearby phones should be placed off the hook or unplugged. And remember to run equipment with a battery instead of AC power in case the power fails.

e. Tell your interview guest *in advance* approximately how long the live interview is expected to last.

f. Since interview time is limited, ask only one or two key questions of *immediate* interest to the live story covered.

g. Predetermine how the interview will end.

h. After your last question has been answered and before you conclude your live report, take a short step away from your interview guest. This will signal that the interview is over and that the next part of the report should begin.

Live news coverage requires extraordinary teamwork, organization, flexibility, and concentration. Quick decisions must be made; ever-changing events and coverage situations must be anticipated accurately and controlled carefully.

Planning, Coordinating, and Producing Live Reports

Successful live reports are based on thorough planning, careful coordination, and skillful use of production capabilities. Although the following information applies to both radio and television live reports, more attention is given to television because radio live reports parallel the process already outlined in Chapter 12, ''Radio Reporting.''

Planning

Newsrooms that regularly do live shots eventually develop a plan of action for each type of story covered regularly. This ''game plan'' outlines the personnel responsibilities, equipment needs, on-air procedures, and so forth associated with a specific kind of story. Examples include: hostage situations, major traffic accidents, and natural disasters appropriate to the area.

The more planning done in advance, the smoother one should expect each live broadcast to be. Such planning information is useful only if it is based on actual prior coverage experiences. Planning information should be in writing and should be evaluated and updated on a regular basis.

Full scripts are not used for every part of a live report. If time and facilities permit, scripts can be expected for in-studio segments and some in-the-field portions of live reports such as a lead-in to a VO or package segment, closing, and Q & A suggestions. But the extemporaneous nature of live reports often precludes use of extensive script material. Ad-libbing (discussed later) is necessary. Use notes, but avoid reading directly from a full script on paper. A reporter's notebook works well for live reports.

Todd Smith is a correspondent in the Washington News Bureau of Bonneville International Corporation. He provides numerous radio and television reports daily from Washington, D.C., for stations in Seattle and Salt Lake City. He follows two essential rules for live reports:

(1) Keep things simple. (2) Rehearse out loud.

The best TV live shots are those that are tightly focused. Always, without exception, have an outline, at a minimum, worked out before going on the air. Scribble the 1-2-3 points in your notebook. If you don't, odds are you will fail, because your report will be long and rambling. I prefer to have an outline in my hand rather than a full script. If the live shot has a tracked insert [a recorded and edited segment or story] . . . put most of the story in the insert so you don't have to deal with a ton of complicated facts live. Generally, with a tracked insert, you only need to deliver a quick line or two going into the insert and coming out.

Radio live reports are more demanding because producers can get you on the air quicker than maybe you'd like. Again, scribble some quick notes at a minimum before going on the air. Since eye contact isn't important on radio, a little script can make a live report even easier, if you have time to scribble one out.[1]

Todd Smith, correspondent in the Washington News Bureau of Bonneville International Corporation, gathers material for one of many radio and television news reports filed each day. Photo courtesy of Todd G. Smith.

Phil Witt, News Anchor and Senior Reporter at WDAF-TV in Kansas City, suggests using your surroundings during live reports:

> The reason a reporter is "live" is because something has happened at the location. . . . Refer to where things happened. Walk around the area a little (keeping in mind the restrictions of cables, etc.) That gives the report context and meaning for the viewers. It's also a wonderful way to help a reporter ad-lib.[2]

If Q & A is planned, let on-the-scene reporters suggest questions for newscasters to use. Mutual Broadcasting System anchor Frank Gentry says:

> Plan whatever you can. Even a 15-second exchange between anchor and reporter prior to going live can make a big difference. If the reporter will be questioned, discuss what will be left out of the report to form the basis of questioning.[3]

Coordination

The result of good planning is smooth coordination of people and machines. KXLY-TV of Spokane, Washington, has won more than seven nationally recognized awards, especially for its documentary and continuing coverage work. KXLY-TV won a television spot news award in the annual RTNDA international competition for its coverage of one of the longest and most expensive sieges in U.S. history. News Director Robin Briley Cowan described events surrounding the coverage:

> It began with a blast of gunfire piercing the quiet stillness of the North Idaho forest. White supremacist Randy Weaver was wanted on federal firearms charges and had been living with his family in a mountain cabin

so remote it was virtually inaccessible by car or truck. Federal marshals spent many months trying to find ways to capture Weaver and keep his family alive. . . .

A surveillance team climbing the mountain was suddenly caught in a fire fight with the family. A deputy marshal was killed along with fugitive Weaver's young son, though we [KXLY TV] didn't learn that part of the story for several days. . . .

More than 200 federal agents and military soldiers descended on the remote mountain area. It was a top national story that didn't stop for eleven days and nights. There were angry protests and widespread fears of civil unrest, as a majority of local residents strongly objected to the heavy government response. . . .

We were the only station to keep two reporters and photographers on the scene around the clock for the duration. The location was two hours away and dangerously remote with rocky ridges, swarms of armed federal agents, radicals and locals. We had use of a borrowed satellite truck but devised a chain of microwave links to deliver developments within seconds to the viewer. . . .

This story was the ultimate challenge for our small newsroom. Reporters became instant engineers, hand-cranking a generator that ran our mountaintop remote microwave gear, and running breathlessly 75 yards downhill to grab a mic and go on the air. We are very proud of our performance during this marathon story.[4]

What are some of the key lessons news crews have learned from extensive coverage of hurricanes, floods, earthquakes, major ice and snowstorms, and other natural disasters in the 1990s? One is to develop a plan well in advance. You should have written procedures for each natural disaster your newsroom is likely to cover. Remember to specify the equipment and personnel you might need. Indicate where machines and people would be stationed for the best coverage. Speculation is not tolerated. Err on the side of caution, especially in the early stages of coverage when the least amount of accurate information is available. During coverage of natural disasters, your audience wants everything they can get, so plan to go on with extended coverage. Be prepared; do research about the local activities that a natural disaster would affect. Above all, make clear that the threat of danger is real.

When several reporting teams are used to provide extensive coverage of a breaking story, each team must know what part of the story to cover and how to handle cues (often called *tosses*) to other teams in the field. A coordinating producer can help guide each reporter who may be required to pick up the thread of the story, report on another aspect, and then cue still another reporter who has prepared another angle on the same story. For example, multiple live reports could be prepared for a police shooting. One reporter might be stationed at the hospital where the officer is brought. A second team could report from the scene of the shooting. And a third reporter might be prepared for reactions from fellow officers and police officials. For such a "round robin" of reports to work, *each* reporter must know the general content of each report and how each reporter will be cued to begin. Be sure to plan a *roll-cue* so everyone involved knows what will be said just before going to another live report location or an edited package. Roll-cues must be specific and direct. For example: *The problems started about noon when the tank car started leaking.*

Production

The broadcast journalist eventually must face the reality that equipment is an essential reporting tool, just like a notepad and pencil. Although the beginning journalist is not expected to be proficient with all of the equipment found in each newsroom, he or she is at least expected to understand the production processes followed, the terms and technologies commonly used, and the capabilities of the equipment used in live reporting.

Various vehicles are used for live reporting. Specially equipped cars and vans work well for radio. Although the same kinds of vehicles can be used for television, helicopters and special satellite newsgathering units are often used.

Helicopters can transport news crews quickly to the scene by overflying obstacles and ground traffic. They can also be used to: relay a live signal from units on the ground to receiving units back in the newsroom; provide surveillance from an excellent vantage point; and (for television) add aerial shots to a live report.

Ground vehicles are often used as "uplinks" to send audio or audio and video signals to a satellite ("the bird") about 23,000 miles in space, back to a dish at a studio location for taping or "live" use. The transportable (Ku-band) uplink unit typically consists of a small, 2-axle vehicle with a foldaway antenna, video production and uplinking equipment, and voice communications equipment that includes several two-way voice channels. Voice channels are used during SNG (Satellite News Gathering) transmissions to coordinate access to the satellite, to connect the vehicle to a central coordinating point back in the newsroom, and to cue the on-site reporter for transmission of live reports (see Figure 14.1). There are also *flyaway* uplinks that fold neatly into one or more suitcase-type containers that are shippable on airplanes for rapid deployment to remote sites.

When covering stories outside the regular coverage area, news cooperative arrangements can provide ground vehicles for uplinking as well as space and time on a distant satellite. Networks can help make SNG affordable even for small-market stations. The average cost of existing satellite newsgathering vehicles (SNVs) exceeds $500,000. Satellites are readily available, cost effective, and offer capabilities that make quality live coverage possible.

Radio live reports require minimum additional equipment beyond the gear used for general radio reporting. The news scene must be linked to the newsroom via cellular or standard telephone, two-way radio, or some other

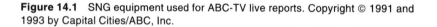

Figure 14.1 SNG equipment used for ABC-TV live reports. Copyright © 1991 and 1993 by Capital Cities/ABC, Inc.

means. The flyaway crews usually carry two extra suitcases that include telephone uplinks. Sometimes the phone that you carry is the only phone you can get. This same link can be used for information updates before the live report and also to cue the reporter just as the live report begins. Some newsrooms provide off-air signals using headphones and a portable radio or over the audio link established between the news scene and the newsroom.

Television live reports require more elaborate facilities. Most SNVs are equipped with video editing equipment, cellular telephones, flexible microwave capabilities, and production mixers for controlling sound and picture as well as creating basic graphics. Gasoline-powered generators are commonly used to run the equipment and provide crucial heating and air conditioning. Accessory gear such as microphones, cables, and monitors is also needed.

Live television reporting requires the use of IFB (interruptible feedback or foldback)—an earpiece the live reporter wears that feeds off-air programming until an assignment manager or newscast producer interrupts to provide instructions and cues for the live coverage. IFB can be used to finalize coverage plans, provide additional story information from other sources, and also provide instructions while a live report is under way! Television reporters must develop the ability to listen to one idea on the IFB while delivering another idea smoothly and effortlessly on-camera. Some larger news operations provide two IFB lines—one for engineering and technical personnel to align dishes and signals, and another for news personnel such as reporters, photojournalists, field producers, and assignment managers, so that the two groups will be ready as soon as possible for a live broadcast.

A special problem arises when IFB is used during satellite feeds. The time required to get a signal from a satellite and back causes a one and one-half second delay in the programming line. Engineers can provide a second

KIRO reporter Essex Porter doing a live broadcast in front of a quake-damaged medical building in Northridge, California. Photo credit, Brian Miller.

delay as well as other adjustments so that reporters are not distracted hearing themselves as an echo on the IFB or looking less than alert when a noticeable pause occurs between an anchor's question and a reporter's response. This technical adjustment is often labeled ''mix-minus.''

Handling On-Air Performance

For a broadcast journalist, on-air work (like production) is an integral part of the job. It represents the final stage of reporting what you know.

Prospective employers will expect on-air competency from broadcast reporters, but proficiency is preferred. Your on-air abilities will improve proportionate to how frequently and how carefully you practice, record, and critique your performance. Large newsrooms often hire consultants to advise on-air talent about their presentation skills.

Several aspects of on-air performance will be discussed. The comments provided here apply to all on-air reporting, live or recorded, but are directed to reporters, especially those involved in live reports, working in radio *or* television. Note, however, that being an anchor or newscaster requires substantially more practice and training and involves additional techniques too numerous to include here.

Reporter's Skills and Techniques

Worthwhile information must be available to present. Even the best on-air work will falter if good writing and reporting skills are not used.

Here are specific skills that broadcast reporters should develop and techniques that they should practice to enhance *live* on-air presentations:

a. Stay well informed about a variety of subjects. Successful reporters read many different publications on a regular basis to better prepare themselves for future news coverage assignments.

b. Be sensitive to what you observe at the news scene. Report the mood and atmosphere of the story, but remember to keep your personal opinions and emotions in check.

c. Train yourself to analyze specific newsgathering situations quickly and then to identify how to best gather accurate, newsworthy facts and comments.

d. Use good news judgment, which is very important during live reports when you must decide quickly what to say or what to show.

e. Be versatile in the way you approach and cover stories. Try different techniques even on routine stories (especially interviews) to refine your story coverage flexibility. Your on-air presentation should be an outgrowth of the specific story you cover.

f. Practice writing in the field amid the congestion, confusion, and noise that usually surround the reporter.

g. If a particularly striking phrase occurs to you as notes are being prepared, write that phrase down. Just the act of writing it down will help you to remember it under pressure during a live report.

h. Cultivate a sense of timing and pace. Begin to gauge the length as well as the flow of information in reports that you prepare. Practice using notes to organize and deliver reports extemporaneously.

i. Develop a ''conversational vocabulary.'' Word choices and sentence structure should reflect regular conversational usage.

Voice

You should be aware of several characteristics of vocal delivery that can be identified and monitored. Noticeable improvement in your vocal delivery style and technique will come only with consistent practice and knowledgeable critique from an experienced professional.

A good breath supply provides the ''power'' you need to control other aspects of your voice. Breathe deeply and regularly from your diaphragm. You were probably taught this technique in choral and speech activities. Stretching muscles, taking deep breaths, and momentarily dropping your head and shoulders can release tension.

Vary the pitch of your voice. Nothing dampens audience interest in a story more than a voice that sounds dull and monotone. One way to vary pitch is to lower speaking volume. The apparent intimacy with the audience should increase while your pitch will tend to vary and follow natural, conversational patterns.

Your voice should be expressive and lively. Varying the pitch of your voice will help. But you must also understand and then convey the key ideas of each story that you want to tell. Several techniques can help convey key ideas. When you read aloud, group words into logical clusters, or ''thought units.'' Some reporters underline a key word or two in each sentence to remind themselves to emphasize these words when reading their copy aloud. Vocal expressiveness makes stories more interesting and information more easily understood and meaningful for the audience.

Your vocal pace or rate of speaking needs to be slow enough to make words and ideas readily understood, but fast enough to sustain interest. Generally a reporter's reading speed will be a little faster than in regular face-to-face conversation.

For the audience to hear your report, you not only must speak clearly and distinctly (enunciation), you also must pronounce the words you say correctly. To improve enunciation, some on-air talent find it helpful to exaggerate jaw and lip movement at first, and then to use less distracting facial movements once enunciation becomes more natural and automatic.

On-the-air, voices with deep resonance have been joined by voices that are at least reasonably pleasant but communicate ideas clearly and effectively. Some moderate regional accents are acceptable if they don't detract from story content. Standard or general American speech patterns are preferred and required if you hope to move to large markets or network on-air work. Work with your *natural* voice quality. Special training may be needed if your voice displays severe voice-quality problems such as nasality and hoarseness.

Marking your copy may improve the effectiveness of your on-air delivery. No universal set of symbols is used. Each on-air talent uses a personalized system. Here is a basic system of marks to use: slash marks for pauses; underlining key words for emphasis and added expressiveness; and arrows up or down above words to indicate rising or declining inflection patterns. Not everyone marks news copy before going on the air. Mark your copy if it helps your on-the-air vocal delivery.

Appearance should be important to *all* reporters, not just those who appear on television. How you look influences your credibility with news sources and also your confidence in working as a professional reporter in a competitive industry. **Picture**

Good grooming is always important. For men this means well-trimmed and neatly combed hair, and usually no facial hair. For women this entails moderate use of makeup and a short, reasonably conservative hairstyle. For television work especially, ''thin'' is in.

Dress for success and practicality. Select simple, tasteful, professional-looking clothing; avoid extremes in color, texture, and design. Dress in ''business'' fashion. Match story coverage circumstances to clothing worn. For example, more informal clothing is acceptable when reporting in extremely warm surroundings.

Your general visual attitude is also important. On television, stand up straight. While on-camera angle or turn your body slightly to avoid a ''flat'' appearance; also control tendencies to rock from side to side or back and forth. Keep your hands at your sides unless gesturing to emphasize a point. Gestures should look natural and be motivated by story content. On radio, exaggerated body movement is encouraged to provide lively reports. But on television, such movement is distracting and should not be used.

Establish quality contact with your audience. In radio, this means using your voice to reach listeners effectively. In television, this means not only using your voice well but also using video equipment as channels of communications to reach the audience with a worthwhile *visual* message. Television reporters use teleprompters to increase eye contact with viewers. Smooth use of such equipment requires skill developed with practice.

Ad-libbing

Reporters must improvise and ad-lib a large portion of their live reports. Here are ways to improve your ability to ad-lib and to speak extemporaneously and, thus, improve your live reports:

a. *Think* about what you want to say.
b. *Organize* yourself and your thoughts. A short list of "talk points" taped to the camera front, in field shoots, might help.
c. *Determine the sequence of ideas* (not the specific words) you want to communicate.
d. *Write* as much of the report as possible. Note cards or a reporter's notebook are useful. Some reporters are "quick studies" and can memorize small portions of a live report.
e. *Rehearse* what you will say, if at all possible.
f. *Emphasize what is happening now.* That is what live reporting does best and probably why a report is ad-libbed rather than recorded in advance. Don't be afraid to say you don't have all of the details. If it is an accurate statement, indicate that you expect to have more complete details later.
g. *Include activity surrounding the story.* During your live report on a fire, walk over to the firefighter for that interview you want; be certain not to interfere with firefighting efforts! During your story on car scams, kick the tires. Hold the snake during your story about the local zoo. Although it is easier to show story activity and involvement on television, a creative radio reporter can also use natural sound to "demonstrate" the environment surrounding a story.
h. When ad-libbing on radio, *describe vividly* the scene where you are. Audiences will understand and remember what you report when they experience it—firsthand or through your words and images.
i. *Remain calm and be prepared* for inevitable distractions and technical difficulties.
j. *Focus on the story, not on yourself.* Remember, you are the storyteller, the audience's link to a news story or event. But *you* are *not* the story!

Here are some suggestions to help improve your overall on-air delivery: Practice! practice! practice!; know as much as possible about the stories that you cover; think about what you are reading to give meaning and sense to what you say.

Frank Gentry of MBS offers additional suggestions for delivering news copy on-the-air:

> I find it helpful to rest my left arm on the studio console and cross my legs during casts, much as I would in dining informally. The routine has become second nature now, but years ago I would conjure up an image of a favorite restaurant where a good friend asks ''Well, what happened today?'' The cast was aimed at *that* listener in *that* setting. . . .
>
> On-air attitude should match the image of your station. If the format is adult contemporary, then you should sound the part. Since our [MBS] affiliates range from classical to country and urban, I've got to sound generic. I try to be friendly yet authoritative, and I suppose that is universal enough to work in almost any format.[5]

Nan Siemer provided insightful coverage under extremely difficult and physically threatening circumstances when WTOP Radio covered the Mount Pleasant riots. Here is a transcript of some of her live coverage that helped WTOP Radio win an international RTNDA spot news award:

SIEMER: I just got hit with a couple of bottles that just showered me with glass as I tried to walk a few streets over. They are throwing rocks at a police car right across the street from me now. A whole gang of people are taking off down the street. The police are diving for cover. Oh oh . . . something just hit a police officer's shield and knocked it right out of his hand. I don't know what that was. I can't tell at this point. [short silence]

BRUCE ALLEN: Nan, are you still with us?

SIEMER: Still with you, Bruce. I'm hearing some kinds of shots. O.K. it's another gas canister. It's just been fired right across the street. Luckily, the wind is blowing the other direction, so quickly, if you have any questions, this would be the time to ask.

BRUCE ALLEN: O.K., as these little roving bands move through, are they continuing to cause property damage as they move from block to block, Nan?

SIEMER: I was one block down Columbia a moment ago, and there are piles of debris burning in the street, there is glass everywhere. I mean, we have our own little war zone on a couple of these streets over here.[6]

Summary

This chapter has explained how to prepare live reports from the scene of breaking hard news stories.

Live reports add suspense and immediacy to news coverage. However, some loss of control over the contents and presentation of stories reported live from the field also occurs.

Live reports can be structured in various ways using only the reporter, the reporter with someone else, the reporter with recorded material, or combinations of reporting and scripting formats illustrated in earlier chapters.

Interviews pose special problems during live shots. Special techniques are needed to make live interviews more worthwhile and easier to produce.

Successful live coverage requires thorough planning, careful coordination, and skillful use of production capabilities. Newsrooms often develop a plan of action for each type of story covered regularly. Good planning results in smooth coordination of people and machines. Broadcast reporters must understand the production processes followed and the equipment used. Live news coverage generally involves the use of specially equipped vehicles as well as sophisticated satellite systems.

On-air performance is an integral part of the broadcast reporter's work. How you look and sound is important. Develop the ability to ad-lib and report extemporaneously. On-air work will improve only with constant monitoring, diligent practice, and thoughtful, professional critiques on a regular basis.

Exercises

1. Record on audiotape or videotape two news stories you have already written. Critique your presentation based on the criteria presented in this chapter.

2. Ad-lib and record either a 30-second radio voicer or a television stand-up report based on one of the following:

    a. Facts listed in one of the exercises at the end of a previous chapter

    b. A local newspaper article that contains several quotes

Critique your writing, reporting, and presentation skills based on criteria described in this and other chapters. Be sure to comment on the following: lead sentence; story structure; words used; sentence structure; accuracy; clarity; completeness; delivery style and technique. Record your ad-lib report again and repeat the critique process. Indicate the improvement you have made.

3. Follow the directions in Exercise 2, but *use only the notes that you can write on* **one** 3 × 5 inch index card.

Notes

1. Reprinted by permission of Todd G. Smith.

2. Reprinted by permission of Phil Witt.

3. Reprinted by permission of Frank Gentry.

4. Undated information sheet entitled ''Deadly Mountain Siege'' from Robin Briley Cowan, KXLY TV, Spokane, Washington.

5. Reprinted by permission of Frank Gentry.

6. Transcript from audiotape sent to the author by Nan Siemer on September 10, 1993. Reprinted by permission.

Part Four

Coverage

Chapter 15

Routine Coverage

T his chapter concerns coverage opportunities that reporters encounter regularly. Reporting is still a creative profession. Thus, you should not accept the advice given as representing a formula for writing a particular kind of story. Each story is different and should be treated as such. However, you should become familiar with techniques and procedures that tend to work well in routine situations.

In this chapter, specific reporting situations have been isolated for the sake of discussion. However, governmental agencies as well as police departments and political candidates schedule meetings, speeches, and news conferences. Law enforcement activities often lead to court coverage and may involve follow-up stories from governmental agencies.

Meetings, Speeches, and News Conferences

Much of the business of community life is handled through meetings, speeches, and news conferences. These are three situations in which someone is likely to say something that may be newsworthy. Issues are discussed. Concerns and attitudes are expressed. All of this may ultimately affect public opinion or cause public reaction, which makes such coverage potentially newsworthy.

But newsworthiness must be measured carefully. Follow the advice of Bob Priddy, News Director of the Missouri Network and former Chairman of the Radio-Television News Directors Association:

> Time does not necessarily equal newsworthiness. . . . If the people at a press conference say nothing new, or make allegations of no merit, the reporter should not justify reporting the *non*-story by thinking that something should be written because the reporter has spent his time at the event. . . . We sell ourselves, our professional souls, and our integrity cheaply when we justify a news story on the basis of the time we spent watching nothing newsworthy happen.[1]

These three reporting situations have some similarities: the types of events **Similarities** covered; the initial sources of information; the reporting and coverage techniques used; and the story information included.

Two types of events can be identified on the basis of the nature of the group scheduling such sessions: (1) civic/social/professional and (2) political/governmental. Some overlap may occur between these two categories; for example, a local civic group may host a speech or news conference by current or prospective elected officials as part of its monthly luncheon meeting, or the regular meeting of a governmental agency may include a special citation to a civic organization for some meritorious project.

Initial sources of information are similar. Generally a newsroom is alerted to such events by a telephone call or written material such as agendas, news releases, and handouts of prepared remarks that the sponsoring organization sends in advance. The newsroom future file, a reporter's beat contacts, a news tip, or a wire story may have prompted coverage. All of these initial sources of information help the newsroom evaluate the news value of an event and determine the amount of coverage needed.

Similar reporting techniques are used to cover meetings, speeches, and news conferences. These include the following:

a. *Thoroughly cover what you can.* Since you cannot attend every available event, determine which will receive full, in-person coverage. For those not covered in-person, call someone beforehand who is directly involved and ask (essentially) "What will I miss?" Call again after the event and determine what you missed. If the event appears newsworthy, then make several calls to round up the facts needed to write the story. Follow-up calls may also be needed if you must leave an event before it ends. Phone calls, however, are no substitute for personal attendance.

b. *Come prepared.* Anticipate what you may encounter regarding a topic or issue to be discussed as well as the facilities available. Use the news instincts you have developed from experience. Get insights from regular news contacts as well as other reporters in the newsroom. If the advance copy of the city council agenda indicates a major decision about a street widening project, record the reactions of residents along the route *before* you attend the meeting. You will understand the issue better and provide a more insightful story about issues that affect your audience directly.

c. *Get to the event early.* You will need time to set up equipment, get a preview or update about what is expected to occur, and perhaps conduct an interview about the main issue or topic to be covered in time to file a preliminary story. A postevent interview can be arranged, but this request must be made in advance, *before* the event begins. These one-on-one interviews have some advantages: Shorter, more usable comments can be obtained on complex issues often involving long-winded descriptions and discussion; and comments can be recorded on story angles or topics not scheduled for discussion but that may be more newsworthy and not available to competing news media.

d. *Rely on your equipment.* Don't rely exclusively on ''mult boxes'' that provide a common audio signal from the main area where comments are made. If possible, set up, test, and rely on your own equipment.

e. *Be quiet and unobtrusive as you set up and tear down equipment.* This is especially important if you arrive late or have to leave early.

f. *Protect yourself.* Before an event begins or soon after it is under way, record a short stand-up for television or a voicer for radio. This material can be written from your advance information about the event and will be handy when assembling your final report.

g. *Record more than you need.* Once you leave the scene, you cannot edit recorded comments you don't have. Take enough notes and record enough material to file a meaningful story. You can always toss out unwanted material later if not needed.

h. *Check the tape before you leave.* You cannot use what you don't have. If technical problems were encountered, obtaining a quick interview or recording a brief voice report after the event might salvage your coverage.

i. *Consider alternative coverage techniques.* For example, use one machine to record the entire event, and then use another machine to get crowd reactions during a speech or to feed the newsroom early recorded segments of the event. Be prepared to ''go portable'' with your equipment at all times. Sometimes the best part of a story happens outside the obvious event.

j. *Adjust to the reality of abbreviated broadcast coverage.* Reports of these kinds of events generally include a brief interview before or after the session and a short recorded segment from the event. This is not the ideal coverage approach, but it becomes necessary when broadcast reporters race to complete often conflicting assignments under extreme deadlines. Use your time and energy efficiently.

k. *Use a combination of notes and recordings.* Sit next to your recording equipment. Set the counter to "000." Take notes on what is said. Cultivate the technique of listening to a statement while noting the contents of the previous statement. When a potentially useful statement develops, note the counter number as well as the incue, outcue, and approximate length. This makes it easier to review and find recorded excerpts to use in the story.

l. *Keep a tight focus.* Determine the central purpose of the event. Identify the important topics. Stay until they are presented and until you have the information needed to write a meaningful story.

m. *Scrutinize what's presented.* Sometimes your best story comes from what is left unsaid (the governor not commenting on a controversial tax bill), from what is mentioned only briefly (the dismissal of a longtime state employee), or from what conflicts with what the same person previously stated (e.g., the police chief changing his policy about handling juvenile cases).

n. *Ask questions* to better understand issues and technical terms and to probe for more details if needed.

o. *Stay in touch with the newsroom.* During a break in a meeting or a closing question-answer session after a speech, leave your recorder running and contact the newsroom. Indicate what is happening at the event that you are covering and find out about story assignment changes and updates. Be prepared to provide a brief, but complete, over-the-phone voicer report.

The approaches used to determine what information to include in stories from meetings, speeches, and news conferences also share several similarities. These include the following:

a. *Focus on what is said rather than only the event.* Report who said what, not simply that the event occurred. The event is only the setting for the comments to be made.

b. *Understand before you write.* Before you can write a meaningful story, you must understand what has been said and determine what it means to your audience.

c. *Construct a coherent story from "pieces."* Pull together comments that may be scattered throughout a presentation. Very seldom will a broadcast story report what happened in the same order in which events occurred.

d. *Place the comments and ideas into a meaningful perspective.* Make some sense out of what happened and what was said. Find the focus or theme of the session. Provide supporting information as needed. This is especially important when the subject matter is technical or controversial, or when it is linked to a previous news event. Tell the audience what it all means to them, directly.

e. *Get reactions to what happened* whenever possible and if time permits. A disgruntled property owner or a displaced city employee may provide interesting counterpoint to the mayor's statements made during a speech, news conference, or at the weekly city council meeting.

f. *Verify crucial information.* Those conducting the session or those most directly involved in the important issues considered can clarify details or fill informational gaps to help you avoid errors and provide accurate information.

g. *Write the story while it is fresh in your mind.* Think about the event, and identify what is important. Determine how you will organize and present the information. *Then* write the story.

Although the coverage of meetings, speeches, and news conferences shares several similarities, the coverage of these events also has differences that you must understand. These are described in the following sections.

Meetings

In most states, access to governmental meetings is ensured. However, each state determines the degree of access reporters will have. Chapter 19 discusses the laws regarding open meetings. Access to the meetings of civic, social, and professional groups is not ensured and must be determined by the reporter.

The reporter packages most meeting stories as summary reports (a voicer in radio or a package in television) or as edited comments recorded at the meeting or shortly afterward (an actuality in radio or soundbite in television).

Your best sources will be the officials who conduct the meetings as well as your regular news contacts. Your experience with a particular group will provide added insight about how the group operates at meetings, the personalities involved, and so forth. Don't forget to contact those *affected* by the decisions made at a meeting.

If the issue to be decided at a meeting is important enough, consider writing a preview story.

It could be a historic decision for the City of Phoenix . . . a major transportation issue to be decided. . . . The Phoenix City Council is set to decide the route of the Paradise Parkway. . . . A controversy over the route of the parkway is a quarter of a century old. . . .

KTVK-TV, Phoenix

This copy preceded a live report from the Phoenix Civic Plaza that included a prerecorded package of comments from a school principal and from parents of students who faced the possibility of a freeway 100 feet from their school playgrounds. The intensity of the controversy was evident when KTVK-TV's Tom Olson used the following to lead into a map showing the two routes proposed:

```
Tonight, expect fireworks. . . . Every Paradise Parkway
hearing before the council draws a thousand or more. . . .
Tonight, expect more.
```
                                        KTVK-TV, Phoenix

Report only the significant items from the meeting. Significance includes impact. Demonstrate the effect of the decisions made on those most directly affected. The impact of the Phoenix City Council's decision was clear from the story broadcast at five the next afternoon.

```
Almost 5-thousand Phoenicians are tonight facing the reality
of losing their homes. That's because the Phoenix City Council
has chosen a route for the Paradise Parkway. Tom McNamara is
visiting one of the neighborhoods that . . . in a few short
years . . . will become a six-lane freeway.
```
                                        KTVK-TV, Phoenix

McNamara's report focused on a resident along the route who expressed frustration after investing in major home improvements and refinancing her home. The story concluded with a review of the route and comments from a councilman and another homeowner. Just before a homeowner's concluding statement, McNamara placed the council's decision in perspective:

```
The focus for now is along the approved route . . . and on the
lives that will change because of Paradise Parkway.
```
                                        KTVK-TV, Phoenix

For comparison, here's the lead-in from another Phoenix station reporting the same city council decision:

```
More than a thousand people who live south of Camelback Road
are faced tonight with the prospect of finding new places to
live. They now know they are in the way of the Paradise Parkway.
```
                                        KPNX-TV, Phoenix

Both stations stressed the impact of the council's decision and used comments from those most directly affected.

Here are some *additional suggestions for covering meetings:*

a. At some point as the meeting progresses, decide the key topics or issues that you are likely to include in your story.
b. Disputes often arise. Get statements from all sides.
c. Don't ignore the audience at the meeting. Note the crowd size as well as the spectators' reactions and comments.
d. Follow up on the items considered at a meeting and destined to be included in your story. Was an item tabled for later consideration? When will it be reconsidered? Is this the first or last official reading or hearing for a particular piece of legislation? Is a public hearing scheduled on the issue? When will a final vote be taken on the issue? All of these kinds of questions help you guide the listener or viewer through an often confusing maze of procedures and terms and also point the way to follow-up stories you could pursue.

Speeches

Some speeches are newsworthy. The president assesses the latest congressional spending package in a televised speech to the nation. At a state convention of teachers, a governor pledges her support to increased aid to education. An internationally respected biologist tells a local college audience that landfills pose serious environmental dangers. Again, someone is saying something that may be potentially newsworthy.

Advance copies of a speech make the reporter's work easier. Mark the speech text for potential audio or video excerpts to be used. But remember to record the entire speech and follow along with the speaker, who may deviate from the prepared text or sound emphatic on a particular point that you may have overlooked.

If a question-answer session follows the speech, ask questions that are concise and direct. Your questions should ask for clarification or defense of key points made in the speech. Pursue issues that the potential newsmaker may have chosen to ignore or deemphasize.

The lead sentence in a speech story could emphasize the occasion, the speaker, or the topic. All three elements can be included in the lead:

```
At the Point Center Chamber of Commerce luncheon today, the
mayor said his downtown redevelopment plan needs citizen
input.
```

A few sentences that support or elaborate on the central theme or topic of the speech follow the lead. Then, depending on the length and importance of the speech, the story continues to present other key ideas the speaker offered, using recorded excerpts inserted in the copy. Select excerpts that feature the speaker's unusual, profound, attention-getting, or humorous comments.

Some news conferences and interviews are conducted in the field, at the site of the news story. Photography by Robert Buchar, KSL-TV, Salt Lake City, Utah.

Avoid stagnant writing. Vary sentence construction so that every sentence does not begin with the speaker's name. Mix verb tenses (as illustrated in earlier chapters), even though the speech occurred in the immediate past.

Note the credentials of the speaker early in the story and indicate what the speaker *said,* not the fact that the speaker simply came and spoke. Remember to attribute comments to the speaker. Also note whether the comments were made during the speech or in a personal interview afterward.

Demonstrate the significance of the speaker's main theme or message to the audience attending as well as to those hearing your story.

Include information about the occasion of the speech. Was it the regular meeting of a particular group? Was it a special presentation or a major announcement? Were the remarks made at the dedication of a building or new expressway? And make notes about the audience (size, responses, etc.).

News Conferences

A news conference sometimes precedes a speech. The speaker or the person featured at the news conference answers questions from a number of reporters in a group interview.

Generally news conferences are called for a single purpose; for example, the state treasurer responds to embezzlement charges, or the mayor fields questions after announcing he is resigning for health reasons.

Most news conferences are staged events managed by people who want publicity and an inexpensive way to get a point of view across to the public. Lobbyists often use what are labeled ''preemptive'' news conferences within hours of a vote on a sensitive issue. Shortly before the critical vote, a lobbyist or agency or organization spokesperson briefs the media with a positive or negative spin on the issue. The same technique is often used when legislators or legislative aides are briefed on upcoming legislation. The preemptive news conference provides spokespersons one final opportunity to use the media to convey a specific perspective on an issue. Remember that reporters are generally *invited* to a news conference. Be aware of who invited you to the news conference.

Unfortunately, news conferences may be used to cover up and stifle reporters' questions about sensitive issues. What passes as a news conference may be someone reading from a prepared statement distributed to reporters who are then not allowed to ask questions.

Earlier you were encouraged to consider using alternative coverage techniques for news conferences as well as meetings and speeches. Even if it looks like a news conference or brief statement from a news source will provide the information you need for a particular story, stay alert! Follow your instincts! Perhaps the news conference or statement is a diversion meant to distract you from a more newsworthy development.

Here's how Richard Warner, General Manager of the Georgia Radio News Service, bypassed an available news conference and got a stronger news story:

> We learned that Atlanta Police were about to make an arrest in the murders of more than 30 black youngsters one night in 1980. The world's press converged on Atlanta's police headquarters to learn what it could from vantage points outside. . . . At one point, the police commissioner stepped outside to address the crowd, but instinct told me that enough people were present to get his remarks, so I left and circled around behind the police building. Only a photographer and newspaper reporter were standing by the exit to the underground police parking garage, when we noticed some commotion, back in a far corner. Police officers were surrounding someone with a coat over his head, stuffing him in the back seat of an unmarked car, and speeding toward the exit. While every other reporter in the city was covering a press conference several hundred yards away, I got a look at Wayne Williams, lying down on the back seat of a police car, as it sped away. . . . Of course, it was a shining moment for our radio station when I went on the air, after the press conference, to describe what had REALLY been going on.[2]

Laurie Krueger at KVOO Radio in Tulsa has learned that:

> It never hurts to do your own homework before attending a press conference. Old news copy, newspaper articles, and notes can refresh your memory on the background information.
>
> Have a list of prepared questions you might want to ask. You may find, however, that a lot of them are answered in an opening speech. In addition, you're most likely to come up with more as you listen to the speaker.

Know your faces. Attending a conference in which a person announces his or her candidacy for an office and not knowing what he or she looks like can be awkward. This applies to those . . . officials already in office. . . .[3]

Remember that a news conference is no more productive than the questions asked and the answers given. The news conference should be guided by *reporters'* questions. No questions should be "off limits." Clarify what's been said or left unsaid, and probe into areas not included in the original call to the news conference. *Pursue* until your question is answered.

Do not avoid "dead spaces" at a news conference. Waiting a moment before asking the next question makes editing the tape easier and might provide useful afterthoughts when the potential newsmaker jumps in to fill the void.

News conferences offer both advantages and disadvantages. The give-and-take between a potential newsmaker and several reporters provides comments on topics a single reporter may not have thought to obtain. Unfortunately, all who attend a group interview share the comments made.

If time permits, arrange a personal interview. Try to find an unusual angle to the story. Follow up on a passing reference made; for example, read the document the newsmaker held or interview the county employee mentioned as a key to the success of his department. Balance your desire for exclusivity with a thoughtful determination that what you have obtained individually is indeed newsworthy.

The structure of the news conference story is similar to that recommended for speeches—lead sentence featuring the speaker, key topic, or occasion followed by significant details using recorded excerpts whenever possible. Assimilate scattered but related comments and present them in a coherent manner. The news source will flit from one subject to another and then return to an earlier subject when a follow-up question is asked. Monitor the progression of opinion on key topics and pull together the pieces that make the story more readily understood.

Governmental Agencies

An unlimited number of governmental agency activities receive regular news coverage at the municipal, county, state, and federal levels—legislative, fiscal (budgets, audits, taxes, bid letting), public works and utilities (gas, electricity, water, sanitation), energy and natural resources, education, health, transportation and traffic, legal, housing, recreation and parks, labor, planning, social services, and personnel.

Covering such diverse activities well is difficult, but not impossible. Establish strong contacts using the beat system. Understand the structure, authority, responsibilities, and range of activities of each governmental agency covered. Budgets, for example, often indicate priorities as well as who wields power within an agency. Learn to uncover, interpret, and then report often complex and confusing laws, ordinances, policies, procedures, and recommendations. Learn how to digest routine public records and documents. Show how information that most people do not easily understand or appreciate affects their lives directly.

Northwest Airlines is an important Minnesota-based company. Figure 15.1 shows how WCCO-TV in Minneapolis used its investigative team to report a federal transportation agency story that had significant local impact.

Law Enforcement

A variety of private and public agencies are involved in law enforcement activities. Newscasts often include stories about crimes, protests, riots, terrorists, accidents, disasters, and fires. Small- and medium-market stations report virtually all such activities. Larger markets in which such events occur frequently tend to overlook all but the most serious situations. Determining the uniqueness of each event and its significance to the audience listening to a particular newscast is always important.

The sources and coverage techniques used to cover various law enforcement activities have similarities. We will examine the similarities first and then offer specific considerations for each type of law enforcement story.

Similarities

Law enforcement stories have common sources of information. Cultivate law enforcement agency news sources. Encourage them to call *you* when a newsworthy situation develops. When you arrive on the scene, follow this priority scheme for contacting sources and recording comments: first, officials for the facts they know now; second, eyewitnesses for a personal perspective about what it was like; third, rescuers for specific observations about what it was like helping to cope with a situation; and, finally, survivors and relatives for personal insights about the event that has affected them directly.

Similarities in how sources should be handled include the following:

a. *Do not interfere with law enforcement personnel.* Your job is to report what is happening and not stand between the event and those responsible for handling it. Do not endanger yourself, your equipment, or your newsroom's reputation by becoming a participant. Remember that you are a reporter gathering information from which to report events and viewpoints as objectively as possible.

b. *Talk first, then record.* If the situation permits, talk off-mike or off-camera to your sources at the scene. They will be less distracted by the equipment and can offer a more coherent recorded comment about what happened.

c. *Be sensitive to your sources.* Remember that police officers and rescue personnel operate in a highly charged, occasionally dangerous, often highly politicized world. They have a job to do. They often don't know how reporters fit into this scheme.

NORTHWEST REPORT P.1.
DAVE READS
A BOX ADDA, SS FAA REPORT (NEW)
 	
TAKE VT ___11___ NAT   :15
	(DAVE/___3___)
	   TODAY, THE FEDERAL
	AVIATION ADMINISTRATION
	RELEASED A REPORT ON
	NORTHWEST AIRLINES.
	   IT (VT/NAT)
	   X̶X̶X̶B̶O̶X̶X̶E̶X̶ SAYS
	NORTHWEST DELAYED
	IMPORTANT REPAIRS . . .
	   ALLOWED PILOTS TO
	FLY TOO LONG . . .
	   AND FAILED TO CONDUCT
	REQUIRED SAFETY INSPECTIONS
	ON SOME PLANES.
	   THE REPORT DREW
	IMMEDIATE REACTION FROM
	THE HEAD OF A PRIVATE
	AVIATION SAFETY WATCH-
	DOG GROUP:	

		1-9

VT GOES SOUND FULL   :17/:32
TITLE: JOHN GALIPAULT
         AVIATION SAFETY INSTITUTE
VT GOES NAT   :20/:52 *6105*
DAVE READS
	(((((SOT)))))
	(IN: THEY GOT A REPORT
	(OUTCUE: MUCH MORE TROUBLE
	(DAVE/NAT VT)
	   X̶X̶X̶B̶O̶X̶X̶E̶X̶ NORTHWEST
	OFFICIALS DECLINED TO
	DISCUSS THE REPORT ON
	CAMERA, BUT IN A WRITTEN
	STATEMENT THE AIRLINE
	SAID IT HAS ALREADY
	            (MORE)
		14:24:13

2.

Figure 15.1 Example of local follow-up to a federal transportation story. Courtesy of WCCO-TV, Minneapolis, Minnesota.

NORTHWEST REPORT P.2. DAVE READS NAT VT ROLLS	(DAVE/NAT VT) CORRECTED MANY OF THE PROBLEMS CITED BY THE F-A-A. THE INSPECTION REPORT MUST STILL BE REVIEWED BY GOVERNMENT LAWYERS, BUT SOURCES TELL THE WCCO TV I-TEAM THAT THE REPORT COULD LEAD TO ONE OF THE LARGEST FINES IN AVIATION HISTORY.	 *1-10* *T-3*

DAVE READS
X̶X̶B̶O̶O̶B̶X̶ A, CU
	(DAVE/___3___)
	   THE F-A-A REPORT WAS
	RELEASED AFTER THE
	X̶X̶B̶O̶O̶X̶ I-TEAM FILED
	A REQUEST UNDER THE
	''FREEDOM OF INFORMATION
	ACT.''
	        -0-
		
		par
		
		ठ℥H3
		
		19

Figure 15.1 continued.

Remember, too, the personal and emotional shock of survivors and relatives of victims who now face the reality of coping with the aftermath of this event. Show compassion and respect when gathering personal accounts of what happened. Most newsrooms recommend that reporters avoid interviews with survivors of accidents or other tragedies or their relatives unless these interviews are essential to the story; examples include when they help explain what happened or drive home a point that might help avoid future tragedies. Always get an interviewee's permission for the interview and then exercise restraint in what you ask and how you report what you obtain.

Similarities also exist in how various law enforcement activities should be covered and reported. These include the following:

a. *Respond quickly.* Assess the situation. Determine your approach. Be flexible in the use of your time, energy, and equipment.

b. *Prioritize your coverage* (as recommended at the beginning of this section). For television coverage, for example, get the shots that evaporate quickly, such as burning buildings, rescue workers leaving, demonstrators walking past the state capitol. *Then* shoot SOT interviews and cutaways. Similar radio coverage techniques are described and illustrated in Chapter 12.

c. *Avoid speculation, rumor, and accusation.* Wait until the facts are confirmed before reporting that the bank president may have been involved in the bank robbery or that a large section of town will have to be evacuated because of toxic fumes. Just report the facts!

d. *Use names cautiously.* Do not use the names of suspects or fatalities until officials release them. There may be exceptions; a prominent government official may be involved. Be aware of the fair trial-free press guidelines that should be followed when releasing the names of suspects. These are described in Chapter 19.

e. *Choose words carefully.* Be precise about the criminal charges filed, the size and nature of a group of demonstrators (should they be labeled a crowd or a mob? Is it a disturbance or a riot?), the condition of the survivors, the extent of fire damage, and so forth. Be careful not to say a person has committed a crime until formal charges have been filed. Then you could write *He was charged with driving while intoxicated.* Be accurate. Be precise.

f. *Update the story.* Follow up and report the cause of the fire, the latest number of fatalities from the earthquake, the responses from those criticized by protestors, the amount of money taken in the convenience store robbery.

Crimes

Several specific sources of information are used to cover crime stories. These include police radios, the ''blotter,'' and investigative reports.

Monitor the police scanners for breaking stories. Some police agencies use what are called *standard mobile 10 signals*. Your newsroom can monitor police scanners and stay alert for a 10–40 (drug violation), 10–50 (traffic accident), 10–55 (dispatch ambulance), 10–56 (dispatch fire truck), 10–59 (attention all units), 10–65 (probable death), 10–80 (bomb threat), or any number of other coded messages. Most police agencies simply relay messages in plain words and avoid using the 10–code.

At the police station, check the police ''blotter'' that lists events occurring during a particular shift, or ''watch.'' The blotter generally indicates the circumstances of each incident reported to police. This might include time, place, nature and source of the complaint, parties involved, charges filed, arrests made, and suspects identified.

Examine investigative reports, accident, and arrest records that provide more details about each incident. This might include what happened, names of witnesses, suspects, officers involved. These must be requested from a police department representative. They are not readily available to the general public.

The information included in crime stories depends on the nature of the crime reported. Essentially you need to know what happened and the circumstances involved. This checklist of items might include: nature of the crime; names of those involved (victims and suspects); when and where events occurred; description of the police investigation; arrests made (how many? by whom? on what charge[s]?); identity of witnesses; unusual circumstances surrounding the incident; amount of loss or damages (for burglaries, robberies, and property damage accidents).

Juveniles present a special situation. Most newsrooms do not use the names of juveniles unless they are involved in serious crimes such as murder, assault, or rape or will be prosecuted as adults. It is best to record and note the information about juveniles involved in crimes and then discard this material if it is determined later it should not be used.

Go beyond the formal account the police provide. If circumstances warrant, illustrate the facts by retracing the crime using expert comments, eyewitnesses, neighbors, or relatives who can help re-create the emotion and drama surrounding the incident.

KTVK-TV used this lead-in to a live, on-scene report:

A bank robbery turned into a shootout on the streets of Phoenix today. When it was all over, the suspect and his hostage were wounded.

The reporter arrived at the scene within minutes of the shooting and traced the events for viewers. The report included recorded comments by an eyewitness as well as one of the hostages.

Protests and demonstrations involve issues that need to be identified precisely and reported as objectively as possible from all sides of the controversy. Terrorist situations generally involve hostages, may cause death and destruction, and almost always involve complex demands and charges.

Follow police instructions. Do nothing that jeopardizes lives or interferes with authorities' efforts to contain the situation. Any police action that appears designed to limit or suppress legitimate news coverage should be resolved in the field with the appropriate police official. If that doesn't work, report the circumstances to your newsroom supervisor.

Be unobtrusive. This means using unmarked vehicles and being restrained and neutral in what you say and what you do at the scene.

Do not allow yourself and your newsroom to be used as a vehicle for stories involving insignificant issues or small numbers of people. Assess thoughtfully the nature and extent of the situation.

Cut through the rhetoric that often surrounds such incidents and report only significant, verifiable incidents and comments. Get all sides of the controversy involved, and attribute statements carefully. Do not add to the problem by reporting rumor and speculation. Report the effects of such incidents on the community or area involved.

Determine the cause of the incident as soon as possible. Explore the background of the situation and the issues and circumstances that led to the incident. This might have to be done in a later report, but at least make an effort to determine the causes.

Use restraint. Report what happened in a cool, calm, factual manner. Consider the consequences of what you report. For example, all reported bomb threats do not need to be announced; this might cause undue panic and encourage others to seek the same amount of media attention. However, when bomb threats prompt increased building security or protection of public officials or create a large public disruption, such as the evacuation of a major shopping center, then coverage may be merited.

Cover the incident exactly as it happens. Do not use staging, simulation, reenactment, or other means that in any way influence the participants and insert you *into* the story. Live coverage of such incidents needs to be handled judiciously.

Protect yourself and your equipment. These kinds of situations can lead to violence and may endanger you and those around you. Be alert!

Here's how KGAN-TV led into a report on protests surrounding the use of Iowa National Guard troops in Honduras:

```
Iowa City Police arrested one person this morning as about 50
protestors tried to prevent a bus carrying Iowa National Guard
troops from leaving the armory in Iowa. Bruce Tiemann reports
the confrontation capped months of protests and controversy
surrounding a national guard training mission in Central
America.
```

                                        KGAN-TV, Cedar Rapids-Waterloo

Tiemann's report included SOT comments by protestors and a Guard representative, previewed the stops the Guard detachment would make on the way to Honduras, and indicated what was next.

The *ABC News Policy Book* offers the most useful advice for the coverage of protests, demonstrations, and terrorists: "All of these are good guides, but they cannot substitute for the judgment, discretion and integrity of newspersons covering explosive situations.[4]

Accidents and Disasters

Accidents and disasters include home and industrial mishaps (falls, electrical shock, burns, poisoning), roadway accidents, airplane crashes, train derailments, fires, drownings, and various natural phenomena (hurricanes, tornadoes, earthquakes, major snowstorms, etc.).

These two story situations are linked because the coverage used and the information collected are similar. They differ in the severity of the incidents reported and the number of people involved.

Because these kinds of events do happen regularly, newsrooms often devise specific coverage plans. This is especially helpful for natural disasters. News crews can be dispatched more efficiently if a thoughtful plan has been developed in advance for each kind of natural disaster that is likely to occur in a specific geographical area.

Unfortunately, accidents are unplanned events. Their impact on a community often requires immediate and organized response. This is how WIFR-TV in Rockford, Illinois, earned an Associated Press spot news award for its coverage of a local explosion:

> About 10:00 in the morning we heard on the scanner that there had been an explosion in a small factory on Broadway. At that point, we pulled a reporter/photographer crew off the story they were working on, and sent them to the scene. Before they got there, we heard on the scanner that officials were asking people to leave their nearby homes, and one person was dead. We quickly got in touch with a second crew and cancelled their story. At this point, we knew we had a major story on our hands. We decided to cancel all the rest of the stories scheduled for the day, and concentrated on the explosion and the clean up. As a result, we filled the entire news hole for the 6:00 P.M. version of Action News with stories about the explosion. Since we do not have a live truck, we called the anchorman in early and sent him to the scene to do opening and closing standups and bridges. These were used to tie together the various reporter packages.[5]

You often have to enterprise accident stories. Here's how Richard Warner, General Manager of the Georgia Radio News Service, used initiative to cover a plane crash:

> At Chicago's O'Hare Airport, a passenger jet loaded with people, baggage, and fuel, lost its left engine and crashed upon takeoff. Not more than a half hour later the story cleared the wires around the country, but

none of the networks had managed to get reporters to the scene and feed tape out on their newscasts. I was manning the ''slot desk,'' or radio assignment desk at Atlanta's WSB when the story broke, and decided to go after some tape myself. I called Chicago information, and got numbers for a couple of businesses with the word ''airport'' at the beginning . . . ''Airport Gulf Station,'' ''Airport Dry Cleaners,'' whatever. On the first call, I talked with someone who had not only seen the crash, but had just returned from the crash site. The live interview on WSB radio went so well, NBC radio news used some of his comments on their hourly newscast; tape gathered from Atlanta hundreds of miles away from the scene of the tragedy.[6]

Not all of the following facts will need to be gathered for every accident or disaster story, but they should be included as appropriate and *always* verified with official, reliable sources before they are released:

   a. *Casualties* (dead and injured): names, ages, addresses, nature and extent of injuries, hospitals involved, animals or livestock involved (if any)
   b. *Property damage:* description (vehicles, buildings), estimate, how damage was sustained, insurance and recovery, other property threatened
   c. *Causes:* discovery, alarm sounded, precautions taken, negligence suspected, other circumstances; for example, in traffic accidents— road conditions, direction of the vehicle involved, visibility
   d. *Time and place event occurred*
   e. *Rescue, heroism, relief:* names, description of what happened, equipment used, handicaps encountered in rescue effort
   f. *Other details:* current status at the scene, cleanup efforts under way, investigation details, legal action pending, similarity to other accidents and disasters, effect of the incident on the community, such as after a heavy snowstorm or major earthquake.

Story structure is predictable. The summary lead indicates the essentials of what happened. The lead generally features what is happening *now* concerning the story. The rest of the story ''layers in'' the other details—deaths (if any), injuries, lives saved or endangered (if any), significant damages, circumstances of the event, odd or unusual occurrences, what happens next.

This is the first portion of a report by Adrienne Abbott on a massive fire:

Nine hundred firefighters are battling the Woodfords fire today, trying to get a line around the blaze that has devastated over six thousand acres near the Nevada-California border. Homes around the small community of Woodfords were evacuated yesterday when a wall of flames fifty feet high swept through the area. Firefighters are being assisted today by

five air tankers, a lead plane and three helicopters. At the
height of yesterday's drama, an air tanker crippled by a faulty
landing gear made an emergency landing at the Douglas County
Airport in Minden.

KBUL, Reno

An actuality from the pilot of the air tanker described the emergency equipment available. The story concluded with the reassurance that the crew landed safely.

Here's a typical drowning story:

Burt County authorities still have not released the name of a
32-year-old Omaha man who drowned in a lake just west of
Tekamah over the weekend. A fisherman discovered the body just
below the surface of the lake. Authorities say the man
apparently drowned late yesterday morning.

KKAR, Omaha

Hospitals

If casualties are associated with law enforcement stories, hospitals and medical facilities need to be contacted. Most medical officials respect the journalist's informational needs but also feel they are obligated to protect the privacy of patients under their care.

Most medical facilities have established procedures for releasing information in person or over the telephone. A typical set of guidelines for releasing patient information to news media appears in Figure 15.2.

Courts

Many stories lead to the courtroom. Some originate with crimes (criminal cases). Others (civil cases) originate when charges are filed between prominent individuals or companies or involve substantial amounts of money or issues that seem particularly significant or likely to set a legal precedent.

A reporter assigned to courts as a regular beat assignment must understand the law and judicial processes and must write accurate, interesting stories about court actions that, on the surface, may appear dull and unnecessarily complex. Court coverage requires concentration, energy, and patience. See Chapter 19 for a discussion of legal issues and regulations associated with court coverage.

This book cannot provide the background necessary for a thorough understanding of the court system; however basic court structure and the criminal justice process are summarized, as well as specific sources of information and coverage suggestions that might prove helpful if you are assigned to cover the courts. An abbreviated list of legal terms often used in such stories is also provided.

General Guide for the Release of Patient Information by the Hospital

The following guide was adapted from the "Release of Information" section of Hospitals and the News Media: A Guide to Good Media Relations, *by Mary Laing Babich, copyright 1985 by American Hospital Publishing, Inc. (out of print). The guide is now available under the title* General Guide for the Release of Patient Information, *catalog number 166851, from the American Hospital Association, P.O. Box 99376, Chicago, Illinois 60693.*

The following information may be released by the hospital for any inpatient or emergency department patient [depending on state statutes]:

- Name
- Address
- Occupation
- Sex
- Age
- Marital status

However, the restrictions described should be observed whenever possible or practical before any information is released.

Author's Note: This guide is general. It is important to be aware that laws regarding patient privacy, confidentiality, and "public record cases" vary from state to state. The PR manager should consult with the organization's legal counsel before finalizing any policies on release of patient information.

☐ Condition of Patient

Except for the following one-word conditions, no information about the patient may be released without the patient's permission. Only a physician may discuss the patient's diagnosis and/or prognosis, if the patient has given permission for the physician to do so. The following terms can be used to describe the patient's condition:

- *Good.* Vital signs are stable and within normal limits. Patient is conscious and comfortable. Indicators are excellent.
- *Fair.* Vital signs are stable and within normal limits. Patient is conscious but may be uncomfortable. Indicators are favorable.
- *Serious.* Vital signs may be unstable and not within normal limits. Patient is acutely ill. Indicators are questionable.
- *Critical.* Vital signs are unstable and not within normal limits. Patient may be unconscious. Indicators are unfavorable. [Note: By definition, a critical patient cannot be stable.]
- *Unconscious.* The hospital may release information that the patient was unconscious when brought to the hospital.
- *Dead.* The death of a patient is presumed to be a matter of public record and may be reported by the hospital after the next of kin has been notified or after a reasonable time

has passed. Information regarding the cause of death must come from the patient's physician, and its release must be approved by a member of the immediate family [when available].

[Note: Although often used, the terms *stable* and *guarded* do not have universally accepted definitions and, therefore, should not be used.]

☐ Nature of Accident or Injury

The hospital spokesman may give out only limited information about the various kinds of accidents or injuries in order to protect the privacy of the patient.

- *Battered children.* The spokesman may not discuss possible child abuse. However, the injuries sustained by the child may be described as indicated below.
- *Burns.* The spokesman may state that the patient is burned, but the severity and degree of burns may be released only after a physician's diagnosis.
- *Fractures.* The spokesman may provide information on the location of the fracture only if a limb is involved and may say whether the fracture is simple or compound.
- *Head injuries.* The spokesman may state that the injuries are of the head. It may not be stated that the skull is fractured until diagnosed by a physician.
- *Internal injuries.* The spokesman may state that there are internal injuries, but no information may be given as to the location of the injuries until a physician has made a diagnosis.
- *Intoxication or drug abuse.* The spokesman may not provide information that the patient was intoxicated or had abused drugs, or characterize the patient as an abuser. The spokesman should be wary of indicating a diagnosis that might imply substance abuse; for example, saying that a patient had cirrhosis could indicate alcohol abuse.
- *Poisoning.* The spokesman may state only that the patient is being treated for suspected poisoning. No statement may be made concerning either motivation or circumstances surrounding a patient's poisoning. The suspected poisonous compound may be identified only by the patient's physician.
- *Sexual assault.* The spokesman may not say that the patient has been sexually assaulted nor provide information regarding the nature of the sexual assault or injuries. Only the condition of the patient may be given.
- *Sexually transmitted and communicable diseases.* The spokesman may not provide information that the patient has a sexually transmitted or communicable disease. The spokesman should be careful not to indicate a diagnosis that might imply a communicable disease. For example, saying that a patient has Kaposi's sarcoma could indicate the patient has AIDS.
- *Shooting or stabbing.* The spokesman may provide the number of wounds and their location if these facts have been definitely determined by a physician. No statement may be made as to how the shooting or stabbing occurred.
- *Suicide or attempted suicide.* The spokesman may not provide any statement that there was a suicide or attempted suicide.
- *Transplant recipients and organ donors.* The spokesman may release information regarding the nature of the transplant and the condition, age, and sex of the recipient. However, the release of the names of the recipient and/or donor requires prior consent. If the donor is deceased, the name may not be given out without the consent of the legal next of kin.

Figure 15.2 Typical guidelines for releasing patient information to the news media. Reprinted with permission from *Public Relations in Health Care: A Guide for Professionals*, published by American Hospital Publishing, Inc., Copyright 1991.

☐ Matters of Public Record

Matters of public record refer to those situations that are by law reportable to public authorities, such as the police, coroner, or public health officer. Examples of matters of public record are the following:

- Persons under arrest or held under police surveillance
- Persons brought to the hospital by the fire department or by any law enforcement agency
- Persons who have been shot, stabbed, poisoned, injured in automobile accidents, or bitten by dogs or other animals
- Persons with any other injuries that are usually reported to governmental agencies regardless of the mode of transportation to the hospital

☐ Coroner's Cases

Generally, in accordance with state law, the hospital must provide the coroner with information in any of the following circumstances:

- When the body is unidentified or unclaimed
- When a sudden death is not caused by a readily recognized disease or when the cause of death cannot be properly certified by a physician on the basis of prior [recent] medical attendance
- When the death occurred under suspicious circumstances, including those deaths in which alcohol, drugs, or other toxic substances may have a direct bearing on the outcome
- When the death occurred as a result of violence or trauma, whether apparently homicidal, suicidal, or accidental [including those resulting from mechanical, thermal, chemical, electrical, or radiational injuries or from drownings or cave-ins] and regardless of the time elapsed between the time of injury and the time of death

- When there is a fetal death, stillbirth, or death of any baby within 24 hours after its birth and the mother has not been under the care of a physician
- When the death has resulted from an abortion, whether therapeutic or criminal, self-induced, or otherwise
- When operative and perioperative deaths are not readily explainable on the basis of prior disease

The hospital should check with its attorney to find out what other types of situations are required by state law to be reported to the coroner.

[Note: When the media ask questions about such cases, the hospital spokesman should not attempt to answer them (beyond the basic information described in this guide) and should refer reporters to the coroner.]

☐ Accidents and Police Investigations

The spokesman may release the name, address, age, nature of injury, condition (if determined), and the disposition of such patients, that is, whether they have been hospitalized. No attempt should be made to describe the event that caused the injury, and no statement about any of the following should be made:

- Whether a person was intoxicated
- Whether the injuries were the result of an assault, attempted suicide, or accident
- Whether a patient was poisoned (accidentally or deliberately)
- Whether a patient is suspected of being a drug addict
- The circumstances that resulted in a patient's being shot or stabbed
- The circumstances related to an automobile or industrial accident

Figure 15.2 continued.

Structure	Each state has its own highly autonomous court structure. The names and responsibilities of state trial and appellate courts vary.

Criminal Justice Process	The flowchart shown in Figure 15.3 will help you to identify the essential steps involved in a criminal case.[7]

Legal Terms	Bob Priddy, the News Director of the Missouri Network and former Chairman of the RTNDA, offers sound advice about the use of legal terms in news copy:

> We're convinced most people don't know what a writ of habeas corpus is, and they think a corpus dilecti is a murder victim (it isn't). Instead of using a phrase you don't understand—and if you don't understand it, your listeners probably won't either—find a reference that will tell what it is. Then use regular English. If a lawyer seeks interlocutory judgement, don't tell that to your listeners. Say he seeks a temporary court order. That's what an interlocutory judgement is.[8]

Basic Steps in the Criminal Justice System

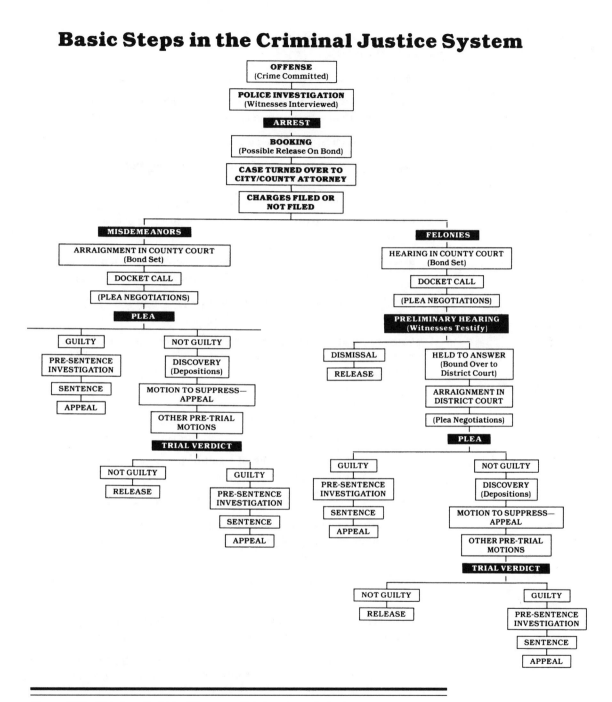

Figure 15.3 This flowchart identifies essential steps in a criminal case. Courtesy of The Nebraska Crime Commission.

Here is a selected glossary of legal terms that are often used when reporting court stories:

acquit—to find a defendant not guilty in a criminal trial.

affidavit—a written, sworn statement of facts made voluntarily, usually in support of a motion or in response to a request of the court.

appeal—a request to take a case to a higher court for review.

appellant—the party appealing a decision or judgment to a higher court.

arbitration—the hearing and settlement of a dispute between opposing parties by a third party whose decision the parties have agreed to accept.

arraignment—in a criminal case, the proceeding in which an accused is brought to the court to hear the charges read and to enter a plea.

arrest—to take into custody; to deprive a person of liberty by legal authority.

bail—to set at liberty a person arrested or imprisoned on security (or bail) being taken for his or her appearance in court on a specified day and place.

bind over—to hold for trial.

brief—a written document a lawyer presents to the court that usually sets forth both facts and law in support of his or her case.

change of venue—the moving of a suit begun in one district to another district for trial, or from one court to another in the same district.

charge—formal accusation of having committed a criminal offense.

civil action—a lawsuit between or among private parties for declaration, enforcement, or protection of a right, or for redress or prevention of a wrong.

common law—the law of a country based on custom, usage, and the decisions of law courts.

concurrent sentence—sentences for more than one crime in which the time of each is to be served concurrently rather than successively.

contempt of court—any act calculated to embarrass, hinder, or obstruct a court in the administration of justice, or calculated to lessen its authority or dignity.

conviction—the finding that a person is guilty beyond a reasonable doubt of committing a crime.

crime—conduct declared unlawful by a legislative body and for which the punishment is a jail or prison term, a fine, or both.

damages—financial compensation claimed by or ordered paid to a person who has suffered injury or loss through the unlawful act or negligence of another.

decree—a decision or order of the court.

defendant—a person sued or accused.

deposition—the testimony of a witness not taken in open court.

discovery—a proceeding whereby one party to an action may learn of facts the other parties or witnesses know.

docket—a list of cases to be tried by a court.

due process—law in its regular course of administration through the courts of justice. The constitutional guarantee of due process requires that every individual have the protection of a fair trial.

eminent domain—the lawful power to take private property for public use by the process of condemnation.

extradition—the surrender from one state to another of an individual accused or convicted of an offense outside its own territory and within the territorial jurisdiction.

felony—a crime of a graver nature than a misdemeanor; generally, an offense punishable by death or imprisonment in a penitentiary.

grand jury—a body of persons sworn to inquire into a crime and bring an accusation (indictment) against the suspected criminal if warranted.

habeas corpus—''You have the body''; name given a variety of writs whose object is to bring a person before a court or judge. In most common usage, it is directed to the official person detaining another, commanding him or her to produce the body of the prisoner or person detained so the court may determine if such person has been denied his or her liberty without due process of law.

hearing—an in-court proceeding, before a judge, generally open to the public.

indictment—an accusation in writing found and issued by a grand jury, charging that a person named has done some act, or is guilty of some omission, which by law is a crime.

insanity—a complete defense to a crime; exists when at the time of the commission of a crime, the accused was not aware of the nature and quality of his or her criminal act, or if the accused did, [sic] was not aware that the act was legally wrong.

judgment—the official decision or decree of the court upon the rights and claims of the parties.

jurisdiction—the legal power to hear and decide cases; the territorial range of such power.

jury (or petit jury)—a jury of 12 (or fewer) persons, selected according to law, who are sworn to inquiry of certain matters of fact, and to declare the truth upon evidence laid before them.

libel—a method of defamation expressed by print, writing, pictures or signs; in its most general sense, any publication that is injurious to the reputation of another. (See Chapter 19 for a more complete discussion of libel.)

lien—an encumbrance upon property, usually as security for a debt or obligation.

mandamus—the name of a writ that issues from a court of superior jurisdiction, directed to an inferior court or a public officer, commanding the performance of a particular act.

manslaughter—the unlawful killing of another without malice; may be voluntary, upon a sudden impulse, or involuntary in the commission of some unlawful act.

misdemeanor—offenses less than felonies; generally those punishable by fine or imprisonment other than in penitentiaries.

mistrial—an erroneous or invalid trial; a trial that cannot stand in law.

murder—the unlawful killing of a human being by another with malice aforethought, either expressed or implied.

no bill—in the opinion of the [grand] jury, evidence was insufficient to warrant the return of a formal charge.

nolo contendere—a pleading usually by defendants in criminal cases; literally means ''I will not contest it.''

parole—the conditional release of a convict from prison before the expiration of his or her sentence.

peremptory challenge—the challenge that the prosecution or defense may use to reject a certain number of prospective jurors without assigning any cause.

perjury—the willful assertion as to a matter of fact, opinion, belief, or knowledge that a witness makes in a judicial proceeding as part of his or her evidence . . . and known to such witness to be false.

plaintiff—the person who brings an action.

plea—a defendant's official statement of "guilty" or "not guilty" to the charges made against him or her.

plea bargaining—the process by which the prosecutor and the defense counsel attempt to resolve a criminal case by a guilty plea.

preliminary hearing—the hearing given a person charged with a crime to determine whether he or she should be held for trial.

probable cause—a constitutionally prescribed standard of proof; a reasonable ground for belief in the existence of certain facts.

release on own recognizance—an alternative to bail; release upon certain conditions that the court sets.

search warrant—an order in writing that a judge issues in the name of the state, directing an officer to search a specified house or other premises for stolen property; usually required as a condition precedent to a legal search and seizure.

sentence—a judgment that a judge formally pronounced upon a defendant after his or her conviction in a criminal or civil prosecution.

stay—a stopping or arresting of a judicial proceeding by order of the court.

subpoena—a process to cause a witness to appear and give testimony before a court.

summons—a writ or order directing the sheriff or other officer to notify the named person that an action has been commenced against him or her in court and that he or she is required to appear, on the day named, and answer the petition or complaint in such action.

testimony—evidence a competent witness gives under oath, as distinguished from evidence derived from writings and other sources.

venue—the particular county, city, or geographic area in which a court with jurisdiction may hear and determine a case.

verdict—in practice, the formal and unanimous decision or finding that a jury makes, reported to the court and accepted by it.

writ—an order from a court of justice requiring the performance of a specified act or giving authority and commission to have it done.[9]

Sources of Information

Several key sources can be used when covering and writing court stories. In most cases, judges are inaccessible to the media, but prosecuting and defense attorneys can be helpful, especially for explaining procedural actions during a trial or giving reaction comments after a verdict (if the judge has not restricted them from talking, or if the case is not likely to be appealed). After a trial, jurors are fair game for interviews about how the verdict was determined, compelling evidence that swayed jurors, and so forth.

One of the best sources is the clerk of court, who is primarily a record-keeping official within the judicial system. Each criminal case that reaches the court level necessarily involves many documents, including arrest or search warrants; indictments; defendant pleas; subpoenas; jury duty notifications; verdicts; sentences passed. The clerk is responsible for maintaining these records and providing access to the general public under state and federal freedom of information or public records guidelines.

Coverage Suggestions

Broadcast reporters are not likely to cover most trials from start to finish because dedicating so much time and personnel to all but the most important cases is difficult. The testimony is often lengthy, and the issues are often too complex to handle within the time limits of a broadcast news story. Procedural debates and delays are also frequent.

However, when you are assigned to cover a trial, the following guidelines will be helpful:

a. *Review the paperwork ahead of time.* This will help place in perspective the trial testimony that is covered.
b. *Feature the latest and most newsworthy items.*
c. *Prepare stories on specific phases of a case.* For example, write separate stories on the charges or indictments; the start of the trial (charges, potential penalties, alleged criminal circumstances); a crucial day of testimony; final arguments and the judge's charge to the jury; the verdict (followed by reactions from the defendant, attorneys, spectators, jurors as well as a summary of major testimony and an indication of what is likely to follow: sentencing? appeal?); sentencing (sentence issued followed by verdict and charge along with what has already happened and what is likely to happen next).

A former employee of the state Franchise Tax Board has been sentenced to five years in prison. KFBK's Edd Fong joins us live and reports that the man was busted for cheating on his taxes:

- - - - - - - - - -

The Franchise Tax Board is the state's income tax collection agency. According to board spokesman Jim Reber, Douglas Himebichner was fired as a board staff member about two years ago. A subsequent federal investigation revealed that Himebichner fraudulently claimed 780,000 dollars in income in 1986 as an employee of Apple Computer and claimed a refund of more than 250,000 dollars:

REBER 1 :09 Q: ''board as well''

Himebichner pleaded guilty to charges of filing false income
tax returns in September and today was sentenced to 5 years in
prison along with 5 years probation and 11,000 dollars in
restitution to the state and U.S. governments.

Edd Fong, KFBK Newsradio 1530.
KFBK, Sacramento

    d. *Don't be judge and jury.* Don't convict the accused in your story
until the trial is completed and an official verdict has been issued,
because a danger of libel always exists.

    e. *Follow up on court stories.* If you announce a charge against
someone, you owe it to the suspect as well as your broadcast
audience to follow through and report the outcome. Were charges
dropped? Were charges filed? What charges? By whom? When?

Most federal courts prohibit access to cameras and microphones. Some
states allow extensive electronic media court coverage; other states are more
restrictive. To overcome these access problems, television stories often use
artists' sketches that highlight important witnesses and testimony, or file
footage of the original story that led to the court case.

Politics

Politics receives regular broadcast news coverage. From the time candidates
file for office to the time the winners assume their official duties, stories are
written about campaign speeches and issues, polls and surveys that purport to
reflect current attitudes toward candidates, strategies, debates, charges and
countercharges, results of election day voting, and statements of winners and
losers. Political coverage at the local, state, and national levels is an important
part of a broadcast newsroom's commitment and responsibility to the audience
that it serves.

Each phase of politics is reported:

Chicago businessman William Farley says he'll announce next
week whether he'll enter the presidential race. Farley told
Waterloo business leaders yesterday he will announce his
intentions during a speech in Des Moines.

KIMT-TV, Mason City, Iowa

Debate-mania goes one step further in the second-district
House race. Republican Congressional candidate Ally Milder
says she's invited Democratic candidate Peter Hoagland to
debate. . . . Milder says since Democratic House candidate
Cece Zorinsky has refused to debate Hoagland, she'll extend
the opportunity. Milder filed her nomination papers today
(Tuesday). She joins Jerry Schenken, Chris Abboud and Carl
Jennings in the race for the Republican nomination.

KKAR, Omaha

> Today, Jesse Jackson brought his presidential campaign to
> Minnesota. . . . He drew an overflow crowd at a pancake
> breakfast in Osakis. Jackson has been campaigning hard to win
> the farm vote. . . . Today, in Minnesota, Jackson offered no
> specific plan to help farmers, but said he alone among
> Democratic candidates has paid his dues in rural Minnesota.
>
> WCCO-TV, Minneapolis

> North Iowa voters are going to the polls today to elect city
> officials. Mayors, new council members and other city
> government positions will be elected today in many north Iowa
> communities.
>
> KIMT-TV, Mason City, Iowa

Eric Engberg, correspondent in the Washington bureau of CBS News, concludes that the news media have ceded too much authority to some of the presidential candidates covered. Engberg recommends that the ''real campaign'' be covered—the part that does not involve just the candidate's public appearances. According to Engberg, this would include a check on the kind of advertising the candidates are using, the consistency of candidates' statements to various constituencies, the candidates' voting records on key campaign issues, and the sources of campaign funds. Engberg's advice should be applied to *all* political campaigns, not only to those for the U.S. presidency.[10]

Political coverage must be balanced, fair, and objective. Some reporters become attached to a particular candidate's personality or viewpoints. A healthy dose of skepticism is always recommended. Step back periodically from the campaign. Assess the balance of your coverage, and determine what you *should* be covering. Resist rumors and the legitimizing of rumors.

Identify and report significant campaign issues. If you're reporting a candidate's economic platform, be certain you understand the economic concepts included. If you're doing a story on a candidate's position on the environment, be sure you understand something about toxicology, epidemiology, and the difference between global warming and the ozone layer hole.

Tell how candidates are communicating themes and issues to prospective constituents. Indicate the impact a candidate's proposals would have if enacted. Compare a candidate's position on key issues with those of opponents, and compare a candidate's campaign statements with voting records (if now in office).

Take a look behind the scenes. How is the campaign organized and financed? Who runs the campaign? What insights can you report that will provide a more complete assessment of the candidate?

Use surveys and polls cautiously. These research tools are better designed today and more frequently used in political coverage, but that does not necessarily mean they are better reported or understood, or that they accurately measure the current popularity of political candidates. Polls and surveys should not substitute for reporting, and they should not lead reporting. They should support it. (See Chapter 9 for a discussion of the use of polls and surveys in news stories.)[12]

Obits

And finally obituaries. If you ever work in a small-market newsroom, you will write obits. Bob Priddy offers good advice.

> The first thing to remember about obituaries is this. People *DIE*. They do not: pass away; enter into rest; pass on; become deceased. They die. Plain and simple. . . . There's no reason for us to use most of the stuff they [funeral homes] send us. . . . Several years ago, we covered a murder-suicide. Man shot his wife, then himself. The funeral home told us she died ''unexpectedly'' and he died ''suddenly.'' At least they died. There's nothing wrong with saying they died the way they died. Suicides are doubly tragic but there's nothing wrong with saying in your obituary that someone died of a self-inflicted wound, or was found in their garage with the car's engine running. . . . Obituaries sometimes mention that memorial donations may be made in lieu of flowers to various organizations. . . . While it is not necessary to rush through an obituary, there is no reason to let a funeral notice consume more time on the newscast than the story about the cable television franchise the city council revoked last night. Here's a simple format we came up with once: ''Funeral services for 74 year-old John Milquetpast of 24–18 Squalid Drive, who died Tuesday, will be at 2 o-clock tomorrow afternoon at the Plantemdeep Funeral Home. Visitation for John Milquetpast will be after 6 o-clock this evening.'' That's the essentials. Who it is. When they died. When the funeral will be. When mourners can call. Move on to the next story.[13]

Summary

This chapter offered suggestions for covering stories that broadcast newsrooms report regularly.

Meetings, speeches, and news conferences present similar situations in the sources contacted, coverage and reporting techniques used, and story information included.

A variety of governmental agencies receive regular coverage. Maintain regular contacts and learn to interpret and report the contents of various kinds of documents.

Law enforcement stories include reports about crimes, protests, terrorists, accidents, disasters, and fires. Identify the stories worth covering and have a plan of attack. Also determine who to contact and what information to obtain.

To cover court cases well, you must know basic court structure, the essentials of the criminal justice process, key legal terms often used in court stories, and who to contact for the information needed.

Politics receives regular broadcast coverage. Reporting should focus on key issues and offer a balanced account of each phase of political activity.

Obituaries must be brief and include only essential information.

Exercises

1. Cover one of the following: a major speech by a nationally recognized expert at a nearby college; a news conference scheduled by an elected official; a meeting of a local governmental body such as school board, city council, county commissioners. Record and edit two actualities for radio or two soundbites for television. Write and record a voicer wrap for radio or a package for television using the material gathered. Compare your story with those used on local newscasts.

2. Follow the directions for Exercise 1 but also arrange for a personal interview after the event covered. Incorporate into either a radio or television report (as specified above) comments made in *both* settings.

3. You are writing for the next newscast on a local broadcast station where these events occurred. Write a 30-second radio voicer report based on the following facts obtained at the monthly meeting of the local board of education:

- Richard Krueger, 3845 Eagle Blvd., was named by the board to fill the vacancy that the resignation of board member Dr. Bernard Lynquist created. Krueger will serve through December 1999, completing the unexpired Lynquist term.
- Krueger was chosen from five applicants. He is a '65 graduate of Fairmont High

School locally and is plant manager of Silver Products in Cedar Point (four miles away).
- Lynquist resigned last month when reports circulated that he opposed renewal of Dr. Paul Richards' contract. Richards is the current Superintendent of Schools.
- The board also voted to place a 9-mill operating levy on the next local general election ballot.
- Tony Ulman, clerk-treasurer for the board, reported that the school system will be more than $1,000,000 in the red by next spring if additional money is not made available for operations. Ulman blamed a shrinking tax base (caused by lower reevaluations of downtown properties) for the loss in revenue.

4. Contact the clerk of your state legislature or assembly. Examine a copy of a bill that is scheduled to be debated soon in the assembly or that is scheduled for hearings within the next few weeks. Read the bill carefully. Record an interview with one of the legislators who introduced the measure, or an individual or organization the proposed law affects directly. Prepare a 30- to 40-second story that uses at least one soundbite. This story could be prepared as a single soundbite story or as a voicer wraparound/ package report. Turn in your news copy, your finished taped report, and the copy of the bill you examined.

Notes

1. Bob Priddy, memorandum to Missouri Network affiliates (6/25/86).

2. Reprinted by permission of Richard Warner.

3. Reprinted by permission of Laurie Krueger.

4. From "Coverage of Riots and Other Civil Disorders," *ABC News Policy Book* (n.p., n.d.), p. II.8.

5. Reprinted by permission of Arles Hendershott.

6. Reprinted by permission of Richard Warner.

7. The American Bar Association, in collaboration with the Society of Professional Journalists, has produced several videotapes and collateral instructional material to help reporters understand the U.S. court system. For a complete listing of available material, call (312) 988–5555 or write the American Bar Association, 750 N. Lake Shore Drive, Chicago, IL 60611.

8. Bob Priddy *Newstips,* October 1987 (Jefferson City, MO), 1.

9. Selected glossary of legal terms prepared by County Judge F. A. Gossett (Blair, Nebraska), *Citizens' Guide to Nebraska Courts* (Nebraska Supreme Court, Court Administrator's Office, updated July 1986), 17–38.

Contact your state bar association to obtain written material concerning the court system in your state and a more complete glossary of legal terms.

10. Eric Engberg, ''The Way We Choose the President,'' *Communicator* 41, no. 11 (November 1987): 36, 38–39.

11. Several issues of *Communicator* in 1988 and 1992 discuss the evolution of political news coverage.

12. Several issues of *Communicator* in 1988 and 1992 discuss the evolution of political news coverage.

13. ''Obits,'' *Newstips,* July 1987.

Chapter 16

Specialized Coverage

Good jobs are difficult to find in the broadcast news business. Writing and reporting skills constantly must be refined and enhanced. Consolidation of duties is a newsroom reality. Yet newsroom supervisors want employees who demonstrate flexibility in their skills. Changing technology and intense competition continue to make the job search increasingly difficult.

One way to respond to this problem is to create a newsroom franchise. Make yourself distinctive and invaluable. The reporter who can stand out from others in the newsroom, who has some particular specialty or expertise that is needed on a regular basis may be able to find and land a better job now and in the future. This will likely lead to a valuable, lucrative, and fulfilling franchise in the newsroom and could protect your job when future personnel cuts are made.

Some special area reporters contend, however, that it is better *not* to have a specialized background that matches the stories covered. They argue that an experienced reporter can better explain technical information and complex processes, that an expert gets too technical and understands so much about a subject that it is difficult to explain it to the general audience. They add that such an expert would find it difficult to remain impartial and not have a vested interest in the information and comments provided. Without such a specialized background, you might then be more aware of terms and processes that need an explanation for the casual listener or viewer. You might also be better prepared to tackle explanations of complicated terms and processes. If you do not develop a reporting specialty, you would need to regularly contact experts to help make sense out of what is covered in stories.

Generally, opportunities are likely to develop if you take steps to acquire the knowledge and skills associated with a specialty that a broadcast newsroom can use. Specialization generally develops after extensive professional news experience, additional education or training, and refinement of basic reporting and writing skills. Specialized reporting opportunities usually develop after reporters have been on the job for a few years.

Mastering a second language is an excellent way to improve your employment opportunities. A working knowledge of a second language, especially Spanish, will improve your ability to compete for jobs in the border states and in Florida, New York, and parts of New England. Your English language skills will also likely improve as you study another language.

This chapter is designed to expand your newswriting and reporting talents, to explore specialized areas that will help refine your basic skills, and to examine additional career options. It may also help you develop a newsroom franchise.

Some of the more common specialties are examined. They are often identified as regularly assigned beats or receive regular emphasis in reporting. The results of such coverage often become regular newscast segments.

You should note that the labels attached to the traditional reporting specialties discussed in this chapter are not the same in all broadcast newsrooms. Sometimes the labels are simply different. Sometimes specialties are combined. As operating budgets become tighter, small-market newsrooms usually have one person handle weather, agriculture, science, and even special community events coverage.

The specialties examined in this chapter include: weather, agriculture, business, consumer affairs, health and science, education, sports, and traffic reports. The following information is provided for each specialty: sources of information, contents of reports, and suggestions for writing and reporting.

Other interesting types of specialized reporting are not included in this chapter either because they have already been covered or because space is not available to give even adequate treatment to essential techniques and processes associated with such specialties. For coverage of these additional specialties, review Chapter 10 or consult the bibliography provided in Appendix C, ''Supplementary Reading,'' at the end of this text.

Weather

The weather often influences our daily activities and plans. We depend on accurate and timely weather information. Lives literally have been saved because people responded to early weather warnings received on radio or television sets. Decide in advance how each weather situation common to your geographical area will be handled. Determine sources to contact, coverage to complete, and reports to be prepared.

Weather forecasting and reporting are critical services. The stakes are high. During severe weather situations, lives are at stake. Amateur weathercasters could do more harm than good.

If you want to secure your newsroom franchise as a *meteorologist* and not as just a weathercaster, earn your American Meteorological Society (AMS) certification. The AMS seal is issued only to those who meet specific education and on-air requirements. Details are available from: the American Meteorological Society, 45 Beacon St., Boston, MA 02108 (617/227–2425). While in college, consider completing the requirements for a minor or major in Meteorology/Climatology, Earth Sciences, or a related field.

Sources of weather information have become expansive and increasingly sophisticated. Newsrooms with a serious commitment to weather reporting go beyond the resources that wire services, the national networks, or even the National Weather Service (NWS) specialized wire provide. Some newsrooms have their own weather monitoring and radar systems. Doppler® radar and computer forecasting are staples of radio and television weathercasts. One of the many NWS radio stations can be monitored and direct reports used during weather emergencies. NWS warnings and forecasts are transmitted to a communications satellite and can be received anywhere in the country by subscribers equipped with appropriate receivers. Newsroom computers can tap advanced database and graphics systems that private weather services maintain. These systems receive and then package a variety of weather information from individual National Oceanic and Atmospheric Administration (NOAA) radar sites several times daily. Ready-for-broadcast satellite data can help properly trained and experienced forecasters better track and predict such things as air pollution concentrations, snowfall amounts, and severity of storms that may threaten a particular area. Television weather forecasters can design weather graphics that feature such techniques as colorization and animation to better explain and illustrate developing weather patterns and systems.

Weather information is not always received in such a sophisticated manner. A telephone call to a highway patrol office can provide current road conditions during severe weather. Some newsrooms round out their weather coverage by receiving regular reports from trained volunteer spotters positioned throughout the coverage area. And do not neglect one of the most inexpensive but reliable sources of weather information—your own senses. Look out of the window to confirm what sophisticated weather equipment indicates is happening on the street outside of the newsroom.

Although the *current local* weather conditions and forecast are used most often, other weather items are also used regularly. These include air quality and soil condition; road conditions; weather records; and ski slope conditions and forecasts. Some newsrooms devise preprinted forms on which this and related information such as school closings, street repairs and closings can be quickly noted and reported during scheduled newscasts.

Local weather must always be emphasized. But "local" could mean a large piece of geography if a station's coverage area extends over several hundred miles. Provide weather information that a majority of the audience needs on a daily basis. National and regional weather information can be provided in occasional in-depth weather summaries.

Keep the facts simple and terminology accurate. A word like *precipitation* becomes more meaningful if replaced with *rain* or *snow* during appropriate times of the year. Make weather information more manageable, more interesting, and more informative. Use statistics sparingly.

Weak: "We've had 1.34 inches of precipitation so far this month, compared with 1.02 inches last month, but that's still more than the .67 inches this month last year when things were so dry."

Weather data must be analyzed carefully. Photo courtesy of WITI-TV, Milwaukee, Wisconsin.

Better: "The rain gauge for the month shows a little over one and one-third inches. That's a little more rain than last month and twice as much as last year at this time when things were so dry."

Agriculture

Knowing the agricultural interests of the area in which you work is important. In one way or another, practically every area of the country is oriented to agriculture. There are timberlands in the northwest; citrus crops in California and Florida; ranching interests in the southwest and along western mountain ranges; hog, cattle, and grain industries in the great plains; dairy businesses throughout the Mississippi Valley; sugar cane and rice crops in Louisiana; tobacco in the Carolinas; eggs in New York State, and so forth.

Agriculture has become big business. Many people depend on a particular agricultural crop or industry for their livelihood. Agriculture often becomes intertwined with general news events; for example, the balance of trade deficit, bank failures linked to agricultural bankruptcies, and controversies about the effect of pesticides on general health.

Several sources can provide the necessary agricultural orientation. Contact one of the 10,000 plus county agents hired by the U.S Department of Agriculture to help with consumer, agriculture, and business stories; agents know their counties well and can help arrange interviews with people affected most by the stories you are covering. *Local* ag market (like local weather) information is crucial. Find out who to call to get price quotes several times each day. Stay in touch with area agricultural organizations such as 4-H, FFA, State Grange, American Farm Bureau, National Farmers Union, and livestock- and grain-marketing associations. Attend agricultural events and fairs regularly. Read agribusiness journals, state and national agriculture department news releases, and national and specialized wire service copy to stay informed. Data Transmission Network (DTN) Corporation provides daily ag-business news items and interconnects hundreds of National Association of Farm Broadcasters (NAFB) members nationwide. Sources will tend to multiply as you become acquainted with agricultural terms, concepts, and processes.

What should be included in a regularly scheduled agricultural report? Although time of year and the agricultural concerns of each area will determine what needs to be used, here are items often included in a regularly scheduled Midwest agricultural report: weather forecast (short- and long-range) and current conditions (including soil temperature and moisture level); world/ national/state news items that relate directly to agriculture such as governmental regulations, international trade agreements, new uses for standard agricultural products; *local and area* grain and livestock market reports (throughout the day); commodity futures reports; calendar of future events and issues; features about people and events associated with agriculture.

A balanced approach is needed when preparing agricultural stories. Those involved directly in ag industries expect accurate and complete information. *All* listeners and viewers want to understand clearly how ag topics and issues might touch their lives. Therefore, provide specific, meaningful information for the first group, yet do not neglect those in the second group, who also need to understand what is happening.

Kim Dlouhy Agri-Service Director at WOW Radio in Omaha, put it this way:

> Know your audience. Know the demographics of agricultural production in your listening audience. Also know the consumers or non-farm audience that you serve, and don't forget them. Agricultural information can be useful in the hands of non-farm consumers, but you have to give it to them in their language, without being too basic for your farmer listeners.
>
> Much of the ag information you have to convey is scientific. Ask questions until you understand the science, and then find a way to translate it in non-scientific terms. A question I often ask is "What does this mean to the farmer?"[1]

Here is a sample of Kim Dlouhy's work: one program in a multiple-part report on corn sales to Japan. Listeners receive current information culled from a variety of sources. Nat sound is used throughout. Soundbites help anchor or shape the report. Transitions help guide listeners from one soundbite to another. A transcript of the soundbites is provided.

```
In the next three days, we'll tell you about an innovative
program to market technology to Japan that could increase
sales of corn to that country. Jim Parker is Ag Counselor to
Japan at the U-S Embassy in Tokyo.
```

FARM CART SSS :23 ''VERY VERY LARGE''

[One thing that U-S corn farmers can look at is the new uses of corn and I know the Feed Grains Council here in Tokyo is studying the possibility of biodegradable plastic products using corn as a base and the Japanese are quite excited about that and the potential in terms of bushels. I don't have the number right at my fingertips, but it's, you know, five . . . ten years down the road. It's very very large.]

Tim Tierney is Director of the U-S Feed Grains Council's Japan office.

FARM 203 :16 ''TO DO SOME OF THAT''

[Japan is now facing a waste management crisis. They are having problems in terms of disposal of waste. They're looking at opportunities to reduce those pressures. Biodegradable plastics offers a very, I think, unique opportunity to do some of that.]

Don Hutchens is Executive Director of the Nebraska Corn Promotion Board.

[Very selfishly, what we're looking at is transfer of technology in using corn for industrial purposes. So we hope to create more demand for Nebraska corn in Japan with this project and at the same time we realize that the potential just in the biodegradable plastic market is very good in the Asian countries with a high population and a very low land mass for agricultural production. So we think it's a benefit for both countries.]

Tomorrow, we'll tell you about the agreement that has been forged between Nebraska farmers and the Japanese Corn Starch Association. I'm Kim Dlouhy.

Business

Agriculture and business news have several similarities. These include noticeable intertwining with general news developments; use of specialized sources; contents of reports influenced by time of the year and geographical area; and reports that must inform those directly involved while also appealing to those without such direct interests. The popular term *agribusiness* underscores this deepening correlation.

A variety of sources can be used to gather business and financial news. Domestic news wires help monitor world and national events that could affect business developments. Consult local business organizations such as the builder's association or chamber of commerce as well as local public interest and consumer groups. Middle-level business executives and government workers as well as local economists, analysts, and brokers can provide potential story ideas and useful insights.

Bill Flanagan, Money Editor at KDKA-TV in Pittsburgh, suggests additional sources of information:

> For background I read the [Wall Street] Journal, [New York] Times, and local financial sections daily. I also follow Business Week and Money, since they distill the subject almost simply enough for TV.
>
> The station [KDKA-TV] has contracted with a local stock analyst to call us on a daily basis with an update on what's happening in the financial markets. I have other contacts in real estate, construction, and finance who will turn me in the right direction on a story. We also plan to buy the Directory of Wall Street Research, which lists analysts for every corporation traded publicly in the United States. . . .[2]

And what kind of news judgment does Bill Flanagan apply to available business stories?

> The most difficult stories to decide to do are those that represent the most traditional kinds of business news: corporate take-overs, earnings reports, business trends; the bread and butter of the Wall Street Journal. Television is not the Journal, nor is it the New York Times. I don't even believe that as a broadcast business reporter I should try to be like the financial section of a local newspaper. My audience is inescapably broader.
>
> I look for business news that has a grass roots impact. If a company's misfortunes affect its employees in a direct way and if the number of employees is large enough, we'll do a full-blown story on it. Similarly if business trends affect prices or availability of certain products, they deserve a mention, because they potentially affect a large number of viewers. I apply a viewership test to business news: if I don't think the bulk of the viewers of a story will benefit in some way from its being on the air, I don't run it. . . .[3]

Steve Crowley has been providing money and personal finance coverage to local stations and networks since 1982. Crowley reaffirms Flanagan's comment and says the business stories that are in the biggest demand but in the shortest supply are ones that affect how people live—how to get a good deal on a mortgage, how to finance a college education, how to pay off a large personal debt. What works best and what viewers want the most is a hybrid of business, finance, consumer, and economic news, especially local economic news that affects them directly.[4]

Notice how Bill Flanagan creates interest, provides clarity, and emphasizes a local angle in the introduction to this story about seed money for small, developing local companies:

`Pittsburgh's small, new businesses may find it a bit easier in`
`the future to break into the ranks of their bigger competitors.`

New money's available to help them pay their start up
costs. . . . The new program's geared toward those proverbial
people who build the better mouse traps . . . entrepreneurs
who may have a great idea, but who lack the money they need to
grow.

KDKA-TV, Pittsburgh

Explaining economic terms clearly is important. For example, *trade deficit* might be easier to understand if you wrote *Americans purchase vastly more from the rest of the world than they are able to sell.* *Wholesale price index* might mean more if you explained that *a selection of items costing ten dollars two decades ago would cost 34 dollars and 20 cents today.* Sometimes you should describe a common economic term *before* you use it: *The government's main economic forecasting gauge — the Index of Leading Indicators — rose just one-tenth of one percent last month.* Use the appropriate terms, but take a moment to explain concepts that are important to understand clearly.

Bill Flanagan suggests creative use of computer graphics to make economic concepts easier to understand and more compelling for viewers. He explains it this way: "You can't make a concept too simple if you want all your viewers to understand it and especially if you want them to remember it. This doesn't mean that television reporting should be superficial. Good reporting is good reporting, whether you're gathering information for print or broadcast media. You can't make too many calls; you can't follow up enough leads.[5]

In Chapter 9, video news releases (VNRs) were described as a growing news and information source available from syndication and newsfeed services. Figure 16.1 is an example of a VNR that Investment Company Institute (ICI), the national trade association for the mutual fund industry, prepared. Local station consumer affairs and business reporters receive VNRs regularly from ICI and similar financial associations and organizations.

Consumer Affairs

People want the most for the money they spend. They want to know that others care about them and their role as consumers and are looking out for their best interests. The consumer affairs reporter handles these concerns and others that deal directly with the effects of business and industry and their products on the consumer. Sometimes this specialty is included in the business beat just described.

Consumer reporters cover a wide range of stories. Here is a sampling: scams and frauds; unfair business practices; false advertising; product recalls; consumer-related laws and practices; brand preferences and comparisons; wise money management; consumer services; effects of technological developments. Much of what is covered resembles the work of investigative reporters who research a situation thoroughly and then reveal information previously unknown.

SCRIPT

TOTAL RUN TIME:

SLATE #1:	This material is provided by the Investment Company Institute for your free and unrestricted use Package plus b-roll
SLATE #2:	Package soundbites:
	Frank Richter Investor
	Jennifer Lynch Investor

SLATE #3:

SUGGESTED LEAD: Middle Income Americans often think of investments as something only rich people can afford. Consequently, they may never learn much about the subject.

If you want to start investing, but don't know how, one good place to begin is to determine your investment objective: growth income, security or a combination of the three? Correspondent Doris McMillon has more.

VIDEO	AUDIO
Video of Richters walking their dog	Frank and Sally Richter have just retired.
Richter bite 00:09:00	"I'm not going to earn any more money other than social security. . . ."
Lynch and Weitzel fixing dinner	Jennifer Lynch and Derek Weitzel are about to be married.
Lynch bite 00:01:00	"I'm just trying to accumulate money for retirement and college education for whenever we have kids. . . ."
video of two couples split screen?	Two couples with two very different investment goals. Lynch is just starting out and has decades to accumulate a nest egg. Right now she wants her money to grow. So she's invested the bulk of it in growth stock mutual funds.

Figure 16.1 A video news release (VNR) prepared by Investment Company Institute. Used by permission.

VIDEO	AUDIO
computer graphic	Statistics show that while stocks may be more volatile over the short term, they tend to provide more growth than bonds over periods of seven years or more.
Lynch bite 00:05:21	"I take the risk because I have the time to recover. If I lose money, then you know I have twenty years to recover and build up my assets again."
video of the Richters	The Richters, on the other hand, need several things from their investments: income to supplement social security, growth so that their investments keep up with inflation and security to protect their principal. To meet these goals they've invested in a mix of mutual funds: bond funds for current income with relatively low risk and conservative stock funds so their money keeps growing for the twenty to thirty years they're likely to live in retirement.
Richter bite 00:13:07	"Hopefully, the income you derive from your investments will not only provide the basics--heat, rent, light and so forth--but allow you to do the things with that added time that you have from retirement, like to travel, go to Redskins games . . ."
video of Lynch and Richters/possible closing shot would be Richters walking away from the camera	To choose between stock, bond or money market mutual funds, and the different degrees of risk and reward they entail--the first step is to determine your investment objective. Then pick the fund type or types that best meet your individual goals.
	DM, Washington
Suggested anchor tag	Keep in mind that you don't have to be rich to invest in mutual funds. Many mutual funds let you open an account for as little as one or two hundred dollars.
SLATE	For more information contact:
	Malin Jennings 202-955-8415
	Susan Stolov 202-638-3400

Figure 16.1 continued.

Sue Breding, a freelance medical reporter based in Los Angeles, interviews a University of Southern California Medical Center researcher about the testing of a cancer vaccine. Photo courtesy of Sue Breding.

Some types of sources at the local, state, national, and even international levels are especially helpful for this specialty: court cases and laws related to consumer concerns; regulatory agencies at all levels, especially the Federal Trade Commission and the Food and Drug Administration; consumer groups; product testing labs; and local consumer consultants.

Consumer reporters base their success on several factors. These include knowing the interests and concerns of the audience by examining the results of questionnaires, surveys, personal encounters during public appearances, and so forth; identifying important consumer developments and interests by reading regularly a wide selection of publications and by completing specialized training and education; building a varied list of experts who will provide the accurate information needed to form objective judgments about consumer affairs.

Health and Science

Health and science considerations have become crucial for many daily decisions that we make: what we eat, where we live, the work and leisure activities we pursue, and so forth. This fast-growing specialization occupies a regular time slot on many newscasts, especially on television and notably in larger markets where proximity to medical and research facilities is more likely. If the need is evident and if sufficient personnel are available, health and science coverage could become separate specialties.

People are your best sources. Patients, physicians, scientists, and researchers can provide a human perspective and practical applications for the results of health and science developments that you uncover.

Sue Breding is a freelance medical reporter based in Los Angeles. Whenever possible, she recommends that:

When setting up a medical story, try to think beyond just interviewing a doctor or researcher. Ask if a patient can also be located to add his or her perspective. I have found this can add a very important element to your piece. It can give viewers something they can relate to in your story. It can also enhance your piece when someone explains how a new procedure or medicine has affected their life or how they have been able to overcome odds against them. . . .

Arrange to meet that person [the patient] in a non-medical type setting. I recently interviewed a boy with cystic fibrosis on his own living room couch. He was much more at ease in his own home, and it allowed us a chance to get some footage of how his mother has to help him clear his lungs by pressing on his back several times a day. While we were there, they also were sharing with us a family photograph. We were able to get video of that photo and use it in my piece.[6]

Professional associations as well as various public interest groups concerned with scientific and medical developments hold meetings or conferences that you should attend.[7] Many of these organizations also publish journals and magazines that you should read regularly. You could begin by reading *Science,* JAMA (*The Journal of the American Medical Association*) or *New England Journal of Medicine*. These types of publications can also help you monitor government agency regulations and activities relating to health and science. Many of these groups will also provide broadcast materials.

Story ideas associated with this specialty are expansive. Here is a sampling: health and medicine (cancer research and therapy, health care costs, AIDS, nutrition); environmental issues (toxic waste disposal, oil spills, air and water pollution); life sciences (genetic experimentation, biotechnology); high technology (robotics, artificial intelligence, fiber optics); energy (recycling, nuclear power, conservation programs). Subspecialties could be developed focusing on these key topic areas.

Clarity and precision should be the hallmarks of this specialty. Explain medical and scientific terms in clear and simple language. Verbs like *suggests, appears to indicate,* and so forth allow you to be precise without overstating the significance of scientific discoveries and developments.

Sue Breding stresses the need for clarity in medical stories:

Your viewers only have one chance to hear your report. . . . The jargon and complicated explanations that are a necessary part of the professional medical world may be unfamiliar to many of your viewers. . . .

Medical pieces can be a visual challenge. . . . Graphics can also enhance your piece. I have used them often when I am explaining a complicated procedure or talking about how a new drug works. They're also great if your producer wants to give viewers "tips" as part of your story, for example, tips on how to avoid getting sick during the cold and flu season. Sometimes just having a physician describe something while using a medical model will help.[8]

Dr. Brian McDonough speaks with eight or ten physicians to prepare each of his daily one-minute reports for KYW NEWSRADIO in Philadelphia.

Dr. McDonough says, "I usually get from these interviews what I wasn't even looking for. Through a conversation, a subject might come up that's actually more interesting than what I was going to speak to them about. And I take it from there. Then I break them [the interviews] down and use the cuts as I like—cross-checking them with medical references.[9]

Here is one of Dr. McDonough's reports:

Most of us have heard of the CAT Scan, but Dr. Leon Malmud, a physician at Temple University Hospital, explains just how it works. . . .

[''The word CAT stands for computerized tomographic scanner. It is an x-ray tube that rotates around a patient and takes a series of x-rays, and these images are then fed into a computer which generates a single image.'']

Now, CAT Scanners are being used in patients' treatment planning, particularly in x-ray therapy.

[''These new imaging devices give us images of the patient and data about what's inside the patient that we didn't dream was possible only a decade ago.'']

With information provided by the CAT Scan, surgery is often avoided, extra studies are not performed, and physicians' decisions are often made easier. I'm Dr. Brian McDonough, K-Y-W NEWSRADIO.

Education

Educational issues often evoke strong emotional responses from parents who are interested in the quality of the education their children receive and from local property owners and taxpayers who provide a large share of the money used to support education.

The best education reporters cover the obvious stories—school board meetings and features on administrators, teachers, and students—but then also look beyond these routine items into other stories. Here are a few possibilities: disputes and controversies about how the school system is operated and how well children are learning; curriculum developments and adjustments; the implications of a bulging or shrinking school age population; long-range school system planning and budgeting; teachers' training and educational programs, as well as union activities; laws and regulations affecting education; results and uses of standardized testing; processes and results of evaluations of students, teachers, administrators, or even the entire school system.

Personal contact is one of the best ways to gather the information needed. Students and teachers can offer tips and insights about in- and out-of-class activities. Administrators and public information officials can provide facts and opinions about budgets, central administration planning and operation, and so forth. Parent-teacher, home-school, and local citizens groups are helpful when trying to identify key issues and concerns.

Printed material is another useful source of information. Agendas for school board meetings help track issues and projects. Public documents provide statistics that might be useful. Periodicals like *Education Week* report on elementary and secondary schools, while others, like *Chronicle of Higher Education,* cover college and university interests.

Sports

At all levels, sports has become big business. Sports news is important and a growing number of people take it seriously.

Some activities related to sports coverage have already been covered; for example, news conferences and recorded interviews. Other topics related to sports coverage are beyond the scope of this book such as play-by-play sports broadcasts and full-game highlight programs that feature continuous commentary. Regularly scheduled sportscasts are the subject of this section. Sports features relate more directly to techniques described in Chapter 17, "Features."

Effective local sportscasts combine various kinds of information to spark interest. The key ingredient is *local* sports coverage, since it affects and interests local sports fans most directly. Such coverage involves previews of upcoming matches as well as scores and highlights from completed games and contests. Preview stories could focus on any number of elements: profiles of key players, coaches' projections, league standings, special activities or rules, medical updates on players, and so on. Stories that include game highlights use techniques similar to those described in Chapter 15 for summarizing issues discussed at meetings and news conferences. Other kinds of items are included regularly in sportscasts; for example, controversies involving suspected criminal activity or union negotiations, recruiting prospects and results, signings and deals, player trades, job changes by coaches or team executives, awards and recognitions received, records broken or established, and even sports trivia questions and answers.

People and paper probably are the sports reporter's best sources. Coaches, players, school officials, or team owners can be interviewed personally, at scheduled news conferences that are often combined with lunches or dinners, or even at arranged times before or after games and matches. Determine the preferences of the people involved. Paper sources are also important. These include daily newspapers, sports magazines, media guides and brochures, sports trivia books and almanacs, news releases sent throughout a season, and wire services, including special sports wires.

Other sports sources are electronic—network news feeds, satellite transmissions from news cooperatives and other stations. Many sports information offices provide players' and coaches' comments on videotape or via satellite feeds as well as on audiotape using automatic telephone-answering machines.

Here are suggestions to make sports coverage more effective:

a. Know what you report. Use the sports sources just listed. Learn the rules of the sports that you cover.
b. Get firsthand information, but avoid close, personal involvement with sports sources that could cloud your objectivity.
c. Control your on-air enthusiasm for local teams.
d. Keep things in proper perspective. Remember it is *only* sports!
e. Simulate the action, thrills, and excitement that sports fans enjoy. Provide sports stories that place the viewer or listener in the best seat in the arena or in the stands.
f. "Humanize" sports by emphasizing the *people* involved—who they are, what they do, how they feel, what they hope for, and so forth.
g. Look for story ideas and angles that go beyond routine facts.

```
The price of athletic shoes may be going up, after what's going
down today in pro football. . . . Paul Fireman is buying the
New England Patriots football team, for a reported 100-million
dollars. . . . Who is Fireman? He's the President of the
Reebok Shoe Company. . . . Get the connection? Details of the
deal are sketchy. . . . We should know more tonight at eleven.
              KMST-TV, Monterey/Salinas/Santa Cruz, California
```

Admittedly, special terms (*jargon*) are associated with sports. When used sparingly, jargon can add fun, color, and life to sports copy, but you don't need to use an action verb *every* time a score is reported. Avoid strained and unnatural word choices like *maul, kill, annihilate, destroy, whitewash,* or *massacre.* Keep it simple, quick, clear, and conversational; for example, *Everett High beat Moss Point, 56–20 . . . Explorers over the Eagles, 13–10 . . . It was the Bears 30, Wolves 21.*

Traffic Reports

Commuters depend on frequent traffic reports to help get them to and from work safely and on time. All motorists appreciate the accuracy and immediacy of such information, especially during bad weather.

Traffic reports can be handled in several ways. At some stations, one person in the newsroom monitors police and emergency frequencies, and coordinates coverage with another reporter in a news car or a helicopter. Occasionally, the reporter in the field files live voicers on major traffic accidents. KXL Radio in Portland uses in tandem several short reports from different locations throughout the city. KKAR Radio in Omaha uses reporters and off-duty law enforcement officers in ground and airborne vehicles to monitor traffic conditions during morning and afternoon drive times. Some auto clubs offer recorded reports on the condition of major state highways. Motorists

Helicopters provide quick access to news stories. Photo by Manny Garcia, courtesy of KTVK-TV, Phoenix, Arizona.

with cellular telephones may be encouraged to call when they see traffic problems develop or want to give firsthand accounts of newsworthy events.

In some large metropolitan areas, a small army of off-duty law enforcement personnel, journalists, and authorized volunteers monitor traffic conditions and then provide stations with frequent and brief reports. An alternative is to pool resources: Stations in a market that offer traffic reports hire the same company or group of traffic reporters who customize daily traffic reports for each subscribing station. Airborne reports are common, even in small and medium markets.

Although brief (sometimes less than 15 seconds), each traffic report should indicate street conditions (icy, snowy, etc.) as well as sites of major accidents along with alternate routes available. Some reports also include street repair and closing listings; commuter bus and railway service updates; and brief safety tips. Almost anything that disrupts normal traffic flow is worth mentioning: stalled cars, large debris in roadways (wood, boxes, garbage, furniture), construction and road repair sites, water main breaks, unusually slippery or wet roads, and so on.

Traffic reporters need special skills. Know your city *thoroughly;* learn the location of major arterials as well as hospitals and schools for times when special emergency warnings are given. Learn to juggle your time and attention so that you can monitor several emergency frequencies (police, fire, rescue units), identify, and then report important information while writing notes, driving or flying safely, adjusting volume levels on different machines, staying in touch with the newsroom, even covering other news stories! You must also be able to organize information quickly and report facts accurately using only brief notes or simply your memory.

Here is a snapshot of how Laurie Krueger handles her traffic reports at KVOO Radio in Tulsa, Oklahoma:

A typical afternoon drive requires monitoring scanners, writing down accidents and trouble spots, driving by those areas so I can determine which lanes are most affected and alternate routes for drivers, and reporting those traffic conditions eighteen times within two hours through use of a two-way radio.[10]

Specialized Coverage Reporting Techniques

Here are suggestions that will help you handle various kinds of specialized coverage assignments and prepare effective news reports:

a. *Keep the specialized material interesting but also understandable.* Make sure that you decide who you are trying to reach with your specialized stories and that the ideas and terms you use are clear to those who may not have an extensive background in the particular field you are covering.

b. *Have someone outside the newsroom review your story.* This extra pair of eyes and ears might spot a troublesome or sensitive idea or an unsubstantiated opinion or statistic, or might point to a particular piece of audio that is difficult to understand or a segment of video that may overwhelm a sensitive viewer.

c. *Use current news events and issues to present specialized pieces of information.* If police report that a recent shooting suspect had been using antipsychotic medication, such as lithium, and that such medication may have caused a psychotic reaction leading to the shooting, a medical-health reporter could use this incident as an opportunity to show the consequences of the use and misuse of this medication in situations such as a shooting. By tying this specialized information to a specific current story, listeners and viewers will understand better the circumstances surrounding a particular incident.

Summary

Experienced reporters who have mastered basic broadcast newswriting and reporting skills and acquired special knowledge and training produce specialized coverage. Such coverage is accomplished via the beat system or allowing reporters to cover special types of stories on a regular basis.

Several specialties were examined in this chapter: weather; agriculture; business; consumer affairs; health and science; education; sports; and traffic reports. The following information was provided for each type of specialized coverage: sources of information; contents of reports; reporting and writing suggestions.

Developing a specialty keeps a reporter's life interesting and challenging and often provides a competitive edge when the search begins for that next broadcast news job opportunity.

Exercises

(*Note:* The following exercises can be used for either radio or television stories.)

1. Produce a local enterprise/follow-up story based on recent national or international events relating to one of the specialized areas covered in this chapter. Provide clippings from relevant publications as well as your news copy and edited tape.

2. Write a story based on information gathered after developing a story idea suggested in this chapter for one of the following specialties: agriculture; consumer affairs; health and science; education.

3. Obtain a copy of the current budget for a local public school district or public hospital. Assume that this budget has just been approved and released to the news media. Based on personal research as well as interviews with education or health officials, produce a story about this budget and its potential effect on your city or locale.

4. Congratulations! You are the business reporter this week! The assignment manager and newscast producer agree that they want to begin a series of reports on ''the health of local publicly held businesses'' (i.e., ones in which the public can own shares). You will need to obtain financial statements directly from one of the prominent local companies or from an office of the Securities and Exchange Commission, and maybe complete interviews with key local business leaders. No rush! Just make sure your copy and edited tape are ready for *tomorrow's* late-night newscast!

5. For an upcoming local sports event, prepare a preview story based on published reports. When the event concludes, prepare another story that includes highlights from the event. Provide *all* of the written material used to prepare *both* stories.

Notes

1. Reprinted by permission of Kim Dlouhy.

2. Reprinted by permission of Bill Flanagan.

3. Reprinted by permission of Bill Flanagan.

4. Comments summarized from Malin Jennings, ''Why So Little Business Reporting?'' *Communicator* 46, no. 2 (February 1992): 16–17.

5. Bill Flanagan, excerpt from the first draft of an article prepared for the *Pittsburgh Post-Gazette*.

6. Reprinted by permission of Sue Breding.

7. The AMA's Annual Health Reporting Conference offers medical reporters and broadcasters an opportunity to develop and enhance communications skills. For information, call 312–645–5102.

8. Reprinted by permission of Sue Breding.

9. Reprinted by permission of Dr. Brian McDonough.

10. Reprinted by permission of Laurie Krueger.

Chapter 17

Features

Feature stories offer insights about the people, places, things, or events that surround us each day but to which we may pay little or no attention. We relate to them because they often expose human emotions or feelings and are generally told in an engaging manner from a personal point of view, the reporter's or some other person's. Feature stories allow the reporter to look beyond the obvious, to linger for a moment, to explore an interesting or intriguing idea that may not necessarily relate to a breaking story.

In the rush to get today's breaking stories on the air, feature story ideas often get pushed aside in the hope that they can be produced sometime in the future, "when things settle down." If the newsroom staff is large enough, a reporter may be assigned to develop local features on a regular, full-time basis. Many nationally distributed features are produced originally by local reporters.

You may think that features are all "fluff" and not really considered worthwhile journalism. In reality, features can often provide an opportunity for more journalistic enterprise and creativity than the average hard news story.

This chapter examines the various types and sources of feature stories as well as the approaches and techniques used to plan, organize, write, and produce effective broadcast feature stories. Basic broadcast newswriting and reporting principles illustrated in previous chapters also apply to feature stories. However, story structure, angle, emphasis, point of view, and treatment tend to be more flexible and personal when preparing features rather then hard news items.

Types

The categories that will be identified are not rigid and are provided only to help you better develop and describe broadcast feature stories. Most features are blends of information and entertainment and combine some of the categories described.

News features are stories that are newsworthy but are not as immediate and do not require the conciseness and precision expected in a breaking news story. News features could also be follow-ups to previous hard news stories. John Holden's copy shown later in this chapter is best classified as a news feature.

Sidebars are stories that cover in detail one aspect of a larger breaking story. Each sidebar should be a meaningful part of the breaking story and should explore in greater detail only one part of the larger story. For example, if the main news story was a major oil spill, several sidebars could be prepared to explain more fully the various activities surrounding the cleanup. These might include the potential environmental damage, pending lawsuits, and criminal charges as well as the impact of the oil spill on local business or tourist activity.

Special events features are similar to sidebars, but the main story concerns a one-time-only situation. For example, if a major presidential candidate comes to town, features could be prepared for various activities surrounding the visit, such as security preparations, cost to the city and state, itinerary for the candidate, or the candidate's stand on major campaign issues. A variety of reports supplemented extensive live coverage of the pope's activities when he visited the United States several years ago. These included other cities visited; sold-out downtown hotels; traffic problems/road closures; security precautions; weather conditions; medical and heat preparations; profiles of issues facing the Roman Catholic Church; and even a profile about a woman who makes the pope's lunch.

News backgrounders trace the development of a significant *current* news story. Background information and a brief chronology can be presented to help the audience understand how a story progressed to where it is now. Such background may be needed because of the complexity or duration of the news story. Examples include an extended hostage situation or trial, or a long-standing confrontation between neighboring countries.

Historical features attempt to show the importance and relevance of significant past events. Such features review what has happened and assess the current and future impact of the events. If the past event is the anniversary of a major local crime or natural disaster, a feature could be developed that would review the important events surrounding the incident, indicate what has happened since it occurred, and note what it means in human terms for current and future residents. A different kind of historical feature would be developed if the past event was the bicentennial of the founding of a town, state, or organization, or if the birthday of a famous resident was being observed.

Human interest stories offer the odd, unusual, humorous, and offbeat incidents and personalities that help keep life in perspective. This is a very common type of feature story. Here are a few examples: the rookie police officer who found out that his supervisor was the man who delivered him; the fraud suspect arrested after he appeared on a game show; the world's smallest police station, a phone booth topped by a "Police Station" sign; or a just-retired auto worker who saved quarters in a variety of containers for more than 25 years until he transported them to a local dealership, counted his loot, and purchased a truck he had helped build on the assembly line. The Charles Osgood copy shown later in this chapter offers an interesting, heartwarming, and personal human interest story.

In *personality sketches or profiles* the reporter tries to determine what motivates, excites, or discourages one individual to provide a better sense of who and what this person is. Examples include a newly hired coach, a recently elected public official, a former astronaut, or an official spokesperson for a controversial organization or issue. Consult friends, associates, and maybe even "enemies" as well as the individual profiled to establish a noticeable angle or primary theme for the feature—attitudes, philosophy, uplifting spirit, current interests and activities, lifestyle, accomplishments, and so forth.

Descriptive features focus on places to visit and see and events to participate in or enjoy as spectators. Examples include profiles of recreational areas and tourist attractions as well as fairs, festivals, and pageants or even a behind-the-scenes look at one aspect of a circus, carnival, or theater production.

Seasonal features spotlight specific annual events or observances. The focus of a seasonal feature is often a traditional holiday, from New Year's Day through Christmas (see Chapter 8 for KOTA Radio copy segments from multiple stories on Memorial Day observances). The seasonal texture might highlight a particular annual harvest, fair, festival, or activity and be associated with any number of topics, even environmental topics such as a salmon run, a timber harvest, or a tree planting on Arbor Day.

Sources

Where do ideas for feature stories originate? Some are based on suggestions by viewers or listeners, even friends or regular news sources. Many evolve from hard news coverage that you or even other media have completed. This may produce sidebars and special events features discussed earlier. Other stories simply occur to you during the course of your day. The best source is you and your sensitivity to the world that surrounds you.

Here are ways to heighten your sensitivity to potential feature story ideas:

a. *Never stop looking* for good feature stories. Consciously search for story ideas. *Everything* is a possible feature story, even items found on a bulletin board, in classified ads, or in a weekly or daily newspaper.

b. *Cultivate an interest in a variety of subjects* by becoming knowledgeable about a variety of activities and issues. Expand your circle of friends. Explore a new hobby. Read several articles in one issue of a magazine you have never read.

c. *Look beyond the obvious.* What most people would view as only routine and commonplace, an alert feature reporter will find intriguing and interesting as a possible feature story idea.

d. *Listen carefully* to what people say as well as what they do *not* say in recorded interviews and in casual conversation. Their interests, problems, concerns, and questions provide clues for potential feature stories.

e. *Watch carefully* what people do, how they react with their eyes and posture.

f. *Observe with a purpose* by making notes when something that you hear, see, or read sparks a feature story idea.

Sensitivity as well as creativity will help guide you through the selection and development of feature story ideas. Sensitivity will alert you to potential stories. Creativity will help you shape the stories that you decide to develop.

Approaches and Techniques

Features require extra measures of curiosity, interest in people, and flexibility. You have to be especially curious and wonder about why things work the way they do, or what it is like to live a particular way, or how a particular task is done. Anything that makes you curious could be developed into an interesting feature story, if you take the extra time to explore an intriguing story idea. You must also have an overwhelming interest in people, all kinds of people. The most memorable features are those that center on people—who they are, what they do, and so forth. Features require flexibility; you need to approach stories without preconceived notions or viewpoints, offering a fresh and creative treatment for each story that you develop.

Here is a suggested process to follow to nurture and develop a feature story idea:

1. Create a tentative story outline or structure.
2. Continue to shape and adjust this outline as you gather facts and comments (generally more details than for hard news stories).
3. Arrange recorded comments and notes into a rough sequence and revise the outline.
4. Write the first draft of the feature story, molding words, sounds, and images into the finished piece.
5. Refine and polish the script and edited tape.

In following this or some similar process, you need to consider several factors: structure; length; emphasis on people; point of view; and refinement of elements such as tone, mood, pace, and rhythm.

Structure and Length

Although flexibility is encouraged, feature stories, like *all* stories, must have a structure. The beginning, middle, and end should be obvious.

But the structure of a feature story can be molded creatively, with flexibility, as the reporter assesses and places the story's elements into a pattern that will secure interest, convey information, and capture the emotions that may surround the story. This might mean identifying the ending of the story and working back to the lead. It could involve telling a story chronologically or topically, or maybe highlighting contrasting viewpoints.

```
                        ((NAT SOUND FULL))
The music of Mozart, Haydn, Bach contrasts with the
surroundings—the Indian teepees and covered wagons of an
untamed west. In Woolaroc, cultures have been put aside.
People are joined as one in appreciation of music far removed
from this time and place. . . .
                                            KWTV, Oklahoma City
```

Many features are anecdotal—short narratives about an interesting or unusual person, incident, or situation. The reporter, like a good storyteller, tries to create instant interest with intriguing people and locales, and then carefully peels away, teases, and delays story developments and details:

```
One thing about the town of Waldo . . . It's got nearly
everything one could want in retirement. It's quiet, rural
. . . and already home to an entire village—of retirees!

But not a retirement village for humans. . . . No, this is a
retirement village for animals—wild animals!
                                            WTVJ-TV, Miami
```

Like good fiction, good feature stories come complete with suspenseful events, turns, twists, and surprises, and even dramatic endings or comic punch lines.

Devise at least a tentative story structure *before* gathering material for a feature. Even a brief outline will help to identify the "spine" of the story. This is the essential structure of what you expect to report. Once you know even the tentative angle or direction of the story, you can determine where to look, who to contact, what to ask, and what to emphasize as you gather information. This technique will help you identify what is important and what is not, what to keep and what to discard, which leads to pursue and which to disregard, and so forth. Unless you use at least a tentative story structure or outline when developing features, you will need to reexamine all of the material you have gathered and then devise a story structure or pattern that may not be effective or "natural" for the story covered.

The outline or story structure should remain flexible until the various story elements come together and are assessed in the editing room or at the keyboard.

Content and available air time determine the length of feature stories. Radio features range from 30 to 60 seconds. Television features tend to last 1:30 to 3:00, although most are under 2:00. But feature stories can be any length; they are not necessarily or automatically longer than hard news stories.

Listeners or viewers can become involved in a story if they can identify with **Emphasize People** or focus on *people* and their concerns:

```
The strain shows in their faces. . . . Rhonda and Bob McClure
are enduring the toughest week of their life so far. . . . They
sit in silence at the bedside of their nine year old son . . .
Jeremy. . . . His skin has yellowed from jaundice. He twists
and turns . . . and they know he's uncomfortable. . . .
                                    KTVK-TV, Phoenix
```

Place the audience in the shoes or in the position of the person, place, event, or thing that is the principle focus of the story. What is it like to *be* or to *experience* what the audience sees or hears? Even if about some*thing,* all successful features focus on *people.*

People telling their own stories are always stronger than a reporter telling their stories for them. Know when to be quiet and let the subject carry the story. When the material is properly edited, the people who are subjects of the feature can often carry the story without voice-over narration by the reporter:

```
The search to find Ethel Bell has become almost a nightly
routine for her son and grandchildren. They have driven nearly
every street, every alley . . . looking for a sign . . . or
someone who might have seen her. . . . So far, there's been
little hope. . . .

          ((NAT SOUND-PASSING OUT FLYER))

Back on the road . . . to keep looking. . . .

SOT (LINDA, BELL'S GRANDDAUGHTER): ''We can't give up. She's
the mainstay of the family. She helped raise me. She helped
raise my daughter. My father's her only child and we can't do
without her.''
                                    KWTV, Oklahoma City
```

A sensitive approach will often produce a more recognizable, human emphasis. People whom you interview for features are not accustomed to the abrupt interview techniques often used when covering hard news stories. For most feature stories, leave your gear in the car or van. Take a few minutes to get to know the persons you hope to interview. Talk about things that interest them. Learn who they are and what they have to say or show. This will help guide you about the content and angle of the feature story. Then, once you are familiar to them and have gained their confidence in you as a reporter, bring out the gear. Explain that these are simply tools that will help you tell their story better. Talk as you set up the gear to make the setting more natural and less intimidating.

Point of View

A key element in a successful feature story is the point of view, angle, or perspective from which the story is told. Features are generally told from the reporter's or some other person's viewpoint. A singular point of view is the most effective.

An individual's point of view can be used even when explaining or exploring a complex or expansive subject. By examining carefully one small part of such a subject, you can typify the rest of the story that is not examined. For example, instead of trying to report on an extended and bloody border dispute, focus on one person or one family caught up in the struggle and magnify what you discover to reveal what the story is really about, how specific *people* have responded to the situation. A complex presidential campaign or a local controversial issue may be best explained by seeing the situation from *one* person's point of view. Use one strong central character to illuminate the larger issue or story.

Point of view should be identified early and sustained throughout the same feature story. A recognizable point of view will help reinforce the theme, focus, or "spine" of the story and also help place into perspective the personal opinions that are often expressed.

Refinements

Feature stories provide an opportunity for a special kind of shared experience between reporter and audience. The reporter can share a sense of adventure and discovery, guide listeners or viewers through the story, prepare them for what is about to happen, respond to what has just been seen or heard. But accomplishing this requires conscious control and refinement of story elements such as tone, mood, pace, rhythm, and flow.

Charles Osgood

You may have seen him occasionally on CBS television newscasts on weekends, wearing his distinctive bow tie. But Charles Osgood is at his very best when he writes and delivers his weekday morning features under the banner "The Osgood File" on the CBS Radio Network.

Osgood is a master storyteller. He uses a variety of techniques to grab attention and develop an interesting and human look into a particular subject. He is famous for his rhyming verses and his original lyrics written to melodies that are familiar to his many listeners. Sometimes soundbites punctuate his commentary on current events. What may appear to some to be an unimportant or dull wire story evolves into a masterful description of an event or issue that now has new meanings and a very human perspective.

Many of Osgood's features focus on important national and international issues. His insights into human emotions and responses are also striking. Once in a while, he shares a personal moment, a little insight into himself and his life. He did just that in this piece (see Figure 17.1) about a special evening in which fellow employees honored his late father. Notice the use of ellipses (series of three dots) to ensure pauses at critical places in the piece. And notice, too, the smooth writing style and strong emotional appeal of this feature story.

The Osgood File. Sponsored in part by Lennox Heating and Cooling. I'm Charles Osgood.

Last night at the University Club in New York, I attended a reunion dinner of 60 people who used to work for the same company my late father did. There were books of pictures, and in some of them I could hardly recognize Dad because he was so much younger then than I am now. Made me feel like Michael J. Fox in Back To The Future. And amongst the memorabilia, I found something that impressed me so much I wanted to share it with you . . . which I'll do in a moment. Stand by.

My father was in the textile business. His boss, at a company called Indian Head Mills, was a dynamic young man named Jim Robison. Dad thought the world of Jim, not only because he was so smart and successful, but also because he was such a straight shooter. He never wanted to outdo or get the better of anybody in a business deal. If both parties didn't benefit from the deal, he didn't want to do it. My Dad died several years ago, but last night I was invited to a reunion of Indian Head people. Some of them I hadn't seen since I was a kid. Jim Robison was there . . . retired now and no longer a young man . . . but still sharp as ever. But looking through some materials they had there, I came on a company policy statement he issued forty years ago . . . and I took a copy of it because I wanted to share it with you. Here's what it said:

"There is one basic policy to which there will never be an exception made by anyone, anywhere, in any activity owned and operated by Indian Head. That policy is as follows," Jim Robison wrote, "Play it straight, whether in contact with the public, stockholders, customers, suppliers, employees or any other individuals or groups. The only right way to deal with people is forthrightly and honestly. If any mistakes are made, admit them and correct them. Our commitments will be honored and we have the right to expect the same performance from those people with whom we do business. This is fundamental. We will not welsh, weasel, chisel or cheat. We will not be a party to any untruths, half-truths or unfair distortions. Life is too short. It is perfectly possible to make a decent living without any compromise with integrity."

I think I'm going to frame that and put it on the wall.

The Osgood File. Charles Osgood on the CBS Radio Network.

The Osgood File. Tuesday November 24, 1992.

Figure 17.1 Charles Osgood, THE OSGOOD FILE, CBS Radio Network, Copyrighted by CBS Inc. All rights reserved.

John Holden

With less staff than a few years ago, newscast producers look to several sources to fill the space that expanded newscast time has created, especially in early morning hours. Local news staff coverage assignments can be monitored carefully to produce more stories using fewer people. You can often make better use of network and co-op material. Syndicators can supply a variety of news-related items. Freelance reporters can help customize and expand a specific station's needs.

John Holden is a freelance reporter. His features have been seen for many years on networks such as the NBC News Channel operating in Charlotte, North Carolina. Co-op groups, such as Conus Communications in Minneapolis, have also distributed his work.

Holden enjoys a challenging, diverse, and invigorating professional lifestyle. He admits that picking and choosing the kinds of stories that he does is a luxury, but he quickly adds, ''It's up to you to make them interesting enough to air for a national audience.''[1]

How does Holden approach the production of his features?

I always have a preconceived notion of how a story will be put together before we ever shoot the first frame of video . . . but the elements of that story will change as we're on site. My main source of inspiration in writing a story is the interview or interviews with the participants. If I get a ''soundbite'' from someone that's especially emotional or funny, or maybe is spoken with a special expression on the face that will make a great ending to the story . . . I'll write a voice-over to lead into that soundbite. Viewers may not always remember what any specific story was about . . . but they do remember emotional comments and visual expressions, which may change an informative story into a memorable story.[2]

And what is a typical day for freelance reporter John Holden as he produces and processes his feature stories?

My typical day is now spent flying to a different city every week . . . hiring a freelance production crew (many of whom are former photographers and soundmen from TV stations) to shoot a story in one day . . . flying back to Miami to have the video transferred to Hi-8 [newstape] with burned-in time code for me to log interviews and video on a portable Hi-8 player . . . logging the story on my next plane flight and writing the story on [a] laptop computer . . . then faxing the finished script by cellular phone to the editor when I land. The editor can then edit the story based on time-coded scripts, even while I'm away on another story.[3]

Freelance work is *not* recommended for beginning reporters. Your livelihood depends on quick thinking, flexibility, professional responses to stress and competitive services, and durability. These characteristics generally come after years of reporting experience. One of Holden's underwater feature stories, entitled ''Underwater Archeology Class,'' involved

> following students from across the country who had come down to the Florida Keys for an unusual class offered by the same people who had researched and uncovered treasure from the sunken Spanish galleon called the Atocha. Since the waters far off [the] coast are always unpredictable . . . it was important to shoot interviews and B-roll of class preparations before we took off on the dive boat, as you can never be sure you'll be able to get this done at sea. As it turned out, conditions were miserable underwater: you couldn't see a few feet in front of you! So the underwater cameraman had to shoot all video from only a few inches away in order to get an image . . . and he was in no shape to tape interviews after the dive. But we had shot enough video and interviews before [the] dive to put a nice feature together.[4]

Figure 17.2 is the production script for the television feature entitled, ''Underwater Archeology Class.''

Many reporters find features harder to write than routine hard news stories, since features do not follow a specific copy format or preferred writing style. But a good way to begin writing effective features is to continue to use the essential writing principles already illustrated in this book—simple and precise words, concise and direct sentences, easy-to-follow story structure. Then enjoy the opportunity to go beyond a routine, hard news story treatment. Features provide opportunities for creative and lively writing that can reflect the vividness and color in the world around us.

You can also further your career by working on the feature niche. Just as some reporters enhance their careers by building health, sports, or other ''franchises,'' a creative feature reporter who can tell stories in an interesting way can be in big demand. Certainly you won't be hired in your first job as a feature reporter, but if opportunities arise, go for them. Broadcast news careers are covered in Appendix A, ''Careers.''

```
Reporter: John Holden
Date: 9-18-93

VIDEO                          AUDIO

                               (ANCHOR LEAD)
                                    WHEN IT COMES TO DISCOVERING SUNKEN SHIPWRECKS
                               . . . ONE NAME PROBABLY COMES TO MIND: MEL FISHER
                               OF KEY WEST!
Suggested lead . . .                WELL, EVEN IF YOU HAVE TROUBLE FINDING YOUR CAR
                               IN A PARKING LOT, YOU CAN LEARN THE ART OF MAPPING
                               THE OCEAN BOTTOM. IN FACT, REPORTER JOHN HOLDEN
                               TELLS US MEL'S OWN ARCHEOLOGISTS HAVE THE PERFECT
                               "WET COURSE" WAITING!

                               ------------------------------------------------
                               VO1
s/ Key West 00-04                   IT'S A COMMON DREAM IN THE FLORIDA KEYS: TO FIND
   (Florida Keys)              A SUNKEN SHIPWRECK OR TREASURE AT THE BOTTOM OF THE
s/ John Holden reporting       SEA. ONLY A SELECT FEW ARE SO LUCKY . . . BUT YOU
   04-08                       CAN ALWAYS LEARN HOW TO DO IT!

                               (NAT SND Instructor)
                               "We're just bringing back the information. Not the
                               artifacts themselves . . just the
                               information!" :05

                               (SOT K.T. Jones)
s/ K.T. Jones                  "We're basically teaching things that they're not
Underwater Archeology          going to find in a textbook . . . tried and true
   Instructor 21-25            methods that we've developed through the years
                               that have worked for all situations.'' :09
                               VO2
                                    THIS IS MARINE ARCHEOLOGY 101 . . . A WEEK-LONG
                               CERTIFIED COURSE IN DIVING SHIPWRECKS IN THE
                               FLORIDA KEYS: UNDER THE SUPERVISION OF SOME OF THE
                               SAME ARCHEOLOGISTS WHO HAVE DOCUMENTED THE GOLDEN
                               FINDS OF FAMED TREASURE HUNTER MEL FISHER!

                               (SOT Syd Jones)
s/ Syd Jones 44-49             "We've had a lot of experience in this type of
Marine Archeology              field. It all incorporates the same type of
   Instructor                  techniques . . . so we're pretty well versed in
                               it." :08

                               (STANDUP-Holden)
                               "Now it's only the second time this class has ever
s/ Holden Standup 54-1:00      been offered . . . and students have come from all
                               across the country to take it. But they're not here
                               to find underwater treasure or underwater
                               artifacts . . . they're here to learn the science
                               behind it." :11
```

Figure 17.2   Script of a freelance feature story produced by John Holden. Courtesy of John Holden.

VIDEO   AUDIO

                                               (SOT'S STUDENTS)
s/ Frank Fechteler 1:02-1:05   "I mean, I have an interest in scuba diving
   Connecticut Dive Student   obviously . . . but this is more of historical
                                               interest to me." :04

s/ Corley Thompson 1:06-1:11   "There are only so many shipwrecks in the world
   St. Louis Student   . . . and it's interesting to learn something
                                               about them!" :05

s/ Ron Barth 1:12-1:15   "And this encompasses the art of the way things
   Wisconsin Student   are done . . . right!" :04

                                               VO3
                                                   HERE A STUDENT DIVER CAN LEARN THE BASICS OF
                                               DOCUMENTING A SUNKEN SHIPWRECK: FROM MAPPING AND
                                               MEASURING A SITE . . . TO MARKING A FIND.
                                                   AND THAT'S WHAT MAKES THIS CLASS UNIQUE: EVERY
                                               STUDENT WHO PASSES COMES HOME A CERTIFIED
                                               ARCHEOLOGICAL DIVER OF THE SEA!

                                               (SOT Jim Willsey)
s/ Jim Willey 1:36-1:43   "If they go out and do this on their own, which
   DiveMaster/Instructor   hopefully they'll be able to . . . then they can
                                               apply these techniques and not become what we
                                               call treasure hunters. They won't go down and
                                               just start digging up treasure . . . they'll
                                               actually do it archeologically and
                                               scientifically." :13

                                               VO4
                                                   BUT THAT DOESN'T MEAN THERE'S NEVER A CHANCE OF
                                               FINDING SOME LOST GOLD OR SILVER IN THESE FEDERAL
                                               WATERS . . . EVEN IF YOU'RE NOT ALLOWED TO KEEP
                                               IT!

                                               (SOT Peggy Thompson)
s/ Peggy Thompson 1:53-1:57   "Oooh, you bet! I spent my life looking for four-
   St. Louis Student   leaf clovers. Think of all the time I've wasted!
(Underwater Archeology   (laugh)" :06
Student)

                                               VO5
                                                   NO . . . THE TREASURE HERE IS NOT A GOLD BAR:
                                               IT'S KNOWLEDGE. . . . AND A CERTAIN PRIDE IN
                                               SAYING YOU KNOW HOW TO FIND SUNKEN TREASURE!

TRT: 2:08

Figure 17.2 continued.

Summary

This chapter examined broadcast feature stories: types; sources; and approaches and techniques.

Several kinds of features can be developed from hard news stories, beat assignments, and simply careful observation. To develop effective feature stories, heighten your sensitivity to potential ideas and follow a workable plan of development.

Essential broadcast news writing and reporting principles apply to *all* stories, including feature stories.

But effective feature stories use additional approaches and techniques, including flexible, creative story structure; a focus on the human aspects of the story; a noticeable and consistent tone, mood, and point of view; a conscious manipulation of pace and rhythm through words and images.

Additional suggestions were offered for planning, organizing, writing, and producing effective broadcast features.

Exercises

1. List five specific topics that you find particularly interesting, ones that you might have already explored but about which you are not yet satisfied that you know all you could or want to know. For each topic, write a short paragraph in which you describe *why* the topic interests you and *what* you still want to know.

Outline at least three possible feature story ideas related to *one* of the topics you have described. For radio or television, produce *one* of the feature stories you have outlined.

Turn in the list and description of the five topics; the outline of three story ideas based on one topic; the script and edited tape for the feature story produced; and any notes, editing logs, and so forth used to produce the feature story.

2. Select *one* item from a local daily or nearby weekly newspaper. This item could be a hard news story, but it could also be a headline, personal column, feature story, classified or retail ad, or a photograph. Describe at least three story angles that you could develop for this item. Produce a radio or television feature story based on *one* of the angles described.

Turn in the newspaper item, your description of the three possible story angles, the final script, and the edited tape for the one story angle you developed.

3. Develop a local feature story based on one of the hard news stories written for an assignment found at the end of an earlier chapter.

Notes

1. Reprinted by permission of John Holden.

2. Ibid.

3. Ibid.

4. Ibid.

Chapter 18

Newscasts

T he newscast—the end product of all newsroom planning efforts—
represents the news judgment, journalistic skills, production expertise,
thought, energy, and commitment of all involved. To be effective, newscasts
require the close coordination and cooperation of all personnel in the newsroom, and even personnel *outside* the newsroom. News content and production
must receive equal attention. The newscast producer and the newscast director
together shape the newscast presentation. The effort must be cooperative if it
is to succeed.

Local news is one of the most expensive activities for most stations.
Nevertheless, it can also be profitable. Some stations generate as much as 40
percent of their gross income from news programs. Local news represents a
station's commitment to the community and is of major importance when
evaluating the results of periodic audience ratings reports. Technological developments have made the production of newscasts easier and less uncertain
for all involved. Television newscasts, for example, now look and sound better
than ever before with enhancements such as creative color graphics, compact
live report units, robotic cameras, remote location cameras, and attractive and
functional news sets.

Radio newscasts generally are heard on the hour and half-hour, often
adjacent to a network newscast. These newscasts tend to be longer and more
frequent on weekdays during radio's primetime, so-called drivetime (approximately 6:30–9:00 A.M. and 3:30–6:30 P.M.). Stations often produce a local
noon newscast.

Television newscasts are scheduled less often but are longer. Network-
affiliated stations tend to schedule local newscasts in the early morning adjacent to network morning news and entertainment programs, at noon, early
in the evening adjacent to network newscasts, and late at night immediately
after primetime network evening programming. In the early evening (5–8
P.M.), small-market stations generally offer one half-hour local newscast adjacent to a network newscast, whereas large-market stations tend to broadcast
half-hour or full-hour local newscasts surrounding network newscasts.

This chapter focuses on the guidelines and considerations used to select stories for newscasts and the steps and techniques used to build or plan effective newscasts. More attention has been given to television than radio because of the complex nature of television newscast production. However, the principles apply equally to both media.

This chapter picks up the thread of continuity described and illustrated in Chapter 11: Individual news stories have been assigned and covered; copy has been written and timed; tape has been edited; details and contingency plans have been devised. The newscast pulls together the resources of the newsroom to present one installment, one report highlighting the day's news events.

Selecting Stories

This section touches on several guidelines and considerations used to select stories for newscasts. With experience, productive critiques, and association with quality newsrooms, most newscast producers develop intuition and their own set of priorities for selecting stories.

Guidelines

The principles of news judgment discussed in Chapter 1 (proximity, prominence, timeliness, impact, human interest, etc.) apply equally to assigning potentially newsworthy stories as well as to selecting finished stories for a newscast. But instead of selecting the pieces of information to include in an *individual* story, the newscast producer evaluates the *total merits* of *many* individual stories and selects those that are the *most* newsworthy to include in the newscast.

The "yardstick" used to measure newsworthiness varies, based generally on the coverage area and the audience reached. For the most part, broadcast audiences are more interested in what is happening in their own area than in another country. Thus, *local* news needs to be a priority for *local* newscasts. Networks do cover local events, but they are looking for stories with more general nationwide appeal because they are serving millions throughout the country.

Every day, newscast producers and reporters review an overwhelming amount of information as they assemble newscast items. They must identify the information needs of the newscast audience and assign priorities to available stories. These priorities might be arranged in this sort of scheme: stories of immediate need (approaching tornado); stories essential to daily activities and livelihood (traffic bottlenecks, major local factory closing); stories essential, but not necessarily immediately, to a substantial portion of the audience (new tax law passed); stories of interest to a large portion of the audience (features).

According to Bill Wagner, Executive Producer of WUSA-TV's 11 P.M. newscast in Washington, D.C., there are common denominators for news story selections:

I don't think there is a neighborhood in the nation where a proposed school closing is not an issue of concern. The construction of a new prison or a toxic waste site will create controversy anywhere in the nation. An abduction, a search for a missing child, a trapped worker, a savage murder, an indicted official, a coming storm or a home-team winning an important game will all be big news anywhere in the country. And the closer any of these events are to your hometown, the more significant they become.[1]

Time of day often determines how important and appropriate a story is to your audience. This factor also influences story length, placement, and treatment. Toward the end of a local 5 P.M. newscast, this lead sentence was used for a consumer report on tartar-controlling toothpastes:

```
Right now, you probably have dinner on your mind . . . but
we're going to skip ahead a bit . . . to later tonight, when you
brush your teeth.
                                              KIRO-TV, Seattle
```

A noticeable continuum and flow can be identified in the audience throughout the day. Early morning newscasts attract an audience that is probably sleepy, rushed, and maybe late; the day is just beginning. The audience is changing constantly. Thus regular news updates, traffic reports, weather forecasts, and late-night sports scores occur. By midday, newscasts compete with other activities for a mixed audience at home and at work. At noon, newscasters report about what has happened in the morning, rewrite important early-morning stories, update weather and market reports, and preview upcoming sporting events. By late afternoon and early evening, the audience wants to know what they have missed since early morning; thus brief, hard news stories as well as partial sports scores, periodic traffic and weather reports, and final market reports are presented. By 10 or 11 P.M., the audience has heard or read about most of the major news events of the day. These last newscasts each day provide a roundup and update of the day's newsworthy events and offer special features and stories to round out the news day.

Newsroom philosophy or policy may influence story selection. An effort may be made to use more investigative stories about local corruption or irregularities in government. Maybe the crime beat receives special consideration because the newscast airs in a larger market facing severe competition from several other stations. Perhaps community activities are to receive more attention. At KIRO-TV, a conscious effort is made to channel specific kinds of stories to a particular late afternoon local newscast. Hard news stories and features are presented in a magazine approach in the 5 to 6 P.M. weekday newscasts; features and background stories tend to be used in the 6:30 to 7 P.M. local newscast that follows the network newscast. At times news philosophy or policy extends to overall newscast content and presentation.

How much news is available is also a factor. For example, weekend and early Monday morning newscasts often use items that might be rejected during other weekday newscasts because fewer news items usually are available from which to select on weekends and Mondays. Governmental offices are closed, and businesses are also closed or operate on a restricted schedule. However, weekends and Monday mornings can be just as hectic on occasion, requiring difficult decisions about the contents of newscasts.

The availability of sound or picture must be determined. Some stories are more likely to get used because they include sound or picture and help balance the production aspects of a newscast. The danger is using a story *only* because it contains sound or picture; it may have no other redeeming news value.

Along with the preceding guidelines noted, several considerations should be remembered when selecting stories for a newscast: commitments, format, and the lead story.

Considerations

Commitments relate to a variety of situations. For example, competitive local ratings periods may dictate the use of more investigative stories or live reports during the newscast, which might bump other worthwhile stories. The names of newscast sponsors as well as the placement and length of commercials are important. You would not want to run the story about a local furniture store fire adjacent to the scheduled commercial for this same sponsor. To avoid embarrassment and poor taste, check the commercial program log for potential problems.

The format of the newscast must also be considered, since it influences the lineup, which is a term discussed later. Some newscasts are arranged in "blocks," with each block, or segment, allotted a specific amount of time during a designated portion of the newscast. Typical newscast blocks include local, state, world-national, sports, weather, markets, and features. Although this format makes it easier to plan and time individual segments, it does not hold audience interest throughout the newscast. Also, if followed strictly, it does not allow for late story updates. More common is an integrated, or magazine, approach to newscasts in which stories are presented in clusters, or interest areas, designed to maintain audience interest throughout the newscast. Although this approach requires more thoughtful and precise planning, it provides flow and movement to the newscast.

One of the most crucial decisions is choosing the first, or lead, story in a newscast. This story sets the pace and tone for what follows; thus the story must have significance, interest, and importance. It might be an exclusive story.

The best guideline (not a rule) is to lead with a strong local story that includes picture or sound, grabs audience interest, affects your audience most directly and immediately, and reports what is about to develop or is still developing. If the top story is sports or weather, the lead story should provide a capsule of that local sports scandal or the impending severe weather. Details and updates can be provided during the regular sports or weather newscast segment. The same guidelines could apply to a strong local business story about layoffs at a major manufacturing plant. The lead story should be *the* top story, no matter where it occurs.

Building the Newscast

Although selecting stories carefully is important, using those stories to build a newscast that is easily understood, memorable, and significant for the audience is just as important. The newscast producer follows several steps to coordinate the building of a newscast.

Essential Steps

First, identify what is available. Check with the assignments desk to see what is being covered. Review previous newscasts. Monitor the wire services, network and satellite feeds, and competing stations' newscasts.

Second, determine how much time you have in the newscast. In a 30-minute newscast, the "news hole" is generally about 21 minutes, after you deduct time for commercials that precede and follow the newscast as well as those within the newscast, the open and close, bumpers and teasers (discussed later), transitions, and banter between on-air anchors. Generally, sports and weather segments are controlled by those particular on-air talent. Once these 7 or 8 minutes are deducted, the news hole is now down to about 14 to 15 minutes. Not much time to provide a comprehensive report on the day's news events!

Finally, construct the newscast segments. Approximate times are assigned for each story that might be used. Story developments and importance change, so story lengths are adjusted regularly. The newscast producer tries to fit the stories selected into the narrow "window" available and to make the order of presentation logical, meaningful, and interesting. Anchor Frank Gentry notes that "hourly newscasts for both MBS and NBC Radio, while billed as 'five minutes,' are actually 2:45 when commercials and format language are taken out. So creativity takes a back seat to brevity. . . . The process is, at times, akin to stuffing a whole cow through a sausage grinder! The goal is to get 8–12 stories into a typical hourly cast, along with 3–5 tape cuts."[2]

Planning and Coordination

Cooperative teamwork, intense dedication, and precise planning are necessary for all of the components to come together for the production of an effective newscast. The assignment editor and newscast producer are constantly monitoring news coverage during the day. Stories that looked promising earlier when assigned after the morning news staff meeting may have failed to materialize or taken a different turn than expected, or other stories may have developed that take the place of the stories assigned.

Producers' dias in KUSA-TV main control room. Producers have their own bank of monitors showing sources such as remotes, cameras, and talent prompter copy. Producers also use phone lines and communications systems to contact anchors, the assignment desk, editing area, master control, etc. Photo courtesy of Barb Simon and KUSA-TV, Denver.

Planning a newscast is almost like creating an original jigsaw puzzle in which the edges of the puzzle are known (the time limitations of coverage and presentation), but the individual pieces inside of the puzzle (the news events of the day) vary each time for each puzzle (or newscast). Each puzzle piece (shape, size, color, dimension) must fit tightly to form a mosaic that is colorful, interesting, informative, and significant—a structure that provides variety in pace, tone, flow, and impact.

The newscast producer has overall responsibility for assembling the newscast components. The *details* of the newscast must be controlled: how it looks or sounds, what it says, how much information it provides, how memorable it is, how the pace and flow of the newscast progresses. The producer organizes the content and divides or delegates the workload to accomplish the task. The result is a lineup, or *rundown sheet* (discussed later), that, with the script, becomes an essential production tool and guide for the on-air look and content of the newscast.

The producer provides several pieces of the puzzle for the newscast director. These include the lineup; complete script or copy with timing and technical information noted; a list of graphics to be used (if television); and a stack of tape material (carts for radio or videocassettes for television), all labeled and keyed to the newscast copy.

The newscast director uses the producer's materials in guiding the technical personnel to present the newscast as the producer has planned and envisioned it and as the news staff has written and reported it. The director plans the technical execution of the newscast. Although both the producer and the director work together in the control room when the newscast is broadcast, the director is in charge once the newscast begins. On-camera talent receive directions from the producer via a *PL* (private line)—tiny, barely visible earpieces.

Timing

Broadcast news is a time-driven industry. Thus each story and each element in a newscast must be timed precisely. Commercials have to air when logged, and the newscast must end when scheduled. Accuracy is important. One mistake causes unnecessary problems for the newscast producer and director. The producer constantly battles the clock to get stories written and edited, to finalize the lineup, to resolve constant requests for more time from reporters.

Newsroom computer systems not only can compute the length of each newscast element but also can provide cumulative or progressive running time. Using this system, a newscast producer or director knows exactly how much time has been used, how much time is left, and what would happen if a late-breaking story was added to an already full newscast lineup. The use of computers in broadcast news is described more fully in Chapter 2.

Although mechanical and electronic timing devices are available, an experienced producer soon cultivates the ability to convert a set of timing notations into minutes and seconds without such devices. Each reassessment of a potential story for the newscast prompts the producer to make quick calculations to measure the impact of changing story length or placement. Often stories are moved or eliminated for timing purposes.

As indicated earlier, scheduled breaks must be accommodated when formulating the lineup. A 30-minute newscast usually contains five segments, with each of the four breaks lasting 1 to 2 minutes. A 60-minute newscast generally has eight segments or blocks, with each of the seven breaks lasting 1 to 2 minutes.

Backtiming is one technique used to make newscast timing more precise. The last few items in a newscast are read aloud and timed. Tape material (if included) is timed. The total length of this backtimed material is noted at the top of this set of copy, so that when this point is reached in the newscast, the on-air talent will go to this material and end the newscast on time. This technique helps ensure that a particular story gets used no matter how many changes are made during the newscast.

The producer may also provide on-air talent with *pad copy,* two or three minor stories kept in reserve in case the newscast runs short for whatever reason. It is best to provide anchors reader-only copy of varying lengths for less critical news items. Stories can then be selected based on length once the producer determines how much time is needed to finish on time. Reader-only copy avoids hectic technical adjustments.

Lineups

A newscast *lineup,* also called a *rundown* and *budget,* is the written plan that guides those involved in getting and keeping the newscast on-the-air. Lineups are used primarily for preparing television newscasts. Some computerized radio newsrooms also prepare lineups (see Figure 18.1).

9News newsroom and anchor Gary Shapiro at the update news desk. Photo courtesy of Barb Simon and KUSA-TV, Denver.

Here are the typical phases involved in preparing the lineup for a 6 P.M. television newscast (similar steps are used to prepare newscasts at other times of the day):

Morning

Dispatch news crews after the morning news planning meeting. Prepare preliminary lineup. Monitor news developments.

Noon

Update lineup. Continue monitoring news developments.

1 P.M.

Meet with assignment editor, anchors, writers, editors to discuss latest lineup. Plan segments for weather, sports, markets, and so forth. Start writing. Update lineup.

2 P.M.

Work on electronic graphics to be used. Update lineup.

3 P.M.

Write headlines, bumpers, teasers, features. Continue monitoring.

4 P.M.

Review unedited videotape and copy. Revise lineup. Push the crew!

5 P.M.

> Push for final edits on copy and tape. Finalize graphics. Distribute final script and lineup to technical personnel. Brief newscast director.

6 P.M.

> Meet in the control room with the director to get and keep the newscast on-the-air.

Producers use various methods to prepare lineups: preprinted forms that note segment positions, commercial placements, and so forth, with handwritten notes added; index cards containing specific information about each story or newscast item that can be shuffled until the lineup is finalized; a menu board with slots into which story information is inserted, rearranged, and photocopied when a final lineup is ready; in-newsroom computer systems that prepare custom rundowns that identify and time individual stories as well as newscast segments, specify studio cameras and tape sources, provide backtiming, and offer many other useful features.

Lineups need to provide essential information about each item in the newscast. There are variations in the format or layout as well as the information included in a written lineup.

Figure 18.1 shows lineups for both radio and television news and sportscasts. In some lineups each newscast item, or *event,* is numbered consecutively. In others a three-digit number or a letter-number combination indicates the position of each item in a specific segment. Thus the first three items in segment 1 could be numbered 101, 102, 103 or A1, A2, A3. If multiple reports are associated with the same story, often called *folos,* or if a single story is written on several consecutive script pages, the lineup would indicate 101A, 101B, 101C, and so on (if the first story in the first segment was a folo). Other notations are generally included for each item in a newscast lineup: the length of each item and often the cumulative time also; the story slug or event designation (e.g., *open, commercials, tease*); the initials or abbreviated name of the on-air talent who reads or handles each item; the initials of the reporter, writer, and/or editor responsible for preparing each item; source(s) for video or audio to be used; and the production or presentation format to be used, such as VO/ENG, PKG WRAP, and SOT.

Variety, Pace, and Flow

Variety, pace, and flow are three concepts that form the glue and provide the power or movement for the newscast. Experienced producers develop a sixth sense about offering enough variety in story content and presentation format to spark audience interest and avoid making the pace of the newscast stagnant, dull, or boring while at the same time guiding the audience through the flow of the day's news events in a logical and meaningful way.

NEWS 4 ST. LOUIS — KMOV-TV

NEWSCAST __5P__ DAY __MONDAY__ DATE __11/2__ RUNDOWN PAGE # 1-1-1-1-1-1-1
PRODUCER __DK__ REVISION _____

PG	AN	SHOT/GRAPHIC	SLUG	W/E	VIDEO	PB	AUDIO	TIME	UTILITY	
0	H/C	CK CREDITS	HEDLINES							
			COMMERCIALS		ACR		SOT			
			OPEN		ACR		SOT		*JHarkop* 48	15
1	C/H	2 SHOT								
	H	FATAL FIRE	MADISON IL FIRE	LL	VTR		LL PKG	1:30	2²⁵	1 45
1T	H	OC	TAG							

--- KMOV-TV, St. Louis

SLUG	ANCHOR	WRITER	CART NO.	COPY	TAPE	TOTAL	CUME
OPEN				0:13			0:13
MISSING RENO WOMAN 2	DILLON	petersen	30	0:48	00:23	1:11	1:24
TEASE				0:10			1:34
COMMERCIAL				0:60			2:34
CUBAN PRISONERS	DILLON	dillon	34	0:28	00:22	0:50	3:24
2ND SPONSOR CREDIT				0:07			3:31

--- KFDI Radio, Wichita, Kansas

```
ouohe.i  Fri Nov 20 16:15  page  1
                                              FINAL
                   CABLE NEWS NETWORK RUNDOWN
SHOW   DAY    DATE     REV PRODUCER   ANCHOR      ANCHOR       STATUS
NEWSWA LAST DAY 10/20   1  JERRY KRIEG LOU WATERS  MARY ALICE    HOLD
PG SLUG        ANC FORM   WR VTR TAPE#   GRAPHIC         TIME TOTAL
===============================================================
HELLO EVERYONE  THIS IS NEWSWATCH
THIS IS A ONE-HOUR FORMAT 5:00 TO 6:00

WRITER:BEDINGFIELD
=================
A0   PRESHOW       WEATHER IS SPONSORED               :55
     WEATHER COMMERCIAL                               35
     CNN PROMO                                    :20/58:45
     CNN NETWORK ID                               05/00:00

A1   OPEN          LOU      VO_____                :15/00:20
                                   G-NEWSWATCH FULL SPLIT
A2   BUDGET/WHOUSE  MAW                               :20    40
     BIERBAUER     PKG OR LIVE                      2:30/  310
       this will be the white house angle...any announcement or lack there of.
                   FULL SCREEN ADDAS  G FULL SCREEN:BUDGET NUMMBERS
A3   BUDGET-WHAT??  LOU  BOX          G BUDGET TALKS     1:30/  440
                                      G BUDGET TALKS/CAPITOL HILL
                   SOT    _
```
--- Cable News Network

10PM SPORTS NOV 5 NOLAN

Cam3	Tal	Page		SOURCE Type	Shots	Production Details	Reporter Writer	SS1
			SLUGS:					
	M	F-1	BRONCOS/SMITH	vo/eng	S			
	M	F-2	NFL/NEWS	L	BOX	NFL		
	M	F-3	PREP/FOOTBALL	vo/eng	BOX	PREP FOOTBALL		
				vo/cg	/			
	M	F-4	NUGGETS/ROSTER	vo/eng	BOX	NUGGETS		

--- KUSA-TV, Denver

Figure 18.1 Portions of various types of radio and television newscast lineups.

Here are some ways to infuse more variety into a newscast:

a. Vary the length, treatment, and presentation format of stories. A short on-set story could be followed by a longer reporter package, followed by a few brief anchor reader stories, followed by anchor copy using tape, and so on.

b. If the newscast has coanchors, vary how many stories each anchor reads consecutively. Changing anchors gives the audience a nonverbal cue that the story subject or focus is changing.

c. Begin each segment with a strong story that is interesting and significant.

d. Use features or background pieces to ''bridge'' between stories or to end a segment and lead into a break. These bridge stories should have something in common with the story they follow or precede.

e. Use related stories throughout the newscast. For example, use the longer story about the local election day results or the major local disaster in the first segment; then use additional story angles or feature items (sidebars) later in the newscast.

f. Update major breaking stories later in the newscast if events warrant.

Many of these suggestions, illustrated in Figure 18.2, also apply to pace, that is, the speed with which the newscast seems to progress. The newscast must be slow enough to be understood but fast enough to maintain interest.

Pace and variety must operate in tandem. One influences the other. A rhythm or pulse develops in a newscast but the audience may not be aware of it. The producer, however, *must* remember to monitor and control the rhythm of the newscast.

Manipulating the flow, or apparent connection, between stories ensures variety and controls the pace. The producer weaves the fabric of the newscast by clustering or grouping related stories. Each segment in a newscast is like a mini-newscast in that an effective use of pacing, variety, peaks and valleys of interest and intensity, and especially flow should occur between stories.

This clustering or grouping can be done according to subject matter (politics, education, medicine, accidents, crimes, courts); geography (local, state, national, international); newsmaker (president, congress, governor, mayor); or any number of other cluster or interest-area designations.

KMOV-TV in St. Louis strung together these stories in one segment of a newscast: a 37-second anchor reader item about a local man who died after getting the wrong heart transplanted into him; a 30-second anchor VO story about the successful five-organ transplant into a 3-year-old girl; a 35-second anchor VO story about the dedication of a new St. Louis health clinic; a 15-second anchor reader/VO previewing a special report about losing weight scheduled for a later newscast.

A danger does exist that a newscast could become too predictable, with *all* stories in each cluster presented at one time in a newscast. The use of this clustering concept must be tempered with a desire to make the stories flow or progress naturally from one to another *throughout* the newscast. The flow may not be apparent to the audience, but it helps lead the audience *through* the events that are reported. Follow the advice WMAR-TV in Baltimore offers:

> You don't want to be a stacker, you want to be a block builder . . . an architect of something watchable and compelling. Even on slow days our broadcasts can be interesting and memorable. Those are the days the programs must sing just as strongly. You are the composer! . . .
>
> Make your show segments well-rounded. An all-crime block becomes repetitive and depressing for viewers. Spread it out . . . include a variety of stories which can be transitioned into your newscast . . . don't get stuck in a ''theme block'' that leaves the viewer feeling like he's not getting all of the news in those first vital few minutes of a broadcast. And even when you are past your ''top news'' material, don't tip your hand to the viewer that there is no news left by only mentioning that sports and weather are ahead. Work news into each block, where appropriate, and keep the general viewer interest high.[3]

Some stories defy this clustering effort. No amount of the producer's twisting, bending, or pushing will make the story fit into a cluster. These stand-alone stories can be used as bridges between clusters as long as they do not disturb the flow of the rest of the newscast.

In Figure 18.2, notice how stories 2, 3, 4, 5, and 6 provide a cluster of stories about the summit treaty. Stories 7, 8, and 9 pull together items about crime and police. But also notice that additional crime stories are not in the same cluster. Items 14 and 15 relate to holiday crime prevention and are placed in segment 2. The connection between the crime items was made back in item 10 when the holiday crime profile was previewed or ''teased,'' going into the first break. Items 12 and 13 form a third cluster—a story about a PSA crash that leads into an item about a pilot being captured in another country; both stories relate to airplanes, crashes, and pilots.

Here are the lead sentences for three stories relating to aviation that Dan Dillon tied together so that the stories progress both geographically (from world to national to local) and topically (from airplane crashes to an important local aviation industry item):

```
The wreckage of a South Korean jetliner that carried 115 people
has been spotted in the thick jungle on the Thai side of the
Thailand-Burmese Border. . . .

There's been another near-collision involving a domestic
airline flight. . . .
```

PAGE	TLNT	SLUG	VISUAL	LENGTH
		SHOW: 10 PM **DAY:** TUESDAY **DATE:** 12/8		
1		Open-Alyce	Vtr sot	:45
2	B/A	Intro Treaty Signed	2-Shot, 3-Shot, ON SET	:15
3	LE	Treaty Signed	ON SET, Dve Fz, Vtr pkg	1:30
4	LE	TAg/Toss. Back	ON SET	:25
5	B	Intro Summit Impact	Dve Fz	:15
6	MS	Summit Impact	Vtr pkg	1:45
7	A	Intro Murder/Kidnapping	Dve Fz	:15
8	CK	Murder/Kidnapping	Vtr pkg	1:30
9	B	Cops Fired	Dve Fz, Vtr vosot	:45
10	B/A	Tease PSA Crash	Vtr vo	
		Tease Holiday Crime	Wipe to Vtr vo	:15
11		BREAK ONE		1:00
12	A	PSA Crash	Dve Fz, Vtr vosot	:45
13	B	Pilot Captured	Dve Fz, Vtr vo	:25
14	A	Intro Holiday Crime #2	Dve Fz	:15
15	LF	Holiday Crime #2	Vtr pkg	1:30
16	A/B	Tease Sports	Vtr vo	:15
17		BREAK TWO		1:30
18	SM	Sports	MICRO/UNIT ONE?	4:20
19	B/A	Tease Weather	Vtr vo	
		Business Wrap	Wipe to Vtr	:30
20		BREAK THREE		1:30
21	HT	Weather	Vtr vo	4:15
22	A	Southland Buyout	Dve Fz	:20
23	A/B	Tease Kicker	Vtr vo or ON CAM	:15
24		BREAK FOUR		1:00
25	A	Copy	Medium	:20
26	B	Kicker	ON CAM OR Vtr vo	1:00
27	B/A	Bye	2-Shot, wide	:15

C I T Y

Figure 18.2 An example of a finished television newscast lineup or rundown.
Courtesy of KXAS-TV, Fort Worth, Texas.

```
Wichita may soon host the first jumbo jet to become part of the
fleet of the U-S President. . . .
```
KFDI Radio, Wichita, Kansas

Transitions help add variety, balance the pace, and highlight the flow or connection between stories in a newscast. They contribute to the continuity of a newscast by guiding the audience from one story to another and creating the feeling of an integrated presentation of news rather than a set of stories selected and arranged at random.

Once the lineup has been finalized, transitions can be inserted at the *beginning* of a story. After a story about the demolition of a local drive-in movie theater, this was the first sentence of the next story about the lighting of the traditional Christmas tree:

```
In Seattle's Pioneer Square right now, it's what's GONE UP
that's making news.
```
KIRO-TV, Seattle

These *segues, bridges,* or *coupling pins* can also be used *within* stories to guide the audience by showing the connection between various parts of a story:

```
Besides talking about higher gas taxes, the state
transportation department today approved spending money for
roads near the new Navy homeport at Everett.
```
KIRO-TV, Seattle

A transition at the *end* of a story can help wrap up details and point to the next story development:

```
Meanwhile, fire investigators are trying to find out what
caused the fire that killed her brother and grandmother.
```
KMOV-TV, Saint Louis

Transitions can be short phrases keyed to geography: *Elsewhere in Washington . . . ; Also in Oregon today . . . ; Meanwhile, at the state capitol . . . ; and at the White House. . . .* They could be keyed to subject matter: *In other action, the board . . . ; Turning to reforms of a different sort. . . .* Transitions may also simply serve as signposts for the audience: *In other news tonight . . . ; Turning to sports . . . ; In news closer to home . . .* (see Chapter 5, ''Story Structure,'' for more details about the use of transitions in news stories).

Transitions also can be made without using words. Shifts in on-air talent or changes in camera angles in a television newscast alert the audience that a change in direction or topic is about to happen. Don't forget to provide time in the lineup for these ''hand-offs'' between on-air talent.

Remember to use transitions with skill and discrimination. Identify the places in the newscast that *need* transitions. Look for logical and natural tie-ins that can provide a smooth flow of language and thought. Keep them simple. Use them sparingly, but effectively. Avoid detracting from the stories or calling undue attention to the transitions by creating arbitrary and artificial bridges.

Bumpers and Teasers

Some transitions alert the audience that a break is coming and may add brief, *stand-alone* pieces of information, such as a market summary, pollen count, or weather forecast; these are called *bumpers:*

```
KFDI Newstime is (time). This portion of the news brought to
you by (sponsor). It's currently (conditions) and (temp).
                                KFDI Radio, Wichita, Kansas
```

Other transitions may preview an upcoming story and entice the audience to stay tuned by whetting their curiosity and interest; these are called *teasers:*

```
Still to come on Channel 12 News at six . . . Details of the
biggest drug bust ever for Phoenix. . . . And in the east
valley . . . authorities are set to round up drunk drivers this
holiday season. . . . We'll have a live report.
                                          KPNX-TV, Phoenix
```

Teasers are often used over the closing credits in the adjacent program to preview the top stories in the upcoming newscast:

```
DVE OVER CREDITS          ------CAMERON------
                          Coming up on
                          Newschannel Three. . . .
                          A Phoenix police officer
                          is shot while trying to
                          foil an apparent robbery
                          attempt. . . .
DVE OVER CREDITS          ------HEIDI------
                          And the bodies of three
                          people are discovered in
                          a north Phoenix home. . . .
                          It's all next on
                          Newschannel
                          Three.
                                          KTVK-TV, Phoenix
```

This is sometimes referred to as a "squeeze tease" since the closing credits of a program are "squeezed" into a portion of the television screen while the video for the teaser occupies the rest of the picture. Credits usually return to full screen after the squeeze tease is finished.

Teasers can also be used at the end of a newscast to promote coverage in a later newscast (see the WTVJ-TV example under "Opens and Closes").

Remember *why* teasers are used. "Teasers tease, not tell. The purpose of the tease is to make the viewers curious so they'll stay tuned, not to rob the story of its main elements."[4]

The importance of teasers cannot be overlooked. As WMAR-TV points out, "Teasers cannot be throwaways! You need to work as hard or maybe harder on your teases than anything you do for your newscast. They need to be a priority, not an afterthought. They have to complement the video portion of the tease . . . and the CG [character generator] material must take it all a step further. It's all designed to help the viewer choose to stay with us . . . instead of turning to our competition."[5]

WMAR-TV goes on to offer this advice:

1. Sell the story.
2. Satisfy viewer needs (tease the story with an eye toward answering the question, "What's in it for the viewer?").
3. Whet the viewer's appetite for more.
4. Reassure viewers that the story will meet their expectations of what they want from the news.
5. Always try to avoid:
   Giving the story away
   Using weak words, convoluted sentences
   Vague, generalized teases
   Duplication in copy/CG material[6]

Opens and Closes

Having an opening that grabs attention and clearly identifies the start of the newscast is important. At a minimum, the newscast opening needs to identify the station or network and the newscaster. Music or electronic effects may be used. Upcoming stories could be previewed as part of the opening. A few stations (like KXAS-TV in Dallas-Fort Worth) have copyrighted their openings. KRNT Radio uses this standard opening that also integrates the name of the newscast sponsor:

```
SOUNDER (except when following CBS News)

KRNT News (continues). (Sponsored by _____ .)

I'm _____ . At _____ , we have _____
        (name)         (time)        (sky condition)

and _____ degrees in Des Moines. KRNT Weather is calling

for _____ .

        (brief look at day's/night's weather)

                                KRNT, Des Moines
```

The closing finishes out the newscast by reestablishing identity. Production credits could be used at the end of a weekend newscast when more time might be available. Some closing segments tease, or preview, stories on upcoming newscasts.

```
JOHN TWO SHOT              (JOHN)

                           Thank you for having us in for
                           news . . .
SUSAN TWO SHOT             (Susan)

                           We'll have election coverage
                           throughout the evening. And join us
                           again at 11 for complete
                           returns. . . .
                                             WTVJ-TV, Miami
```

WTOP Newsradio 1500 in Washington, D.C., uses an hourly lineup labeled "Anchor Language." This semiscript newscast format guides newscasters each hour as they begin and end various types of news and information segments.

ANCHOR LANGUAGE

:59:30 INTO HEADLINES:

GOOD MORNING/AFTERNOON/EVENING!! I'M _____.
_____ IS AT THE EDITOR'S DESK. IT'S ___ DEGREES UNDER
_____ SKIES, AT ___:___, ON (DAY, MONTH, DATE). IN THE
HEADLINES AT THIS HOUR . . . (TWO HEADLINES & WEATHER BRIEF)
WTOP NEWSTIME ___ O'CLOCK.

:05:00 OUT OF CBS:

GOOD MORNING/AFTERNOON/EVENING!! I'M _____.
IT'S ___:___. HERE'S THE WTOP 3-DAY WEATHER FORECAST. . . .

:20:10 INTO HEADLINES:

GOOD MORNING/AFTERNOON/EVENING!! I'M _____.
IT'S ___DEGREES UNDER _____ SKIES, AT ___:___, ON
(DAY, MONTH, DATE). IN THE HEADLINES AT THIS HOUR . . . (TWO
HEADLINES & WEATHER BRIEF).

:30:30 ONLY OUT OF PROMO ON EVENINGS AND WEEKENDS WHEN THERE
ARE TWO ANCHORS.

GOOD MORNING/AFTERNOON/EVENING!! I'M _____. WTOP
NEWSTIME ___:___.

```
:40:10 INTO HEADLINES:

GOOD MORNING/AFTERNOON/EVENING!! I'M _____. IT'S ___
DEGREES UNDER _____ SKIES, AT ___:___,
ON (DAY, MONTH, DATE). IN THE HEADLINES AT THIS HOUR . . . (TWO
HEADLINES & WEATHER BRIEF).
```

Kickers

A *kicker* is a story about the odd, unusual, surprising, often humorous events that happen in the news. It can be used at the end of a newscast to bridge back to entertainment programming or at the end of a segment to provide a pleasant contrast to the generally serious tone of the rest of the newscast.

Kickers should be in good taste. Do not treat serious subjects lightly or ridicule people or their beliefs and habits.

Summary

This chapter outlined the steps and techniques used to select stories for a radio or television newscast and then use those stories to plan or build an effective presentation.

Several guidelines and commitments influence the selection of stories. These include newsworthiness; coverage area; target audience; time of day; newsroom philosophy and policy; availability of news items as well as the availability of sound or picture; newscast format used; commitments the newsroom has made; and the lead story in a newscast.

Building or planning a newscast involves three key steps: (1) becoming informed about the day's news events; (2) calculating available newscast time; and (3) writing copy and the lineup. The lineup is the producer's written plan for the newscast. The director uses the lineup and other material provided to produce a newscast that will be smooth, informative, clear, and satisfying for the audience. Within the newscast, evidence of variety, pace, and flow should occur. Transitions can be used to show the apparent connection between news items. Bumpers and teasers are special kinds of transitions. Kickers can be used to provide a lighter approach to the day's news. Using backtimed and pad copy can ensure ending on time.

Exercises

1. Use the next edition of a local daily newspaper for one of the following exercises.

   a. Circle in the newspaper the items used to write and then record a two-minute radio or television newscast (all anchor copy only). Turn in the entire newspaper, your copy, and tape.

   b. Circle the major national-international stories featured in the newspaper. Record a comparable network newscast; for instance, use a morning newspaper with a morning newscast or an afternoon newspaper with a noon or early afternoon newscast. Determine the similarities and differences between the two reports (story selection, length, placement, use of illustrations vs. graphics or tape, etc.). Report your findings. Turn in the complete newspaper for evaluation.

c. Follow the directions for Exercise 1b, but circle local, state, and regional items. Then monitor a local radio or television newscast. Turn in the same material as for 1b.

d. Follow the directions for Exercise 1c, but *before* you monitor the local newscast, prepare a lineup of stories that you would *expect* to find included. Report your findings and analyze the discrepancies that arose.

2. You have been assigned to write the one-minute segment of world-international news to be used in your station's ''Week in Review'' program. Use the principles illustrated in this chapter and Chapters 4 to 8 to write your one-minute segment for radio or television. Use these story headlines from the week's events:

a. An accident Sunday involving a truck carrying about 22 tons of dynamite has prompted the evacuation of hundreds of people in Westfield, Massachusetts. A tractor-trailer split open after striking a railroad overpass.

b. Train travel across Italy has come to a virtual halt due to a 24-hour strike by Italian rail workers.

c. On Sunday, network newswriters and editors ratified a new contract and are expected to be back in the newsroom within a few days.

d. Sirens sounded in Israel Sunday morning marking Holocaust Day. Residents of the Jewish state stopped what they were doing to remember the six million Jews killed by Nazis during World War II.

e. The search continues for 13 people believed buried in the wreckage of last week's Bridgeport, Connecticut, building collapse.

f. Tens of thousands of marchers around the world joined forces Monday to mark the anniversary of the Chernobyl Nuclear Power Plant disaster.

g. Japan's trade minister pledges to do more to trim Japan's huge trade surplus after coming under frequent attack during a two-day meeting of international trade officials in Japan.

h. A demonstration outside CIA headquarters in suburban Washington Monday led to the arrest of more than 500 protestors.

i. South African police used whips, tear gas, and birdshot in battles with black and white students during an antigovernment demonstration Monday at the University of Cape Town.

j. Ten deaths were reported Tuesday in the crash of a Salvadoran military helicopter.

k. The head of the National Transportation Safety Board Tuesday called for a reduction in flights because, he says, the air traffic control system cannot handle all of the scheduled flights.

l. It was reported Wednesday that new home sales dropped last month as prices climbed to a record high.

m. Clouds of ammonia were released from a broken pipe Wednesday in Bells, Tennessee—forcing evacuation of about 50 people from their homes.

n. On Thursday, police surrounded a mountainous area near Wolf Creek, Montana, and planned to go in after three heavily armed men who have been on the run since Monday.

o. On Friday, Israel and Jordan reportedly reached agreement on guidelines for Arab-Israeli peace talks.

p. The Senate Appropriations Committee Friday endorsed the addition of nine billion dollars to federal spending this year. Most of the money would go to the Commodity Credit Corporation, which is running low on funds for farm subsidies.

Notes

1. Bill Wagner, "Producer's Corner," *RTNDA Communicator* 40, no. 12 (December 1986): 30–31.

2. Reprinted by permission of Frank Gentry.

3. "Producers," *Channel 2 News Stylebook* (Baltimore, MD: WMAR-TV, n.d.), p. 2.

4. *Cable News Network Style Book* (version 4.0), writ-5 (n.d).

5. "Producers," *Channel 2 News Stylebook,* pp. 4–5.

6. Ibid.

Part Five

Laws and Ethics

Chapter 19

Laws and Regulations

T his chapter and Chapter 20 are companion chapters. This chapter reviews various requirements and restraints as well as rights and privileges extended to the broadcast journalist. Chapter 20 examines ethical issues and situations often encountered and for which there are usually no easy solutions or answers.

Specifically this chapter covers the following topics: libel; privacy; protecting sources; access; copyright; Section 315; and the fairness doctrine. Legal references made in this chapter are clarified in Chapter 15, ''Routine Coverage.''

This chapter can only introduce the essential obligations faced regularly by the broadcast journalist; details about each topic have had to be curtailed. Many other requirements confront the journalist as well as others working in the communications media.

Stay informed! Many of these laws and regulations are complex and subject to change. Also, state rather than federal laws often control various aspects of news coverage. Consult qualified counsel *before* serious legal problems develop. Stay current by completing a media law course and by reading trade publications such as *Broadcasting & Cable, The Quill,* RTNDA's *Communicator,* and *Columbia Journalism Review.*

Libel

Defamation is a false statement—spoken (slander) or written (libel)—that damages the character or reputation of a person or group. States generally incorporate slander in their libel laws.

You should know the following about libel: essential elements; precautions to take; and defenses available.[1]

Five specific legal requirements must be present for libel: "publication"; identification; false statement; damage; and fault. Most libel claims will fail unless all five elements are present.

Reputations cannot be harmed unless others (third parties) become aware of the offending material. Publication must occur, which includes written *or* oral statements as well as pictures and other communication. If you call a co-worker a drunk and a liar in the privacy of your home where no one else can hear your accusations, libel has not occurred. But libel may have occurred if the charges are false and if they are made to a third party by being used on-the-air.

The plaintiff must also be identified for libel to occur. This could involve using the name or showing the specific activities of a particular person or group. However, identification could also be established if the plaintiff (the one bringing the suit) can show that the statement clearly refers to him or her, or that those who know the plaintiff think that the statement refers to him or her.

To be libelous, a statement must be false. Although true statements may not be libelous, public disclosure of private facts may give rise to a charge of invasion of privacy; this is discussed later. You should always be able to prove the accuracy of the information that you report. Be prepared to verify your charges, for example, that a particular bus driver has a long string of drunk driving convictions or that a certain political candidate has a history of psychological problems.

The plaintiff must show that a libelous statement has damaged his or her reputation. The plaintiff could be awarded any of three types of damages: general or compensatory for the humiliation or shame suffered as a result of the defamatory statements, actual or special for verifiable economic losses sustained, or punitive, intended to punish defendants.

In most cases, the plaintiff must prove, according to a state's libel laws, that a false statement of fact was "published" due to the negligence of the defendant. Public officials and public figures such as notable entertainers, sports stars, and community leaders must prove not only that a statement was false but also that malice was intended, that the defendant knew it was false or proceeded with reckless disregard about the truth of the statement.

Several precautions will help minimize the risk of a libel suit:

  a. Be attentive when processing potentially sensitive information. Routine reporting chores require the most precision and care.
  b. Review and verify all facts and comments, especially those made in official proceedings such as in court.

c. Be certain someone has been tried, convicted, and sentenced before labeling him or her as a *thief, murderer, bigamist, drug addict, perjurer,* and so forth.

d. Be cautious when reporting business failures or statements.

e. Avoid unscripted comments or remarks.

f. Never insert personal opinions into a straight news story.

g. Never use stories from another news outlet, for example another station or local newspapers, without rechecking potentially libelous information. You could be held responsible for "publication" of the same libelous statements.

h. Try to obtain face-to-face rather than telephone interviews to ensure more direct contact with news sources. More accurate reporting should also result.

i. Record on tape the name (with correct spelling) and title of each person interviewed. Use written consent forms if news coverage is extensive, complex, or involves sensitive issues, for example, in documentaries and investigative reports.

j. Get another opinion about stories that *might* lead to libel suits.

k. If in doubt, don't! If you *think* there might be a libel problem, stop. Talk to your news director, newscast producer, station manager, or a qualified attorney.

Defenses

In most cases, a formal charge of libel can be avoided if an authorized newsroom spokesperson such as the news director or general manager, but *not* an attorney, responds seriously, courteously, fairly, and sensitively to every libel complaint received. Initially, the person voicing such a complaint is probably concerned more with reputation than with money. The potential plaintiff simply wants to set the record straight. Response from an attorney at this initial stage might unnecessarily alarm the person complaining.

If you acknowledge that a clear case of libel has occurred, always demonstrate, at least, that an honest and reasonable effort has been made to solve the problem. An official newsroom spokesperson could offer to provide an apology on-the-air or in a letter; do a follow-up story based on the complaint; or at least to mark or flag the story for reference to avoid future lawsuits. Avoid the legal entanglements of libel suits if at all possible.

Several defenses can be used if a formal libel charge is filed. All of these options should be considered with the advice of qualified legal counsel:

a. *The statements made are substantially true.* However, knowing that something is true and proving it in court can be two different things.

b. *The plaintiff consented to publication.* A written or recorded consent from the plaintiff will make this defense viable.

c. *The statements made were "privileged," involved an item of public interest, and were made without malice.* Generally stories about criminal trials, public meetings, police reports, and other governmental documents are privileged or protected from libel suits, so long as they are accurate, involve issues and concerns of the general public, and are nonmalicious (i.e., not intended to do harm).

d. *The plaintiff has waited too long to bring the libel suit.* Each state sets the statute of limitations for the filing of libel suits.

Most media analysts agree that libel charges have become very common and damages from libel decisions have increased noticeably as listeners and viewers increase their involvement in programs on-the-air, especially controversial talk shows in which telephone calls are received from audience members. These heated on-air discussion situations increase the likelihood that libel charges may develop.

Privacy

Invasion of privacy charges sometimes accompany libel suits. Four categories of activities are associated with invasion of privacy: intrusion; public disclosure of private facts; false light; and misappropriation.

Intrusion

Intrusion occurs when someone intentionally disrupts or invades the solitude, seclusion, or personal privacy of another. Intrusion, like libel, is a matter of state law. An experienced local attorney can help you handle intricate intrusion questions.

Three factors should be considered when deciding whether a certain activity constitutes intrusion and might produce an actionable invasion of privacy claim: consent; use of public places; and newsworthiness.

Consent should be obtained before you go onto private property: *expressed* consent from the legitimate owner or the owner's representative, or *implied* consent when a newsworthy disaster has occurred, for example, the crash of a light plane in a farm field. Get the story, but be courteous and considerate of others. If asked to leave, do so. An attorney should review the circumstances under which implied consent is used to avoid charges of intrusion or trespassing.

Use public places. Avoid going on private property. Record interviews in the open, in public view. Accurate reports about what transpires in public pose no potential invasion of privacy. Thus a shot of someone on the steps of a public building during a public demonstration could not be considered an invasion of privacy. Charging into a private medical facility that is under fire for medical fraud and demanding answers on tape could lead to intrusion problems. The solution? Try to get the interview in public view. Use a public sidewalk or a public park. Restaurants, theaters, stores, and similar private establishments open to the public generally protect the privacy of customers inside, since they have not subjected themselves to public view.

Newsworthiness is influenced by many factors and determined by several people, including the reporter and other newsroom supervisory personnel. Obviously, those considered public figures have less of an expectation of privacy than those who are involuntarily thrust into the limelight. These victims of circumstances should be handled with care and sensitivity.

Telephone calls pose a potential privacy problem. (Chapter 10, "Developing News Sources," described ways to obtain the required prior permission from everyone involved in telephone conversations broadcast live or recorded for later use.) Permission is not needed for employee calls to the newsroom.

Another potential problem area is using electronic eavesdropping such as hidden microphones and cameras. Obtaining the prior consent of all parties involved in any electronic recording is best.

Public Disclosure of Private Facts

If you reveal an embarrassing private fact about someone that is not newsworthy and that you have no permission to reveal, you could be sued for invasion of privacy. As noted earlier, public figures surrender many of their rights to privacy. But for them, as well as for holders of public office, reveal only the private activities that directly influence public and legal responsibilities and that relate to the story being reported.

Public office carries with it public trust, and that means increased public scrutiny. For example, a privacy suit might develop if you report that the governor has a mistress. But such a suit is not likely to develop if you report that the governor's mistress has been added to the state payroll!

The broader the public mandate, the more heightened the public need and desire for accountability. The higher the public office, the closer the scrutiny of private facts.

False Light

This type of invasion of privacy can occur when a news story creates a false impression about a person's character, background, or connection with a controversial issue or group. This could happen when reporters attempt to sensationalize, embellish, or dramatize a story. It could also occur when pictures taken for one purpose are used to illustrate a different type of story. For example, you could have problems if you used file footage of a congested street scene shown several months earlier in a documentary about downtown redevelopment for a story today about increased drug use on downtown streets, especially if a particular person is shown clearly in a shot just as the narrator says, "And some of the drug addicts are in desperate need of help!" Think about *potential* privacy problems and complaints!

Use file footage carefully! Make a clear verbal or visual reference to the source of the footage shown. On-screen references could indicate that the shots were used on a different date or are simply stock or file footage.

Using a person's name, picture, or likeness in a bona fide (i.e., genuine or authentic) news report is not an invasion of privacy. This type of invasion of privacy, misappropriation, occurs most often in advertising and commercial applications.

Misappropriation

Privacy laws vary from state to state. Here are a few questions to ask as you consider questionable situations or prepare to meet with an attorney about potential privacy issues:

    a. How newsworthy is the information you are thinking of gathering or releasing?

    b. How important is it for the public to know this information?

    c. How public a person is the subject of your story?

    d. Are you certain that your information is completely accurate? Can it be verified by another source?

    e. Is there a safer but still journalistically sound alternative available for collecting or disseminating the information?

If the signs are alarming and the problem cannot or should not be avoided, consult an attorney.

Chapter 10 offered several suggestions for handling requests for confidentiality, anonymity, and privacy rights when news sources are contacted and interviewed. An informed journalist should also know about subpoenas, newsroom searches, and shield laws, since they concern protection of information sources.

Protecting Sources

A subpoena is the court's official request for someone to testify or provide information concerning a particular case. If you receive a subpoena as a reporter, treat it seriously; consult a qualified attorney. Ignoring a subpoena could lead to a fine or even a jail sentence. You do not have to provide any documents, tapes, or materials until you actually testify on the witness stand. Although it seldom happens, some courts have voided a subpoena after it has been issued.

Congress enacted the Privacy Protection Act of 1980 to prohibit both federal and state searches of newsrooms as well as journalists' homes or offices in all but the most limited circumstances. Such limited circumstances include seizing material related to a crime or needed to prevent death, serious bodily injury, or a breach of national security. Material generally protected under this law includes original as well as edited audiotape or videotape, reporters' notes, initial drafts of news copy, and photographs. If a search warrant is served, take immediate action: Notify the news director or station manager; try to delay the search until an attorney has examined the warrant; record the scene on videotape if the search continues.

Some states have enacted *shield laws* to further protect reporters from having to provide private documents or divulge their sources of information. Such state statutes do not apply in federal courts. Even in states with shield laws, reporters have spent time in jail for contempt of court when they refuse to turn over documents and records or reveal their sources of information. Short of subpoena or other court order, no Federal Communications Commission (FCC) or other federal government requirement calls for retention of news programs, video or audio outtakes, scripts, or reporters' notes.

Access

Access is the reporter's ability to gather information easily and openly. Reporters enjoy the same access rights and privileges as ordinary citizens. However, reporters tend to use available access rights more often than the general public.

Reporters regularly encounter challenges to access rights. Some of these are examined in the following sections: disaster and crime scenes; voluntary coverage guidelines; courts; and open records and open meetings laws.

Disaster and Crime Scene Access

Reporters and news photographers want to be as close to the action as possible during a disaster or tense police situation like a shootout, kidnapping, or hostage-taking incident. But even with a solid working relationship and understanding between law enforcement agencies and your newsroom, news media access at disaster and crime scenes may be limited.

The circumstances surrounding each incident will determine the media access provided. Generally, media access restrictions are imposed when any of the following are endangered: news personnel; crime or disaster victim(s); law enforcement or rescue operations; or evidence. Although the appointment of a police/press or media liaison officer designates a specific contact who might be more sensitive to journalists' needs and provide at least some information on the scene, some contend that such a system encourages the "filtering," or screening, of the information that a reporter gets about police operations and stifles the use of personal and more direct news sources.

Determine how to handle these kinds of restrictions *before* you encounter them. Should you agree to stand behind a particular police line at a disaster or crime scene? Should you obey an official police directive not to tie up the only telephone available to police to contact a man holding several children hostage in a school? Ask your newsroom supervisor, news director, or assignment manager for specific guidelines and preferences.

Voluntary Guidelines

Internal newsroom guidelines will help handle some of the situations just mentioned. Other kinds of guidelines, especially those for regular coverage of law enforcement agencies, medical facilities, and the courts, can help establish a set of expectations and standards for both the news media and certain categories of news sources. Although they do not ensure legal guarantees, these types of voluntary guidelines may save time when access to information is urgent. (Chapter 15, "Routine Coverage," provided terminology and suggested guidelines for gathering information from law enforcement agencies and hospitals.)

Legal and media ("bar and press") representatives in some states have formulated voluntary guidelines for disclosing and reporting information related to imminent or pending criminal litigation. Examples of information generally considered appropriate to report include biographical information about the arrested person, such as name, age, and residence; the specific criminal charge; conditions of bail; identity of the investigating and arresting agencies and the length of the investigation; circumstances of the arrest; and description of the physical evidence seized. Items often considered *not* appropriate to release include the existence or contents of any confession the accused made; statements predicting or influencing the outcome of the trial; and statements or opinions concerning the credibility or anticipated testimony of prospective witnesses.

Voluntary guidelines can only begin to answer access questions reporters may have when dealing with the courts. You must know the legal access you should expect when covering court cases and also how fair trial-free press concerns influence your local access to courtrooms and court records.

Courts

Over the years, the courts generally have extended First Amendment protections to the media to help shelter reporters and newsrooms from prior restraint situations. But courts have not been as generous in extending First Amendment rights of access to trials. Some access privileges are extended to some news media, but not to others. For example, courts may permit print reporters with pen and pad, but not broadcast journalists with microphones and cameras. Regrettably, five U.S. courts of appeals have held that no First Amendment right for electronic coverage exists.

Most state courts continue to extend full access rights to all news media, print *and* broadcast. Approximately 40 states permit electronic coverage in both trial and appellate courts in both civil and criminal cases. Although access has increased, most states rule out whole categories of sex-crime, juvenile, and domestic relations cases and/or witnesses, or give the trial judge broad discretion to close trials or portions of them to cameras while print reporters remain in the courtroom.

Media groups have lobbied for federal court access. As an experiment, for three years in the early 1990s, cameras were allowed into eight federal courts, but only for civil cases. RTNDA President David Bartlett cited the civil-only nature of the experiment as the main reason for low usage of the federal court access granted from 1991 to 1994. Another problem was finding reporters who were able to cover the federal courts well.[2]

What access situations are you likely to encounter if you cover the courts regularly? Grand jury hearings and judges' deliberations generally are closed to the public and to the media. As a rule, trials are open to the public unless compelling reasons merit closing these public proceedings.

Judges also have the power to control the activities and statements of attorneys and witnesses involved in a particular case. On occasion, when a judge is concerned about pretrial publicity and how it might affect a defendant's right to a fair trial, *gag orders* can be issued. These directives forbid reporters to use certain information or testimony presented in court. Although a higher court can overturn most gag orders, this decision often comes too late for the reporter to use the restricted information. Judges cannot restrict access to court documents or records considered a part of the public record. This is discussed later in this chapter.

Cameras and microphones are allowed in some trial and appellate courts and in some government buildings, but not routinely in federal courts and federal buildings. Several conditions are often imposed in states where cameras and microphones are allowed in courtrooms. For example, pool coverage is used to avoid cluttering the courtroom and distracting witnesses or the jury with excessive equipment; jury members must not be shown on camera; the presiding judge authorizes coverage on a case-by-case basis. Many states restrict broadcast coverage of particular cases or classes of witnesses.

News personnel may be held in contempt of court for disregarding or disobeying court directives or for using material that tends to ridicule the court or obstruct justice in some way. Contempt of court charges can be filed in federal or state courts and usually carry a fine, a jail sentence, or both.

Federal Freedom of Information (FOI) Act

The federal Freedom of Information Act establishes a procedure for obtaining access to government documents and restricts the government's right to withhold documents from the public. The FOI Act allows the government to restrict access to certain kinds of information, including properly classified documents, files from ongoing criminal investigations, and personnel and medical files. Disputes are settled in court.[3]

State Open Records and Open Meetings Laws

Every state has statutes governing public access to records and meetings. The provisions of these *sunshine laws* vary from state to state.

Open or public records laws generally specify the rights of the general public and the news media to inspect and copy specific kinds of documents and records from specified agencies or commissions. Such laws also indicate the penalties imposed if such access is denied.

Open meetings laws usually indicate the public's access to various kinds of public body activities and documents, such as agendas and minutes; the meanings of key words like *meeting* and *public body;* how advance notice of a meeting is given; when closed sessions are permitted; and the legal penalties for violating provisions of such laws.[4]

Copyright

You will probably write a news story one day that will require the use of a particular photograph or an excerpt from a motion picture for a movie review or an obit of a famous entertainer. When a local player or team receives special recognition late in the year, you might want to use excerpts from a special sports documentary broadcast earlier in the season. Or you might want to use spot news coverage that another broadcast facility provides. All of these situations involve copyright regulations and the need to obtain permission to use copyrighted material.

The copyright law has many facets. Only those that apply directly to routine broadcast spot news coverage are discussed here. Practically all works fixed in tangible form, such as newscasts, news wire copy, newspapers, and magazines, are protected from the moment of creation until 50 years after the death of the author. ''The author'' could be an individual as well as a company.

Permission to use copyrighted material must be obtained from the owner of the copyrighted material. The two most common exceptions to this requirement are material in the *public domain* and *fair use,* which is a complex legal doctrine allowing use of copyrighted material under specific conditions. A work is in the public domain if it was never copyrighted or if the copyright has expired. For works published prior to 1978, copyrighted material loses its protection after 75 years. Material more than 75 years old is now in the public domain. U.S. government publications are generally in the public domain and may be photocopied or reproduced without permission. However, these materials may contain copyrighted material from other sources. Consult an attorney if either the fair use or public domain exceptions are used.

How can the situations suggested earlier be handled? Syndicated news services and networks often provide excerpts from new theatrical releases for on-air movie reviews and edited highlights from older movies for use in obits. Motion picture production companies can provide publicity photographs and news releases. Generally, copyright clearances have been obtained for individual station use of this material.

You will need permission to use material already broadcast. If the sports excerpt you want is from one of your company's broadcasts, verbal permission from the documentary producer is probably all that is required. But if you need material prepared by another source such as a station, network, or even individuals who might have recorded material with their own equipment, you should obtain written permission. Generally, oral consent is satisfactory until confirmed in writing. Video piracy is a growing problem for radio and television news operations, mostly due to unauthorized use of satellite-delivered material. If a station broadcasts game highlights from another station, crediting and having permission from the source station may not be enough. One of the stations should have a copyright license from the sports team or league that permits such further showing on the second station.

Permission is not needed to rebroadcast the signals of stations originating emergency communications under an emergency broadcasting system (EBS) plan. Permission is also not needed before using National Weather Service messages, to which special identification requirements apply, or Citizens Band (CB) and amateur radio messages.

Section 315

Broadcasters face several special obligations and responsibilities regarding political broadcasts. News stories, documentaries, investigative reports, and other broadcasts often use material that features political candidates.[5]

Section 315 (a) of the Communications Act of 1934 indicates that

> no station licensee is required to permit the use of its facilities by any legally qualified candidate for public office [except for federal elective office], but if any licensee shall permit any such candidate to use its facilities, it shall afford equal opportunities to all other candidates for that office to use such facilities. Such licensee shall have no power of censorship over the material broadcast by any such candidate. Appearance by a legally qualified candidate on any (i) bona fide newscast, (ii) bona fide news interview, (iii) bona fide news documentary (if the appearance of the candidate is incidental to the presentation of the subject covered by the news documentary), or (iv) on-the-spot coverage of bona fide news events (including, but not limited to political conventions and activities incidental thereto) shall not be deemed to be use of a broadcast station [under provision of these regulations].

Thus, routine spot news coverage is exempt from Section 315 requirements. Candidate debates and news conferences are exempt from Section 315 obligations as long as the format of such debates is adversarial (i.e., no candidate has free rein to advance his or her candidacy). Section 315 exemptions apply even if such events are not covered live or in their entirety. *Special* programming such as call-in shows and town meetings could trigger equal opportunity obligations. Even news interviews could necessitate following Section 315 requirements unless they (1) are part of regularly scheduled and well-established program series, (2) follow a question-and-answer or interview format and do not blatantly advance an individual's candidacy, and (3) are controlled in content and participant selection by your newsroom or station. The *program,* not the interview itself, qualifies for the exemption provided in Section 315.

The Fairness Doctrine

On August 4, 1987, the Federal Communications Commission (FCC) voted to eliminate the fairness doctrine, which had imposed an obligation on broadcasters to address "controversial issues of public importance" and afford reasonable response time to parties with significant contrasting viewpoints. Thus, broadcasters are no longer *required* to follow fairness doctrine requirements. At this writing, the FCC decision is on appeal in the courts. Also, attempts to codify the doctrine are under way in Congress. Responsible journalistic practice as well as financial good sense have retained both the appearance and the reality of fairness and balance in the majority of news broadcasts.

Several other fairness-related aspects of broadcasting, specified in the fairness doctrine, do not apply to newscasts, news interviews, and on-the-spot news coverage, which constitute the focus of this book.

The Federal Communications Commission (FCC) still enforces the *personal attack rule,* which requires generally that response time be offered on a station when a person's honesty, character, or integrity is attacked on-the-air during the discussion of a controversial issue of public importance. Although editorials and documentaries are not exempt from the personal attack rule, bona fide news interviews, on-the-spot coverage of news events, and newscasts are exempt from the personal attack rule.

Pressure groups and citizens committees continue to lobby for more opportunities to influence what appears on radio and television sets around the country. Be conscious of these efforts, and track the legislation that will alter some of the specific information contained in this chapter.

Summary

This chapter reviewed rules and regulations as well as rights and privileges that affect the routine work of the broadcast journalist. Topics included libel; privacy; protecting sources; access; copyright; Section 315; and the fairness doctrine. Broadcast journalists must know current federal and state laws that apply to common news coverage situations. Qualified attorneys should answer intricate legal questions.

Only basic principles of *libel law* were explained: essential elements needed for libel to occur; precautions necessary to avoid libel problems; and defenses to use if a libel suit develops.

Four categories of activities associated with *invasion of privacy* were examined: intrusion; public disclosure of private facts; false light; and misappropriation. Special attention was given to potential privacy problems caused by use of telephone calls, electronic eavesdropping, and file footage.

The *protection of sources* (as determined by subpoenas, newsroom searches, and state shield laws) was also examined. The contents of the Privacy Protection Act of 1980 were reviewed.

Attention was given to *access rights* at disaster and crime scenes; for certain categories of routine coverage as determined by voluntary guidelines; as influenced by fair-trial/free-press concerns about access to courtrooms and court records; and as determined by the federal Freedom of Information Act and state "sunshine laws," open records and open meetings laws.

The chapter concluded with a review of *copyright, Section 315,* and *fairness doctrine* requirements.

Be vigilant and sensitive in news coverage situations that could provoke legal problems. Know your responsibilities and obligations as well as your rights and privileges as a journalist.

Exercises

1. Provide a one-page summary of your state's laws or regulations concerning one of the following: libel; privacy; open records; open meetings; newsroom searches; protecting news sources; cameras and microphones in courtrooms. Sources to use to gather the necessary information include the reference section of a public library, a local law library, or the clerk of your state legislature or supreme court.

2. Rewrite as a 20-second radio or television reader report, the following news release delivered personally to you in your newsroom by Rodney Bankston, a deputy sheriff in your local sheriff's department. Bankston says that all of the facts are correct but admits that he probably added a few personal comments about the case and about the accused. He says he knows that you will "clean up the news release to avoid any potential legal problems." Here is the news release you receive:

John Chambers, 24, of this city, killer of a local retired couple, faces trial tomorrow for his crime in district court. He will be arraigned on murder charges. He apparently murdered Mr. and Mrs. Charles Trent last July while robbing them in their home at 84–84 Trendwood Lane, this city.

Investigators have said that Chambers was vicious in killing the pair. A coroner's report states that Mrs. Trent, 74, was stabbed 19 times with an ice pick. Mr. Trent, 76, died of multiple head wounds likely inflicted by Chambers with a fry pan.

This cold-blooded killer is not expected to have an easy time of it before a jury. This crook's life story is one of crime and anti-social behavior. After two years in a reformatory, law enforcement officials in this state say that this deadbeat graduated to the "big time" and served five years for robbing a milk truck driver of $14.21. This ex-convict's employment record is rather spotty. Past employers have labeled Chambers "a slacker." Chambers was arrested last July 25 at the Torrid Sheik Drive-In (this city), where this bum worked as a dishwasher.

Mr. Chambers may soon learn that crime does not pay when a jury evaluates his repeated claims of innocence.

Notes

1. The National Association of Broadcasters has prepared a 60-minute videotape, "Staying Out of the Libel Stew," and offers a booklet, *The Journalist's Handbook on Libel and Privacy.* Both are available through the NAB Publications Department, 1771 N Street, N.W., Washington, DC 20036.

2. Tony Mauro, "Use It or Lose It," *Communicator* 47, no. 8 (August 1993): 9–11; and "Cameras Banned from Federal Courts," *Broadcasting & Cable* (September 26, 1994): 7.

3. An excellent step-by-step guide for filing FOI Act requests (*A Citizen's Guide on Using the Freedom of Information Act and the Privacy Act of 1974 to Request Government Documents*) is available from either of these sources: The House (of Representatives) Document Room, H226, The Capitol, Washington, DC 20515 (ask for House Report 100–199); or The Superintendent of Documents, U.S. Government Printing Office, Washington, DC 20402 (the GPO stock number is 052–071–00752–1 and the price is $1.75 per copy).

For easy-to-use summaries of laws concerning newsgathering issues, contact the Reporters Committee for Freedom of the Press, Suite 504, 1735 Eye St., NW, Washington, DC 20006 (202/466–6313).

A videotape entitled "The First Amendment: A Journalist's Guide to Freedom of Speech" is available from: American Bar Association, Commission on Public Understanding About the Law, 541 N. Fairbanks Court, Chicago, IL 60611 (312/988–5745). The tape reviews basic definitions and illustrations of such topics as libel, privacy, free trial versus fair press privileges.

4. To obtain a copy of any state's open meetings/open records laws, send $5 with a request for the *Tapping Officials' Secrets* volume for that state to the Reporters Committee for Freedom of the Press, Suite 504, 1735 Eye St., NW, Washington, DC 20006 (202/466–6313).

5. A comprehensive treatment of Section 315 as well as the fairness doctrine is in the latest edition of *Political Broadcast Catechism,* available from the National Association of Broadcasters, 1771 N Street, NW, Washington, DC 20036.

Chapter 20

Ethics and Judgment

Ethics in journalism is not just deciding between two choices, right and wrong, when facing an ethical dilemma. True ethical decision making is much more difficult and complex. It's about developing a range of acceptable actions and choosing from among them. It's about considering the consequences of those actions. And it's about basing decisions on obligation, on the principles of the journalist's duty to the public. True ethical decision making is also about public justification, the ability to explain clearly and fully the process of how and why decisions are made.[1]

Whereas laws and regulations stipulate what a journalist *must* do, ethics can provide essential moral principles or values that form rules of conduct or behavior for what a journalist *should* or *might* do. Essentially, one's ethics represent one's views of right and wrong.

Why be concerned about ethics? The author presupposes that you have or will develop pride in your craft and care about your work as a journalist— to make what you do more meaningful and significant to the audience, the ones that you serve. That kind of professional spirit and commitment requires a well-defined set of ethical guidelines and standards. Acquiring and maintaining a sense of professional ethics will help convert the job of reporter to the craft and profession of the journalist.

Awareness of ethical concerns and issues is the first step in resolving sensitive situations in a fair, truthful, accurate, compassionate, and responsible manner. Ethical guidelines can help a journalist resolve moral dilemmas with speed and certainty. No time is available to debate ethical values in the heat of intense news coverage, under deadline pressure. *Now* is an ideal time to assess key ethical issues and concerns.

As noted in the preface of this book, you should not infer from the placement of this discussion of ethical concerns and situations that ethics should be your last concern as a journalist. Indeed, they should be your *first* concern. The discussion in this chapter will probably be more meaningful now that you have spent some time wrestling with the coverage and writing of news stories.

Ethical concerns and practices can be viewed from several levels, perspectives, or vantage points. *Professional ethics* influence your work as a journalist. These are suggested by the codes of ethics or conduct that professional news associations and organizations recommend (see Appendix B). Newsrooms often provide written guidelines and policies as well as rules of conduct and decision-making processes to be followed in certain kinds of newsgathering situations; these may involve ethics. Some of these situations and guidelines received attention in previous chapters. *Personal ethics* probably are the most meaningful, since they are rules that you impose on yourself and that influence you personally on a regular basis, regardless of your job or responsibilities.

Ethical principles and standards may be applied universally or situationally. *Universal* application is done without regard for specific situations. *Situational* application is done based on a particular set of circumstances. Universal or constant application offers a secure ethical foundation or framework for the journalist, but it is difficult to establish and maintain. Situational ethical applications may be more realistic, because they provide the flexibility needed in broadcast newsgathering.

Many factors influence ethical standards, including the quality and level of your professional experiences, relationships, and influences, as well as those factors based on your education and association with family members and friends.

Some of the ethical concerns and questions examined in this chapter may be considered unique to broadcast journalism. Most are common to all forms of journalism and are independent of technological changes and practices. The main topics in this chapter are *responsibilities and privileges* associated with political coverage, use of rumors, allegations and embargoes, the need to monitor taste and decorum, and the problems posed by misrepresentation by news personnel; *conflicts of interest* as exemplified in concerns about a journalist's civic involvement, opportunities for outside employment, and advertising pressures that may influence news judgments; *impartiality of coverage* as threatened by manipulated news coverage, use of "spin doctors" and "checkbook journalism," and acceptance of gifts and special privileges; and the *ethics of confidentiality and privacy* as applied to the use of information that identifies crime and accident victims and juveniles in news stories. Many of these topics interrelate and sometimes present overlapping, often conflicting concerns. Often it seems that there are more questions to ask than answers to give. The exercises at the end of the chapter will help you to better identify and resolve typical situations involving both ethics and broadcast news coverage.[2]

Personal viewpoints inevitably filter into the comments and suggestions offered here. However, the intention is not to impose rigid personal ethical standards. The comments contained in this chapter are intended to *guide* you, to help you identify and consider several common but very important situations in which personal and professional ethics are involved. A variety of viewpoints and solutions are presented for several perplexing ethical concerns and situations that may influence the daily work of the broadcast journalist.[3]

Each reporter must follow his or her own conscience when resolving conflicts involving ethics. These conflicts and the resultant decisions are not always clear-cut. Not every journalist will make the same decision. Make the decision that you honestly believe is the best for all involved. The way that you respond to ethical situations will say a lot about the kind of person you are and the kind of journalist you are or hope to become. No one can impose on you a concern or interest in ethics. And only you can determine how ethics will influence your reporting and writing talents.

Responsibilities and Privileges

Responsibilities are attached to the privileges that journalists enjoy. Some of the ethical concerns associated with these opportunities are examined in the following sections.

Political Coverage

Political coverage often evokes ethical concerns. How do you keep potential voters informed about a candidate's background and yet not invade a candidate's privacy? How close should a candidate get to the reporters covering his or her campaign? What, if any, concerns are raised by journalists who openly admit that they bring noticeable biases to their political coverage?

Should voting results be announced and winner projections be made before all polls close? Does releasing results early prejudice or even preclude further voting before all polls close? Resolving these kinds of dilemmas is usually difficult.[4]

Rumors and Allegations

Rumors and allegations about politicians as well as others must be handled with care and restraint. Not only are legal rights involved in such situations but ethical principles as well.

Remember to maintain initial presumption of innocence of the accused. Collect solid evidence of fact from multiple sources—people as well as documents and records—*before* you either confirm or reject rumors and allegations. Too much is at stake to do otherwise.

Embargoes

An *embargoed* story is one that is held until an agreed upon or specified time. On the surface, this does not appear to pose any ethical concern. Most newsrooms abide by embargoes because they are generally arbitrary release times for noncontroversial material.

But what happens when controversy is involved? Should you release embargoed information if it affects a majority of your audience, especially when you can get the same information from other sources that do not insist on an embargo? Should you take a chance on releasing such important information even if it means ''burning'' a reliable news source that you might need in the future? Should a journalist be concerned about the *reason* an embargo is imposed? Should this make any difference in determining whether or not to abide by the embargo?

Occasionally embargoes are self-imposed by journalists or their supervisors. Some have delayed for a time the use of footage of police brutality in hopes that an already volatile situation would not erupt into further violence that would endanger lives and property. Others facing the same decision might recommend showing all the footage that you could, in hopes that it would demonstrate an urgent and dangerous situation that could cause further injuries and property damage.

Taste and Decorum

Providing uniform guidelines for decisions about the use of material that may be considered offensive to a substantial portion of an audience is difficult. Sometimes morbid or sensationalistic details are used to "hype," or inflate, the value of a story. Generally, the more newsworthy the event or situation, the more understandable and acceptable the use of potentially offensive words, pictures, and references. Be guided by local tastes and standards as well as your best judgment about what is appropriate and acceptable.

A journalist may have to approach some situations with extra measures of sensitivity and compassion for the feelings of others. Should you show a drowning victim being pulled from a lake? Is it all right to shove microphones, lights, and cameras into the faces of grieving parents who may have just witnessed the drowning or shooting death of a child and ask their reaction to what they have just seen, heard, and felt? Should your personal or your professional ethics guide your decisions about handling such situations? Would the coverage requirements of your news department influence your decision? How do you balance the right to privacy with the public's right to know and be informed? Where do you, or can you, draw the line?

Some reporters dismiss concerns for compassion on the basis that aggressiveness produces more competitive, interesting, and intense stories that satisfy the audience's needs. Competitive demands do complicate the resolution of ethical issues!

Misrepresentation

Truth, accuracy, objectivity, and credibility are only some of the many hallmarks of reputable journalism. Misrepresentation of situations and events can threaten these honorable principles.

File footage should be labeled as such. Avoid creating the false impression that the scenes shown were shot today when, in fact, they were not.

Identify material that sources outside your newsroom supplied. Such sources include other stations, government agencies, and congressional delegations. Your audience should know the sources of the information that you use.

Are there times when you can or should shield your identity as a reporter? Journalistic "sting" operations, in which reporters often hide their identity in hopes of acquiring more newsworthy information, have been justified on the basis that the information gathered could not have been obtained in any other way and that, in the end, the public good will be better served in some significant way. The argument certainly could be made that sources deserve to know who you are and what you might do with what they say or provide. Some reporters insist on making it clearly understood that *anything anyone* says or does might be used in a news story at any time. On occasion, reporters have spoiled friendships and close associations when they do not make it known that they are journalists *all the time!*

Keep stories in perspective. Report what happens, but try to place issues and events into context. Show the small group of protestors on the sidewalk, but also show the larger scene to indicate that most passersby showed disinterest and that less than ten protestors were there, not a mob of hundreds as the use of only close-up shots might have implied.

Despite your efforts to not misrepresent the facts of a story, sometimes determining the result of your reporting efforts is difficult. For example, will showing the results of vandalism in local public schools encourage or discourage this criminal activity? Would you be providing undue publicity to vandals who cost taxpayers thousands of dollars when they destroyed hundreds of tree limbs overnight on public property? Would antiwildlife advocates be receiving extra attention if you showed what happened to an endangered bird that was nailed to a tree next to a sign advertising the proper way to watch the birds' annual migration through the area?

Misrepresentation might also result from the distortion that such techniques as omitting or re-creating natural or location sound in a radio actuality cause. If thunderous applause occurred after a significant statement heard on tape, even a brief portion of that applause should be heard after such an actuality to give listeners some perspective about the response to that statement. Be honest with your audience and with yourself about the material that you use.

Conflicts of Interest

Conflicts of interest impair the objectivity, fairness, and accuracy expected of professional journalists. Conflicts of interest can evolve for many reasons and in many kinds of circumstances.

Citizen versus Journalist

Here is a dilemma that most people working in news face: How do you get involved in community activities so that you do not become an isolated, elitist reporter, and at the same time avoid creating conflicts of interest in which your community ties interfere with or unduly influence the way you do your job as a professional journalist? Is it possible to be active in your community and still avoid conflicts of interest as a journalist? Where do your rights and responsibilities as a citizen end and your duties and obligations as a journalist begin?

The solution to the dilemma may be to acknowledge the requirements and restrictions of your journalistic responsibilities and then try to carefully balance these with the civic or community commitments and obligations you may accept voluntarily or that station or newsroom management require you to consider accepting.

A potential conflict may also arise because of sexual, gender, or racial orientation. Two perspectives are represented by the way journalists are assigned stories. One perspective is to assign journalists with the *same* affiliation or orientation as those involved in the story; thus, black journalists would cover sensitive conflicts surrounding the local black community and gay reporters would cover gay events. The other perspective is to *not* assign journalists with the same viewpoints as those who are covered in the story; thus, men are assigned to cover events surrounding women's rights issues and white reporters are assigned to stories that take them into the black community. The perspective or approach that you accept depends on whether you believe that reporters having specific, shared insights as those people covered in the story will provide an objective, fair, and balanced report. The choice depends, to some extent, on the nature of the story and the maturity and life experiences of the reporter assigned.

Outside Employment

It is an unfortunate reality that those in journalism often find it necessary to work part-time at additional jobs to make financial ends meet. Much of this additional work involves using journalistic skills, talents, and contacts. A potential conflict of interest may develop when outside employment or business activities challenge, impair, obstruct, or unduly influence a journalist's responsibilities to provide news stories that are fair, objective, and balanced.

Many journalists contend that no conflict of interest occurs when they research, write, and narrate programs for nonprofit and civic organizations. But a conflict of interest might be suspected when you offer (even part-time) the same journalistic talents to governmental agencies or even more specialized employers, like hospitals and schools, and yet continue to cover stories originating from the same sources that provide extra income to you. In such a situation, keeping your two employment obligations and responsibilities separate would be difficult. You may have to eliminate outside employment to maintain minimum ethical standards of journalistic conduct.

The appropriateness of news personnel becoming actively involved in various kinds of commercial activities is an issue that still generates heated debate. Such involvement could include working as the talent for commercial messages on-the-air as well as in other advertising media; testimonials and endorsements for products, services, industries, companies, and causes, even nonpartisan causes; and personal appearances and writings. Most journalists contend that the integrity of news requires that journalists avoid being tainted by commercialization in any way. Others argue that news personnel should be expected to do their part to attract more revenue to the newscast in which they work and earn their living.

Competition to capture available advertising dollars pushes some in broadcasting to try to compromise the sensitive position of the newsroom and the need to maintain credibility, objectivity, fairness, and so forth. In some commercial broadcast stations managers, sales executives, and others in and out of the newsroom exert noticeable pressure to merge the concerns and eventually the activities of news and advertising. Other facilities establish policies against sales department interference with newsroom practices and priorities.

The logical connection between news and advertising in a commercial broadcast station should be recognized. Advertising provides the revenue needed for news operations. News personnel report on issues, events, and people that affect business activities, especially *local* business activities.

Also, remember that in most towns a broadcast station is a part (usually an active, major part) of the *local* business community through promotion of community improvement programs, projects, and so on. Legitimate concern exists that a current or prospective advertising client be shown in a positive light on a station's newscasts. The station manager will encounter advertising clients at local social gatherings or meetings, for example, and be expected to respond to criticisms about his or her station's news coverage, especially as it relates to the *local* business community.

What kinds of advertising demands might news personnel encounter? Perhaps an advertiser will request you to withhold a story that places the advertising client, your community, or even your employer in a negative light. Perhaps you will be asked to cover a story that is not truly newsworthy (a "puff piece") and only pleasing to the advertising client who requested the coverage. In some newsrooms, refusing to do such stories or doing a noticeably weak job on such assignments results in a reprimand and, in a few cases, loss of employment.

Follow *legitimate* news developments *wherever* they lead. Self-serving puffery often causes an undesirable chain reaction to develop: The news department cannot cover *real* news when reporting such puff pieces; eventually your audience will become suspicious if such "light" stories are peppered throughout *all* newscasts; finally, your audience will turn elsewhere for credible news coverage. This shift could result in loss of audience, a drop in ratings, and a resultant decline in advertising support; ultimately, money is lost!

Here are a few ways to help resolve dilemmas arising from conflicts of interest caused by various kinds of community involvement, personal affiliations, employment activities, and advertising pressures:

   a. Monitor judiciously your civic activities and business
      relationships. Avoid even the appearance of a conflict. Your
      journalistic credibility is too valuable.
   b. Do not place yourself in a compromising position. For example,
      do not agree to manage the political campaign of a local candidate
      (even if a longtime friend) while assigned to cover that same

political campaign. And do not write news releases for a local hospital or medical facility (even part-time) if the health beat is your current assigned news beat.

c. Avoid being identified with a particular side in a controversy. Make an effort to present *all* sides of an important issue, no matter what your personal beliefs might be.

d. Do not cover stories in which you have a vested interest. Try to exchange stories with another reporter or get the day off.

e. If a conflict or potential conflict of interest becomes obvious, sever the relationship or activity and disqualify yourself from stories involving that conflict.

Remember that a conflict of interest is a conflict of interest no matter what amounts of money, time, products, or services are involved. A high level of personal and professional integrity is required to acknowledge that a conflict of interest has developed and then to have the courage to do something about the situation.

Impartiality of Coverage

Ethical reporting standards not only should encourage the formation of responsible attitudes and the avoidance of conflicts of interest but also should promote impartial coverage that is fair, objective, and as unbiased as possible.

Several reporting practices can impede impartial coverage: manipulation of news events that heighten or dramatize what happened; the use of "spin doctors," who generally provide biased viewpoints; payments ("checkbook journalism") to obtain facts and comments from prominent, reluctant, or elusive news sources; and acceptance of freebies and "perks" that may cloud or blur a journalist's responsibility to report news stories fairly and objectively.

Manipulating News Events

News coverage can be managed, controlled, or manipulated by altering or falsifying events and statements through techniques like staging and reenactments. Manipulation leads to distortion about what happened. Why might this be considered unethical? Is it sometimes acceptable, even helpful, to manipulate news coverage?

Do not cross the line separating the news observer and the active news event participant. Journalists observe, record, and report news events. They do not change, shape, or manipulate situations by staging events that never occurred or by re-creating events that reporters did not observe.

Staging events is not *always* unethical, however. Use good judgment and reasonableness. For example, having a Coast Guard boat make another pass near the dock when shooting a feature on holiday boat safety would be all right. And it would be acceptable to ask someone to walk through a door again to get cutaways, reverse angle shots, or just better shots to use in a story.

Some simulations or reenactments are useful. They can help viewers understand the sequence of events in an important robbery-murder case or get a long-winded state senator to rephrase and abbreviate a key statement that took several minutes to record. But use these techniques sparingly and *cautiously*—when actual sounds or pictures from a news scene are not available, and when a simulation or reenactment might clarify the story you are trying to tell. Make it very clear to the audience, by the way the reenactment is introduced and used, that a simulation of the event is being broadcast and that the reenactment is an accurate reproduction of the original event.

Professional journalists would never intrude into a story and attempt, for example, to manipulate news developments by asking street gang members to destroy property or injure someone just to capture the scene on tape for a story about increasing crime rates in the city. Waiting for protestors to call friends to come carry protest signs before recording interviews about the nature and scope of a local labor protest would also be inappropriate.

At times, legitimate news coverage leads to a manipulation of events. For example, the presence of bright lights and news cameras has been known to transform a peacefully assembled crowd into a more active, potentially dangerous mob. Just pointing lights and microphones into the face of a frightened hostage just released from a captor alters, in some way, the natural course of events and can influence the behavior of those involved. Some reporters keep equipment and even themselves out of sight until a volatile situation can be assessed and a plan of action finalized.

Spin Doctors

During political campaigns, reporters often turn to what are called *spin doctors* for comments and opinions. These current or former politicians, their associates, and even acquaintances provide a highly partisan "spin," an unflappable optimism and none of the absolute truth reporters say that they seek about the candidates, issues, and events in a political campaign.

In recent national political campaigns, candidates have often avoided reporters' questions by targeting friendly audiences assembled in smaller, more intimate town hall meetings. In such a friendly setting, easier, less controversial topics can easily replace tough campaign issues and questions.

Checkbook Journalism

Should you ever pay for news material? Some contend that paying for *any* information or opinion makes that source and that information-gathering process suspect. In addition, opponents insist that *checkbook journalism* seriously jeopardizes the credibility of a news organization and could distort the quality and value of the information provided.

Other journalists believe that payment may be appropriate in some circumstances. Situations often judged acceptable include paying informants and others who provide liaison or information services for news stories, although some news organizations insist that these paid sources be identified as paid consultants if their comments or information are used on-the-air; paying prominent or even nonpublic experts in specialties such as economics and foreign relations who may not be available unless paid; paying for access to newsworthy events such as telethons and fund-raising concerts; and paying for private home movies or videotapes of events such as tornadoes and plane crashes.

Payments for access to news material may not necessarily ensure a particular type or level of coverage. If you start paying news sources for their information, audiences may begin to suspect potential bias or lack of objectivity in general news coverage as well as coverage of the specific news event for which payment was offered. Think about the potential consequences when considering paying for the material used in news stories.

Freebies, Perks, and Privileges

Most newsrooms pay whatever costs are associated with gathering the news—the equipment, transportation, even housing and food if needed.

Some journalists do not think that accepting certain gifts and favors endangers their journalistic integrity. They contend that it is appropriate to accept a free lunch while covering a speech, to accept free passes to a theater performance or other event if you will be reviewing the presentation, and to ride with other media representatives in a vehicle leased by a candidate's campaign committee, even if the reporter is covering that same candidate.

Freebies and perks are given for a reason, the same reason journalists should refuse to accept them—to obligate reporters to news sources in the hope of obtaining at least some coverage or of obtaining more favorable coverage than planned or expected. Freebies, perks, and privileges have become a serious ethical problem when you find yourself giving a second thought to calling a certain source that has been especially generous or being very careful about how a certain story is written in an effort not to offend someone you like.

Do not compromise your journalistic independence, integrity, and responsibilities. Do not make yourself and your work suspect by accepting anything of value from someone who may be involved in a news story you may cover.

The Ethics of Confidentiality and Privacy

Shield laws as well as regulations governing the use of subpoenas and newsroom searches were described in Chapter 19. Chapter 10 outlined *techniques* used to provide confidentiality, anonymity, and privacy to news sources. The *ethical considerations* surrounding such actions also need attention.

Crime and Accident Victims

Almost all newsrooms withhold the names of those who have died until the identity of each victim is confirmed and relatives are notified. Many newsrooms have decided not to use the names or addresses of *any* crime victims—not just the names of sex, murder, and suicide victims or their families. One newsroom decided not to identify robbery victims in any way to avoid encouraging other robberies of the *same* victims![5]

Be compassionate and become sensitized to the information that you process routinely. Delay using a crash story until all essential information, such as the flight number, train destination, or identity of all victims in the car, has been confirmed. If such a story touched your life, you would expect and appreciate the same kind of careful attention to accuracy and consideration.

Most newsrooms have special policies for handling stories involving juvenile crime. These WMAR-TV guidelines are followed in most newsrooms:

Juveniles

> Normally, we don't mention the names of juveniles accused of crimes nor do we show their pictures. However, when a juvenile is involved in a particularly brutal crime the state will often petition the court to try the alleged offender as an adult. In these instances, we show pictures and mention names.[6]

The journalist must resolve a common conflict surrounding the ethics of providing confidentiality and privacy—the duty to inform the public about people and events it needs to know about versus the responsibility to protect the vulnerable and comfort the afflicted in times of great personal sorrow and loss. A sense of humanity and caring *can* be a part of a professional journalist's code of ethics.

Summary

This chapter explored some of the ethical concerns that broadcast journalists face regularly: *responsibilities and privileges* associated with political coverage, the use of rumors, allegations, and embargoes, the need to monitor taste and decorum, and misrepresentation by news personnel; *conflicts of interest* that may develop due to a journalist's civic contacts, personal associations and involvements, opportunities for outside employment, and advertising pressures that may influence news judgments; *impartiality of coverage* that is impeded by manipulated news coverage, use of spin doctors and checkbook journalism, and acceptance of gifts and special privileges; and the *ethics of confidentiality and privacy* as applied to the use of information that identifies crime and accident victims and juveniles in news stories.

No code or set of ethical standards and guidelines can apply to every newsgathering situation. Common sense and good judgment, based on sound professional experience and education, are required to apply key ethical principles and standards to each reporting situation.

Following an ethical course of action is not always the easiest, most pleasant, or popular course to take. But applying ethical standards wisely to your work as a journalist will lead to increased satisfaction for you and your audience.

Exercises

1. Develop a written statement of your personal code of ethics that you plan to follow as a professional journalist. Include at least five key principles.

2. A news source that you have found reliable in the past tells you that the new director of the state health department will begin making surprise inspections of local restaurants. Your source asks you to withhold using this information until inspections actually begin. Would you withhold using this story? Would you include this story in the next newscast? What, if any, ethical considerations and implications are involved in resolving this situation?

3. Soon after you become news director, one of your reporters discovers that for several months, some varsity football players at a major local university have received free personal use of new automobiles from a local dealer. The reporter has taped interviews with two players in which they admit having accepted free use of the cars and another taped interview with the dealer admitting that all he wanted to do was "help in any way that I can to recruit and hold good players for the team."

While the reporter is in your office pressuring you to run this exclusive story involving a serious NCAA violation your general manager calls and says he has heard from the president of the university's citizen support group as well as from the school's sports information director. The general manager says that both callers know the station has this sensitive and potentially damaging information. They ask that the story *not* be run at this time out of consideration for the many years of close cooperation between your station and the university, especially in light of your station's exclusive rights to broadcast all football games of this university for the next three years.

What do you do? Do you run the story now? Wait for the O.K. from the university or the sports information director or the general manager? Do you wait to see if other stations in the market run it? What do you tell your boss if you *do* run it? What do

you tell your reporter (and other journalists working in your newsroom) if you do *not* run it? And what will you tell *yourself* about your decision when you drive home from work today?

4. While working on an in-depth report about the increase in local crimes affecting children you find a court document filed two months ago. The document indicates that a principal at a local elementary school was charged with child molestation. This principal just recently resigned from this local school and withdrew from the education or school board race that will be decided next Tuesday. Although the former principal has already been arraigned on the child molestation charges, there has been no trial yet and certainly no conviction. If not already known in the community, would you reveal the child molestation charges? Why?

5. You have collected information about this morning's supreme court ruling denying a local man's request to have the court overturn his conviction for incest. As you are preparing the first draft of the story, the man's former wife calls you and asks that you kill the story or at least not use her former husband's name. She says the local community already knows who he is and that the family does not need to experience unnecessary grief and turmoil again. You tell her you plan to run the story. As you fine-tune the final draft of the story, the man's son calls and says that his fiancée does not know about his father's conviction and recent appeal and adds that running a story about this latest court appeal will wreck his pending marriage and further erode his limited success at finding work in the area.

Do you run the story? Do you run the story, but not the name of the man convicted of incest? In your judgment, who is affected most by this story? The convicted man? His family? Your audience? Your newsroom?

What would you report if the man involved or one of his family members threatened or followed through with suicide threats?

(Note: Recommended solutions or responses for many of the ethical dilemmas presented in these exercises can be presented individually in writing or in groups using role-playing techniques in which individuals interact spontaneously. Each development would be dramatized extemporaneously and later analyzed in terms of ethical issues, considerations, alternatives, and decisions.)

Notes

1. Jay Black, Bob Steele, and Ralph Barney, *Doing Ethics in Journalism: A Handbook with Case Studies* (Greencastle, IN: The Sigma Delta Chi Foundation and The Society of Professional Journalists, 1993), 29.

2. Interesting contemporary ethical issues are reviewed in *FineLine,* a monthly newsletter on journalism ethics. Subscription information is available from *FineLine,* 600 East Main Street, Louisville, Kentucky 40202–9723.

   Real-life scenarios are presented in ''You Be the News Director,'' a traveling workshop presented around the country by Radio-Television News Directors Association members. For those who work in news, the sessions present opportunities to ''second-guess'' news decisions that others made. For those in radio or television who do not work in news, the videotape examples illustrate the difficult news decisions that field reporters and newsroom personnel often must face. For more information about these innovative workshops in ethics, write RTNDA, 1000 Connecticut Avenue, NW, Suite 615, Washington, DC 20036.

3. Broadcast newsrooms often handle ethical concerns, issues, and situations in customized policy and procedure manuals. Excerpts from several of these documents have been used throughout this book.

4. In 1990, CNN and the news divisions of ABC, CBS, and NBC agreed to pool their resources, share exit poll results, and provide uniform election winner projections. See *Electronic Media,* vol. 9, no. 10 (March 5, 1990): 4.

5. Two interesting cases may help you to examine the ethical question: Should victims be identified when the crime is sexual assault? The William Kennedy Smith rape trial is examined in several national publications, including: The *Communicator,* June 1991, pages 10–12. The public testimony of rape victim Nancy Ziegenmeyer is discussed in a variety of publications, including: *Time,* April 9, 1990, page 71, and in *The Des Moines Sunday Register,* April 1 and July 1, 1990.

6. ''News Policy,'' *Channel 2 News Stylebook* (Baltimore, MD: WMAR-TV, n.d.).

Careers

Television news may change more in the next five to seven years than it has in the past 50. The advent of 500 channel cable, the expansion and possibilities of video delivery by satellite, fiberoptic telecommunications, HDTV and interactive television all will have huge impacts on broadcast news careers.

—Phil Witt, News Anchor Senior Reporter, WDAF-TV, Kansas City[1]

The broadcasting news industry has changed over the last few decades. New technologies are evolving and challenging today's broadcast journalists. Opportunities in the field have diversified. Flexibility has become the watchword for broadcast journalists and the broadcast news industry. The *business* of broadcast news has responded to audience demands for quality, diversified material delivered in an efficient, convenient, cost-effective manner. The focus is on the intensely competitive and changing technological and economic marketplace of fiber optics, the broadcast-cable wars, FCC regulations, and the resultant effects on market share.

Demands have also intensified. Broadcast audiences want more flexibility in how they consume news and information. They want to participate in the selection and pursuit of broadcast news coverage. Although basic reporting and writing techniques generally have remained constant, new, more powerful and flexible delivery systems require broadcast news journalists who possess a variety of skills. The packaging of broadcast news material is evolving to meet a changing landscape of delivery systems and audience demands.

If you want to succeed in this challenging, ever-changing environment, you'll need some help. You'll need to know how to prepare for a broadcast news career, where to look for jobs, where to begin working, what to consider when job searching, and what steps you should take to land your first job in broadcast news. You'll need to determine the value of part-time and internship experience versus full-time employment. You'll also need to assess the current state of the industry and learn how to keep an eye on future developments to protect your job prospects.

Only the basics can be covered in this appendix. Career placement and planning centers, and personal academic and career advisers can supply details and help complete some of the steps recommended. Several working broadcast journalists have provided comments for this appendix; their newswriting and news reporting work is featured in other sections of this book. Each quotation is identified with the name and news affiliation of the contributor at the time each comment was received.

The Changing Broadcast News Industry

Generalizing about a career in broadcast news is difficult. The number of variables precludes offering specific suggestions that will be useful in every situation. Positions, titles, and job responsibilities vary from station to station. The route traveled through the job market is as varied as the number of people who begin the journey. Chapter 11 describes the principal jobs and responsibilities in the typical broadcast news operation as they relate to assigning, covering, writing, producing, and preparing stories for the air. Identifying specific job objectives and employment tactics will be easier after you review this information.

Trends

Several trends have affected jobs prospects in broadcast news. Ownership changes and federal deregulation of broadcasting have resulted in cutbacks in news staffs and budgets, and, in some cases, decreased emphasis on local news coverage. Local marketing agreements make it possible for corporations to own portions of several stations in the *same* market! Although this generally produces a steady flow of black ink, it also causes less money to be spent to sustain a strong commitment to local news coverage. This has also caused layoffs in news departments, particularly in radio news, and especially in small markets. In some markets, news has been labeled unprofitable and, thus, expendable. Some stations have decided to discontinue local news coverage. Some commercial broadcasting industry representatives are preoccupied with profits, ratings points, sophisticated delivery systems, and technological change. Radio and television news is a critical part of the broadcasting *business,* a business that must consider the bottom line—success, especially financial success. In most markets, local news is still a vital part of stations' operations and service to the local community.

Consultants, talent agents, and coaches have helped newsrooms respond to these regulatory and ownership changes. Advice on content, presentation, style, and appearance has helped newsrooms achieve higher ratings and justify deeper commitments to news operations.

Personnel Shifts

The job situation has changed in the last 15 to 20 years. Before cable systems and regional news operations began offering news broadcasts, young broadcast news professionals would identify and pursue a broadcast news career in a local radio or television station newsroom. Although that possibility still exists, the employment "window" is now much narrower.

Many news directors now want maturity—people over 35, with track records. They want not only good on-air performers but also reporters and anchors who know lots of things. Unfortunately, the pay for these enhancements has not also increased proportionally in the last few decades. Six-figure anchors and reporters are being replaced with younger employees who work for a lot less money.

Many broadcast news jobs and responsibilities have been consolidated. Reporters must now be prepared to also edit, process, and, often, air their news stories. Less people are doing more work for essentially the same or less pay. Although local television news operations kept growing in the early 1990s, the typical radio news staff looked about the same as it had for many years—about one and one-half staffers. Radio news staff size differed little by market size; more of the radio news coverage is handled by part-time rather than full-time personnel.[2]

Mutual Broadcasting System anchor Frank Gentry says job consolidation often produces job insecurity:

> The ease of radio format changes, coupled with management turmoil, almost guarantee job insecurity. Forced job changes can lead to all sorts of tensions in personal relationships and can leave you shuffling between temporary jobs at age 40 with no home equity or pension vesting . . . only a Lifetime Achievement Award from U-Haul. . . . Regardless of market size, this is almost never a very secure line of work.[3]

Salaries vary widely with the market size, type of station, skills that each applicant offers, and the requirements of each job. The pay tends to be short and the hours long. Expect modest pay during the first few years when you are gaining experience and developing your talents. However, opportunities for advancement generally exist either within a news operation or at another facility.

Here is the salary perspective offered by Barb Simon, News Producer at Gannett's KUSA-TV in Denver:

> Expect to take a vow of poverty, for a long time. My first job in Oklahoma City paid $5.25 an hour, in 1989. People who wait tables make more money! Don't get into the business if you want to make money, but look at the other "benefits" to the job—the opportunity to work with creative

Nan Siemer checks audio material before a newscast. Photo courtesy of Nan Siemer.

people, to make a difference in your community, to learn about your world and see it change before your eyes! The anchors who make six-figure salaries are the last of their kind. Stations are cutting back and more often than not, they will hire only for part-time work, so they don't have to pay benefits and they can have you work all kinds of schedules at their convenience.[4]

In markets of every size, print journalists earn more than television reporters, and much more than their radio counterparts. For example, in 1992 reporters averaged $21,000 at small-circulation daily newspapers, about $6,000 more than at small-market television stations in 1993. Only television anchors in major markets earn more than comparable print journalists. The disparity is expected to continue.[5]

Television and radio news operations lead daily newspapers in the employment of minority journalists. A 1992 survey by the American Society of Newspaper Editors found that 10.3 percent of all daily newsroom professionals were members of minority groups. That compares with 11.3 percent for radio and 18.5 percent for television news operations. Minority employment was highest in large markets, were minority populations tend to be concentrated. Black and Hispanic journalists have accounted for most of the increase in minority employment.[6]

The status of women in broadcast newsrooms has remained essentially unchanged for several years. In the early 1990s, women composed just over a third of all the news staff in television and just under a third in radio. Those shares have changed little since the mid-1980s.[7]

Despite this disappointing overview, women have made some progress in broadcast newsrooms. Nan Siemer of WTOP Radio in Washington, DC, believes women are making positive strides.

I find many are working harder than men to balance work and family lives, but I am also finding more and more women are successful at achieving this balance. While a change towards putting more women in management positions is a slow process, I believe there is some progress. Hopefully, as more women move into management, they will afford the women and men on their staffs equal opportunities.[8]

Ann Pedersen Gleson, Operations Director/News at WCCO-TV in Minneapolis, believes that

we have broken the ranks in every position at every level. If the position is a union position, the salaries are comparable to male counterparts. If the position is a personal service contract position, at least in my experience, the salaries are also comparable. The one area that I still believe there is a need for more women is in the area of news management and station management.[9]

Later in this appendix, Pedersen Gleson suggests the background needed for management positions.

Evolving Technologies and Delivery Systems

The technology revolution has had a noticeable impact on broadcast news operations. Sophisticated electronic tools have made the broadcast news reporter's job more complex as well as exciting. Digital audio and video equipment, cellular telephones, nonlinear video editing, laptop computers, fiber-optic transmissions to field and home locations, and electronic database systems are some of the technological enhancements now available in broadcast newsrooms.

Electronic news reports no longer originate only from local radio and television stations. Local and regional all-news cable channels have grown beyond the experimental stage and now compete with stations and newspapers for news audiences. Partnerships have formed between local newspapers and cable systems, and between local stations and cable systems. The result has been a consolidation of news staff duties and a repeat of local station newscasts on local cable systems. In some markets, early evening television newscasts are simulcast on local radio stations. Integration and consolidation of the news product has become part of the changes in the broadcast news business.

Qualifications

So why should you be attracted to this industry? What makes the broadcast journalist's work so enticing that you would be willing to overlook the dark clouds that hang over future job prospects and embrace this profession with all of the enthusiasm you have ever had for any undertaking? Barb Simon provided a few reasons earlier. This profession should be considered, however, for many other reasons.

The work of a broadcast journalist is interesting and challenging. It offers rewards, but it also requires dedication and commitment. It holds out the opportunity to influence the daily lives of many people but also requires a professional attitude and a sustained effort by those in the profession.

Broadcast journalists need specific skills. Some of these are developed with experience. Others are expected of any employee in a professional news operation. Many are simply the marks of a good employee in any job. Take an inventory of yourself as you read the following discussions of these qualifications.

Learn to write well. Writing is at the heart of a solid news operation. Your ability to write well often determines your success in this field. Good writing is at least as important as your ability to handle equipment associated with newsgathering. Kim Engebretsen, Senior Editor for CNN, emphasizes the importance of knowing how to write well: "It's a very basic foundation to so many jobs: reporting, producing, copyediting. I firmly believe that anyone with good writing skills can get their 'foot in the door' of so many media outlets."[10] Learn how to apply the basic rules of grammar and composition to broadcast news. Build on writing skills learned in other situations. Critically evaluate your writing each time you write a story.

Be curious about the world around you. You are in the communications business. Read newspapers daily, including local papers and a national daily newspaper of substance. Monitor radio and television newscasts on a regular basis. Stay informed about current events.

Acquire a broad liberal education. Show that you have the potential to learn and grow as a journalist because of the background and experience you have consciously acquired. What courses should you take? How should you prepare for your career in broadcast

WTAE-TV anchor/reporter
Sheila Hyland reports live
from Harrisburg at the
Pennsylvania Governor's
mansion. Photo courtesy of
Sheila Hyland and WTAE-
TV, Pittsburgh.

journalism? Here are the recommendations of a few professional broadcast journalists:

> If I were in college now, . . . I would diversify. Writing and communications skills are valuable in many fields. Basic courses on journalistic ethics are important. Basic science courses are helpful in many fields of journalism.
>
> —Kim Dlouhy, Agri-Service Director, WOW Radio, Omaha[11]

Study a wide range of subjects, especially political science and economics. Also familiarize yourself with the court system. Writing, writing, writing— is of the utmost importance. Take as many courses as you can! Practice makes (almost) perfect. I would try to have a specialty in one area— medicine, or political science, for instance, to give you an edge, and to allow you to develop that knowledge in someday becoming a beat reporter.

> —Sheila Hyland, News Anchor/Reporter, WTAE-TV, Pittsburgh[12]

Understand how the news operation functions and coordinates its efforts with other divisions within the broadcast facility. This will help you determine how your work meshes with that of others and also will give you insight into the objectives and policies of management. Each news organization has a distinctive organizational structure. However, newsrooms have essential similarities. If you want to move from broadcast news to management work, Ann Pedersen Gleson of WCCO-TV in Minneapolis advises that you acquire ''a broader understanding of the entire station, which could mean courses in other areas beyond broadcasting. More business classes should be required which would assist reporters in terms of reporting on what is currently a very hot beat . . . business, finance, and consumer reporting.''[13]

Know the capabilities and limitations of the equipment used in news production. For the broadcast journalist, equipment is one of the reporting tools used. Recorders, cameras, microphones, editing facilities, and so forth become an extension of the broadcast journalist's ability to mold and shape a story.

Develop the ability to capture the essence of a complicated story and then present the essential facts in a clear, concise, and interesting way. This helps the audience understand and digest what is presented. Todd Smith, a correspondent in the Washington News Bureau of Bonneville International Corporation, emphasizes that you should never be afraid to ask questions: "Know what your story is about. You can't write a good story unless you understand it. And you can't understand it unless you do a good job of reporting. That means asking questions and asking them again if you still don't understand something."[14]

Learn to work under pressure. Broadcast news deadlines are demanding and exacting. With experience, you will learn to grasp a complex idea quickly and without misinterpretation and then meet excruciating deadlines with consistent, professional, quality material. This requires rigorous discipline and personal commitment to your job, because distractions will always interrupt your focus at the most critical moments when you are developing a story.

Be versatile. There is a premium on a person who can report, write, and present a story on-the-air. Develop a reporting specialty, but remember to remain a generalist who can cover a variety of stories well without much extra preparation.

Become a self-starter who can take the initiative on a story with minimum supervision. You will need to be fast and efficient in your journalistic habits and to remain calm at all costs, even when it may seem that the world is falling in on you. Despite the pressures, remember to smile. It will lighten your load and the burdens of those around you.

Develop strong people skills. A good journalist likes people. They are the sources for the stories that you write. Listen to what people say, the concerns they express, the feelings they reveal, because these elements form the basis for your news stories.

Become tenacious. Learn to pursue a story until you know the crucial facts. If one source is uncooperative or shields necessary information, search for other sources until you acquire the information needed. Do not be satisfied with the preliminary information you gather. Learn to develop other possibilities to gather what you need to know.

Treat people fairly. Show consideration as well as empathy. Pursue a story aggressively, but remember to be considerate of those who supplied the information that you use. Kathryn Christensen, Senior Broadcast Producer and Managing Editor of "World News Tonight with Peter Jennings," suggests that you be fair: "Not just technically fair, fair in your heart. That means not taking advantage of the people you're dealing with, whether an ordinary citizen, a government official or the biggest crook you've ever met. Be aware of the impact, the power you have. Use it carefully. . . . Be mindful of your responsibilities."[15]

Learn to type reasonably well regardless of the system used to process your stories. All news copy is typed. Broadcast newsrooms are shifting from the use of standard typewriters to computerized word-processing systems.

Maintain good health and energy. You cannot function at full capacity if you suffer from poor health or lack of energy. The pace expected in broadcast news operations is too fast to allow for significant health problems. Broadcast news work requires physical and emotional stamina.

Learn the laws and regulations that influence how you cover and report stories. Broadcasting is a heavily regulated industry, filled with requirements and recommendations. You will need to know what is permitted and what is not, what is preferred and what is optional.

Exercise good judgment when covering stories. Respond in a calm, professional manner. Formulate sound ethical standards in advance, *before* events confront you.

Commit to professionalism. Your appearance, attitude, enthusiasm, mannerisms, and general decorum often will influence news sources more than your reporting ability. If you look, sound, and act like a professional, you will establish yourself as someone who cares enough to maintain professional standards. Professionalism also extends to how you conduct yourself as a news reporter. Demonstrate your dependability by being punctual and alert at all times. Develop a positive, cooperative attitude about your work. Be conscious of your physical appearance and attitude when on assignment and in the newsroom.

Demonstrate your personal commitment to broadcast news excellence by participating in professional news organizations. Two prominent groups are the Society of Professional Journalists and the Radio-Television News Directors Association. Both organizations strive to improve the professional standards of news and information presentations and to foster the principles of journalistic freedom for those working in all sizes of stations and markets, from major networks to the smallest local stations. Both organizations offer student memberships, publish monthly newsletters that keep you informed about people and issues relating to your work, sponsor annual awards competitions, and host annual conventions and workshops to update your information and refine your professional skills. RTNDA offers placement services; local, state, and regional news organizations offer similar opportunities. Several national organizations are available to match your general or specific career interests.[16]

Career Planning

Even if you make diligent efforts to develop the qualifications needed for a broadcast news career, you still must consciously plan your career so that you secure employment in this very competitive field. How should you prepare? Where should you begin working? Where do you look for jobs? How should you prepare application material such as résumés, audition tapes, and cover letters? What should be considered when you get a job offer? How valuable is an internship and part-time work? What about developing specialties? All of these considerations require your serious attention and action.

How to Prepare

Get a broad education. Enroll in a reputable college-level academic program that combines liberal arts courses with broadcast news skills training. Yours will be a diverse job requiring broad knowledge as well as specific skills. You will need to know about several areas. These include: history and the development of society; how government works; fine arts, literature, and culture; how science affects daily living; writing and communicating skills; and people (their concerns, interests, and heritage). Do not neglect special interest areas such as computer science, personnel management, economics, and business and finance. Use your education and extracurricular activities while in school to help you understand people better.

Be flexible, both in your skills and your job requirements. Learn about meteorology to develop your talents as a weather forecaster. Understand the basic economic structure and develop the background that a good business or consumer affairs reporter needs. Be flexible, too, in your job requirements. Your first job may not be your ideal job. Choose a position where you can practice your craft and refine your skills to become a polished broadcast journalist.

Know the current situation in the industry. Read trade publications such as *Broadcasting & Cable*, *Electronic Media, The Quill* (published by the Society of Professional Journalists), and the *Communicator* (published by the Radio-Television News Directors Association). These publications will keep you informed about developments within your profession.

Practical newsroom experience is also important. Dan Dillon, News Director at KFDI Radio in Wichita, Kansas, says that "although a lot has changed in broadcast news, one thing has stayed the same: You still have to pay your dues. . . . Get some experience."[17] Ben Hall, a WTVF-TV reporter in Nashville, Tennessee, agrees: "Hundreds of people graduate with broadcasting degrees each semester. Internships help set you apart."[18] Mutual Broadcasting System anchor Frank Gentry says that "the best combination would be a well-rounded college degree and *practical* on-the-job experience. Very few stations are set up along the lines of college radio. And experience doing long NPR-style reports and features is not terribly relevant at most small commercial stations."[19] Internships and part-time employment are discussed later.

Critique your work. Todd Smith encourages interns who work with him in the Washington News Bureau of Bonneville International Corporation to continue to develop their writing and reporting style.

(1) Find someone out there whose broadcast style you like and study it. Don't copy it, but study it. Transcribe scripts so you can see what they're saying and how they say it. (2) Look for an independent person to critique your work, not somebody you currently work with, but say a former colleague . . . or a former teacher. There are also folks out there that critique work for a fee [among them are consultants and coaches]. Getting an independent critique regularly can be

very helpful. (3) Take time to look at your own work with a critical eye. Go over old scripts. Rewrite some. Ask yourself how you might cover the story differently now to make it better. Then do it that way the next time you're assigned the same or a similar story.[20]

Frank Gentry offers a practical way to critique your work:

Absolutely the best *investment* you can make in a career is an AM-FM-cassette recorder, along with six cassettes. One cassette is used each day of the work week to tape your performance from the air signal. You can also use the recorder to monitor and tape 'casts from a larger market and analyze how *they* do it. . . . You might also transcribe the taped work of people you admire to gain insights into writing style, inflection, reading speed, and story selection.[21]

Where to Begin

Be realistic in your job search. Limit yourself to stations where you can realistically expect to be considered for an opening and where you really would like to work. Your first job probably will be in a small news operation in a local broadcast station; you probably won't get a job in a large news operation in a large market.

The small news operation provides opportunities for you to refine your writing and reporting skills and acquire insight into the daily workings of a news operation. In a small- or medium-market station you will likely be involved in all aspects of news—gathering facts, writing and reporting stories, operating studio and field equipment, and delivering newscasts. A small- or medium-market news operation is the best place to begin. ABC-TV's Kathryn Christensen echoes that advice:

At ABC in New York, the few just-out-of-college graduates we hire start out as desk assistants. Most have graduated at the tops of their classes. They start out answering telephones, sending and receiving faxes, assembling scripts and—if they're good—after about a year, they may start working in research or in the tape room. Eventually, some

of them will become producers and correspondents. . . . If you're lucky enough to have a choice about that first job, I'd always go for the one that allows me to get started as quickly as possible in real journalism. . . . I'd rather do that in a small place, where I could learn from DOING, than start at a bigger place where the closest thing I came to real journalism was answering everyone else's telephone.[22]

Part-time work is an excellent way to continue your education and still acquire necessary experience. You might do rewrites of stories, monitor police radios, clip or file news copy, or cover night meetings of local governmental groups. Perhaps you can arrange for an internship in the newsroom that would provide pay and/or academic credit for your work. This kind of experience introduces you to broadcast news and helps identify the job you eventually would like to have. In the process of gaining experience, you also have a chance to talk informally with those in the newsroom and get a better sense about what goes on. Part-time work could lead to full-time work. It is a good place to begin. Details about internships and part-time work are covered later.

Laurie Krueger's path to her job as a reporter at KVOO Radio is typical of many young broadcast journalists:

I began my radio reporting career as a part-time reporter for WOW Radio a few months after graduating from college. It was definitely not the ideal job . . . working six hours on the weekends and working holidays. However, I discovered I enjoyed radio reporting and considered it a possible career. I then met with the news director and we discussed the possibility of full-time work, job openings of which he knew, and the radio reporting job market in general. His reference to sister station KVOO in Tulsa, Oklahoma, led me to my first full-time job. My experience was still somewhat limited, but I had the "know-how" and by practice, I improved my skills.[23]

Volunteer work is also a possibility. Campus radio stations offer a chance to work in news. Perhaps a production group active at your local cable system prepares programs for the community access channel. You could volunteer to work as a reporter or newscaster and gain experience, and a reference, for future full-time positions in news.

Where to Look

You can use many sources to learn about broadcast news openings. Each has its advantages and usefulness. You may not need to use all of the sources discussed here. Use the sources that are appropriate for your employment situation.

Networking is an excellent source. Who you know *is* important. Personal contacts you make now will pay dividends over the long term. Someone you know who works in a local newsroom may tell you about a potential opening. Job notices often are posted at stations or listed in classified sections of a local newspaper.

Trade publications usually include help wanted columns in the back pages of most issues. Become familiar with general electronic media publications such as *Broadcasting & Cable* and *Electronic Media.* Review specialized media publications such as RTNDA's *Job Information Service,* which is available free to RTNDA members and *Current,* which lists openings in public broadcasting.

Professional placement services can put you in touch with prospective employers, but for a fee; specialized placement services might be an alternative for your second or third full-time position, but not usually for your first job. Exceptions would be placement services associated with specific professional groups and organizations in which you hold current memberships.

If you have identified a specific geographical area you want to consider, you can find specific station listings in publications such as *Broadcasting/Cablecasting Yearbook,* which is available in the reference section of most large libraries.

Remember to stay flexible. Consider job alternatives in fields that relate to broadcast news. Look beyond regular broadcast or cable operations. Consider corporate and institutional communications opportunities that would provide a chance to use your writing and reporting skills and work in an environment much different from a traditional broadcast newsroom.

What to Do

How do you apply for a broadcast news position? What should you expect to provide? What will you encounter from those who review your application? You should know how to write an effective cover letter, prepare a concise and positive résumé, compile a quality audition tape, and survive a personal interview.

You can contact a prospective employer by telephone or by letter. A telephone call would be best if the job will soon close or if you are in the same town as the newsroom and the opening is for part-time work. Do *not* call near newscast deadlines!

If you *call* about a possible job: Read the job listing or posting carefully; double-check the name, title, and telephone number of the person who should be contacted; rehearse aloud the words you plan to use when asking about the job; sound professional; identify yourself clearly and confidently; briefly identify the job you find interesting; schedule a specific date and time for a face-to-face appointment; express enthusiasm for the possibility of the job and appreciation for the chance to visit about job prospects. Be *sure* to arrive for the interview at the scheduled date and time. Suggestions for interviewing with a prospective employer are discussed later.

If you *write* to a prospective employer, you should prepare several items: a cover letter, a résumé, and an audition tape. This written and electronic introduction of your credentials could lead to an in-person or over-the-telephone interview as well as a live audition in the newsroom where you hope to work.

Cover Letters

Cover letters help introduce you to prospective employers. Use good-quality bond paper to write a brief, businesslike letter that indicates why you want the job, why you think you are qualified, how you will contribute something meaningful to the newsroom's success, when you would be available to begin working, and refers the reader to any materials such as a résumé and audition tape you might have enclosed. In the final part of your letter indicate your desire for a personal interview and your flexibility as to the time and place.

Be sure to personalize each letter with the name and title of the person reviewing your application. Find out

March 12, 1997

Mr. Shawn Pettus
News Director
WCCC-TV
1818 Fourth Ave.
Murfreesboro, TN 37130

Dear Mr. Pettus:

I am applying for an internship in the WCCC-TV newsroom. My recent professional experience has centered on our campus radio station. Last summer I completed an internship with WTTT Radio in Oakview. I opened the newsroom each day and prepared and delivered four morning newscasts. My other duties included covering local meetings and breaking stories overnight. For two weeks, while the news director was on vacation, I was the only person in the newsroom. I actually enjoyed the twelve-hour days. I especially appreciated the opportunity to show that I had the skills to do the job. I am ready to build on my radio experience and sharpen my television writing and reporting skills.

I have enclosed a resume and a recent audition tape. I would be pleased to provide additional information. I hope I can begin my summer job soon after the current semester ends June second.

I have always admired the work of the WCCC-TV news staff. Channel 42 has an excellent news reputation. I want to improve my professional skills by working with dedicated professionals. I want to work at WCCC-TV news.

I plan to be in the Murfreesboro area during spring break. I would appreciate a chance to tour WCCC-TV and briefly visit with you about the prospects of an internship. I can meet at any time that is convenient for you.

Thank you for your consideration. I look forward to talking with you.

Sincerely,

(Written signature)
Jennifer Mirasky
5151 "R" St., # 14
Oakview, TN 37130

Enclosure

Figure A.1 Sample cover letter.

who should receive the letter. In most cases, you should contact the news director. Be sure to spell the name correctly. Make your cover letters clean, clear, and complete. Figure A.1 shows a sample cover letter written in a full block format.

Résumés

Include a résumé with your cover letter. This is a one or two-page summary of your education, past employment, professional experience, activities, and personal information such as age and address. Some résumés are written without references; most are written with full identification of at least two or three individuals who can be contacted by letter or phone to discuss your potential as an employee. List dates for all professional work that might relate to your application. Provide pertinent information that is concise, well organized, easy to read, neatly typed, and reasonably complete. Stress your positive activities.

An effective résumé should quickly identify: who you are, what you have done, what you would like to do, what you know, and what you can offer. You will want to have several clean copies of your current résumé on hand, especially when you go for personal interviews. Figure A.2 illustrates the contents of typical résumés. Complete details about both cover letters and résumés are available from local placement services and career development centers, and reference works that are available from your local library.

Audition Tapes

Audition tapes help a news director or producer determine how you look or sound on-the-air. Your prospective employer wants to know that you are an effective communicator. Many applicants include audition tapes with their cover letters and résumés. Many send them only when requested. Despite their good intentions, most news directors do not return audition tapes. When making the audition tape, be sure to use fresh audio- or videotape. Label the tape with your name, address, and telephone number; list the stories and their length on the inside cover of the tape box. Demonstrate the variety of your skills by including several kinds of news stories, features, and in-depth pieces. Length and quality are important. Submit a 3- to 5-minute tape for

radio or an 8- to 15-minute tape for television that features only your best work. Make the first item on the tape your strongest, most compelling story. Air checks (material recorded off the air) could be sent in edited form. Be sure to include the copy for the news stories included on the audition tape.

Here are additional suggestions for audition tapes, especially television audition tapes:

a. Consider beginning the tape with a slate listing your name, home address, and telephone number(s).

b. Remember that the first 30 seconds of the tape are especially important. This is about the amount of time you have to sell your journalistic skills to your prospective news director.

c. Avoid on-tape bios: ''Hi! I'm Jane Smith and I really want to be your next anchor!''

d. Do not include newscast opens on the audition tape.

e. Even for anchor jobs, include reporting examples.

f. Be sure to include a variety of stories.

g. An ideal audition tape for a reporter's position would include:

1. an on-set introduction to a package or a strong spot news story that includes a stand-up segment (if this is a television audition tape)
2. a live shot for a breaking news story
3. one segment from a series produced for a sweeps or ratings period
4. a hard news package
5. a softer or specialty reporting package
6. anchoring work (if available)

This suggested lineup would have to be adjusted, of course, if your specialty was sports, weather, business reporting, government news, and so forth.

Live Auditions

It is important for your prospective employer to know how well you will work in the environment of a particular newsroom. The best way to determine this is to place you into a situation where your work habits can be observed and the quality of your work evaluated. That's what the live audition will help accomplish.

JILL KELLEY

ADDRESS
621 Mehring Way #1010   WKRC-TV
Cincinnati, Ohio 45202   (513) 763-5453
(513) 579-8972

EDUCATION   **University of Nebraska-Lincoln**
                     Bachelor of Journalism, May 1986.
                     MAJOR: Broadcasting, College of Journalism.
                     MINORS: English, Sociology, Geography.

                     Lewis Central High School, Council Bluffs, Iowa, 1982.

EXPERIENCE   **WKRC-TV,** Cincinnati, Ohio, "Good Morning, Cincinnati", anchor/
                     general assignment reporter, September 1990 to present.

                     KCCI-TV, Des Moines, Iowa, Police/Courthouse Reporter, substitute anchor,
                     January 1989 to September 1990.

                     KGAN-TV, Cedar Rapids, Iowa, Johnson County Bureau Chief, general
                     assignment reporter, July 1987 to December 1988.

                     KIMT-TV, Mason City, Iowa, Full-time morning cut-in anchor/producer,
                     general assignment reporter, May 1986 to July, 1987.

                     CABLEVISION, Lincoln, Nebraska, Intern - producer, director, reporter,
                     photographer, editor, writer, May 1985 to May 1986.

                     KNCY, Nebraska City, Nebraska, Legislative stringer, January 1986 to May 1986.

                     KRNU, Lincoln, Nebraska, Legislative reporter, January 1986 to May 1986.

                     KRNU, Lincoln, Nebraska, News reporter, August 1984 to December 1984.

                     DAILY NEBRASKAN, University of Nebraska, General assignment reporter,
                     August 1983 to December 1983.

OTHER   Iowa Broadcast News Association.

                     National Broadcast Honorary Society/Alpha Epsilon Rho, University of
                     Nebraska chapter.

                     Mason City Chamber of Commerce, on-camera promotion, 1986.

                     Iowa State Fair Queen, public speaker, promotions, 1981.

REFERENCES   Dave Busiek   Shirley Brice
                     News Director/ KCCI-TV   TV News Consultant
                     Des Moines, IA   6413 Fleetside Court
                     (515) 247-8888   Alexandria, VA 22310
                                                          (703) 719-5680

                     Judy Thomas   Dave Polyard
                     Tom Melia   Former Asst. News Director/KGAN-TV
                     Broadcast Performance Counsultant, Inc. Associated Press/Broadcast Services
                     Cincinnati, OH   Alexandria, VA
                     (513) 244-3109   (703) 719-5680

Figure A.2 A typical résumé that includes a list of references. Reprinted by permission of Jill Kelley.

Live auditions may be a part of your job application. For writing or reporting jobs, you may be asked to re-write (under deadline pressure) a stack of wire copy into a five-minute newscast or to cover a local story with another reporter already on staff and file a story for the evening newscast. Many newsrooms require language usage, cultural literacy, or current events tests to determine your writing skills, general knowledge, and familiarity with the local area (major landmarks, local officeholders, and so forth).

Personal Interviews

A personal interview is one of the final stages in the application process. An interview is often arranged after your résumé and audition tape have been evaluated. Occasionally, interviews are done over the telephone. Generally, they are done in person, on site, in the newsroom area.

Before your interview, research the station, news operation, and your potential interviewer. Ask colleagues who have worked there what they think about the people and operation. Monitor the station's newscasts before you are interviewed. You might be asked your opinion about what you have observed. Research such as this may answer many of your questions, thus saving valuable interview time. It will also help you formulate specific questions you will want to ask. In addition, your obvious knowledge about the news operation and the local community will demonstrate your ability to prepare well for an assignment, especially a news story assignment.

During the interview, project a positive, confident image about yourself and about your work. You would not have made it to the personal interview if the interviewer did not believe you showed potential. Present a strong professional attitude and appearance. Avoid discussions of salary or compensation until a job offer has been made. Show interest and understanding about the job you want. Try to incorporate you and your background into each response. When given an opportunity, ask questions that demonstrate your initiative in doing research on the company and its people. Use the last few minutes of the interview time to summarize your credentials, express enthusiasm for the opportunity to discuss job prospects, and reinforce the attitude that you are the right person for this particular job. Ask

when you might be able to learn of the interviewer's decision on the opening. Demonstrate that you are a competent broadcast journalist.

Here are a few questions that are asked frequently during job interviews:

- Tell me about yourself.

- What are your goals and objectives?

- Describe the activities you have enjoyed most in college.

- What courses did you like the best? And the least?

- Why do you want this particular job?

- What do you do in your spare time? What are your hobbies?

- How do others describe you?

You should practice your response to a few of these before an interview.

Be persistent. It takes planning, hard work, patience, and determination to land that first job. Persistence is expected of someone in news. It is also expected of someone applying for a news job.

What to Consider

You should consider a few items before you complete your job search and agree to begin working in a broadcast newsroom. These include: pay versus credit (if your position is an internship); unions; learning opportunities; and potential for advancement.

You may need to decide whether you will work for free, for academic credit, or for pay. The common practice is to have students work for free or as part of a recognized internship program. Some newsrooms combine a scholarship with an internship opportunity or provide the tuition costs of the internship registration. If you work for pay, it is likely that you will work for the minimum wage. It is unlikely that you will be allowed to work overtime or that you will receive overtime pay.

Jobs in larger markets require membership in various unions that control the activities of those in the news operation. Some are talent unions, like the American Federation of Television and Radio Artists

(AFTRA). Others concern writers, such as the Writers Guild of America. Still others involve technical personnel, such as the International Brotherhood of Electrical Workers (IBEW) and the National Association of Broadcast Employees and Technicians (NABET).

You must also consider whether a prospective job will provide strong learning opportunities. You should learn practical aspects of the jobs in a broadcast newsroom. You should see what you have read, studied, and practiced in classes come alive as you work with professional news people who do what you want to do full-time. You should avoid jobs that offer only an "observer" or "go-fer" status and do not provide any opportunity for you to learn by participating and doing the work of the broadcast journalist.

When you consider that first full-time job, determine the potential for advancement. Will your work be reviewed periodically to determine increases in pay and responsibilities? Does this company promote and reward from within? How long should you expect to stay in a job before you would be able to move up? The advantages of working in a small broadcast newsroom were discussed earlier.

Internships and Part-Time Work

Do not confuse an internship with part-time employment. The terms are often used interchangeably, but they are different.

Internships provide students opportunities to learn in a working environment on-site at a station or business. Internships may be part-time (15–20 hours each week), but some are only offered on at least a two-thirds-time basis (30–40 hours each week). Internships are based on formal agreements made on a regular basis. They involve a student, the sponsoring business or station, and the student's academic institution. Depending on the nature of the internship agreement, an internship may be paid or unpaid and may involve academic credit. Choose an internship based on the learning experience that you perceive is available rather than on the amount of money you might receive.

Part-time employment may share some of the characteristics of an internship, but the situation is fundamentally different. Part-time opportunities develop sporadically. When an opening occurs, the best applicant is simply hired. The student's academic institution plays no official role and assumes no responsibility. Learning opportunities are not dictated or required by a formal agreement or contract. A student is usually paid for part-time work. Unpaid, observer jobs are also common. No academic credit is usually offered.

Benefits

Why should you bother trying to get an internship or part-time work? Here are a few reasons:

a. You can gain direct experience and improve professional skills.
b. This experience will add professional credibility and improve the quality of your résumé and audition tape.
c. You can find out the job prospects you like the best and the least.
d. This experience provides visibility for you that could lead to full-time work.
e. This experience will motivate you to perform well in your broadcast journalism classes.
f. This experience helps in your personal and professional maturing process.
g. Your confidence will improve after you tackle a variety of challenges and personalities.

John Holden, a freelance feature reporter-producer, has worked in television stations around the country, from Kearney, Nebraska, to Miami, Florida:

I can honestly say after working in a large-market newsroom with hordes of interns, that to this day I can't remember whether someone was an intern or not. They're not walking around with a sign saying "I'm an intern, I don't know what I'm doing!" In fact, in some cases, I think the intern knew more about the business than some of the seasoned professionals. And you can always use that to your benefit . . . offering to help a reporter or producer or editor or photographer in their daily job, and learn from the experience.[24]

How to Get Internships or Part-Time Positions

Aggressiveness is important for broadcast journalists and for job applicants. There *are* job opportunities, but you have to seek them out. They will not usually come looking for you.

Perhaps your broadcast journalism academic program provides regular notices about internships or part-time work. Maybe your campus has a placement coordinator. You may need to file an application and then complete an interview before you finalize details such as timetable, duties, pay or credit, and so forth.

Don't hesitate to "network." Use family, friends, or simply acquaintances to make initial employment contacts. Who you know *is* important.

After you identify an internship or part-time opportunity, prepare your résumé and audition material and get prepared for a personal interview. Follow the process outlined earlier.

Legal Guidelines

Many stations and networks have elaborate, on-going part-time and internship programs. They want to provide a worthwhile learning experience for possible future employees. These good motives must often be tempered with the reality of federal labor law requirements.

The provisions of the Fair Labor Standards Act (FLSA) apply when a station treats an intern like other employees or employee-trainees. These requirements apply to items such as minimum wage, overtime pay, and record keeping. A student will not be considered an "employee" under FLSA, and thus would not need to be paid, if *all* of the following criteria are included in a student internship agreement:

a. The training, even though it includes actual operation of the facilities of the employer, is similar to that which would be given in a vocational school.
b. The training is for the benefit of the trainees or students.
c. The trainees or students do not displace regular employees but work under their close observation.
d. The employer who provides the training derives no immediate advantage from the activities of the trainees or students; and on occasion the employer's operation may actually be impeded.
e. The trainees or students are not necessarily entitled to a job at the conclusion of the training period.
f. The employer and the trainees or students understand that the trainees or students are not entitled to wages for the time spent in training.[25]

These criteria are the basis for offering formal credit or at least recognition by a college or university for an internship. These criteria generally lead to a formal list of learning assignments that are well defined and closely supervised during an internship. These federal requirements mirror standard union restrictions that limit the type of work that can be done by an intern; unions want to protect the jobs of their members.

The Future

What might you expect in the future? What are the best estimates about the future of broadcast journalism?

When surveyed by the RTNDA, news directors said that in the near future they would expect more emphasis on production, local reporting (especially government news), live reporting, and computerization, and less dependence on networks. Newsrooms are expected to be run as profit centers even more than now. Salaries for most key positions are not expected to keep up with the cost of living, except in large-market television stations.[26]

Technological developments are expected to change the way news stories are written and produced. The transition to computer-based digital video is expected to be the most far-reaching and significant event of the decade. Computer-based video systems, also known as disk-based video, nonlinear editing, or desktop video will revolutionize broadcast newsgathering and reporting processes and techniques. Equipment, staffing, and procedures will certainly change. Phil Witt, News Anchor/Senior Reporter at WDAF-TV in Kansas City, says that those "who work in television news must be willing to adapt to the new technologies which will change the industry dramatically in months, not just years. . . . One-person crews which shoot, report, write and edit stories (with the help of extremely portable video gear, remote equipment and laptop computers) may become the norm."[27] Radio news will share in this digitalization process with the use of equipment such as DAT recorders and systems.

The broadcast journalist of the future will need to be prepared for a hybrid job situation. Instead of only writing and reporting skills, you need to consider adding computer and specialized research skills. Computerized assisted reporting promises to be in every newsroom's future.

Sheila Hyland of WTAE-TV in Pittsburgh cautions that "because so many people are trying to get into the field, only the cream of the crop are going to find jobs. That means, the more you know, and the more experience you have, the better your chances."[28]

Your skills as well as your attitude must be versatile to better match the evolving telecommunications industry. Much of the evolution will be technological, but a noticeable portion will involve consolidation of duties, pressures from group ownerships, federal regulations, and so forth. Prepare for more than one career option.

What is the future for women in broadcast journalism? Laurie Krueger of KVOO Radio in Tulsa, Oklahoma, says "there will always be instances of discrimination and it will not always be an easy road, but I think women just beginning in the field have a better chance now of reaching the highest of goals."[29] Sheila Hyland adds that "the line between journalism and entertainment seems to be getting fuzzy. A pretty face may get you in the door, but it won't necessarily keep you on the job. . . . Good writing, good investigative techniques and a skillful presentation will do more than a pretty face."[30]

KIRO-TV Reporter Essex Porter offers encouragement for young minority journalists:

Mainstream journalism hasn't made room for many minority journalists, so wherever you go and whoever you work for, journalism needs you. Journalism needs your insight and perspective. Journalism needs you to break stereotypes and to include those communities that are easily left out of mainstream coverage. Exercise your influence to make journalism better.[31]

Final Thoughts

Journalism is a serious business. It requires you to maintain a responsible attitude. Essex Porter put it this way:

1. *Journalism is important.* Information is the lubricant of our society, the guardian of our democracy. Need a reminder? Remember that in other countries journalists are routinely exiled or killed for what they write or broadcast. Remember that it's hard to take over a country unless you first take over the radio and television stations. Remember that Chinese troops didn't move to clear students from Tiananmen Square until after the government had chased away the foreign TV crews and pulled the plug on live satellite broadcasts.

2. *Credibility gives journalism its value.* Our society is awash in information from hundreds of sources and hundreds more sources will be available soon, so providing information is not enough. Journalists will have an audience only if we remain credible. Credibility requires that we be free of bias and conflicts, that we are as open to those on the fringes of society as we are to those in the mainstream.

3. *Journalism is a demanding career.* It's seductive. It's a 24-hour-a-day business. It requires your heart as well as your head. If you let it, it may absorb all the time and energy you try to reserve for a personal life. Enjoy journalism, but get a life, too![32]

Notes

1. Reprinted by permission of Phil Witt.

2. Summary of a 1993 survey by Vernon A. Stone, "TV News Work Force Grows," *Communicator* 48, no. 4 (April, 1994): 20–21.

3. Reprinted by permission of Frank Gentry.

4. Reprinted by permission of Barb Simon.

5. Summary of a 1993 survey by Vernon A. Stone, "Pay Gains Top Cost of Living," *Communicator* 48, no. 2 (February, 1994): 68–70. Early each calendar

year, Vernon A. Stone has provided for the Radio-Television News Directors Association an annual news salary report. Staff size changes generally are reported a few months later. The results of both surveys are published in RTNDA's *Communicator.*

6. Summary of a 1992 survey by Vernon A. Stone, "Good News, Bad News," *Communicator* 47, no. 8 (August, 1993): 68–69.

7. Summary of a 1992 survey by Vernon A. Stone, "Good News, Bad News," *Communicator* 47, no. 8 (August, 1993): 68–69.

8. Reprinted by permission of Nan Siemer.

9. Reprinted by permission of Ann Pedersen Gleson.

10. Reprinted by permission of Kim Engebretsen.

11. Reprinted by permission of Kim Dlouhy.

12. Reprinted by permission of Sheila Hyland.

13. Reprinted by permission of Ann Pedersen Gleson.

14. Reprinted by permission of Todd Smith.

15. Excerpt from a speech at J-Days at the University of Nebraska-Lincoln, April 15, 1994.

16. Contact the groups appropriate to your interests. Some groups offer a broad perspective of broadcast journalism, whereas others are more specialized. All of the organizations listed offer individual memberships. Many offer student or associate memberships at reduced rates, scholarships, and job placement services.

American Meteorological Society
45 Beacon Street
Boston, MA 02108

Asian American Journalists Association
1765 Sutter St., Rm. 1000
San Francisco, CA 94115

National Association of Black Journalists (NABJ)
11600 Sunrise Valley Dr.
Reston, VA 22091

National Association of Farm Broadcasters
26 E. Exchange Street
St. Paul, MN 55101

National Association of Hispanic Journalists
529 14th St., N.W., Ste. 1193
Washington, DC 20045

The National Press Photographers, Inc.
3200 Croasdaile Drive, Suite 306
Durham, NC 27705

Native American Journalists Association
School of Journalism and Mass Communication
University of Colorado
Campus Box 287
Boulder, CO 80309

Radio-Television News Directors Association
1000 Connecticut Ave., N.W., Ste. 615
Washington, DC 20036

Society of Professional Journalists
Box 77
16 S. Jackson
Greencastle, IN 46135

17. Reprinted by permission of Dan Dillon.

18. Reprinted by permission of Ben Hall.

19. Reprinted by permission of Frank Gentry.

20. Reprinted by permission of Todd Smith.

21. Reprinted by permission of Frank Gentry.

22. Excerpt from a speech at J-Days at the University of Nebraska-Lincoln, April 15, 1994.

23. Reprinted by permission of Laurie Krueger.

24. Reprinted by permission of John Holden.

25. Quoted from the U.S. Labor Department's WH Publication 1297, "Employment Relationship Under the Fair Labor Standards Act."

26. Summary of a 1993 survey by Vernon A. Stone, "News in the '90s," *Communicator* 47, no. 10 (October, 1993): 33–35.

27. Reprinted by permission of Phil Witt.

28. Reprinted by permission of Sheila Hyland.

29. Reprinted by permission of Laurie Krueger.

30. Reprinted by permission of Sheila Hyland.

31. Reprinted by permission of Essex Porter.

32. Reprinted by permission of Essex Porter.

Codes of Ethics

The following codes of ethics have been reproduced with the permission of the respective organizations. Membership eligibility guidelines and application information can be obtained by contacting each organization: Radio-Television News Directors Association, 1000 Connecticut Ave., N.W., Ste. 615, Washington, DC 20036; Society of Professional Journalists, Box 77, 16 S. Jackson, Greencastle, IN 46135; The National Press Photographers Association, 3200 Croasdaile Drive, Suite 306, Durham, NC 27705. Both RTNDA and SPJ offer special student membership rates and benefits.

CODE OF ETHICS

The National Press Photographers Association, a professional society dedicated to the advancement of photojournalism, acknowledges concern and respect for the public's natural-law right to freedom in searching for the truth and the right to be informed truthfully and completely about public events and the world in which we live.

We believe that no report can be complete if it is not possible to enhance and clarify the meaning of words. We believe that pictures, whether used to depict news events as they actually happen, illustrate news that has happened or to help explain anything of public interest, are an indispensable means of keeping people accurately informed; that they help all people, young and old, to better understand any subject in the public domain.

Believing the foregoing we recognize and acknowledge that photojournalists should at all times maintain the highest standards of ethical conduct in serving the public interest. To that end the National Press Photographers Association sets forth the following Code of Ethics which is subscribed to by all of its members:

1. The practice of photojournalism, both as a science and art, is worthy of the very best thought and effort of those who enter into it as a profession.

2. Photojournalism affords an opportunity to serve the public that is equalled by few other vocations and all members of the profession should strive by example and influence to maintain high standards of ethical conduct free of mercenary considerations of any kind.

3. It is the individual responsibility of every photojournalist at all times to strive for pictures that report truthfully, honestly and objectively.

4. Business promotion in its many forms is essential, but untrue statements of any nature are not worthy of a professional photojournalist and we severely condemn any such practice.

5. It is our duty to encourage and assist all members of our profession, individually and collectively, so that the quality of photojournalism may constantly be raised to higher standards.

6. It is the duty of every photojournalist to work to preserve all freedom-of-the-press rights recognized by law and to work to protect and expand freedom-of-access to all sources of news and visual information.

7. Our standards of business dealings, ambitions and relations shall have in them a note of sympathy for our common humanity and shall always require us to take into consideration our highest duties as members of society. In every situation in our business life, in every responsibility that comes before us, our chief thought shall be to fulfill that responsibility and discharge that duty so that when each of us is finished we shall have endeavored to lift the level of human ideals and achievement higher than we found it.

8. No Code of Ethics can prejudge every situation, thus common sense and good judgement are required in applying ethical principles.

Courtesy of the National Press Photographers Association, Inc.

RTNDA
The Association of Electronic Journalists

Code of Ethics

The responsibility of radio and television journalists is to gather and report information of importance and interest to the public accurately, honestly and impartially.

The members of the Radio-Television News Directors Association accept these standards and will:

1. *Strive to present the source or nature of broadcast news material in a way that is balanced, accurate and fair.*

   A. *They will evaluate information solely on its merits as news, rejecting sensationalism or misleading emphasis in any form.*

   B. *They will guard against using audio or video material in a way that deceives the audience.*

   C. *They will not mislead the public by presenting as spontaneous news any material which is staged or rehearsed.*

   D. *They will identify people by race, creed, nationality or prior status only when it is relevant.*

   E. *They will clearly label opinion and commentary.*

   F. *They will promptly acknowledge and correct errors.*

2. *Strive to conduct themselves in a manner that protects them from conflicts of interest, real or perceived. They will decline gifts or favors which would influence or appear to influence their judgments.*

3. *Respect the dignity, privacy and well-being of people with whom they deal.*

4. *Recognize the need to protect confidential sources. They will promise confidentiality only with the intention of keeping that promise.*

5. *Respect everyone's right to a fair trial.*

6. *Broadcast the private transmissions of other broadcasters only with permission.*

7. *Actively encourage observance of this Code by all journalists, whether members of the Radio-Television News Directors Association or not.*

Society of Professional Journalists

Code of Ethics

SOCIETY of Professional Journalists, believes the duty of journalists is to serve the truth.

We BELIEVE the agencies of mass communication are carriers of public discussion and information, acting on their Constitutional mandate and freedom to learn and report the facts.

We BELIEVE in public enlightenment as the forerunner of justice, and in our Constitutional role to seek the truth as part of the public's right to know the truth.

We BELIEVE those responsibilities carry obligations that require journalists to perform with intelligence, objectivity, accuracy, and fairness.

To these ends, we declare acceptance of the standards of practice here set forth:

I. RESPONSIBILITY:

The public's right to know of events of public importance and interest is the overriding mission of the mass media. The purpose of distributing news and enlightened opinion is to serve the general welfare. Journalists who use their professional status as representatives of the public for selfish or other unworthy motives violate a high trust.

II. FREEDOM OF THE PRESS:

Freedom of the press is to be guarded as an inalienable right of people in a free society. It carries with it the freedom and the responsibility to discuss, question, and challenge actions and utterances of our government and of our public and private institutions. Journalists uphold the right to speak unpopular opinions and the privilege to agree with the majority.

III. ETHICS:

Journalists must be free of obligation to any interest other than the public's right to know the truth.

1. Gifts, favors, free travel, special treatment or privileges can compromise the integrity of journalists and their employers. Nothing of value should be accepted.

2. Secondary employment, political involvement, holding public office, and service in community organizations should be avoided if it compromises the integrity of journalists and their employers. Journalists and their employers should conduct their personal lives in a manner that protects them from conflict of interest, real or apparent. Their responsibilities to the public are paramount. That is the nature of their profession.

3. So-called news communications from private sources should not be published or broadcast without substantiation of their claims to news values.

4. Journalists will seek news that serves the public interest, despite the obstacles. They will make constant efforts to assure that the public's business is conducted in public and that public records are open to public inspection.

5. Journalists acknowledge the newsman's ethic of protecting confidential sources of information.

6. Plagiarism is dishonest and unacceptable.

IV. ACCURACY AND OBJECTIVITY:

Good faith with the public is the foundation of all worthy journalism.

1. Truth is our ultimate goal.

2. Objectivity in reporting the news is another goal that serves as the mark of an experienced professional. It is a standard of performance toward which we strive. We honor those who achieve it.

3. There is no excuse for inaccuracies or lack of thoroughness.

4. Newspaper headlines should be fully warranted by the contents of the articles they accompany. Photographs and telecasts should give an accurate picture of an event and not highlight an incident out of context.

5. Sound practice makes clear distinction between news reports and expressions of opinion. News reports should be free of opinion or bias and represent all sides of an issue.

6. Partisanship in editorial comment that knowingly departs from the truth violates the spirit of American journalism.

7. Journalists recognize their responsibility for offering informed analysis, comment, and editorial opinion on public events and issues. They accept the obligation to present such material by individuals whose competence, experience, and judgment qualify them for it.

8. Special articles or presentations devoted to advocacy or the writer's own conclusions and interpretations should be labeled as such.

V. FAIR PLAY:

Journalists at all times will show respect for the dignity, privacy, rights, and well-being of people encountered in the course of gathering and presenting the news.

1. The news media should not communicate unofficial charges affecting reputation or moral character without giving the accused a chance to reply.

2. The news media must guard against invading a person's right to privacy.

3. The media should not pander to morbid curiosity about details of vice and crime.

4. It is the duty of news media to make prompt and complete correction of their errors.

5. Journalists should be accountable to the public for their reports and the public should be encouraged to voice its grievances against the media. Open dialogue with our readers, viewers, and listeners should be fostered.

VI. MUTUAL TRUST:

Adherence to this code is intended to preserve and strengthen the bond of mutual trust and respect between American journalists and the American people.

The Society shall--by programs of education and other means--encourage individual journalists to adhere to these tenets, and shall encourage journalistic publications and broadcasters to recognize their responsibility to frame codes of ethics in concert with their employees to serve as guidelines in furthering these goals.

CODE OF ETHICS
(Adopted 1926; revised 1973, 1984, 1987)

Courtesy of the Society of Professional Journalists.

Supplementary Reading

The following books and publications provide additional insights into broadcast newswriting and reporting techniques. The readings are arranged into categories that match the organization and content of the chapters in this book. The assignment of a book to a particular category or topic area is arbitrary in some cases.

General

Hausman, Carl. *Crafting the News for the Electronic Media*. Belmont, CA: Wadsworth, 1992.

Shook, Frederick, and Lattimore, Dan. *The Broadcast News Process*. 4th ed. Englewood, CO: Morton, 1992.

Stephens, Mitchell. *Broadcast News*. 3d ed. Fort Worth, TX: Harcourt Brace Jovanovich, 1993.

White, Ted. *Broadcast News Writing and Reporting*. New York: St. Martin's, 1993.

Broadcast Journalism Perspectives and Analysis

Auletta, Ken. *Three Blind Mice: How the TV Networks Lost Their Way*. New York: Random House, 1991.

Bliss, Edward, Jr. *Now the News: The Story of Broadcast Journalism*. Irvington, NY: Columbia University Press, 1991.

Boyer, Peter. *Who Killed CBS: The Undoing of America's Number One News Network*. New York: Random House, 1988.

Donaldson, Sam. *Hold On, Mr. President!* New York: Fawcett, 1988.

Ellerbee, Linda. *And So It Goes: Adventures in Television*. New York: G. P. Putnam, 1986.

Goald, Robert S. *Behind the Scenes at the Local News*. Stoneham, MA: Focal Press, 1994.

Graham, Fred. *Happy Talk: Confessions of a TV Newsman*. New York: W. W. Norton and Co., 1990.

Hewitt, Don. *Minute by Minute*. New York: Random House, 1985.

Hosley, David H., and Yamada, Gayle K. *Hard News: Women in Broadcast Journalism*. Westport, CT: Greenwood Press, 1987.

James, Doug. *Walter Cronkite: His Life and Times*. Brentwood, TN: J. M. Productions, 1991.

Mayer, Martin. *Making News*. Boston, MA: Harvard Business School Press, 1993.

Rather, Dan, and Herskowitz, Mickey. *The Camera Never Blinks Twice: The Further Adventures of a Television Journalist*. New York: William Morrow, 1994.

Savitch, Jessica. *Anchor Woman*. New York: G. P. Putnam, 1982.

Schoenbrun, David. *On and Off the Air: An Informal History of CBS News*. New York: E. P. Dutton, 1989.

Stephens, Mitchell. *A History of News: From the Drum to the Satellite*. New York: Viking, 1988.

Trotta, Liz. *Fighting for Air: In the Trenches with Television News*. Columbia, MO: University of Missouri Press, 1995.

Writing

Bliss, Edward, Jr., and Hoyt, James L. *Writing News for Broadcast*. Irvington, NY: Columbia University Press, 1993.

Block, Mervin. *Rewriting Network News*. Chicago: Bonus Books, 1990.

———. *Writing Broadcast News—Shorter, Sharper, Stronger*. Chicago: Bonus Books, 1987.

Hewitt, John. *Airwords: Writing for Broadcast News*. 2d ed. Mountain View, CA: Mayfield, 1995.

Kessler, Lauren, and McDonald, Duncan. *When Words Collide: A Media Writer's Guide to Grammar and Style*. 3d ed. Belmont, CA: Wadsworth, 1992.

MacDonald, Ron. *A Broadcast News Manual of Style*. 2d ed. White Plains, NY: Longman, 1994.

Mayeux, Peter E. *Writing for the Electronic Media*. 2d ed. Dubuque, IA: Brown & Benchmark, 1994.

Newman, Edwin. *A Civil Tongue*. New York: Warner Books, 1977.

Osgood, Charles. *The Osgood Files*. New York: Fawcett, 1992.

Strunk, William, and White, E. B. *The Elements of Style*. 3d ed. New York: Macmillan, 1979.

Wulfemeyer, K. Tim. *Beginning Broadcast Newswriting: A Self-Instructional Learning Experience*. 3d ed. Ames, IA: Iowa State Press, 1993.

Research and News Sources

Kessler, Lauren, and McDonald, Duncan. *The Search: Information Gathering for the Mass Media*. Belmont, CA: Wadsworth, 1992.

Reddick, Randy, and King, Elliot. *The Online Journalist: Using the Internet and Other Electronic Resources*. Fort Worth, TX: Harcourt Brace, 1995.

Stout, Rick. *The Internet Complete Reference*. New York: Osborne McGraw-Hill, 1994.

Ullman, John, and Colbert, Jan. *The Reporter's Handbook: An Investigator's Guide to Documents and Techniques*. 2d ed. New York: St. Martin's, 1990.

Interviewing

Biagi, Shirley. *Interviews That Work: A Practical Guide for Journalists*. 2d ed. Belmont, CA: Wadsworth, 1992.

Killenberg, George, and Anderson, Rob. *Before the Story: Interviewing and Communication Skills for Journalists*. New York: St. Martin's Press, 1989.

Radio Reporting

Alten, Stanley R. *Audio in Media*. 4th ed. Belmont, CA: Wadsworth, 1994.

Gifford, F. *Tape*. 3d ed. Englewood, CO: Morton, 1987.

NPR Staff. *Sound Reporting: National Public Radio's Guide to Radio Journalism and Production*. Dubuque, IA: Kendall-Hunt, 1992.

Television Reporting

Hamer, Dave, ed. *The TV Storyteller*. Durham, NC: National Press Photographers Association, 1985.

Hewitt, John. *Sequences: Strategies for Shooting News in the Real World*. Mountain View, CA: Mayfield, 1992.

Shook, Frederick. *Television Newswriting: Captivating an Audience*. New York: Longman, 1994.

Ward, Peter. *Basic Betacam Camerawork*. Focal: Stoneham, MA, 1994.

Yoakam, Richard D., and Cremer, Charles F. *ENG: Television News and the New Technology*. 2d ed. New York: Random House, 1989.

Field and Live Reporting

Shook, Frederick. *Television Field Production and Reporting*. New York: Longman, 1989.

Verna, Tony. *Live TV: An Inside Look at Directing and Producing*. Stoneham, MA: Focal Press, 1987.

On-Air Presentation

Hyde, Stuart. *Television and Radio Announcing*. 7th ed. Boston: Houghton Mifflin, 1995.

Utterback, Ann S. *Broadcast Voice Handbook: How to Polish Your On-Air Delivery*. Chicago: Bonus Books, 1990.

Specialized Areas of Reporting

Benjaminson, Peter, and Anderson, David. *Investigative Reporting.* 2d ed. Ames, IA: Iowa State University Press, 1990.

Campbell, Don. *Inside the Beltway: A Guide to Washington Reporting.* Ames, IA: Iowa State University Press, 1991.

Gaines, William. *Investigative Reporting for Print and Broadcasting.* Chicago: Nelson-Hall, 1994.

Hitchcock, John R. *Sportscasting.* Stoneham, MA: Focal Press, 1991.

Johnston, Carla B. *Election Coverage: Blueprint for Broadcasters.* Stoneham, MA: Focal Press, 1991.

Killenberg, George M. *Public Affairs Reporting: Covering the News in the Information Age.* New York: St. Martin's, 1992.

Kluge, Pamela Hollie. *The Columbia Knight-Bagehot Guide to Business and Economics Journalism.* Irvington, NY: Columbia University Press, 1993.

Kuralt, Charles. *A Life on the Road.* New York: Ivy, 1991.

―――. *On the Road with Charles Kuralt.* New York: Fawcett, 1986.

Lavrakas, Paul J., and Holley, Jack K., eds. *Polling and Presidential Election Coverage.* Newbury Park, CA: Sage, 1990.

Prato, Lou. *Covering the Environmental Beat: An Overview for Radio and TV Journalists.* Washington, DC: The Media Institute, 1991.

Spence, Jim, with Diles, Dave. *Up Close and Personal: The Inside Story of Network Television Sports.* New York: Antheneum, 1988.

Wilhoit, G. Cleveland, and Weaver, David H. *Newsroom Guide to Polls and Surveys.* Bloomington, IN: Indiana University Press, 1990.

Law and Ethics

Black, Jay, Steele, Bob, and Barney, Ralph. *Doing Ethics in Journalism: A Handbook with Case Studies.* Greencastle, IN: The Sigma Delta Chi Foundation and The Society of Professional Journalists, 1993.

Denniston, Lyle W. *The Reporter and the Law: Techniques of Covering the Courts.* Irvington, NY: Columbia University Press, 1992.

Holsinger, Ralph, and Dilts, Jon. *Media Law.* 3d ed. New York: McGraw-Hill, 1994.

Limburg, Val. *Electronic Media Ethics.* Stoneham, MA: Focal Press, 1994.

Overbeck, Wayne. *Major Principles of Media Law.* Annual ed. Fort Worth, TX: Harcourt Brace Jovanovich, 1994.

Patterson, Philip, and Wilkins, Lee. *Media Ethics Issues and Cases.* Dubuque, IA: Wm. C. Brown, 1991.

Pember, Don. *Mass Media Law.* 6th ed. Dubuque, IA: Brown & Benchmark, 1993.

Broadcast News Careers

Gross, Lynne Schafer. *The Internship Experience.* 2d ed. Prospect Heights, IL: Waveland Press, 1994.

Sanders, Marlene, and Rock, Marcia. *Waiting for Prime Time: The Women of Television News.* Urbana, IL: University of Illinois Press, 1988.

Index